LOLLARDY AND THE GENTRY IN THE LATER MIDDLE AGES

EDITED BY
MARGARET ASTON AND COLIN RICHMOND

SUTTON PUBLISHING • STROUD
ST. MARTIN'S PRESS • NEW YORK

First published in the United Kingdom in 1997 by
Sutton Publishing Limited • Phoenix Mill
Thrupp • Stroud • Gloucestershire • GL5 2BU

First published in the United States by St. Martin's Press
Scholarly and Reference Division
175 Fifth Avenue, New York, N.Y. 10010

British Library Cataloguing in Publication Data
A catalogue record for this book is available from the British Library

ISBN 0 7509 1194 8

Library of Congress Cataloging-in-Publication Data applied for

ISBN 0-312-17388-1

The editors and publisher gratefully acknowledge the grant towards the
cost of publication from The British Academy.

TM   ALAN SUTTON™ and SUTTON™ are the
trade marks of Sutton Publishing Limited

Typeset in 10/12 pt Baskerville.
Typesetting and origination by
Sutton Publishing Limited.
Printed in Great Britain by
Hartnolls, Bodmin, Cornwall.

CONTENTS

LIST OF ILLUSTRATIONS

MAPS AND TABLES

LIST OF CONTRIBUTORS

Geoffrey Martin is Research Professor of History at the University of Essex, and was Keeper of Public Records from 1982 to 1988. His publications include *Knighton's Chronicle, 1337–96*, which appeared in 1995.

Anne Hudson is Professor of Medieval English at the University of Oxford. She has published papers on various late medieval writers, is the author of *The Premature Reformation: Wycliffite Texts and Lollard History* and the editor of *Two Wycliffite Texts* and (in collaboration with Pamela Gradon) of *English Wycliffite Sermons*.

Fiona Somerset is a Research Fellow at Lady Margaret Hall, Oxford. She is currently working on several articles and books for publication, including 'Vernacular Argumentation in the Testimony of William Thorpe', Medieval Studies 58 (1996) and articles on the dissemination of Wyclif's *Dialogus* in both Latin and English.

John Scattergood is Professor of Medieval and Renaissance Literature in the School of English, Trinity College, University of Dublin.

J.A.F. Thomson is Professor of Medieval History at the University of Glasgow. He has written various works on the Church in the Later Middle Ages, including *The Later Lollards 1414–1520, Popes and Princes 1417–1517*, and *The Early Tudor Church and Society 1485–1529*.

Dr A.K. McHardy is Senior Lecturer in the Department of History at the University of Nottingham. She is the author of *The Church in London 1375–92* and *Clerical Poll-Taxes of the Diocese of Lincoln 1377–1381*, and of many articles on the English Church in the later Middle Ages.

Christina von Nolcken is Associate Professor in the Department of English at the University of Chicago. She is the editor of *The Middle English Translation of the Rosarium Theologie* and has published a number of articles on Lollardy.

Maureen Jurkowski is a Research Assistant on the E179 project at the Public Record Office. She has published articles on Lollardy, the gentry and late medieval lawyers.

Paweł Kras is Assistant to Professor Urszula Borkowska in the Department of History, the Catholic University of Lublin, Poland.

Rob Lutton has been a Temporary Lecturer in Medieval History at the University of Manchester. He is currently completing a doctorate on family piety in pre-Reformation Tenterden.

Dr Norman Tanner is a Jesuit priest who writes and teaches on medieval religion and other subjects, living at Campion Hall in the University of Oxford. Among his recent publications are *Decrees of the Ecumenical Councils*, 2 vols, and *Kent Heresy Proceedings 1511–12*.

Andrew Hope teaches history at Harris Manchester College, University of Oxford. He is the author of an article entitled 'Lollardy: the stone the builders rejected?' and the editor of the journal *Reformation*.

Abbreviations

Arnold, *SEW*	*Select English Works of John Wyclif*, ed. T. Arnold, 3 vols (Oxford, 1869–71)
Aston, *FF*	Aston, Margaret, *Faith and Fire: Popular and Unpopular Religion, 1350–1600* (London, 1993)
Aston, *LR*	Aston, Margaret, *Lollards and Reformers: Images and Literacy in Late Medieval Religion* (London, 1984)
BIHR	*Bulletin of the Institute of Historical Research*
BL	British Library
BM	British Museum
CCR	*Calendar of the Close Rolls* (London, 1892–1954)
CFR	*Calendar of the Fine Rolls* (London, 1911–63)
CPapReg	*Calendar of entries in the Papal Registers: Papal Letters* (London, 1893–1960)
CPR	*Calendar of the Patent Rolls* (London, 1891–1916)
CYS	Canterbury and York Society
DNB	*Dictionary of National Biography*
Dymmok	*Rogeri Dymmok Liber Contra Duodecim Errores et Hereses Lollardorum*, ed. H.S. Cronin (London, 1921)
EETS	Early English Text Society
EHR	*English Historical Review*
Emden, *BRUC*	Emden, A.B., *Biographical Register of the University of Cambridge* (Cambridge, 1963)
Emden, *BRUO*	Emden, A.B., *Biographical Register of the University of Oxford*, 3 vols (Oxford, 1957–9)
Fasc. Ziz.	*Fasciculi Zizaniorum*, ed. W.W. Shirley (RS, 1858)
Forshall & Madden, *HB*	*The Holy Bible . . . by John Wycliffe and his Followers*, ed. J. Forshall and F. Madden, 4 vols (Oxford, 1850)
Foxe, *A&M*	*The Acts and Monuments*, ed. J. Pratt, 8 vols (London, 1877)
GEC	G.E. Cokayne, *The Complete Peerage of England, Scotland, Ireland*, 12 vols (London, 1910–59)
Hudson, *LB*	Hudson, Anne, *Lollards and their Books* (London and Ronceverte, 1985)
Hudson, *PR*	Hudson, Anne, *The Premature Reformation: Wycliffite Texts and Lollard History* (Oxford, 1988)

Hudson, *Selections*	*Selections from English Wycliffite Writings*, ed. A. Hudson (Cambridge, 1978)
Hudson & Gradon, *EWS*	*English Wycliffite Sermons*, ed. A. Hudson and P. Gradon, 5 vols (Oxford, 1983–96)
JEH	*Journal of Ecclesiastical History*
KC	*Knighton's Chronicle 1337–1396*, ed. G.H. Martin (Oxford, 1995)
Matthew, *EWW*	*English Works of Wyclif hitherto unprinted*, ed. F.D. Matthew (EETS, 74, rev. edn 1902)
McFarlane, *JW*	McFarlane, K.B., *John Wycliffe and the Beginnings of English Nonconformity* (London, 1952)
McFarlane, *LK*	McFarlane, K.B., *Lancastrian Kings and Lollard Knights* (Oxford, 1972)
PL	*Patrologia Latina*, ed. J.P. Migne (Paris, 1841–64)
P&P	*Past and Present*
PRO	Public Record Office
Reg. Chichele	*The Register of Henry Chichele*, ed. E.F. Jacob, 4 vols (Oxford, 1938–47)
RES	*Review of English Studies*
RS	Rolls Series
Rot. Parl.	*Rotuli Parliamentorum 1278–1503*, 6 vols (London, 1767–77)
SCH	*Studies in Church History*
Tanner, *HT*	*Heresy Trials in the Diocese of Norwich*, ed. N.P. Tanner (Camden 4th ser. 20, 1977)
TCD	Trinity College, Dublin
Thomson, *LL*	Thomson, J.A.F., *The Later Lollards* (Oxford, 1965)
TRHS	*Transactions of the Royal Historical Society*
VCH	*Victoria County History*
WS	Wyclif Society

INTRODUCTION

The Reformation that succeeded, like the 'premature reformation' that failed, was dependent on the gentry as well as the king for its outcome. The fate of Sir John Oldcastle may have been as decisive for the ecclesiastical future under Henry V as that of Sir Thomas More was under Henry VIII, but twenty years before Oldcastle was tried for heresy, gathered his rebellion and was hanged and burned, an event took place that might well be regarded as the critical peak of Wycliffite ambitions.

The *Twelve Conclusions* of 'pore men, tresoreris of Cryst and his apostlis', made public for the benefit of parliament early in 1395, advertised the call for 'þe reformaciun of holi chirche of Yngelond' as a matter of public secular debate.[1] Posted on the doors of Westminster Hall when parliament was in session between 27 January and 15 February – and reportedly also on the doors of St Paul's Cathedral for the benefit of convocation – this bold move amounted to an open declaration of what had become a widely recognised fact: the issues raised by Wycliffe had moved outside the university of Oxford, far from academic lecture halls, and become the concern of many lay men and women, including some of influential knightly standing.

The sexcentenary of this event was the occasion for an academic debate on the role of gentry in the Wycliffite heresy. A group of scholars from both sides of the Atlantic and from eastern Europe as well as England, met in Newnham College, Cambridge, to discuss a wide range of issues relating to this theme. The twelve chapters printed here are the outcome of that meeting. The editors believe that they make an important contribution to the field of Lollard studies in general, as well as highlighting, in a way that has not been done before, the centrality of Lollard knights and knightly religion to the challenge faced by the fifteenth-century English church.

Twenty-five years have passed since the publication of K.B. McFarlane's influential study of Lollard knights. Subsequent work has both amplified and qualified his conclusions. His main finding, that the chroniclers were right in accusing a group of prominent knights of Lollard sympathy, has stood the test of time, and seems likely to hold. But it has led on to further questions, which are addressed by the contributors of this book. Were there still serious gentry supporters of Lollardy long after the Oldcastle rising? How should we define and judge Lollardy among its gentry supporters? Was the English experience in any way paralleled by developments among the Hussites in eastern Europe? Is it misleading to think of doctrinal deviance as something that moved down the social scale, rather than permeating it in various directions through different kinds of community, sometimes with an upward mobility? Although the sources may be against this, should the historian not consider the gentry household, as much as the artisan hearth, as a potential Lollard forum or recruiting ground?

Those who drew up the 'manifesto' of 1395 knew they had a knightly constituency, and chose their moment carefully. At the time, the reforming landscape seemed highly promising. Wycliffe, ten years dead, lay in a respectable grave in his church at Lutterworth, honourably enough interred for two visiting Bohemians to be able some years later to take chips from his tombstone as relics. Despite the proceedings of the 1380s and the abjuration of prominent Oxford Wycliffites, works by Wycliffe were still to be read in the university and the issue of Bible translation could still be openly debated there.[2] Important textual production was in full swing. The influential Wycliffite theological manual, the *Floretum theologie*, was in the process of completion round about this time,[3] as was the second version of the Bible translation. One of those who owned a fine copy of the earlier version of the Wycliffite Bible was Thomas of Woodstock, the duke of Gloucester, to whom Wycliffe's followers also addressed a dialogue between a friar and a secular clerk.[4] An author himself, the duke was the owner of a huge library that included, in a sizeable collection of religious and theological works, a two-volume English Bible, an English book of the gospels and 'a new book of the gospels glossed in English'.[5] As John Thomson indicates,[6] Lollards might well have looked to Gloucester (as they had to his brother, the duke of Lancaster)[7] as a patron. He was present at this parliament (which was presided over by the duke of York), being sent back from Ireland to give a direct report from the king to the Lords and Commons.[8]

How important was it that the king was not present at this parliamentary session, being out of the country (for the first time during his reign) campaigning in Ireland? Thomas Walsingham, who transcribed the text of the 'unheard of' (*inauditas*) conclusions into his chronicle, believed that the Lollards deliberately took advantage of the royal absence. He saw their action as instigated by four of the suspect group of knights whose names he had already listed under the year 1387 – Richard Sturry, Thomas Latimer, Lewis Clifford and John Montagu.[9] Was it expected that parliament – in which none of these men was sitting – would take notice of this unconventional mode of address? Who were the likely authors of the conclusions, and what can we make of their strategy?

Lollards had never before this attempted to draw parliament into the religious debate by such means. Parliament had of course considered matters closely relating to Wycliffite issues, and Oxonian leaders had gone out of their way to stress in lordly hearing the bearing of their arguments on temporal lordship.[10] Public appeals had also been made by means of scattering or posting handbills, some of which entered Knighton's chronicle (thanks to Philip Repingdon, Geoffrey Martin supposes). But it was an entirely new tactic to take the

ecclesiastical cause to parliament as a whole, declaring to Lords and Commons –
the controllers of financial supply – in the name of impecunious purse-keepers of
the spiritual estate, the corrupt burden of the church. If these petitioners took an
unorthodox – indeed presumptuous – route to address parliament, they did so as
apostles of Christ, pointing out the 'leprouse' effects of 'proude prelacye' and
private religion.[11]

The *Twelve Conclusions* were, as McFarlane says, 'a Lollard bill', not a
parliamentary bill but a posted bill: 'twelve short paragraphs of contentious
matter'.[12] Why was it decided in Lollard circles that parliament should be
informed, as the preamble to the conclusions states, of 'certeyn conclusionis and
treuthis for þe reformaciun of holi chirche of Yngelond'?[13] There are various
possible answers to such a simple question, but the most straightforward is that it
was by parliament, or at any rate king in parliament, that 'reformaciun of holi
chirche of Yngelond' would have to be effected. Yet, because 'there is no proof
that it [the manifesto] was taken notice of by parliament, and . . . it led to no
action',[14] even so straightforward an answer provokes more complicated
questions.

We cannot tell who the framers of the manifesto were; we do know who its
audience was. The most recently published volumes of the *History of Parliament*
contain biographies of all the known members of the Commons in parliament for
the period 1386–1421.[15] It is now an easy task to learn something about those
who were, or should have been, at Westminster in February 1395, those for
whom – whether they took any notice or not – the framers of the manifesto
posted their advertisement. The *Twelve Conclusions* were addressed to 'þe lordis
and þe comunys of þe parlement' but it was neither the brief of the Newnham
essayists nor is it our intention here, to discuss the Lords, especially not the Lords
and Lollardy. The commons, the Commons in parliament, are another matter.
The gentry among the Commons (and the majority of the Commons were
gentry, despite the fact that 'gentleman' in 1395 was twenty or thirty years short
of becoming the word they would use to describe themselves), and the relation of
the gentry to Lollardy, was what was particularly on the minds of those gathered
in Cambridge in 1995. It is not only the parliamentary gentry who are in
question, but the gentlemen of the Commons will occupy us first.

It is characteristic of the suspected Lollard knights that they were not
committed parliamentarians. If they were behind the document of 1395, was it
because they were not themselves familiar with parliament and its procedures?
Did they have to use so clumsy a means as bill-posting to communicate with the
non-Lollard parliamentary gentry because hitherto they had not thought of
parliament as an occasion when, as members of the Commons, they might
disseminate their views, either publicly or privately? If there are too many
conjectures in such a hypothesis, including the initial one of there being a group
which thought and behaved as a group, the fact remains that those whom

historians designate the Lollard knights were not parliamentary gentry; that is, they were not themselves members of parliament or, if they were, they sat neither frequently or regularly. The Cheynes are the sole exception.

Sir John Cheyne I was knight of the shire for Gloucestershire four times in the 1390s, but not in 1395; Sir John Cheyne II was knight of the shire for Buckinghamshire seven times between 1421 and 1445. More typical – of those who sat at all – were Sir John Oldcastle, who was knight of the shire for Herefordshire on one occasion (in January 1404), and Sir Thomas Latimer, who sat twice for Northamptonshire. Sir Thomas Clanvow, probably the son of Sir John Clanvow, and a likely Lollard, sat as knight of the shire for Herefordshire three times in the 1390s, though not in 1395.[16] If Sir Philip de la Vache was a Lollard, his single appearance in the Commons as knight of the shire for Buckinghamshire at the February parliament of 1388 hardly warrants us considering him as a parliamentary one.

The experienced parliament men in the group were also only uncertain, if likely, Lollards: William Stourton, the two Sir Thomas Brookes, and Sir Gerald Braybrooke II. Sir Thomas Brooke the father was undoubtedly a parliamentary gentleman: he was elected as knight of the shire for Somerset on thirteen occasions between 1386 and 1413. One of these parliaments was that of 1395. Another was in 1410, when (probably) the knights of the shire entertained a proposal for the disendowment of the clergy.[17] William Stourton was also elected to the parliament of 1410. Were these two behind the disendowment scheme? So far as we can tell, Sir Thomas Brooke in 1395 did not have a single Lollard companion.

Why, then, were the *Twelve Conclusions* addressed to 'þe lordis and þe comunys' at all? What, apart from publicity, did its framers expect to get from their bill-posting? Perhaps they expected nothing more. There is, however, a point to be made about the conclusions and the parliamentary gentry in the Commons, whether in the parliament of 1395 or any other parliament of the period. Posed as a question it is: does an examination of the parliamentary gentry, those who were in the Commons of 1395 for example, suggest that the Lollardy of the *Twelve Conclusions* might have been gentry orientated? After all, it was uncompromising Lollardy which was spiritedly proclaimed by the conclusions, even, it has been said, uncompromisingly academic Lollardy. What were the Commons in parliament to make of that? Disendowment of the clergy, it has been argued, was much more their glass of wine than iconoclasm, pacifism, or the abolition of purgatory. Whether the gentry in the Commons thought well or ill of such matters, the point which requires emphasis is that they did think of them, or rather that they could think of them, were capable of thinking theologically (as well as morally) and, apparently, were deemed by the framers of the conclusions to be so capable.

To read the biographies of the members of the Commons of the parliament of

1395 is to realise the wide range of experience of those who were active in local and central government, politics national and international, war and peace-making, trade and commerce, and the law. It also shows how cultured they were. That point was made by McFarlane about the Lollard knights: 'career-soldiers though they were, they were cultivated men . . . not all their books were light reading . . . The literacy of the group was exceptional.'[18] What we have to accommodate in Geoffrey Chaucer, in other words, we have also to accommodate in them.[19] The accommodation we have to make in the members of the Commons of 1395 is one between their hard-nosedness and their capacity for theological as well as devotional thought. It is not difficult to do so. Was the church reaching a similar conclusion, or did 'holi chirche of Yngelond' underestimate the literate layman as the French church was doing? Were churchmen in England taking into sufficient consideration that the minds of the laity required sustenance as much as their hearts (and souls) did? 'There remained a persistent refusal in the northern French language', concludes Geneviève Hasenohr, 'to allow theoretical reflection, and this left the faithful defenceless before the Reformers: the church was caught off its guard, at a time when reading acquired a decisive weight in the formation of belief. Literacy, even when it did not foster heresy, might offer little with which to combat heterodoxy.'[20] Was English devotional reading as resolutely anti-intellectual as the French? If it was, where does that place Lollardy in relation to the literate English gentry and their literate English wives?

We arrive at the *Twelve Conclusions*. Some are ultra-puritanical, philistine, and anti-populist: clauses three, five, eight, eleven and twelve are, for example, respectively anti-buggery, anti-supranatural, anti-pilgrimage, anti-abortion, and anti-arts and crafts – the last perhaps particularly topical in 1395, given the preparations for the Irish expedition and Richard II's artistic patronage. Clause four, however, is more than an expression of moral outrage. The question of whether or not transubstantiation occurs at the consecration of the bread and wine is a matter requiring a good deal of concentrated attention. Moreover, whether prayers for named souls (clause seven) and confession and priestly absolution (clause nine) are defensible or not, are questions to be considered in a similar manner, despite the anti-clerical terms in which the arguments against them were couched in the conclusions. As there is no indication either of moral outrage or concentrated reflection being shown by the Commons in 1395, we must suppose the posted manifesto led to neither. The time was not ripe, it seems, for parliamentary acceptance of the church as corrupt in faith as well as morals. Still, while the Commons may have ignored the *Twelve Conclusions*, there is no evidence that the proposals were theologically or morally too demanding for them. Their biographies demonstrate otherwise.[21]

One clause of the conclusions, the sixth, which petitioned for the end of clerical employment in secular government, might be thought to have strong appeal to the gentry. There was, as Anne Hudson points out in her examination of this question, a ready-made parliamentary context for cutting bishops out of the highest secular office. The issue of ambidexterity, of placing in one pair of hands the separate tasks of temporal and spiritual affairs, was discussed at length by Wycliffe and his followers. The growth of lay literacy, and the increasing amount of work performed by a class which one might see (as reformers of a later age effectively did) as itself hermaphroditic – married clergy in lesser orders – meant that change was already taking place. Yet the radical separation proposed by this clause could have affected different gentry differently. Greater lords might have lost where lesser gentry stood to gain. Parliamentary and non-parliamentary gentry alike might have seen its advantages, as could ordinary bureaucrats like Thomas Tykhill and extraordinary councillors like Thomas Chaucer.

It is clause six which appears to signal most strongly that the conclusions were gentry-directed. Roger Dymmok, for one, read the signal in that fashion and, as Fiona Somerset demonstrates, he had gentlemen in mind when making his reply to the whole text. No one could doubt the seriousness of the appeal made in the conclusions, as no one can doubt it of Dymmok's reply. Yet it recalls Alexander Murray's exposé of the call for reform at the Council of Constance, as little more than a demand of graduates for more lucrative jobs.[22] The two cases are different, but they have the same air about them. Was the Lollard call for a separation of church and state really about the clergy getting in the way of good government – 'makin every reme out of god reule'[23] – and about the proper administration of the cure of souls? Or was it simply an anti-clerical swipe? In other words, was there a real issue for the Lollards here or not? And if so, which one was it?[24]

It does not seem that gentlemen themselves regarded their careers as being blocked by clerical holders of office. Maureen Jurkowski points out – as others have done before her – that there was no lack of opportunity in royal, noble, gentry and ecclesiastical administration for careerist laymen, particularly lawyers; indeed it was a time of greater opportunity than ever before. It may be that the 1410 scheme for clerical disendowment had a slightly more subtle appeal than its obvious calculation, as McFarlane put it, 'to tempt the avarice of laymen'.[25] Disendowment would have meant more jobs as well as more lands for the laity. But that issue, whatever its implications for lay employment, is less important here than clause six of the twelve: all clerks out. The hesitation of gentry on this issue could have had something to do with their ambivalent – not to say ambidextrous – position. They were both employers and employees; they were also patrons, and patrons of livings. Clerical labour was cheap, cheaper at any rate than that of laymen. Whether our cultivated gentlemen, let alone cultured kings and nobles, made any sort of calculations, however rough, about or between themselves on the matter is doubtful. Yet most (if aware of it) must have had doubts about the wisdom of the clause, even if they were not voiced: clause six was not implemented; nor did disendowment take place.

The Lollards, clerical Lollards most of all, were well aware of the importance of patrons. John of Gaunt's patronage of Wycliffe was what kept him out of prison, possibly what kept him alive, and the patronage Sir Philip de la Vache seems likely to have exercised on behalf of Lollard knights is one of the 'missing links' in the early history of Lollardy. Just as the hugely influential de la Vache moved into Gaunt's vacant Garter stall at Windsor in April 1399, so he may have replaced him as chief protector of the Wycliffites until his death in 1408. McFarlane wrote of him: 'Lollard or not, he belongs to the group we are considering.'[26] Gentry patronage, like that of the Lollard knights and Sir William Beauchamp (who is considered below), was equally important where the appointment of Lollard priests to benefices was concerned. While it is an obvious point it needs emphasis, as such support was critical to the long history of Lollardy.

Protection was also given in other, more straightforward ways, some of them evidenced in the essays published in this volume. Take what superficially appears a trifling matter: the removal of James Brewster's faggot badge. He and William Sweeting had been condemned in March 1506 to wear such badges for life. Sweeting's badge was removed by his clerical employer, the parson of the parish church of St Mary Magdalen, Colchester, where he was holy water clerk. Brewster's was taken off by the comptroller of the household of John de Vere, earl of Oxford, in which household he was employed as a carpenter. The comptroller was certainly a gentleman, possibly Philip FitzLewis of the important Essex family, according to Andrew Hope, who sees this as part of 'the web of patronage within which William Sweeting moved'. It is not why the heretical badges were removed that is important; it is the fact that they were, and by whom. The FitzLewis family was one of hundreds of greater, or county, gentry families who governed England. They did what they did, and did what they had to, because they were England's governors. If it suited the earl of Oxford's comptroller of household to take off a heretic's badge, he did so. He did not ask anyone's permission; he either thought he did not need to ask, or he did not choose to. Penances, as Norman Tanner shows, were intended to deter as well as to punish. But if the wearing of a faggot badge was conceived as something that would affect employers as well as fellow workers, this example suggests that it had serious limitations. Lollardy survived primarily because gentry patronage of its exponents persisted. A historian might, therefore, want to question the recent statement that where Lollardy is concerned it is 'the roles of the production and dissemination of books, teaching, and literacy [which] are now at the centre of the picture'.[27] For the historian, patronage has always to be in the foreground.

The essay by Paweł Kras, the odd one out in the collection, graphically displays how crucial the protection of the great was for the growth and survival of heresy. It also makes an illuminating comparison with the situation in England and John Oldcastle's influence. In Poland, unlike Bohemia, the nobility generally regarded Hussite developments as a threat to their position. But Alexander Zbąski was able to create a Hussite enclave on his estates, where tithes were withheld and utraquist services introduced, and whence Hussite missionaries were despatched. His support of Hussite priests, and the subsequent withdrawal of that support, meant life and death for Hussitism in Great Poland. Five of the priests Zbąski handed over after recanting his heresy at Poznan in 1440 were burned at the stake. The consequences of the exercise of power in England were seldom so bluntly demonstrated; there was always, even in the aftermath of the Oldcastle revolt, a blurring of boundaries between jurisdictions and responsibilities. That is what the English upper classes had discovered to be the most effective means of government. We might say it was a device for sowing confusion among the lower classes, were it not for the fact that class divisions in England were themselves blurred.

The best illustration of that celebrated aspect of Englishness is relevant here. 'Who was then the gentleman' is a question everyone was asking in this period. Historians of that period are also currently asking: who were the greater and who the lesser gentry? Thomas Chaucer and Thomas Tykhill are evidently gentlemen; they are very different sorts of gentlemen. Questions about those on the margin of gentility, including that margin in towns – especially in small towns like Tenterden or Amersham – and their Lollard allegiances, are posed in some of the later essays in this book, particularly those of Robert Lutton and Andrew Hope. Did Lollardy have a stronger attraction for those on the margins, because of insecurity or for other reasons? Are there any attitudes shared between lesser gentry, such as most of those who feature in Maureen Jurkowski's essay, for example, or the certain northern knight of Richard Wyche's discourse in Christina van Nolcken's chapter (a man who may have been on a different sort of margin, a geographical one), or well-off townsfolk, like the Castelyns and Pellonds in Tenterden (and their lesser gentry friends Edward Walker and Thomas Pytlesdon), or the Bardfields of Colchester? Did such people warm to Lollardy because it offered a more satisfying explanation of the world, as well as a keener criticism of the church, than did the orthodox faith? Lollardy, we know, offered, indeed was, different things to different men and women: that no doubt was its strength. It may not only have been the prospect of more and better jobs which made Lollardy attractive to gentlemen like Henry Bothe and John Finderne, Ralph and Richard Friday, and the fascinating Thomas Lucas. Self-making men, they may have discovered in Lollardy's stress on *self*-salvation the religious security they were looking for.

There were no gentlemen or gentlewomen among those Kentish Lollards against whom Archbishop Warham proceeded in 1511–12, who are discussed by Norman Tanner. It is impossible to imagine a penance such as he describes, which involved having to watch a *gentleman* burn; a gentleman hang, perhaps, as Sir Roger Acton of Sutton, Worcestershire, a tiler's son from Shrewsbury, was hanged for taking part in Oldcastle's rising. Sir Roger, like Sir Thomas Talbot of Davington, near Faversham (a newcomer to Kent), was a veteran of the Welsh wars of Henry IV's reign. Both had done well out of their soldiering and Sir Thomas, like Sir Roger, responded to the call in 1414. These two look very like new gentlemen, as indeed do three other rebels: Robert Harley and Richard Colfox, 'esquires of doubtful antecedents', and Thomas Noveray of Illston-on-the-Hill, Leicestershire. None of them was ever elected to parliament; all of them overwhelmingly qualify as lesser gentry.[28]

They were, or they may have been, exceptions to a rule stated by John Thomson about the gentry: 'They were king's men first, and religious radicals second.' They were not like the Bohemian gentry; above all not like Tomáš Štitný. Not even Sir John Oldcastle was like Tomáš Štitný. In a book of this nature there is no need to go into the reasons why the English gentry did not behave like the Bohemian gentry c. 1400, and no need to expound the very different contexts, political, ecclesiastical, social, economic and linguistic, in which the two groups lived their lives. Nonetheless, what has to be asked is why in Bohemia there was so great an enthusiasm for religious reform to be found among the gentry and nobility, whereas in England religious reform (though a matter for some discussion and, as Jeremy Catto has shown, of some achievement in the reign of Henry V), did not become a major issue, but only a heretical one. There *was* Oldcastle's rising, but what was that beside the Hussite wars? Even *De Heretico Comburendo*, as Alison McHardy points out, was no more than an act of deterrence; it was not 'a measured response to a theological problem'; it was anti-disorder, anti-sedition, not pro-religion, pro-church.

Tomáš Štitný is an extreme but also a test case. He was born in the 1330s and died before 1410. Described as a country gentleman (although after 1381 he lived in a house next door to the Bethlehem chapel in Prague), a philosopher who translated Augustine into Czech, a moralist and mystic, Tomáš was also a father, a widower who wrote handbooks of family instruction for his children, and a lay preacher. He was not university trained. Writing in the vernacular, he was one of the founding fathers of the Czech language and, therefore, of Czech culture. Professor Reginald Betts wrote of him: 'Tomáš was the eloquent enemy of magic, relics, vain repetitions, fastings, masses for the dead, pilgrimages and indulgences.' Here is Tomáš on St Stephen and those who pray to him 'so that they may have success with horses': 'surely', says Tomáš, 'St Stephen has something better to do than concern himself with horses! Were there no horses before St Stephen? Who looked after them then?' Despite, or because of, being both down to earth and something of an historian, Tomáš was a Utraquist.[29]

Tomáš Štitný was by definition an ordinary country gentleman and his piety was part of, as well as a contribution to, the Czech reform movement of the second half of the fourteenth century. Yet the fact that he *was* a gentleman, despite being so exceptional, is what is important. Sir John Clanvow, Sir John

Oldcastle, Thomas Tykhill and Henry of Grosmont, duke of Lancaster, were all exceptional too. It is the nature of his piety which singles Tomáš out, particularly the differences between it and the piety of John Clanvow or Henry of Grosmont, as well as that of Oldcastle or Tykhill. Defining what is characteristic of the devotional life and pious attitudes of the English élite might help us to understand why that élite ultimately rejected Lollardy; for if it did so largely because Lollardy became heretical, there are aspects of the English religious tradition, above all of lay religion, which were antipathetic to Lollard 'culture'. Nonetheless, while what probably prevented the great majority of English gentry from being Lollards in Tomáš Štitný's lifetime was their lack of religion, or their indifference to it, those who *were* devout might have seen their religion as un- or non-Lollard. The idea that religious life was very much the laity's business – an essential Štitný–Wycliffe–Lollard conviction – failed to gain widespread acceptance. Not until the time of Thomas More did the devout household, so central a concept to the practice of religion for Štitný, Wycliffe and the Lollards, become important in English theory or practice.

That knighthood carried spiritual responsibilities was an intrinsic part of Wycliffe's beliefs. To see Lollardy in terms of Wycliffe's *Ordo Christi* (as Michael Wilks has seen it)[30] is to recognise the supreme duty imposed on king and courtiers in undertaking the task of religious reform: 'It parteyneþ to þe ordir of knyȝthod to defende Goddis lawe'.[31] This was something that extended far beyond the conventional duty of the martial estate. 'Secular lords shulden in defaute of prestes lerne and teche þe lawe of God in þer moder tonge.'[32] The defence of Scripture and the direction of reformation could not be undertaken without the positive cooperation of a trusted group of cultivated and experienced royal servants. Lollard knights, on this reading, were central to Wycliffite thinking.

We know that country gentry were involved from early days in burgeoning theological debates, in touch with issues being hammered out in the schools. This was doubtless easiest for those within close reach of Oxford, like Thomas Compworth, dubbed the first 'Lollard gentleman' by Alison McHardy.[33] There were squires and knights who were interested to hear Wycliffe preach, and to talk about matters of topical academic interest. Wycliffe was invited by a devout layman to preach on the ten commandments, and the Cambridge master John Devereux (or Deveros) got caught up in a discussion on images and pilgrimage with a country squire.[34] Such gentlemen were not beyond the pale of Latin learning, though they may not have wanted too much in the way of learned disquisition. Like the narrator of *Pierce the Ploughman's Crede*, some may have shared the limited view of the essentials of textual learning described by John Scattergood. It was Pierce the lettered layman who was able to end the poem's search for the rudiments of credal learning, but Walter Brut (or Brute), the literate husbandman whose unorthodox teaching mustered a team of university opponents, was also praised by this spokesman of the anti-intellectuals for telling 'the sothe'. And Brut was accused of teaching both commoners and nobles.[35] Walter Brut's Latin learning may have been quite exceptional for a man of his standing, but gentry who were unlikely to have shared this capacity for scholastic composition were recipients of Latin texts. Wycliffe wrote a tract for a knight 'striving after the truth',[36] and Devereux sent his gentle conversationalist a Latin summary of the points they had covered.

Touched by the ferment of avant-garde theology, gentry of this breed might be fired by higher ambitions – devotional, spiritual, religious. When reforming talk was in the air, even fashionable in court circles, suggestions for structural changes in the church might come into the hearing of lay lords on country estates. Parliamentary activity was by no means a necessary part of such concerns, though to some it seemed important. But, in 1395 as at other times, sanctity and politics made awkward if not incompatible bedfellows, and for those of knightly status there was another kind of tension: that between Lollardy and chivalry.[37] If the expedition on which two of the suspect knights, Sir John Clanvow and Sir William Neville, ended their lives was of the kind specifically rejected by the *Twelve Conclusions* – with clause ten's condemnation of manslaughter in war or crusade[38] – Wycliffite knighthood had a perennial mission to uphold the law of Christ.

Lollard knights were Wycliffe's *pugiles legis Dei*[39] – gospel warriors. When Sir John Oldcastle wrote, probably in 1411, to congratulate King Wenzel of Bohemia for upholding the Czech reformers, he surely envisaged himself in the same role as that for which he was complimenting his correspondent – the model *miles Christi*. 'O how delightful that the greatest prince has proved the greatest knight of Christ.'[40] It was a term and a concept with a long history. But when Oldcastle found his own king unwilling to follow Wenzel's example, the Lollards who enlisted under him in their chosen field of battle gave such Christian knighthood a damagingly bad name. A sermon that was probably preached before Henry V at Epiphany 1414, when he (also seen as 'Crystes knyght') was about to crush Oldcastle's fatally daring exploit, made some telling remarks about the three kings of the feast. The respect that was owed to them was more clerkly than regal; the gospel called them *magi*, not kings, and they were honoured above all as men of great learning, 'of right gret letture'. 'For it was more fittynge to grounde oure fey3th and believe in þam undir þe name of clergy þan undir þe name of kny3thod.'[41] The most learned knight or warrior for Christ might find himself faced by clerical demarcation zones. Great learning belonged to the ecclesiastical sphere. Innocent III had put it on record with the words of Malachi: 'For the priest's lips should keep knowledge, and they should seek the law at his mouth'.[42]

Though the writers of the conclusions managed to conceal their identity, their text, as Fiona Somerset points out, betrays access to clerical learning and was taken by Roger Dymmok to be a clerical work. This in itself gave great cause for alarm. The document not only aired fundamental criticisms of the church's priesthood, sacraments, sacramentals and institutions, to the extent that it could be seen as aiming at the destruction of churchmen and church.[43] It could also be read as the ultimate *trahison des clercs*. The reference to Wycliffe's *Trialogus* was a signal that pointed to Oxford involvement. A chain reaction of countermoves started against this work and suspect scholars in the university which, though it by no means ended Wycliffite activities there, fundamentally affected official perceptions. Richard II, who at this time gave lapidary expression to his pride in having 'destroyed heretics and scattered their friends', ordered the authorities in Oxford to investigate the errors of *Trialogus*.[44] Dymmok, writing as the church's champion, sought to enlist king, nobility and gentry, and the widest public support against the dangers posed by the Lollard text. Boniface IX's reaction to the *Twelve Conclusions* added to the growing international scope of anti-Wycliffite action. The alliance between gentry and Lollardy, which had stood Wycliffe's followers in such good stead over the previous fifteen or so years, was critically affected.

The publicity stunt of 1395 may have diminished the capacity of Oxford as a Wycliffite generating station, and given adverse publicity to Lollard knights. But it would be very wrong to suppose that either gentry interest in Wycliffite literature or gentry patronage of Lollards came to an end. The papers in this book are revealing of the ways in which the links between Lollard thought and the interests of the gentry continued through the fifteenth century. Building on McFarlane's work it has proved possible to widen its foundations, by extending the methodology and looking harder at the forms of religious belief and behaviour in which the orthodox and less than orthodox blurred and blended.

McFarlane himself showed the way here in the concluding pages of his examination of the Lollard knights. The expressions of worldly loathing for flesh and world which he found in wills, and regarded as a test of religious affiliation, have been shown to have even more hazardous than he suspected. There were more individuals than he supposed whose unimpeachable orthodoxy was combined with such testamentary phraseology, which, though it may reflect a channel of thought sympathetic to Lollard puritanism, reached far beyond the movement. John Thomson's chapter reassesses such testamentary evidence for a wide group of marginal knightly suspects. He shows the broad range of knightly piety which could lie behind such language. Sympathy for evangelical aspirations could take various forms, and there was a lack of clear-cut boundaries between acceptable and unacceptable enthusiasm. His exploration reveals 'a social circle and perhaps also a spiritual ambience which was acceptable to both orthodox and heretics'.

If much of the confusion and controversy of the day was a question of language, much – perhaps too much – has seemed to turn on testamentary phraseology. But this belongs to a wide context, not purely literary. Jeremy Catto has explained such language as having 'its origin in the devotional literature of the later fourteenth century which appeared in the wake of Richard Rolle'; he sees the common phraseology of the wills, summed up by McFarlane as the 'macabre loathing of the flesh', as 'the outward sign of Rolle's powerful, if indirect, influence'. This was not Lollardy (in any shape or form) but the expressiveness of 'men of the world, imbued with the aristocratic values of chivalry – gentlemen, in the language of a later period – but prone to the doubts and torments of a vivid imaginative conscience'.[45] If we were to add to Lollard wills the cadaver tombs of the later Middle Ages, which depict successful, proud, vainglorious men, grand in their robes of estate above, and humiliated as naked, rotten corpses below, together with Henry of Grosmont's *Livre de Seyntz Medicines*, which with such 'disarming frankness' displays the man of the world humbling himself before the reader as he confesses all the sins of a gentleman,[46] we would have more than enough evidence of what Dr Catto calls the 'predicament which must have limited the attractions of a radical religious posture among gentlemen of Sir William Beauchamp's ilk'.[47]

A form of evidence that McFarlane used, but did not exploit (and which still awaits systematic investigation), is the patronage of benefices. Alison McHardy broke new ground here, in showing the importance of college livings in helping to speed Wycliffites on evangelising missions outside the university.[48] Philip Repingdon's house, as Geoffrey Martin points out, was able to provide him with a useful pulpit between Oxford and Leicester at Brackley, where the canons of St Mary's held the benefice. More work remains to be done on Lollard gentry presentations to livings, and on the parishes (or chapelries) in which Lollard developments could take root. The exploration of book-owning and the contents of religious anthologies can also be revealing of gentry religion, and the varieties of devotional interest which could nest together.

Outlying or marginal associates of the named Lollard knights may, as John Thomson suggests, tell us a great deal about the contemporary piety that was attracted to what became deviance. One such man, whose close links with the group placed him in the category of possible guilt by association, was Sir William Beauchamp, Lord Bergavenny. Benefices and books both add to his dossier. The knowledge that Beauchamp presented Robert Lechlade (Lychlade) and William Counter respectively to the rectories of Kemerton in Gloucestershire and Pirton in Worcestershire, is a strong pointer to his Lollard sympathies. Lechlade was one of the men expelled from Oxford in the summer of 1395; Counter owned and perhaps compiled a volume which included Sir John Clanvow's treatise *The Two Ways*.[49] Knowing this makes it the more interesting to find that Sir William was also patron of one of the livings that later featured in the Norwich heresy trials. Burgh Apton (or Bergh as it was then called) was a Norfolk living to which he presented in both 1406 and 1409.[50] Just at this time, after the death of Bishop

Despenser in August 1406, it was argued that Richard Dereham SPP, chancellor of Cambridge University, would make a better successor to the see than Alexander Tottington, prior of Norwich Cathedral Priory, because of the heresy of the Lollards, whose growing numbers and 'rites and heresies' called for the crushing skills of an expert theologian.[51]

After Lord Bergavenny's death in 1411, his long-lived widow Joan presented successively to the parish of Bergh in 1422, 1425 and 1434.[52] None of the men she patronised is named in any extant heretical proceedings, and they all seem to have led quietly obscure lives. But it is hard to suppose that Robert Potter or Roger Philpot (rectors between 1422 and 1434) could have been oblivious of what was going on in their parish, which was the scene of one particularly scandalous event in the reported career of William White. He was said to have presided over an illicit lay celebration of communion in his room in the parish of Bergh.[53] At this time the parish included an attached chapel which seems to have survived until the sixteenth century, and which was to add the name of Apton to the parish.[54] It is intriguing to speculate that a chapel of this kind, with its semi-independent parochial status, could have provided the kind of base for William White that was enjoyed by William Smith, Richard Waytestathe and William Swinderby in the chapel of St John outside Leicester – whence Swinderby moved from another kind of retreat, the hermitage provided by the duke of Lancaster.[55] When she died in 1435 Lady Beauchamp left a long will of conventionally devout last wishes. But they were written in English, and that in itself alerted McFarlane to consider possible lingering Lollard influences.[56] It is hard to suppose that Joan would have approved of William White. But she, like others, including her husband, might have valued vernacular devotional or scriptural reading.

The patronage of parish livings may suggest that Lollard sympathy or allegiance of some kind continued in the Cheyne family throughout the fifteenth century. The case is perhaps stronger for this among the Buckinghamshire Cheynes than it is for the Gloucestershire branch of the family, whose literary interests are considered by John Thomson.[57] The unusually severe treatment of the Cheynes, members of whose family were placed in the Tower in both 1414 and 1431, suggests that there were powerful suspicions of their good faith. The occupancy of their rectory of Drayton Beauchamp by the heretic Thomas Drayton did nothing to help the family's reputation among the prosecutors, and the situation in another Buckinghamshire parish could have added to the picture. Chesham Bois became another seat – and advowson – of the Cheyne family in the fifteenth century. Bishop Chedworth might well have had misgivings when two of the Amersham heretics he examined in 1464 reported that they had learnt their heresy from the rector of Chesham Bois.[58] At this time there were close links between the landowning gentry of Amersham and Chesham Bois. The Brudenells at Amersham had ties of friendship and marriage with the Cheynes. John Cheyne married Elizabeth Brudenell, the daughter of Edmund Brudenell, who in his draft will of 1457 wanted his two Bibles given to 'sum goode honest places in Oxon where most nede is', while the rest of his books were to be divided among his four sons by his executors, one of whom was John Cheyne.[59] Gentry scriptural bookishness mixes suggestively with heretical enquiries.

Suspicions, not exorcised by local connections, may seem to hang over Chesham Bois through the fifteenth century – starting before the manor was bought by the Cheynes early in Henry VI's reign. Patrons, indicted indirectly by the clergy they promoted, might also seem to suffer a degree of incrimination from suspects who lurked near their premises. A sequence of interesting names appears among the holders of the moiety of the church of St Mary's, Chesham, known as 'Chesham Leicester', which is another example of a parochial chapel. The chapel of St Leonard was appropriated to Leicester Abbey, but the lord of the manor gained effective control over the living, with its jurisdictional independence and geographical separation from the mother church.[60] Was the John Wodard who in 1404 exchanged his rectory of Great Hampden (Bucks.) for this Chesham vicarage, the Wycliffite chaplain whose preaching at Chipping Warden (Northants.) caused so much worry to Bishop Buckingham in 1388–89?[61] Some years later Richard Monk held this living for a bare eight months, in 1421–22. His tenure was apparently terminated by a citation for heresy before the bishop of Lincoln – something he admitted when he was accused before Convocation in 1428. Many years later the Chesham living was for six years in the hands of Mr Thomas Cotton, against whom no more serious charge can be laid than his being the recipient of a book of English gospels when he held the vicarage of Rickmansworth in 1521.[62]

This is, admittedly, flimsy evidence, but it raises again the question of the parochial chapel, and its potential for becoming a preserve (perhaps a gentry preserve, halfway to being a private chapel) in which certain freedoms were allowed to operate. A late fifteenth-century example of such an institution – one which really was 'a Gentleman's lending library' of popular reading, mostly in English – is the chapel founded at Pott Shrigley in Cheshire in the 1490s by Geoffrey Downes. The books (both manuscript and printed) available here for reading, borrowing or copying included *Dives and Pauper* and the Wycliffite commentaries on the gospels of Matthew and Mark, which had been given to Downes by John Crowland (who died in 1493 after forty-four years as rector of South Ockenden, Essex).[63] Were there particular livings where those of a certain religious temperament knew they would find easy lodging? Were local gentry sometimes responsible for such settings?

Gentry complaisance (or inertia) might also enable well-established and prospering local artisan families, like those of Tenterden investigated by Robert Lutton, to tip over into heresy. If the piety of Castelyns and Pellonds was unexceptionable, it seems also to have been unexcited by traditional devotions to the saints, and ready to move into the new (more Christocentric) cult of the Jesus mass. It included a borderline unorthodoxy exemplified by the man who switched his offering to the Rood of Grace into alms to a poor man.[64] One wonders how these parishioners reacted to the 'leisurely progress' by which, through the second half of the fifteenth century, their parish church steadily built up its still outstanding feature: the magnificent tower which in its own age gained proverbial status, and humorous mentions in works of Thomas More: Sandwich harbour silted up through the building of Tenterden's steeple.[65] The countryman's derided logic might mask a sardonic jest; were there parochial objectors to the making of this famous landmark?

The location of books and their gentry owners can also tell us much about the cultivated circles to which Wycliffite authors looked for readers, hearers, and support. The will of Dame Margery Nerford, or Narford, an heiress in her own right who died aged about fifty-nine in 1417, is suggestive of the interface between orthodox and heretical. Margery was connected with the Cobham family, probably through her paternal grandmother, with whom she remained close up to the time of the latter's death in 1394. Alice Nerford was a long-lived widow, who died fifty years after the death of her first husband, Thomas Nerford, calling herself, after her third and last husband, Sir John Neville, 'Lady Neville of Essex'. She bequeathed a silver gilt cup to 'my dear lord and cousin Sir John de Cobham', a gold ring and 'my pater nosters' to his wife, while Margery Nerford, her granddaughter, was given her complete chapel, a long list of rich plate and furnishings, and entrusted with the residue of the estate and her soul's care.[66]

The relationship reads almost like that of mother and daughter. Possibly Lady Neville took the place of Margery's parents, who may both have died while she was still young. The death of her father, John Nerford, in 1363 when she was five, left her in the wardship of Peter Brewes, who married her as a teenager to his son John. The unravelling of this unhappy match was probably helped by Lady Neville, with whom Margery Nerford appears to have found asylum when affairs came to a head in 1378. Both parties were cited to appear before king and council at the time of the Gloucester Parliament in the autumn of that year, and Margery (fearing injury at the hands of John Brewes) obtained protection, which was renewed until 1381–2, while her divorce suit (appealed to Rome) was pending.[67] Finally, in May 1383, at the age of twenty-five, Margery Nerford took a vow of chastity before Bishop Braybrooke of London.[68]

Margery, like her grandmother, kept up with her Cobham relatives in Kent. In 1383 she was involved in the conveyance of various Nerford lands in Norfolk (at Narford, Holt and elsewhere), held for life by her grandmother, to Sir John Cobham of Cooling Castle in Kent.[69] Her own will (dated 31 October 1417) shows that she inherited, along with so much else, the services of one of her grandmother's most trusted female servants, Christian Ipstans. Perhaps Margery Nerford had also inherited books. She was clearly very interested in them. Her household included David, the rector of Pilkington, 'living with me', apparently

Section of an early sixteenth-century survey of manors on the Kent salt marshes, showing Cooling Castle and the marshes, reclaimed ('inned') and salt, of Lord Cobham's manor. (By permission of the British Library, MS Harl. 590, f. 1)

as a scribe, who was given her breviary and the 'book of Chrysostom and all the other books which he wrote for me'. Other books went to religious houses. To Christ Church London, 'my book of gospel homilies and another book of mine which belonged to my father'; to the prioress and convent of Denney in Cambridgeshire 'my book about the Blessed Mary called "le Image de nostre dame"'; to John Wateley, London citizen and mercer (one of her executors), 'my glossed Psalter in two volumes', while the anchorite outside Bishopsgate was given the choice of any book or books not otherwise bequeathed. And, 'I give to Lady Cobham, the wife of John Oldcastle, my book which once belonged to Lord Cobham'.[70]

Which Lord Cobham was this? At the time when Margery made her will Sir John Oldcastle, the latest holder of the title, was lost to view. Perhaps even his wife (of whom McFarlane remarked, there is no reason to suppose she was 'anything but indifferent' to her husband's convictions) was unaware of his whereabouts.[71] It is unlikely that Margery Nerford lived to learn the fate of the rebellious John Oldcastle, who was captured a month after she made her will. But she must have known him, the degraded and dishonoured Lord Cobham, to whose wife the family book was being returned. Lady Cobham, it would seem, whatever her personal views, was at least as book-worthy as her husband. Margery herself died as a pious daughter of holy church. There is nothing to suggest that the direction of her devotions and her reading was other than orthodox. But her scribe, her domestic library, including the gospel sermons, the Chrysostom, the glossed Psalter, and the book which went back to Lady Cobham, are suggestive of industrious religious learning of the kind Wycliffites approved and fostered. Indicative as it is of gentry dabbling in theology, Margery Nerford's will tells us about those verges of gentry religion which are so important to estimating Lollardy.

A wealthy gentlewoman like Margery Nerford could exercise patronage and enjoy considerable independence within her household. The evidence of her domestic scribe is unusual, but there were also widows whose ownership of books is interesting. Perrin Clanvow who died in 1422, widow of Sir Thomas Clanvow, bequeathed in her will a copy of the *Pore Caitif* and 'four quayres of Doctours on Mathewe', which might well have been part of the Wycliffite glossed gospels.[72] A copy of the later Wycliffite version of the New Testament, including the commentary on Matthew, was bought in the fifteenth century by a woman after it had been vetted ('over seyne and redd') by Dr Thomas Eborall, a staunch opponent of Reginald Pecock.[73]

Women, of course, might be assumed to be illiterate, above all in the sense of non-Latinate. There was more reason for them to have vernacular books than men, and the nuns of the Brigettine house of Isleworth had the offices translated into English. The author of *The Myroure of oure Ladye* made plain that he had obtained proper episcopal licence for translating the passages of Scripture in these services. But he regarded it as quite natural and likely that the users of his work would themselves have English Bibles. It was for this reason that he had not translated much of the Psalms, 'for ye may have them of Rycharde hampoules drawynge, and out of Englysshe bibles if ye have lysence therto'.[74] Dame Anne Danvers, widow of Sir William Danvers, in 1517 presented a fifteenth-century manuscript of the Wycliffite New Testament to Syon, and the names of two nuns of Barking are in a manuscript now in the British Library, which contained part of the later biblical translation.[75] Other religious houses also owned such Bibles. Henry VI gave a fine Lollard Bible to the London Charterhouse, and the Franciscans of Shrewsbury owned parts of the translation.[76]

More interesting, as raising more questions about contemporary attitudes to vernacular scripture and its readers, is the evidence of gentry ownership of English Bibles, some of which found their way into parish churches. John Clopton in 1504 bequeathed 'my Bible in Englisshe' to the archdeacon of Suffolk.[77] In 1507 two English Bibles were given by Richard Cook, a Coventry mercer and member of the local élite, to the parish churches of Holy Trinity, Coventry, and St Matthew's, Walsall.[78] Richard Hunne's much discussed Bible was 'wont to lie in St Margaret church in Bridge Street', London, 'sometimes a month together', for the edification of all who cared to read it.[79] The very size and layout of many Wycliffite Bibles suggests that their makers intended such lectern use and public reading.[80] Was this always possible in some quarters, or were the strictures of the fifteenth century going by the board in the early sixteenth? But even in the fifteenth century John Lacy, an anchorite of the Black Friars in Newcastle, a recluse who acted as scribe for his lay neighbours and who may have been supported by Lord Scrope, left to St John's church near his cell a copy of the Wycliffite Bible.[81] As A.I. Doyle has pointed out, the large number of surviving copies of English New Testaments seems indicative of a wide market, and production that 'can hardly have been surreptitious, even after 1408'.[82] How do we explain this substantial body of English biblical texts, and their sometimes open use, which seems to conflict so markedly with the church's determination to root out meddlers with vernacular scripture?

Some time after the publication in 1409 of Archbishop Arundel's *Constitutions*, with their restrictions on the making and reading of scriptural translation, an author (a friar, perhaps a Franciscan) wrote a dedication to a set of English sermons. The addressee, of gentle birth and privileged standing, enjoyed an enviable security. The writer, not without a hint of jealousy, drew attention to the advantages bestowed by this lay patron's position, as compared with that of the humble preacher:

> non of hem hath defendit you to connyn the gospel in
> Englych . . . ye that ben in swych sekyrnesse that non
> prelat may lettin you ne dishesin you for connynge ne
> for kepinge of the gospel.[83]

It was a reproach that Margery Baxter or Hawis Moon might have voiced to Perrin Clanvow or Margery Nerford. It's all right for *you*; you don't have to worry about owning or reading Scripture. No bishop is going to harry someone of your estate.

The social conventions of the day discriminated between different kinds of vernacular readers as they discriminated about so much else. An English Bible, New Testament or gospel commentary in the hands of a glover or tailor or skinner, told quite a different tale from such a text in the hands of a knight or gentlewoman. In one case subversion or potential subversion of established belief and order had come to seem inevitable; heresy could almost be equated with vernacular religious reading. Not so for those whose literacy and loyalty could be depended on. The law for gentlemen was not the law for knaves.

The apparent non-prosecution of the English gentry for heresy (Walter Brut or Brute, for all his learning, seems to have been a Welsh husbandman) is notable, because it tells us about the realities of gentry status, not about gentry Lollardy or the lack of it. Just as the gentry could get away with murder in the common law courts because no jury would convict a gentleman, so the gentry could get away with heresy because of bishops' reluctance to bring a gentleman into court on such a charge. Those whose matrimonial and testamentary affairs would be handled at the highest jurisdictional level (before bishop in his court of audience, rather than by official or archdeacon) knew they would never be cited to answer before a tribunal examining the beliefs of local villagers. Sir John Oldcastle, Lord Cobham, who betrayed his class as well as king and country, and overstepped the mark so egregiously that he had to be tried in the highest forum, still enjoyed the delays and procrastinations of rank (as well as courtly connections) to the annoyance of the lower house of convocation.

Gentry, unless proved otherwise by arrantly conspicuous ill-behaviour, were assumed to be on the right side of belief, as of authority. Several chapters in the book illuminate the various ways by which gentry associations with Lollards undermined this assumption. The literate skills which (Maureen Jurkowski suggests) gave lawyers an affinity with Lollardy, inclined some gentry members of the legal profession to heretical sympathies and to lending their support by giving surety for imprisoned suspects. The career of the ex-fellow of Merton, Thomas Lucas, is particularly interesting in this way. Such men could play an important part in the Lollard support system, a network which Alison McHardy's examination of the 1401 statute indicates may already have been coming into being by 1400. William Sawtrey's link with the son of a Lollard squire (Thomas Compworth, a man with an active legal practice in London) could well have given him some sense of confidence in his position. Literate services of another kind were the means by which William Sweeting made his way into gentry service. Andrew Hope's patient reconstruction of this heretic's long career (a rewarding piece of research, which builds a vivid three-dimensional reality on the scaffold of John Foxe's reporting) reveals the opportunities open to Sweeting as holy water clerk and manorial bailiff. On one level he may have instructed local children; on the other he may have converted the widowed gentlewoman who employed him.

Another chapter reveals the working of these links and expectations, as a gentleman's religious sympathies and secular loyalties were tested at the same time as an accused heretic faced the conflict between the philosophical realism of Wycliffite discourse and the real world and words of an episcopal trial. Christina von Nolcken gives us as close a view as we can ever hope to have of a knight's face-to-face mediation between accused heretic and accusing bishop. It is the more revealing in that the heretic in question might be regarded as a key figure in the Lollard movement. Richard Wyche, whose exceptionally long career joins the Oxford origins of Lollardy with four decades of its fifteenth-century history, became Oldcastle's henchman, and a vital link in the chain of connections between Lollards and Hussites. In Wyche's first known trial we can see the knightly negotiator as well as the accused being tried to breaking point. Bishop Skirlaw might be *dominus meus* to both unknown knight and Wyche himself, but in the event it was the knight who proved his obligation to good lordship as he did his best to mediate a compromise on the critical issue of the wording and interpretation of the oath.

There was a double standard in operation. When in 1543 Henry VIII passed an act regulating Bible reading, which allowed free private reading to nobility and gentry and substantial merchants, but prohibited it for the 'lower sort' – women, artificers, labourers – he was legislating old convention onto the statute book. Fifteenth-century authorities, acting on that convention, imposed an imbalance on the historical record which has ever since weighted the balance of historical judgement. We have inherited the evidence of social prejudice which moulded the imprint of heresy. All humble readers of suspect texts were subject to suspicion of heresy; any Bible or scriptural text or commentary might pass muster in respectable places. The weight of contemporary authority, and the posthumous survival of evidence, is unevenly loaded by this deep-rooted double standard. Thomas More was right when he reported on the English manuscript bibles 'fayre and old' which had been allowed to lay men and women of good devotion and sobriety, but removed from 'the handys of heretykes'. He was wrong, however, to put so much trust in the categorisation of tainted books and hands.[84]

Arguably, the legacy of vernacular scriptures was the largest achievement of the 'premature reformation'. But these texts, together with the gospel commentaries and the sermon-cycle, also argue for a large unknown; they 'hint at a strand of gentle Lollardy which never came to court'.[85] Gentry Lollardy eludes us to the extent that, with the sole exception of Sir John Oldcastle, it was never placed under the arc-lights shone on lesser suspects. Perhaps the best we can do is to think about that interface in which spiritual aspirations of the time felt most at home.

It is not easy to summarise the piety of an age. It may be that the surest bearing to take in viewing the piety of late medieval English men and women – Dame Julian of Norwich always excepted – is along the age-old lines of renunciation, of revulsion and flight from the cares and snares of the world: spiritual retreat, not head-on engagement; contemplation, not combat. The appeal of Carthusian spirituality (as Anthony Tuck suggested)[86] may tell us most about the direction of contemporary religious enthusiasm – an enthusiasm of the west European ruling classes about the year 1400 that was impressive in the support it gained among the élite in England.

The qualities of the Carthusian Order are the orthodox face of tendencies that Lollards expressed more doubtfully. Carthusian emphasis on individual rather than corporate devotion, on personal study and meditation and biblical reading, and the rejection of imagery of the saints and rich curiosities of painting and sculpture in their churches, were all shared by Lollards. The boundaries of spiritual aspiration were not always clear cut; for long it was easy to misjudge, to make misguided choices. Philip Repingdon recanted his Wycliffite views and became a bishop; but he resigned his see and wanted to be buried in a sack.[87] It is understandable that Nicholas Hereford, who started his career so close to Wycliffe, chose to end his days in the Coventry Charterhouse. Maybe there were others who moved in the reverse direction.[88] And for whatever reason, the Charterhouses were not included in the Lollards' disendowment bill.

The long-term fate of Lollardy and of reformation depended on ecclesiastical politics in secular hands – on king, gentry, and eventually parliament. What the Commons could entertain was related to what knights of the shire thought, read, believed and hoped for. The Lollard appeal to them included a temporal bribe, the possible distribution of church possessions, that great share option which was to secure the future of the Tudor English church. In the fifteenth century Wycliffites secured from the gentry the patronage that facilitated their proselytising and textual labours. They also won sympathy from gentlemen and gentlewomen whose commitment to evangelism and denial of the world was wide-ranging and deep-seated. Through that broad band of religious piety something of Lollard-related aspirations survived, along with the many books the movement had produced. Publicity and reformation through the sponsorship of parliament was quite another matter. What happened in 1395 may now look like a watershed.

Notes

[1] Hudson, *Selections*, p. 24. The best text of the conclusions is printed here, pp. 24–9, notes pp. 150–5. They are also to be found in H.S. Cronin, 'The Twelve Conclusions of the Lollards', *EHR*, 22 (1907), pp. 292–304, and *English Historical Documents, 1327–1485*, ed. A.R. Myers (London, 1969), pp. 848–50.

[2] Hudson, *LB*, pp. 67–84; Anne Hudson, 'Wycliffism in Oxford 1381–1411', in A. Kenny (ed.), *Wyclif in his Times* (Oxford, 1968), pp. 67–84; J.I. Catto, 'Wyclif and Wycliffism at Oxford 1356–1430', in J.I. Catto and T.A.R. Evans (eds), *The History of the University of Oxford*, ii (Oxford, 1992), pp. 175–261.

[3] Hudson, *LB*, pp. 13–42; *The Middle English Translation of the Rosarium Theologie*, ed. Christina von Nolcken (Heidelberg, 1979), pp. 9, 29.

[4] Thomson, below, p. 108; Hudson, *PR*, pp. 12, 112; Jeremy Catto, 'Religion and the English Nobility in the Later Fourteenth Century', in H. Lloyd-Jones, V. Pearl and B. Worden (eds), *History and Imagination: Essays in honour of H.R. Trevor-Roper* (London, 1981), pp. 43–55, at 45, 54.

[5] For the duke's books see Viscount Dillon and W.H. St John Hope, 'Inventory of the Goods and Chattels belonging to Thomas, Duke of Gloucester', *Archaeological Journal*, 54 (1897), pp. 275–308 (at 300–1); S.H. Cavanaugh, *A Study of Books Privately owned in England 1300–1450* (Ph.D. Dissertation, University of Pennsylvania, 1980), pp. 844–51; Anthony Goodman, *The Loyal Conspiracy: The Lords Appellant under Richard II* (London, 1971), pp. 77–81; V.J. Scattergood, 'Literary Culture at the Court of Richard II', in V.J. Scattergood and J.W. Sherborne (eds), *English Court Culture in the Later Middle Ages* (London, 1983), pp. 34–5; *KC*, p. 1.

[6] See below, p. 108.

[7] A. Goodman, *John of Gaunt: The Exercise of Princely Power in Fourteenth-Century Europe* (London, 1992), pp. 16, 37–8, 60–1, 241–4. For an early fifteenth-century report of Gaunt's defence of English Bible translations see Janet Coleman, *English Literature in History 1350–1400* (London, 1981), p. 321.

[8] *Rot. Parl.*, iii, pp. 329–30.

[9] *Johannes de Trokelowe et . . . Annales*, ed. H.T. Riley (RS, 1866), p. 174; *Thomae Walsingham . . . Historia Anglicana*, ed. H.T. Riley (RS, 1863–4), ii, pp. 159, 216; McFarlane, *LK*, pp. 148–9.

[10] For instance Nicholas Hereford and Philip Repingdon's reported statement to John of Gaunt that the condemnation of the twenty-four conclusions in 1382 was 'to the destruction and weakening of temporal lordship and the king's temporalities'; *Fasc. Ziz.*, p. 318.

[11] Hudson, *Selections*, p. 24.

[12] McFarlane, *JW*, p. 147.

[13] Hudson, *Selections*, p. 24.

[14] McFarlane, *JW*, p. 147.

[15] J.S. Roskell, Linda Clark and Carole Rawcliffe (eds), *The History of Parliament. The House of Commons 1386–1421*, 4 vols (Stroud, 1993).

[16] There is a notable entry by Charles Kightly in Roskell *et al.* (eds), *The History of Parliament*, ii, pp. 576–8.

[17] The issue of ecclesiastical temporalities, the topic of the first of the 1395 conclusions, was of ongoing parliamentary interest (considered in Aston, *FF*, pp. 103–14), coming to a head in 1410. It is interesting that the 1410 proposal (which is not recorded in the parliament rolls) was copied in a sixteenth-century Commons petition, linked with a call to Henry VIII to carry out what Henry IV and Henry V had intended. R.W. Hoyle, 'The Origins of the Dissolution of the Monasteries', *Historical Journal*, 38 (1995), pp. 275–305.

[18] McFarlane, *LK*, pp. 182, 184–5.

[19] *Ibid.*, p. 206.

[20] Geneviève Hasenohr, 'Religious reading among the laity in France in the fifteenth century', in Peter Biller and Anne Hudson (eds), *Heresy and Literacy, 1000–1540* (Cambridge, 1994), pp. 205–51, at 220–1.

[21] The forty MPs of 1395 who were singled out as remarkable in this connection are here listed alphabetically, for readers who wish to pursue them in the three biographical volumes of the *History of Parliament*: Sir William Argentine, Suffolk; Sir William Bagot, Warwickshire; Drew Barantyn, London; Sir Robert Berney, Norfolk; Alexander Besford, Worcestershire; Sir William Bonville, Devon; Sir Bernard Brocas, Hampshire; Sir Thomas Brooke, Somerset; Sir Peter Buckton, Yorkshire; Sir William Burgate, Suffolk; Sir John Bussy, Lincolnshire; Adam Carlisle, London; Roger de la Chamber, Northamptonshire; Robert Cholmley, Hampshire; Sir John Cockayne, Derbyshire; Thomas Coggeshall, Essex; Thomas Coningsby, Middlesex; Sir Philip Courtenay, Devon; Giles Daubeney, Bedfordshire; Sir Gilbert Denys, Gloucestershire; John Doreward, Essex; Edward Durdent, Buckinghamshire; Hugh atte Fenn, Great Yarmouth; Sir Thomas Fitznichol, Gloucestershire; John Gawen, Wiltshire; Thomas Graa, York; Aymer Lichfield, Staffordshire; Sir Thomas Morewell, Hertfordshire; Thomas Norris, Barnstaple; Sir Edmund de la Pole, Cambridgeshire; Hugh Quecche, Sussex; Sir Thomas Rempston, Nottinghamshire; Sir John St Quintin, Yorkshire; Sir Humphrey Stafford, Dorset; Sir William Swinburne, Northumberland; Sir Robert Urswyk, Lancashire; Sir Thomas Walsh, Leicestershire; Sir John White, Norfolk; William Wilcotes, Oxfordshire; William Wilford, Exeter.

[22] Alexander Murray, *Reason and Society in the Middle Ages* (Oxford, 1978), pp. 292–314.

[23] Hudson, *Selections*, p. 26 (clause 6).

[24] The preamble of the foundation charter of Manchester College in 1421 admirably describes the drawbacks of clergy doing secular work; Samuel Hibbert-Ware, *The Ancient Parish Church of Manchester and Why it was Collegiated* (Manchester, 1848), pp. 154–6.

[25] McFarlane, *JW*, p. 155.

[26] McFarlane, *LK*, p. 161. He sat once in parliament, as knight of the shire for Buckinghamshire in February 1388; there is an excellent biography by Linda Clark in Roskell *et al.* (eds), *History of Parliament*, iv, pp. 700–5.

[27] Biller and Hudson (eds), *Heresy and Literacy*, p. 13.

[28] McFarlane, *JW*, pp. 169–70. For Walter Brute see *ibid.*, pp. 135–8 and below pp. 80–1.

[29] R.R. Betts, *Essays in Czech History* (London, 1969), pp. 69, 114–17, 153–4; Wojciech Iwanczak, 'Tomáš Štitný, Esquisse pour un portrait de la sociologie médiévale', *Revue historique*, 282 (1989), pp. 3–4.

[30] Michael Wilks, 'Royal priesthood: the origins of Lollardy', in *The Church in a Changing Society: Conflict-Reconciliation or Adjustment?* (Proceedings of 1977 CIHEC Conference; Uppsala, 1978), pp. 63–70, at 66.

[31] *The Lanterne of Liзt*, ed. L.M. Swinburn (EETS, OS 151, 1917), p. 34.

[32] H.L. Spencer, 'The Fortunes of a Lollard Sermon-Cycle in the later Fifteenth Century', *Mediaeval Studies*, 48 (1986), p. 389, n 104; cf McFarlane, *JW*, p. 91.

[33] Below, p. 119.

[34] M. Aston, *England's Iconoclasts* (Oxford, 1988), pp. 103, 146–7.

[35] Below, p. 81. On Walter Brut see Anne Hudson, '"*Laicus litteratus*": the paradox of Lollardy', in Biller and Hudson (eds), *Heresy and Literacy*, pp. 222–36.

[36] J.I. Catto, 'Religious Change under Henry V', in G.L. Harriss (ed.), *Henry V: The Practice of Kingship* (Oxford, 1985), p. 100.

[37] See here J.I. Catto, 'Sir William Beauchamp between Chivalry and Lollardy', in C. Harper-Bill and Ruth Harvey (eds), *The Ideals and Practice of Medieval Knighthood III: Papers from the fourth Strawberry Hill Conference 1988* (Woodbridge, 1990), pp. 39–48; Michael Wilks, 'Wyclif and the Great Persecution', *SCH*, Subsidia 10 (1994), pp. 39–63, at 62.

[38] Hudson, *Selections*, p. 28; S. Düll, A. Luttrell, and M. Keen, 'Faithful Unto Death: The Tomb Slab of Sir William Neville and Sir John Clanvowe, Constantinople 1391', *Antiquaries Journal*, 71 (1991), pp. 174–90.

[39] Wilks, 'Wyclif and the Great Persecution', p. 55, citing *De ordinatione fratrum* in *John Wyclif's Polemical Works*, ed. R. Buddensieg, 2 vols (WS, 1883), i, p. 95, where the phrase applies to 'faithful priests'.

[40] Edward Powell, *Kingship, Law and Society: Criminal Justice in the Reign of Henry V* (Oxford 1989), p. 147.

[41] *Middle English Sermons*, ed. W.O. Ross (EETS, OS 209, 1940), pp. xxxvi–xxxviii, 226. For Thomas Hoccleve's invocation of Henry V as 'Crystes knyght' see Aston, *FF*, p. 79.

[42] Mal. 2:7, cited by Innocent III in the Decretals, Lib. V, tit. vii, cap. 12; *Corpus Iuris Canonici*, ed. E. Freidberg (Leipzig, 1879–81), ii, col. 786.

[43] *Johannes de Trokelowe . . . Annales*, p. 174; 'quibus nitebantur destruere personas ecclesiasticas et cuncta ecclesiae sacramenta'.

[44] J. Anthony Tuck, 'Carthusian Monks and Lollard Knights: Religious Attitude at the Court of Richard II', *Studies in the Age of Chaucer. Proceedings of the New Chaucer Society*, 1 (1984), pp. 149–61, at 153; Hudson, *PR*, p. 92; M. Aston, *Thomas Arundel* (Oxford, 1967), pp. 332–3.

[45] Catto, 'Sir William Beauchamp', p. 46. There are some interesting observations on 'estate' (in the context of will-making, funerals, and prayers for the dead) in Howard Kaminsky, *Simon de Cramaud and the Great Schism* (New Jersey, 1983), pp. 311–16.

[46] W.A. Pantin, *The English Church in the Fourteenth Century* (Cambridge, 1955), pp. 231–3.

[47] Catto, 'Sir William Beauchamp', p. 48.

[48] A.K. McHardy, 'The Dissemination of Wyclif's Ideas', *SCH*, Subsidia 5 (1987), pp. 361–8.

[49] Catto, 'Sir William Beauchamp', pp. 42–4; McFarlane, *LK*, pp. 200–1, 213–14; V.J. Scattergood (ed.), *The Works of Sir John Clanvowe* (Cambridge, 1975), p. 21; Hudson, *PR*, pp. 90–1, 422–3, 430; Aston, *LR*, pp. 23, 204.

[50] Norfolk Record Office, Reg 3/6 (Henry Despenser), f. 332^{r-v}, institution of William Manstan to rectory of Bergh with annexed chapel of Apton, by exchange with John Curson, June 1406; Reg 4/7 (Alexander Tottington), f. 22^r, Robert Leghum instituted on Manstan's resignation, September 1409.

[51] Bodleian Library, Oxford, MS Arch. Seld. B.23, f. 114^r, cited by Richard G. Davies, 'Lollardy and Locality', *TRHS*, 6th ser. 1 (1991), p. 201, n 41; 'Item est advertendum quod in diocesi [dictis in MS] ecclesie Norwicensis sunt diverse secte et inter alias sunt qui appellantur lollardi qui sunt in multitudine copiosa madentes [*sic*] in diversas hereses et nisi haberent virum theologum et in sermonibus expertum qui eorum ritus et hereses extirparet, de facili ita pullularent quod ad viam veritatis imposterum reduci non possent'. On this letterbook of William Swan see E.F. Jacob, *Essays in Later Medieval History* (Manchester, 1968), p. 60; *Reg. Chichele*, i, p. c, n. 7; on Dereham and his recommendation see Emden, *BRUC*, pp. 184–5.

[52] Norfolk Record Office, Reg 4/8 (John Wakeryng), f. 74^r (Robert Potter, June 1422); Reg 5/9 (William Alnwick), ff. 3^v, 72^r (Roger Philpot, November 1425, William Wyrmod, October 1434).

[53] *Fasc. Ziz.*, pp. 423–4. For White's reported links with Bergh see Aston, *LR*, p. 87.

[54] Francis Blomefield and Charles Parkin, *An Essay towards a Topographical History of the County of Norfolk* (London, 1805–10), 10, pp. 96–100, reports (96) the chapel as being destroyed 'about two centuries past'. Bergh Apton was among the English manors that came to William Beauchamp with his share of the estates of John Hastings, earl of Pembroke. K.B. McFarlane, *The Nobility of Later Medieval England* (Oxford, 1973), pp. 74–5.

[55] *KC*, pp. 294–7, and below, pp. 34–6.

[56] *Reg. Chichele*, ii, pp. 534–9; McFarlane, *LK*, pp. 214–15.

[57] Below, p. 102.

[58] Shannon McSheffrey, *Gender and Heresy: Women and Men in Lollard Communities 1420–1530* (Philadelphia, 1995), pp. 125–7, 213; Thomson, *LL*, pp. 68–70; Davies, 'Lollardy and Locality', pp. 203–4.

[59] Joan Wake, *The Brudenells of Deene* (London, 1953), pp. 8–10, at 10; the will (made twelve years before Brudenell died) is Northamptonshire Record Office, Bru. O.i.2; G. Lipscomb, *The History and Antiquities of the County of Buckingham*, 4 vols, (London, 1847), i, p. 297, ii, p. 178, iii, pp. 153–8, 270, 334; *VCH, Buckinghamshire*, iii, p. 149; *Testamenta Vetusta*, ed. N.H. Nicolas (London, 1826), pp. 282–4, cf. p. 207 for the books of the elder Edmund Brudenell (an uncle) in 1425: for his career see Wake,

op. cit., pp. 1–8, and Roskell *et al.*, *History of Parliament*, ii, pp. 392–4. W.H. Summers, *The Lollards of the Chiltern Hills* (London, 1906), p. 66, supposed the Bibles to be English. Brudenell held lands in Oxfordshire.

[60] *VCH, Bucks.*, i, p. 295, iii, pp. 218–21; Lipscomb, *History of Buckingham*, iii, pp. 270–2; A. Hamilton Thompson, *The Abbey of St. Mary of the Meadows Leicester* (Leicester, 1949), pp. 115–16.

[61] A.K. McHardy, 'Bishop Buckingham and the Lollards of Lincoln diocese', *SCH*, 9 (1972), pp. 131–45, at 135–6; McFarlane, *LK*, pp. 194–5; Hudson, *PR*, p. 79 n. 119.

[62] *Reg. Chichele*, iii, pp. 197–8; Thomson, *LL*, pp. 144–5; Aston, *FF*, pp. 247, 256.

[63] Colin Richmond, 'The English Gentry and Religion, *c.* 1500', in C. Harper-Bill (ed.), *Religious Belief and Ecclesiastical Careers in Late Medieval England* (Woodbridge, 1991), pp. 121–5; J.M. Dodgson, 'A Library at Pott Chapel (Pott Shrigley, Cheshire), *c.* 1493', *The Library*, 5th ser. 15 (1960), pp. 47–53; Emden, *BRUC*, pp. 170, 193. Crowland and Downes were graduates of Oxford and Cambridge respectively. See also Hudson, *PR*, pp. 248–9, 423, which tells of another university man who was given the Glossed Gospels by no less a person than Archbishop Warham. For the library books (not named) of St Anne's chapel in St Mary's church, Halesworth, in 1503, see Colin Richmond, 'Halesworth Church, Suffolk, and its Fifteenth-Century Benefactors', in C. Richmond and I. Harvey (eds), *Recognitions. Essays presented to Edmund Fryde* (Aberystwyth, 1996), pp. 267–8.

[64] See below, pp. 200, 216.

[65] N Pevsner (ed.), *The Buildings of England*, John Newman, *West Kent and the Weald* (Harmondsworth, 1969), p. 540; T.M.C. Lawler *et al.* (eds), *The Complete Works of St. Thomas More* (New Haven & London, 1963), vol. 6, i, pp. 412–13, ii, pp. 720–1; vol. 8, ii, pp. 775–6: 'Tenterden Steeple was the cause of Goodwin sands'; of which Fuller commented, 'the old man had told a rational tale, had he but found the due favour to finish it'; M.P. Tilley, *A Dictionary of the Proverbs in England in the Sixteenth and Seventeenth Centuries* (Ann Arbor, 1966), T 91.

[66] The will is in Reg. Braybrooke, Guildhall Library, London, MS 9531/3, ff. 443v–444r (old 406v–407r), printed in Samuel Bentley (ed.), *Excerpta Historica* (London, 1831), pp. 424–6. On the basis of the will *GEC* surmises that 'she may have been of the family of Cobham'. Thomas Nerford died in 1344 and his widow remarried twice, her third husband dying in 1358; GEC, 9, pp. 470–1.

[67] *CCR, 1374–77*, p. 159; *CPR, 1377–81*, pp. 260, 299, 301, 307, 309, 311, 374, 530; *CPR, 1381–5*, p. 34; Blomefield and Parkin, *Topographical History of Norfolk*, 5, p. 241; William Dugdale, *The Baronage of England* (London, 1675–6), ii, pp. 8–9; *GEC*, 9, pp. 470–1.

[68] Mary C. Erler, 'Three Fifteenth-Century Vowesses', in C.M. Barron and A.F. Sutton (eds), *Medieval London Widows 1300–1500* (London and Rio Grande, 1994), pp. 179–80, 182, 183n, citing Reg. Braybrooke, f. 325v.

[69] Blomefield and Parkin, *Norfolk*, 6, pp. 231–2; *CCR, 1381–85*, pp. 384, 389. One of these manors was Panworth Hall in Ashill (still on the map), all the goods and chattels of which came to Margery by Lady Neville's will.

[70] Guildhall, London, MS 4424, ff. 48v–50r; printed in Edwin Freshfield, *Wills, Leases, and Memoranda in the Book of Records of the Parish of St. Christopher le Stocks* (London, 1895), pp. 8–9. The will was written when death seemed imminent (date of probate is not recorded). Margery Nerford had a house in Hackney, but was a parishioner of St Christopher le Stocks (to which she gave a donation for works in the nave), and requested burial in the chapel 'where I used to sit', before the image of the Virgin. This chapel was given her missal. Vestments were given to Beeleigh Abbey, Essex, 'where the body of Lady Neville lies buried'.

[71] McFarlane, *JW*, p. 145, cf. 161. See below, pp. 101–2, for her licence to choose a confessor in 1421.

[72] For Perrin Clanvow's will see *The Fifty Earliest English Wills*, ed. F.J. Furnivall (EETS, OS 78, 1882), pp. 49–51; Hudson, *PR*, p. 249; cf. McFarlane, *LK*, p. 185, where Elizabeth de la Vache is confused with Perrin Clanvow. Elizabeth de la Vache (widow of Philip who died in 1408) died intestate in 1425; *Reg. Chichele*, ii, pp. 317–18. On the Glossed Gospels see also Anne Hudson, 'The

Variable Text', in A.J. Minnis and Charlotte Brewer (eds), *Crux and Controversy in Middle English Textual Criticism* (Cambridge, 1992), pp. 49–60, at 52–4. See also below, p. 105

[73] Forshall & Madden, *HB*, i, p. lxiii, no. 158; Andrew Hope, 'Lollardy: The Stone the Builders Rejected?', in P. Lake and M. Dowling (eds), *Protestantism and the National Church in Sixteenth Century England* (London, New York, Sydney, 1987), p. 18 and n. 76. On Eborall see Emden, *BRUO*, i, pp. 622–3.

[74] *The Myroure of oure Ladye*, ed. J.H. Blunt (EETS, ES 19, 1873), p. 3, cf. pp. 71, 339–40; R.W. Swanson, *Church and Society in Late Medieval England* (Oxford, 1989), p. 270. On traditional assumptions governing women's lack of access to scripture see Alcuin Blamires, 'The Limits of Bible Study for Medieval Woman', in Lesley Smith and Jane H.M. Taylor (eds), *Women, the Book and the Godly* (Cambridge, 1995), pp. 1–12.

[75] Forshall & Madden, *HB* i, pp. xliv, lxii, nos 38 (BL, Add. MS 10596), and 156 (now John Rylands Library, Manchester, MS Eng. 81); Hudson, *PR*, p. 233, n. 34.

[76] Hudson, *PR*, p. 233, n. 34; Forshall & Madden, *HB*, p. xlvii, nos. 60 (MS Bodl. 277), 64 (MS Bodl. 771). For the Charterhouse Bible (MS Bodl. 277) and library see E.M. Thompson, *The Carthusian Order in England* (London, 1930), p. 324.

[77] Gail McMurray Gibson, *The Theater of Devotion* (Chicago & London, 1989), pp. 29–30.

[78] Imogen Luxton, 'The Lichfield Court Book: a Postscript', *BIHR*, 44 (1971), pp. 120–5.

[79] Susan Brigden, *London and Reformation* (Oxford, 1989), p. 102.

[80] Hudson, *PR*, pp. 198–9.

[81] Jonathan Hughes, *Pastors and Visionaries* (Woodbridge, 1988), p. 108.

[82] A.I. Doyle, 'English Books In and Out of Court from Edward III to Henry VII', in Scattergood and Sherborne (eds), *English Court Culture*, p. 169.

[83] Hudson, *PR*, p. 420; A. Hudson and H.L. Spencer, 'Old Author, New Work: The Sermons of MS Longleat 4', *Medium Aevum*, 53 (1984), pp. 220–38.

[84] Thomas More, *A Dialogue concerning heresies*, in *Complete Works*, vol. 6, pt. i, p. 317, cited McSheffrey, *Gender and Heresy*, p. 43.

[85] Swanson, *Church and Society*, p. 343, and see also the observations pp. 261, 344; cf. McSheffrey, *Gender and Heresy*, p. 41; 'Unless the number of Lollards is very much greater than has previously been thought, not all who owned Lollard Bibles were Lollards'.

[86] Above, n. 44.

[87] On Repingdon's sermons and 'the outlooks that the Wycliffites shared with their contemporaries', see Simon N. Forde, 'Social Outlook and Preaching in a Wycliffite "*Sermones Dominicales*" Collection', in Ian Wood and G.A. Loud (eds), *Church and Chronicle in the Middle Ages: Essays presented to John Taylor* (London and Rio Grande, 1991), pp. 179–91, at 190.

[88] Was the John Parlebien who in 1391 absconded from the Charterhouse of Hinton (south of Bath) and was pursued for apostasy, conceivably the same man who (then of Mountsorrel, north of Leicester) purchased a pardon after Oldcastle's rising? Thompson, *Carthusian Order in England*, pp. 282–3, includes orders to royal serjeants-at-arms for seizure of him and Richard Barbour; James Crompton, 'Leicestershire Lollards', *Transactions of the Leicestershire Archaeological and Historical Society*, 44 (1968–9), p. 28; *CPR 1413–16*, p. 262 (where he is described as chaplain). See also F. Donald Logan, *Runaway Religious in Medieval England, c. 1240–1540* (Cambridge, 1996), p. 215.

1

KNIGHTON'S LOLLARDS

Geoffrey Martin

Henry Knighton's Lollards are, or were in their time, a substantial army. Knighton had an early and privileged view of Lollardy and, being horrified by what he saw, he described it in some detail. He was uniquely well placed to do so, for he had been in uncomfortably close touch with some of Wycliffe's principal disciples in Oxford, and was an unwilling spectator of what was probably the first, the largest, and the most influential of the movement's extra-mural classes.

Knighton's testimony to the beginnings of Lollardy has not received the credit which it deserves, because his work has not been well understood. His chronicle runs from the eleventh century to 1396, with a break in the narrative between 1372 and 1376.[1] It was copied once during the Middle Ages, almost certainly in Leicester Abbey, but was cited then only by John Rous of Warwick. In the sixteenth century it became better known, probably after one or other of its copies (manuscripts Tiberius C VII and Claudius E III) first came into Sir Robert Cotton's library, where both were eventually lodged.[2] It was published in 1652 in a good text by Sir Roger Twysden, who saw that, despite the break in the narrative in the 1370s, it was the work of one mind.[3]

In the nineteenth century, however, a long series of editorial misfortunes overtook the work. When W.W. Shirley set out to edit the *Fasciculi Zizaniorum* as the fifth volume of the Rolls Series, he consulted Knighton as a major commentator on Lollardy. He was concerned only with the later passages of the chronicle, but he concluded that the interrupted narrative signalled the presence of a second author for the following part of the work. He remarked that the original chronicle consisted only of a jejune and derivative summary of English history to the 1360s, which had been continued from 1377 by a foreigner ('no friend to the English language') of Lancastrian sympathies who had intruded himself into Leicester Abbey.[4] In the 1880s Shirley's dictum was taken up by J.R. Lumby, who edited Knighton for the Rolls Series (1889–95). Although Lumby saw that there were anomalies in the notion, with the main narrative referring forward to events in the supposed continuation, he nevertheless established *Cont. Knighton* in the footnotes of those who followed him. For good measure, having chosen to edit the second and inferior of the two MSS, he suggested that both were only copies of a lost original.[5]

The phantom continuator was exorcised by V.H. Galbraith in 1957, and Knighton's chronicle restored at last to his authorship.[6] In the meantime, however, Wycliffe and his followers had been the objects of much close though not always well-directed scrutiny by both historians and literary scholars, and for many years there were more Wycliffes in circulation than there had ever been Knightons, or even Homers. Wycliffe (though the march of mind may yet deconstruct him again) was reintegrated in 1952 by K.B. McFarlane, who wrote authoritatively on the medieval university in which academic Lollardy began,[7] though rather less sympathetically on Wycliffe himself. In the process he naturally consulted Knighton's chronicle. He also looked at the record of the process against William Swinderby undertaken by Bishop Buckingham of Lincoln in 1382,[8] and from what he saw in Buckingham's register came to the conclusion that Knighton was, through malice or stupidity, an unreliable witness to events in Leicester. It was as though W.W. Shirley rode again.

Knighton was a canon of the Augustinian abbey of St Mary of the Meadows, Leicester. He may have been professed by 1363, when he saw Edward III there, and he was certainly a canon in 1370, and in 1377 when he paid the clerical subsidy together with other members of the convent. He began to write his chronicle before 1385, most probably in or very soon after 1378, when Abbot William Clowne died at Leicester. He seems to have begun his narrative with a threnody upon the successive deaths of Prince Edward, Edward III, and Abbot Clowne, and then to have reached back to compile a general history of England from the Norman Conquest, and composed its two parts in parallel. His accounts of the revolt of 1381, the rise of Lollardy, and the political crisis which culminated in the Merciless Parliament of 1387–8 were evidently drawn up quite close to those events. He was, however, simultaneously writing a history of England from the Norman Conquest, with particular attention to the first phases of the Hundred Years' War, and the prowess of Henry of Lancaster in France and elsewhere.[9]

Knighton covered the ground from Æthelred to 1340 by conflating a version of Higden's *Polychronicon* with Walter of Guisborough's history of England, and then launched out on his own composition. He made only small additions to Higden and the extended text of Guisborough which he had to hand in Leicester, but for his independent narrative, from the beginnings of the war in 1337, he used a wide and carefully managed range of sources.

One of Knighton's most striking characteristics is his acknowledgement of the material which he used. It was a misfortune for Lumby that he quite failed to understand Knighton's habits of annotation. Guisborough was available in Leicester in a version that included some local material, and Knighton referred to and quoted that manuscript as Leycestrensis, just as he cited Higden as Cistrensis. Having then successively and explicitly noted the end of Leycestrensis (in 1326) and of the continuation of the *Polychronicon* (in 1340), he remarked that he was about to go on alone, and referred to himself on that one occasion as Leycestrensis, a name to which he had as good a right as anyone.[10]

That coincidental aside unfortunately led Lumby first to suppose that Knighton was laying claim to all that he had been at such pains to quote from Guisborough, and then, when the error was pointed out to him, to conclude that Knighton had deceived him deliberately.[11] That Lumby had failed to recognise Guisborough's text was demonstrated by R.L. Poole in an acerbic review of the first volume of *Chronicon Henrici Knighton*.[12] Poole had himself offered in 1885 to edit the chronicle, only to be told that it had already been assigned to Lumby,[13] and even if he did not actually enjoy the spectacle of Lumby's misfortune he adequately concealed any sorrow that it caused him. Lumby was in poor health by the 1890s, and he was entirely unnerved by Poole's review. The second volume clearly outran his powers, but in the event he died in 1895, and may thus have been spared James Tait's review of it, which appeared in the next year.[14]

The encounter with Poole was not likely to move Lumby to a more sympathetic view of the text. In fact he inadvertently intensified the atmosphere of confusion and unreliability in which he had enveloped the work by misreading a rubric, and thus making Knighton appear to misdate by three years Archbishop Courtenay's visitation of Leicester in 1389, which he had indeed witnessed, and described and dated quite accurately.

McFarlane first came to Knighton by way of Wycliffe, and returned to consider him as he pursued the Lollards.[15] Although he had addressed Wycliffe and Lollardy as a fount of nonconformity, he was chiefly interested in the Lollards as disturbers of the peace in Lancastrian England. He could not help imposing a rational order upon the welter of Wycliffes which he found in the literature, and in the process he corrected a number of current misconceptions about the Oxford of Wycliffe's day.[16] The medieval university has been intensively studied in recent years, and its nature is adequately well understood. McFarlane's lucid account of the role of the colleges in the fourteenth century and the rationale of Wycliffe's movements between them now has a commonplace air, but at the time it was innovative and refreshingly clear-headed. He was, however, a less sympathetic observer of Wycliffe himself. Neither Wycliffe's theology nor the formidable grasp of dialectic which supported it held any great interest for him. On the whole, he felt that Wycliffe could have been better employed, and that even with other interests he would probably have been a thoroughly tiresome colleague.[17]

There was something similar in McFarlane's opinion of Knighton. Knighton (if he was indeed Knighton, and not a near-sighted and incommunicable foreigner, an open question still in 1952), was a man who could not tell within three years when he had seen the Archbishop of Canterbury in his own house. He was also vague, not to say evasive, in his treatment of his colleague Repingdon. If then his account of William Swinderby's activities differed from the material gathered by Bishop Buckingham's clerks, there could be no contest between them. And having perceived Knighton to be unsound, McFarlane was naturally inclined to give Walsingham the benefit of the doubt wheresoever there were differences between them.[18]

Yet Walsingham, like Knighton, did his best with the material which he had, and he wrote at a distance from Lincoln. Even if he had local sources of information they were not necessarily better than Knighton's.[19] The point at issue – whether Swinderby or, as Knighton says, John Aston, preached a particular sermon at Leicester – arises not from Buckingham's account of Swinderby's trial, but from a varied collection of denunciatory material which was assembled at Lincoln before that event. The clergy of the diocese were invited, in an excitable time, to denounce Swinderby as a Lollard, and they duly attributed Lollardy to him.

Swinderby was an ambulant nuisance, a popular preacher of uncertain origins, with a ready line of repartee. At first Buckingham regarded and treated him merely as an insolent oaf, but it took two inquisitorial commissions and the additional efforts of three learned friars to bring him to book. Swinderby's citation and trial began before and ended after Courtenay's proceedings against Wycliffe in the spring of 1382, and it seems from the preliminary and the final charges against him that he defended himself throughout with some acumen. The teachings upon which he was condemned were much closer to the current popular resentments against the clergy than to the metaphysical arguments with which Wycliffe and his disciples had split the university. The accusations gathered against him, on the other hand, bear a close affinity to the Wycliffite opinions condemned by Courtenay's council at Blackfriars. Those to which he eventually admitted also accord better with Knighton's general account of Swinderby's career than with that given by Walsingham.[20]

McFarlane's general mistrust of Knighton was in fact based upon misapprehension. It is interesting to see that when he came to look in more detail at the careers of the knights whom both Knighton and Walsingham denounce as abettors of the Lollards he found only the slightest grounds for his suspicions.[21] Knighton includes Reginald Hilton amongst their number, and Hilton was not a knight but a priest. He was, however, also a royal clerk, and keeper of the wardrobe, and was therefore neither a phantasm nor a figure of minor account. Having made that point, McFarlane moved on, and there is nothing further in his review of the knights and their affiliations and beliefs to suggest that Knighton had misunderstood or exaggerated their sympathies. Their experience, affinities and, so far as they can be ascertained, their beliefs make them very credible sympathisers with the broad spectrum of Lollard teaching, and especially with the Lollards' impatience with the established privileges and conventions of the church.

It seems worth while, therefore, to look at what Knighton says about Lollardy as though he were a close observer of the phenomenon with access to some particular sources of information about it, which is precisely what he was. He may not have seen Wycliffe himself, but like the man who had never been to London he 'knew them as had'. He also was on close terms with at least one of Wycliffe's admirers and associates, whose role in the expansion of the movement was arguably the most influential of them all. The association was both ineluctable and painfully embarrassing to him.

Philip Repingdon was, like Henry Knighton, a canon of Leicester, who became abbot of the house during Knighton's lifetime, and subsequently bishop of Lincoln (1404–19). He was an Oxford theologian, and as his doctorate was new in Trinity Term 1382 he can hardly have entered the university later than 1374. Some of his activities there are independently documented, which is as well, because Knighton carefully refrains from mentioning his colleague's name when he describes his actions.

Repingdon's later career shows that he was able to sustain orthodox doctrine, perhaps the more readily because he was never then openly challenged on it. What was at issue in 1382, when Archbishop Courtenay resolved to impose order upon Oxford, was whether the gifted Repingdon was going to accept the discipline of the church in and out of the university. He was, and in the course of time he became not only a bishop but a cardinal. He duly denounced unorthodoxy in his diocese and argued with Lollards, but he talked unpatronisingly with Margery Kempe, and despite university purges and the sentences of the Council of Constance, Wycliffe's bones lay undisturbed at Lutterworth as long as Repingdon was in Lincoln. At the end of his career he resigned from his see, in a gesture not unique but uncommon amongst bishops, and his last years are undocumented, except that he was eventually buried at Lincoln. Beyond his academic accomplishments he was a man of some persuasive ability, and everything about him suggests that with all his talents he was adequately well pleased with himself.

There were at least two occasions when that quality was important. The first was when Repingdon, with others about whom we are less well-informed, decided to take the message of Wycliffe's teaching out of the university and preach it to the laity. He preached at least twice in Brackley, then a living in the gift of St Mary's abbey, about halfway between Oxford and Leicester, and perhaps more often as he passed through the town. He also preached in Leicester, to Knighton's dismay, and brought one colleague there, and probably others, from Oxford.[22]

The second occasion arose some time later, when Repingdon had made his peace with the authorities, but probably well before he became abbot of Leicester in 1393. He seems to have given Knighton copies both of the fly-sheets with which he and John Aston sought popular support in London in the summer of 1382, in defiance of Archbishop Courtenay, and also of the decree by which, in the previous year, William Barton, chancellor of the university, denounced and forbade the discussion and dissemination of Wycliffe's teachings in Oxford.[23]

It is remotely possible, but very unlikely, that Knighton came by both documents by some other means. He can hardly have obtained them in Repingdon's despite, for at any time after 1393 Repingdon would have been able to forbid further work on the chronicle, and indeed simply to have disposed of it. As it was, the text was preserved in the abbey library, and even copied in the house during Repingdon's lifetime, if not during his abbacy. What is more, Knighton suppressed Repingdon's name in copying the fly-sheet, and again in summarising a sermon which he had heard Repingdon preach in Leicester. Those elementary devices, and the manner in which Knighton introduces the chancellor's decree as though it had followed upon Courtenay's initiative against Lollardy in 1382, instead of preceding it by more than a year, seem to reflect Knighton's own misgivings rather than any later anxieties on Repingdon's part. To judge from his general form, Repingdon was more likely to be amused than perturbed by the proceedings.

The material, embarrassing as it was, was also irresistible, and Knighton devoted his ingenuity to using it without making things worse than they were. He introduced Lollardy by referring to the academic reputation of Wycliffe, who was resident at Lutterworth from 1381 until his death in 1384, adding that John Ball had prepared the way for him as did the Baptist for Christ.[24] He had already described John Ball as a preacher of heresy, or more precisely as one who sowed tares (lolia)[25] amongst the laity, and as a hero of the rebels at Blackheath, before noting his execution in July 1381. In discussing the characteristics of Lollardy, however, he refers neither to the rebellion nor directly to the substance of Wycliffe's teaching, but to the fact that Wycliffe had translated the Scriptures into English. He then turns to the writings of the Parisian master Guillaume de St-Amour on the last age of the world.[26] St-Amour's polemic, which arose from disputes in the university of Paris in the middle of the thirteenth century, saw the mendicants and the followers of the Cistercian mystic Joachim de Flore as the harbingers of Antichrist. Knighton, seizing upon the Joachimite doctrine of the new Gospel, or Gospel of the Holy Spirit, matches it to the actions of the Wycliffites. He then moves on to Courtenay's attack upon Lollardy in 1382, citing two Lollard professions as arguments offered by Wycliffe, and after telling the story of a timely miracle in London, reproduces the text of Courtenay's mandate to the bishops in 1382.

That is followed by William Barton's proscription of Wycliffe's teaching in Oxford in 1381, which is introduced without comment, as though it were a product of Courtenay's campaign. Barton's decree leads on to the professions of Repingdon (described simply as a priest), Nicholas Hereford, and John Aston, and to Hereford's appeal to the pope, his journey to and imprisonment in Italy, and his eventual release and return to England.[27] Knighton then describes the activities of the Lollards in Leicester, beginning with Repingdon himself, disguised this time as 'one whom I heard preach', and John Aston as a visitor, and continuing with John Purvey, and the baleful influence of the Lollard knights as protectors and promoters of the sect. He moves on to an account of the rampant spread of Lollardy in Leicester, with its cell in St John's chapel,[28] and to an angry denunciation of its social effects. Everything about the Lollards infuriated him, not only their dissemination of heresy, but the whole manner in which they imparted their beliefs, including their style, their cohesiveness, and not least their vocabulary.

Knighton rounds off his polemic with an account of the career of William Swinderby, an enigmatic and deeply interesting member of the movement. Swinderby had appeared in Leicester and attracted the patronage successively of the local community (some luminaries of which never lost faith in him), the duke of Lancaster, and the canons of St Mary's abbey. He subsequently joined the company in St John's chapel, and having openly defied Buckingham's authority was rescued from the bishop's prison at Lincoln, if from nothing worse, by the intervention of John of Gaunt.[29]

Swinderby has an emphatic place in Knighton's narrative. Knighton's first object is to expose his infirmity of purpose, though in the process he reveals a good deal of Swinderby's ability. His career, ending with his recantation and subsequent withdrawal from the diocese, can be read as a climax to the local movement, at least in its public phase, though it is clear not only from Knighton's misgivings but from other evidence that Lollardy remained a force long after Courtenay's visitation.[30] All the passages on Lollardy presented Knighton with problems, but the embarrassments were naturally focused upon Repingdon and Swinderby, who had come together in a most troublesome way, and had, as far as possible, to be kept apart.

Even the presentation of the material created difficulties. In the first place the subject was not only painful but positively disgraceful, because of the close involvement of the abbey with the movement. In the second, and quite as important, the fact that Knighton had chosen a starting date as recent as 1376 and had devoted substantial room to the Peasants' Revolt meant that it was difficult to present Lollardy in perspective. Fortunately he could begin with Wycliffe, with a reference back to John Ball, and could then without undue distortion telescope not only events in Oxford in 1380–1 with Courtenay's proceedings in 1382, but also an earlier series of episodes in and around Leicester. He subsequently left it to the rubricator, either by design or inadvertence, to date the whole passage on the Lollards, and the rubricator assigned it to 1382.

It is immediately clear from the narrative that the action was spread over a much longer period. By the time that Swinderby attracted Buckingham's attention in March 1382 he had joined the group at St John's and was preaching there regularly. He had previously lived and preached for some time in Leicester, then in a hermitage in the forest under the duke's patronage (the duke being presumably Gaunt, who had succeeded Henry of Grosmont in 1362), and then – most significantly – in St Mary's abbey itself. There he enjoyed the allowances of a canon, though apparently with a chamber of his own in the church. It was not, it would appear, an anchorite's cell, as he was free to travel and preach, and did so.

As Swinderby's story follows upon that of Waytestathe and Smith, and connects with theirs only at St John's chapel, we cannot readily relate his comings and goings to the other movements of dissent in Leicester. It nevertheless does appear that at least one Lollard cell was well established, and that Swinderby brought some further meed of public admiration with him to the company at St John's. The question then is what else he may have brought.

Philip Repingdon must have been in residence in Oxford, or keeping his required terms there, throughout the 1370s.[31] In the later years of the decade Wycliffe finally declared against the doctrine of transubstantiation, and thereby dismissed the supernatural power of the priesthood as the miraculous 'confectors' of Christ's body.[32] Repingdon was an enthusiastic proponent of Wycliffe's teaching, and most notably of the conclusion that the laity should be encouraged to ponder the faith in their own tongue, and to draw their own conclusions from the Scriptures. His sermons were one response, the Wycliffite Bible was another; both had their repercussions.

Repingdon's evangelism is important because it was early. We know of no one earlier in the field, and the chronology of Wycliffe's thought would hardly allow any considered campaign before the late 1370s. There were others who continued the work – it took more than twenty years to suppress the movement in Oxford – but none of them enjoyed more striking success than the pioneers.[33]

If the word preached by Repingdon had any lasting effect in Brackley we have no evidence of it. Compared with Leicester, with its abbey and a great seignorial household in the castle, it was a very simple constituency, and not a particularly promising ground. His efforts in Leicester, and probably those of the friends whom he brought there from Oxford, found a more receptive audience. It is a commonplace that there was a populist and an academic strand to Lollardy, and it may be indeed that the dichotomy has been overemphasised. Nevertheless there were discontents amongst the laity before Wycliffe's time, and there were many echoes of them long after Wycliffe's doctrines had been suppressed and expelled from the universities. What mattered in 1382 was not so much that academic heresy might infect the laity (though that had already happened), as that the church's authority should not be dismantled and disavowed at its source.

Swinderby is therefore in every sense a central figure. He not only provides a fixed point in the history of Lollardy in Leicester, but also has something to say (as he evidently had on most subjects) about the tides of popular discontent. He was, as the bishop of Lincoln reluctantly recognised, an ordained priest, though he may not have been ordained in the diocese of Lincoln, in which he was probably born. He nevertheless came footloose to Leicester, where he seems at first to have lived upon the offerings of the faithful. In fact he lived after the fashion of a friar, though the Lollards generally were critical of the mendicant orders, and the friars of Leicester rallied to attack Swinderby when he was brought to trial.[34] His early preaching was not to everyone's taste, however, for his denunciation of women's frailties led even the godly matrons of Leicester to threaten to stone him out of town. He turned about to denounce the rich, who offered him no violence, but understandably shunned his sermons.

He then attracted the patronage of the duke, who provided him with a hermitage. He professed for a time to be content with what the duke allowed him, and rejected offerings from other admirers, but eventually returned to the town. Knighton says that he came to regret the austerity which he had imposed upon himself, but it seems likely that the privation which affected Swinderby most was the want of an audience.

He found one in St Mary's abbey, where the canons received and entertained him with some awe, and allowed him to deliver his sermons at large through the eastern half of the county. Even Knighton seems to have been impressed for a time, but once again Swinderby's restlessness overcame him. He left the abbey, and now began to denounce the power of the church and the wealth and abuses of the clergy. He chose the company of the Lollards, who were already numerous in Leicester, and joined the community at St John's chapel. His popular preaching there became so clamantly successful that Bishop Buckingham moved to suppress it, and found himself embroiled.

Several matters of consequence emerge from the story. Knighton attacks Swinderby from the first not for heresy, but for a calculating theatricality. Swinderby had a gift for making trouble for himself, and positively invited it when the bishop came upon him, but he was well able to attract and hold an audience, and to retain the loyalty of at least some of his followers all the time.[35] He was a puritanical enthusiast, and what we know of popular preaching before Wycliffe suggests that there must have been many others like him.[36] What was exceptional about his career was the patronage that he enjoyed, and its timing. Gaunt's interest was obviously valuable to him. Gaunt had other hermits on his estates, and he was notably loyal to his retainers.[37] He also had, as Knighton despairingly admitted, something of a weakness for Lollards.

The canons' patronage is more unusual, and though communities are apt to welcome novelty, Swinderby was something more than a humdrum lodger. It seems, however, that he had something to learn as well as something to impart. Beyond the delicacy of Knighton's touch we are left with a strong impression that Swinderby was not yet a Lollard when he entered the house, and the assurance that he was one when or shortly after he left it. If so, his most likely patron and instructor was Repingdon.

It looks very much as though Swinderby imbibed some Lollard doctrine in St Mary's, before he went on to join, and quite soon to dominate, the other members of the extra-mural class at St John's. He might be said to have been assimilated rather than converted to Lollardy, for despite the preliminary allegations made against him at Lincoln he was not condemned there on any point of eucharistic doctrine. On the other hand his criticism of the clergy goes beyond charges of incompetence and impropriety, and extends to the doctrine of grace. He preached that tithes could be withheld from an unworthy priest, but also that priestly orders were impaired by mortal sin, and the errors held proved against him included a fundamental Lollard doctrine that formal excommunication (and for that matter the withdrawal of a bishop's grant of licence to preach), was invalid unless its subject was excommunicate of God, that is to say excluded by wilful act from the body of the faithful.[38]

The implication is strong that it was Repingdon who brought Swinderby into the house and into the fold, just as he had brought colleagues from Oxford to carry the good news into the Midlands. What the other Lollards in Leicester owed to such instruction is more obscure, but like Swinderby they had probably brought some opinions of their own to the feast. Although Wycliffe's conclusions derived from highly technical arguments, their implications were readily flattering to those who were dissatisfied with the hieratic nature of the church. We cannot tell how closely Repingdon and his friends worked with the other Lollards, but Swinderby must have seemed a rewarding recruit, and worth an exceptional effort.

The consequences of the academics' endeavours were most dramatic where they inspired the unlearned to preach and prophesy, though Knighton, perhaps only conventionally, attributes William Smith's busy literacy to amatory disappointment. However, the message was not confined to those who laboured, as the tally of Lollard knights shows. There was a spiritual ferment in the later fourteenth century not unlike that of the late twelfth. In the earlier period there was also much heresy, but the friars emerged as champions of orthodoxy, thanks in part to the far-sighted enthusiasm of the papacy. In the aftermath of plague and the associated crises of war in the fourteenth century, lay spirituality tended to the support of orthodoxy through private devotions and the work of confraternities,[39] but Lollardy had come to threaten the whole strength of the church as it had developed since the emergence of the universities. Knighton had no doubt about its import. His problem was to describe and emphasise the danger without betraying the part that his own house and colleagues had played in the movement.

All things considered, Knighton shows a remarkable frankness. He published the bloodcurdling texts which Repingdon produced, he described Swinderby's stay in the abbey, he even deplored Gaunt's role as a protector of the sect. At the same time he did what he could to present Lollardy as a native growth,

flourishing across several layers of society. It seems likely that he was writing in
the short interval between Wycliffe's death in 1384 and Courtenay's visitation of
Leicester in 1389. What is less clear is the length of time over which the
movement had been developing before 1382.

Swinderby's odyssey around Leicester could have taken no more than a busy
year or two, but it probably extended over a longer term. The significance of his
ministry in Leicester, however, is not simply that he threw in his lot with the
Lollards after his sojourn in the abbey, though that is interesting enough, but that
he was not drawn to them when he first preached in the town. Given the
puritanical content of the popular movement it seems more likely that Swinderby
arrived before Repingdon and his friends began to proselytise, than that he
ignored what Knighton presents as a vigorous and popular cult. By the time that
he had tired of the duke's hermitage, however, he was ready as Knighton says for
a new style of life, and he found it with a new and impressive patron.

The year was most probably 1381, during the reign of Clowne's successor
Abbot Kereby, a time of excursions and alarms, when Wycliffe withdrew from the
university, and his followers, not conclusively silenced there,[40] had an incentive to
exert themselves wheresoever they could. It may be that the knights' patronage
was also secured at that time. If so, Swinderby had no need of it while he was in
Leicester, but it may have been useful to him later as he made his way westward
to the March.

Swinderby's withdrawal from Leicester must have been a personal relief to
Knighton, who was glad to use it to close his first and principal chapter on
Lollardy. He had found the whole episode distasteful and trying, but he had
turned it to the best account that he could. In the process he made a number of
valuable observations which are not impaired by his reticences. He provided,
almost despite himself, some useful chronology to an obfuscated story, and he
offered both in his character sketches and his other animadversions the earliest
and clearest account that we have of the impact of the cult on the local
community. The outward marks of Lollardy, its consistency of speech and
professions, its uniform, are vividly portrayed, and the observer's impatience of
those tokens, and of the self-righteousness which he imputed to those who
displayed them, carry conviction in the intensity of his feelings. All that was done
against an anxious care to avoid disparagement of his house and his colleagues.
The whole account abounds in interest, but to appreciate Knighton's testimony
to the full, we have to remember what anguish it cost him to offer it.

Notes

[1] *Knighton's Chronicle, 1337–96*, ed. G.H. Martin, Oxford Medieval Texts (Oxford, 1995) *(KC)*.

[2] There are, however, some extracts from Knighton's and some other chronicles in Bodleian MS Eng. hist. c. 380 which appear to have been made before the middle of the sixteenth century. See *Bodleian Library Record*, vii (1962–7), pp. 107–8; and *KC*, p. xviii and nn.

[3] *Historiæ Anglicanæ Scriptores Decem* (London, 1652).

[4] *Fasc. Ziz.*, p. 524 n.

[5] *Chronicon Henrici Knighton vel Cnihtton, Monachi Leycestrensis*, ed. J.R. Lumby, 2 vols (RS 1889–95). Lumby seems to have overrated the difficulty of reading Tiberius C VII, which had suffered only superficial damage in the Cotton Library fire, and which had been very effectively eased and restored in the British Museum before his amanuensis began work. Having chosen Claudius E III, he designated Tiberius 'A' in his notes, for no obvious reason if not to acknowledge its primacy, and then tried to redress the balance by positing an earlier source for both. See further *KC*, pp. xix–xxi.

[6] See V.H. Galbraith, 'The chronicle of Henry Knighton', in D. Gordon (ed.), *Fritz Saxl, 1890–1948: A Volume of Memorial Essays from his Friends in England* (London, 1957), pp. 136–48.

[7] In *John Wycliffe and the Beginnings of English Nonconformity* (London, 1952).

[8] Swinderby, an outstanding and significant figure in popular Lollardy, has now reached the *Dictionary of National Biography* in an entry by Professor Anne Hudson in the additional volume entitled *Missing Persons*, published in 1993.

[9] The structure of the chronicle was decisively analysed by V.H. Galbraith (see above, n. 6). Galbraith decided, however, that the narrative was written in the 1390s, which upon the evidence of the text seems too late. See further *KC*, pp. xxii–xxviii.

[10] See *KC*, p. 2.

[11] See his remarks on Knighton's 'questionable dealings' in a letter to Henry Maxwell Lyte, 21 July 1891, PRO 37/49/14. Aware that his own work is rather behind schedule, he depicts himself as wresting the truth from a duplicitous author, an excuse with at least a touch of originality about it.

[12] See *EHR*, 6 (1891), pp. 172–3.

[13] See PRO 37/16a, p. 1.

[14] *EHR*, 11 (1896), pp. 568–9.

[15] McFarlane, *LK*.

[16] McFarlane, *JW*, pp. 14–21.

[17] *Ibid.*, pp. 10, 30–1. For a recent considered view of Wycliffe's opinions, see M. Keen, 'Wyclif, the Bible, and transubstantiation', in A. Kenny (ed.), *Wyclif and his Times* (Oxford, 1986), pp. 1–16, at pp. 12–14. There is a valuable general review of the whole movement in Hudson, *PR*.

[18] McFarlane, *LK*, p. 149.

[19] Walsingham adds a detail to one of the accusations garnered by Buckingham's clerks: that a particular sermon of Swinderby's was heard by the rural dean of Goscote. That information seems not to have come from Lincoln, but the sermon reads like a conflation of the charges against Swinderby, and perhaps against Lollardy at large. See further *KC*, p. xlv.

[20] See further *KC*, pp. 318–22. Swinderby's second trial, before Bishop Trefnant of Hereford, in 1391, shows him professing a wider range of Lollard doctrines, though he was still comparatively reticent on the eucharist: McFarlane, *JW*, pp. 132–3.

[21] McFarlane, *LK*, p. 151.

[22] Emden, *BRUO*, p. 1566; and *KC*, pp. 282–4, and below, p. 35.

[23] See further *KC*, pp. 270–8.

[24] Knighton speaks of Wycliffe as rector of Lutterworth, and in the past tense: *KC*, p. 242 and n. Although he subsequently refers to John Purvey's activities (*KC*, pp. 290–2) he says nothing to suggest that Wycliffe himself had been active in the locality, though as McFarlane observes he had every incentive to blame Wycliffe for the prevalence of Lollardy in Leicestershire: McFarlane, *JW*, p. 103.

[25] The prevalence of the metaphor in Knighton's work seems to exclude other etymologies of

Lollardy. At the same time, it is interesting that Knighton does not attribute Lollard beliefs to Ball himself, but regards him solely as a harbinger. His mischief, which was to promote mistrust of the clergy, then enabled the Lollards to disseminate their heresies. See also below, n. 39.

[26] G. de Saint-Amour (1202–72), *De periculis novissimorum temporum*, printed at Paris in 1632. See *KC*, pp. 244–50.

[27] The account of Hereford's adventures seems to date from the time of his arrest and imprisonment at Nottingham in 1387, and before his reconciliation in 1391: *KC*, pp. 282–3; Emden, *BRUO*, pp. 913–15.

[28] Knighton names two inhabitants of the chapel as Richard Waytestathe, a chaplain, and William Smith, a layman who learned to read and write and copied a number of scriptural and other texts. It appears from the narrative that they burned an image there before Swinderby joined them, but were expelled shortly afterwards. However, Smith kept his writings, or some of them, until Courtenay's visitation of the diocese in 1389, when he, Waytestathe, and seven other Lollards were made to do penance in Leicester. Swinderby had already moved on, but the cult had evidently persisted. See further *KC*, pp. 296–8, 534; and J. Crompton, 'Leicestershire Lollards', *Transactions of the Leicestershire Archaeological and Historical Society*, 44 (1968–9), pp. 11–44.

[29] *KC*, p. 312; and below, p. 36.

[30] McFarlane, *JW*, pp. 173–5.

[31] That he died in 1424 suggests that he completed his doctorate at the earliest possible time, in his twenties, rather than that he had matriculated young, and returned to Leicester before proceeding to advanced theological studies.

[32] Wycliffe did not deny Christ's presence in the consecrated host, but he assailed transubstantiation as a perversion of Scripture and logic which had led to a blasphemous corruption of clerical power: M. Keen, 'Wyclif, the Bible, and transubstantiation', p. 14.

[33] It is interesting that Repingdon's principal associates were from Merton (John Aston) and Queen's (Nicholas Hereford), the colleges in which the movement was clearly strongest in Oxford.

[34] Buckingham made considerable efforts to assemble evidence against Swinderby, and it seems that he secured the formal representation of each of the three houses of friars in Leicester at the trial: *KC*, p. 316 and n.

[35] He survived another episcopal inquisition at the end of the decade: McFarlane, *JW*, pp. 127–36.

[36] See at large G.R. Owst, *Literature and Pulpit in Medieval England* (Cambridge, 1933); and Hudson, *PR*.

[37] See, for example, *John of Gaunt's Register, 1372–6*, ed. S. Armitage-Smith (Camden 3rd Ser., 20–21, 1911), i, p. 180.

[38] See above, n. 20.

[39] See further M. Rubin, *Corpus Christi: The Eucharist in late medieval Culture* (Cambridge, 1992); and, for some reflections upon pious sentiment and rebellion, M. Aston, 'Corpus Christi and corpus regni: heresy and the Peasants' Revolt', *P&P*, 143 (1994), pp. 1–47.

[40] Barton was succeeded as chancellor by Robert Rigg, whose open association with Hereford after the Ascension Day sermon in 1382 shows that the threats of excommunication in the previous year had not rested heavily upon the university. Arundel was still concerned with the extirpation of Lollardy in the university in 1409–11: M. Aston, *Thomas Arundel: A Study of Church Life under Richard II* (Oxford, 1967), pp. 375–6.

2

HERMOFODRITA OR AMBIDEXTER: WYCLIFFITE VIEWS ON CLERKS IN SECULAR OFFICE

Anne Hudson

'Quid, rogo, pertinet ad archiepiscopum occupare cancellariam regis, que est secularissimum regni officium?'
('What on earth is an archbishop doing as the king's chancellor, an office which is the most secular in the kingdom?')

Wycliffe's question comes in the course of his anguished reflections upon the Peasants' Revolt which form the main theme of chapter 13 to the end of his *De blasphemia*.[1] Wycliffe conceded that the rebels should not have killed Archbishop Sudbury, at least without allowing him the opportunity to defend himself against their complaints, and that they should not have proceeded in anger (p. 196, l. 20–p. 198, l. 30). The main cause of the Revolt, in Wycliffe's account, was the excessive taxation imposed on the laity as a result of the exclusion of the clergy from all liability; but the direction of the rebels' anger against Sudbury was, in his view, not against his ecclesiastical office as such but against his actions as, and indeed tenure of the office of, chancellor. Wycliffe's emphasis on the unsuitability of a cleric in this particular state office echoes a detail in Walsingham's story of John Ball – in Walsingham's view Wycliffe's follower. According to the chronicler, at the end of Ball's sermon to the Kentishmen assembled on Blackheath the company, elated by Ball's words, acclaimed him their future archbishop and chancellor of the kingdom; only Ball was worthy to be *archipraesulatus*, 'the archbishop', since the present archbishop was a traitor to the commons and the kingdom, and should be beheaded wherever he might be found.[2] Walsingham fails to comment on the omission of the chancellorship in the second part of this acclaim, and may, inadvertently or deliberately, have ignored the irony.

The incompatibility which Wycliffe had noted between the two offices of archbishop and chancellor is not one that is limited in application to these two, let alone to Sudbury, the offending holder of both. Elsewhere Wycliffe himself commented at length on the monstrosity of the link between ordained status and secular office, and also on its contemporary frequency.[3] The objection is put in more general terms in the *Twelve Conclusions of the Lollards*, from which the epigraph in my title derives. These conclusions, posted on the doors of Westminster Hall (and possibly also of St Paul's) during the session of parliament from 27 January and 15 February 1395, proclaim as their sixth item:

> a kyng and a bisschop al in o persone, a prelat and a iustise in temperel cause, a curat and an officer in wordly seruise, makin euery reme out of god reule . . . temperelte and spirituelte ben to [two] partys of holi chirche, and þerfore he þat hath takin him to þe ton schulde nout medlin him with þe toþir . . .[4].

The corollary to this, 'þat alle manere of curatis boþe heye and lowe ben fulli excusid of temperel office, and occupie hem with here cure and nout ellis', reveals one reason for Lollard dislike of the practice, namely that tenure of secular office takes a clerk from his cure, and deprives his parishioners of their proper ministry and especially of preaching. Given Wycliffe's contention that preaching is the only proper purpose of the clergy, condemnation of these *ambidexters* is inevitable. Underlying all others, however, is the force of the verse (Matthew 6:24), quoted, like the other key words in the *Twelve Conclusions*, in Latin, *quia nemo potest duobus dominis seruire*: no one can serve two masters; that is, the incompatibility of the service of God with the service of Mammon, even if the latter, as here, could be glossed as the state.

Wycliffe himself returned to the issue later in chapter 17 of *De blasphemia*. Here the recurrent biblical authorities are two; straightforwardly the Pauline injunction *nemo militans Deo implicat se negociis secularibus*: no man fighting for God embroils himself with the affairs of this world (2 Tim. 2:4) and less evidently the implicit force of Christ's questions and observation concerning John the Baptist: *Sed quid existis videre? hominem mollibus vestitum? Ecce qui mollibus vestiuntur, in domibus regum sunt*: But what did you go out to see? a man covered in soft clothes? But those who wear soft clothing live in kings' houses (Matt. 11:8).[5] Wycliffe rehearses and rebuts the traditional arguments produced to justify contemporary practice, citing canon law as well as the Fathers to back his case.[6] The seven petitions concerning the governance of England which end the chapter include one relating directly to this issue: 'Quod rex nullum episcopum vel curatum mancipet suo ministerio seculari. Patet: quia aliter tam rex quam clerus foret proditor Jesu Cristi': That the king should not appoint any bishop or cleric to his secular administration. This is clear, since otherwise both king and cleric would be a traitor to Jesus Christ.[7] The strongest reasons for the objection to the link are explained in *De officio regis*: both tasks are honourable, but the combination is repugnant to the law of God; the task of the priest can never be completed so as to leave time for the secular office, which latter can only be undertaken to the neglect of the former.[8]

Dymmok's later reply to the Lollards' sixth conclusion is one of his briefest and, it seems fair to say, not one of his most persuasive.[9] Some sections reiterate platitudes, that Christ, 'priest of the order of Mechisedec', established *genus electum, regale sacerdocium*: a chosen race, a royal priesthood (1 Pet. 2:9). Another sets out deductions that his adversaries would certainly have fiercely disputed: that the two swords of Peter (Luke 22:38) indicated that the use of each, material and spiritual, is appropriate to the clergy, whilst the fact that Christ adjured Peter to return his sword to its scabbard, rather than to throw it away (Matt. 26:52), implied the compatibility of secular with religious office. Another chapter asserts the relevance of Old Testament examples such as Eli and Samuel to the new dispensation; a later chapter (with a slight air of desperation?) argues that ambidexterity is a virtue revealed by the apostles.[10] The opening of chapter 2 of this section considers a more relevant case, that of a cleric who unexpectedly comes into possession of a crown, or other major secular office, by natural inheritance. Dymmok argues that in such circumstances the cleric may legitimately rule, indeed may legitimately marry and produce an heir; conversely nothing in scripture, he claims, would preclude the idea that no one could properly ascend a throne unless 'promotus ad sacerdotalem dignitatem': advanced to priestly rank ('sicud quidam dicunt de regno Indorum et Presbitero Iohanne': as some say is the case in the kingdom of the Indians and with Prester John); when, he concludes, was England better ruled than under the monk of Winchester?[11] The final chapter returns to the commonplace: that temporal and spiritual functions are two aspects of the same service to the Master, and hence may properly be combined (p. 157, l. 1–p. 158, l. 13).

Only Dymmok's chapter 5 makes any attempt to grapple with one of the central concerns of the conclusions: the legitimacy of the removal of a priest with cure of souls to an office whose duties preclude the performance of the obligations attached to that cure. Dymmok first relies upon precedent, arguing that more good may be done by the cleric who leaves his ninety-nine sheep in their parish whilst pursuing the one errant member of the flock elsewhere (an analogy that might have pleased the noble employer as little as the Lollards?), and that paradoxically more good to the greater number might thus be achieved (p. 153, l. 6–p. 154, l. 13). He then proceeds to rehearse a few of the canon law texts allowing for non-residence, admits that some clerics have contravened the moral requirement that secular office should not be sought for base purposes, but neglects to suggest how this failing could be corrected (p. 154, l. 21–p. 155, l. 28). Those who posted the *Twelve Conclusions* might reasonably feel that the main force of their sixth section remained unanswered.

Complaints about ambidexterity were not new. At the height of the crisis in 1340–1, an administrative and financial crisis for which Archbishop Stratford and other clerics were held by many to be responsible, Edward III was reported to have sworn '*qe jammès en son temps ne serreit homme de seinte esglise, son tresorer ne chaunceler, ne en autre graunt office qe au roy apent; mès tieles persones qe si jammès de fausine fuissent atteints q'il porreit faire trayner, pendre, et descoler*': that never again in his time should a man of holy church be his treasurer or chancellor, nor the holder of any major office belonging to the king; but that such persons should be appointed who, should they be convicted of corruption, could be tortured, hung and beheaded.[12] Edward had, indeed, briefly appointed lay chancellors and treasurers, though by 1345 both positions were back in clerical hands.[13] But the idea did not disappear for long. In 1371 a petition was presented in Parliament asking that clerics should no longer be used by the king in positions where laymen could perform the work.[14] The date is significant, since it precedes Wycliffe's own active participation in royal or ducal government – though it is intriguing to wonder whether this petition influenced Wycliffe in the same way as did that other 1371 parliamentary argument, in favour of the reappropriation of church endowments in time of national need.[15] The petition itself alleges diverse unspecified 'meschiefs et damages' to have arisen from the practice, since the clergy are '*mye justiciables, en touz cas*': not in every case subject to law, and argues that lay people are sufficient and able to fulfil the tasks. The reply was terse: that the king would ordain as it seemed right to him, by the advice of his council. But in 1371, whatever the reason, a change in administration did occur: Wykeham, bishop of Winchester, was removed from the chancellorship, Thomas Brantingham, bishop of Exeter, from the exchequer, and Peter Lacy, canon of Lichfield and Dublin, from the keepership of the Privy Seal; laymen succeeded all three, albeit briefly.[16]

Notwithstanding these brief intrusions of the laity, by the time of *De blasphemia*, and even more by 1395, clerical domination of the administration was fully re-established. Looked at from the viewpoint of the petitioners in the *Twelve Conclusions*, the *procuratores Christi*, the implication of the prelacy in secular affairs must have seemed complete. Of the seventeen English bishops in post for all or most of the period 1390–5, thirteen held or had held some major secular office.[17] In some cases, as for instance that of William Courtenay, this had been only a brief tenure: Courtenay had acted as chancellor for four months after the death of Simon Sudbury at the hands of the rebels in 1381. Equally, tenure in some instances was far in the past: Ralph Erghum, bishop of Bath and Wells, had served as chancellor to John of Gaunt in 1372–5, well before he took up his see in 1388.[18] The Lollard conclusion, and more explicitly Wycliffe's discussion, seem primarily directed against those who concurrently combine ecclesiastical position and secular office. Bishops such as Thomas Brantingham, bishop of Exeter from May 1370 to December 1394, who had acted as treasurer 1369–71, 1377–81 and 1389; John Waltham, bishop of Salisbury 1388–95, and keeper of the privy seal 1386–9, treasurer 1394–5, or, pre-eminently, William of Wykeham, bishop of Winchester from 1366 to 1404 but keeper of the privy seal 1363–7, chancellor 1367–71 and again in 1389–91, were targets that no contemporary could miss. To the Lollards some of the apparent exceptions could only be regarded as proving their case: Thomas Appleby, bishop of Carlisle from 1363–95, might not be a royal or ducal servant, but his work as papal penitentiary involved administration of a not dissimilar kind.[19] Bishop Despenser of Norwich (1370–1406) found the sword a more congenial weapon than the pen, and had led the hated crusade of 1383 allegedly against the supporters of Clement VII, a crusade which the Lollards saw and long remembered as the epitome of the work of Antichrist.[20] Only the bishop of Rochester, the Benedictine William Bottlesham (1390–1400), seems to have been entirely free of the taint of ambidexterity. As has been commented by a critic by no means concerned to explain Lollardy, by 1399 'the episcopacy must almost have come to resemble an extension of the [king's] household'.[21]

The 1371 petition specified five particular offices, those of chancellor, treasurer, clerk of the privy seal, barons and chamberlains of the exchequer, controller (of the exchequer), along with other *grantz officers et governours*, as unfitting for clerical involvement. Wycliffe reproduced the first three, in the same order, at the head of his list, adding the clerks *de parvo bag* (p. 261, l. 8), and 'an infinite number of similar clerkships which it is not useful to specify', clerkships such as those *de coquina*; he went on to note that not only the king and chief lords have such clerks as servants, but also many other nobles and legal officers (p. 261, l. 11). The list was replicated in many early Lollard texts, presumably reflecting widespread outrage at these particular ecclesiastical positions,[22] but it was also frequently extended. Clerks should not hold 'seculer officis, þat is in chauncerie, tresorie, priuy seal and oþere siche seculer officis in þe chekir, neiþer be stiwardis of londis, ne stiwardis of halle, ne clerkis of kichene ne clerkis of acountis, neiþir ben ocupied in ony seculer office in lordis courtis'.[23] Embroilment extends to all levels of temporal administration: 'riche clerkis of þe chauncerie, of þe comyn benche and kyngis benche, and in the Checher, and of justicis and schereves and stiwardis and bailifis' all fall under condemnation, as do priests who are 'stewardis and clerkis of kechene, and resceyuouris and rente gedereris and hunteris', or those who are 'a kechen clerk or a penne clerk, or wis of bildynge of castelis'.[24] The lord may himself be a cleric, but this does not change the unsuitability of the subordinate occupation: it is wrong for a priest to 'go and serue a bisschope or anoþer lord in temperele office, as to be his steward or his countrollore or clerke of his kicchen or his tresorere, or ony oþer seculere office'.[25]

The reasons for the unsuitability are various. Sometimes secular office is merely thought unsuitable to a clerk: citing again 2 Tim. 2:4, those who 'encumbren and entriken [enmesh] hemsilf in worldli bisynesse and office' act 'aȝen þe pure staat of presthod'.[26] One English text that advocates the forceful removal of worldly things from the clergy, and the abuses of clerical state, mentions the extravagance of such men, who take no thought for their cure; such men by virtue of their position are reluctant to criticise lay faults for fear of losing their office.[27] Another writer comments that 'oure prestis ben so bysye aboute

worldly occupacioun þat þei semen bettere [rather] bailyues or reues þan gostly
prestis of Iesu Crist'; yet another notes that bishops who strive to be chancellor,
treasurer or governor of a worldly office in the realm 'may not well togidre do þer
gostly office and worldly'.[28] The author of *Thirty-Seven Conclusions* exclaims
'A! hou abhominable is þe mysusinge of prelatis and seculer lordis þat holden
greete benefisid men in here courtis and seculer officis oþer chapellis, and
wiþdrawen hem vntruli fro here gostli cure'.[29] A rather different objection is
voiced in another text: 'ȝif þei geten hem worldly offis in lordis courtis, summe to
ben stiwardis of halle, summe to ben kechene clerkis, summe to ben lordis
anyneris [stewards], and summe to ben conseilours and reuleris of werris, and
also to bein chamberleyns to lordes and ladies, and *putten out pore gentil men of her
office*' (emphasis mine).[30] Here social, rather than theological or ecclesiological,
reasoning supports the contention.

Most texts proclaim loudly the reason why clerks are so willing to undertake
secular work: 'þe eende of þis seruyse is to come þus to benefycis – and no drede
boþe þe patroun and þe clerk ben þus cursid of God'; 'prestis occupien hem ouer
moche in worldly occupacions and seculer offices aȝenst holy writt for plesynge of
lordis and hope of benefices'.[31] One text carries the analysis rather further: lords
present to benefices within their patronage not learned clerks of good life but
those who have served them effectively in secular position 'þouȝ he kunne not
rede wel his sauter and knoweþ not þe comaundementis of God ne sacramentis of
holy chirche'; lords who act thus grievously err since they have power to install
better, just as do the clerks who get licences to 'couchen in lordis courtis, in lustis
and aise of here flech for to gete moo fatte benefices'.[32] The blame rests both
with recipient and with donor: 'boþe þe lord and þe clerk don gret traiterie to
God and his peple'.[33]

The issue which Wycliffe and his followers were here addressing was by no
means a negligible one. Implicitly, of course, it involves the whole relation of
church and state, and the Lollard solution points the way towards a complete
separation of these two. To some extent the Lollards, in making these objections,
were knocking at a door that was already ajar. Some years ago R.L. Storey, in an
article entitled 'Gentleman-bureaucrats' surveyed the rise of the secular official in
the early part of the fifteenth century, and particularly in the reigns of Henry IV
and Henry V.[34] The period he examined is slightly later than that in which
Wycliffe's comments were made, but it is interesting that many of the offices that
he examined overlap with those mentioned by the Lollard critics. Storey notes
certain difficulties of such an enquiry: that, at least in his period, men who had
been ordained, often but not only to minor orders, might revert to secular rank
later in life, and that holding of minor orders was not incompatible with marriage
at this date – since it is often easier to trace an ecclesiastical career than
advancement outside the church, there is always a danger of overestimating
clerical domination. Looking at some of the offices that Storey covered, it seems

clear that the tendencies that he saw developing between 1399 and *c.* 1430 had already begun in or before the reign of Richard II. As has been remarked, though the office of chancellor and keeper of the great seal was predominantly in the hands of clerics from the reign of Henry III up to that of Richard II, lay holders of the office were not unknown: three knights had successively held the post in the years 1340–3, two more in 1371–7 (after, if not because of, the 1371 petition), and Michael de la Pole, first Earl of Suffolk between March 1383 and October 1386.[35] A similar pattern emerges for the office of treasurer: after an unbroken sequence of clerical holders from Henry III's reign onward, there were two brief tenures by laymen in 1340 and 1341, a slightly longer period of two laymen in 1371–7, a longer single lay tenure from 1381–6, and two brief periods of office in the final two years of Richard II's reign.[36] Other positions remained firmly in clerical hands: despite his title, the king's keeper of the wardrobe was 'the chief clerical officer of the household', and the office during Richard II's reign was filled by two priests, from 1377 to his death in 1390 by William Pakington, archdeacon of Canterbury and dean of St Martin's-le-Grand, and thereafter by John Carp (cofferer from 1376), a canon of St Paul's, London and of York.[37] The keeper of the privy seal was equally a position occupied throughout Richard's reign by a succession of high-ranking clergy.[38] A similar pattern emerges in the households of important but not regal lords. All the chancellors of John of Gaunt's household were ecclesiastics, as were all his recorded treasurers, heads of the wardrobe, receivers general, attorneys general and auditors.[39]

As has often been observed, the origin of the practice by which medieval kings and lords habitually used the clergy to fill positions such as chancellor, treasurer and so forth, lies in the clerical domination of education.[40] Edward III may well have found his early resolve impossible to maintain. For such complex matters as taxation or diplomacy, training of a sophisticated kind was necessary; as long as the majority of university graduates had, before the completion of their education, received ordination (even if only of the lower grades) and hence expected a career within the church, kings and lords were obliged to recruit their staff from amongst the clergy. Whilst *litteratus* retained primarily its sense of 'able to read Latin', and Latin was the almost universal medium of official record, domination of secular administration by clerics was inevitable. But at the end of the fourteenth century that easy domination was beginning to be challenged. By 1393 a *laicus litteratus* might be found in surprising places: the case of Walter Brut revealed this clearly to the shocked bishop Trefnant, who, in his anxiety, demanded refutations of Brut's claims from William Woodford and others.[41] In less contentious quarters, it has been noted that in England by the end of the fourteenth century the quintessentially clerical office of notary was increasingly being filled by men who might be in minor orders but who were, notwithstanding, married.[42] To Wycliffe such a position was unexceptionable –

they were effectively laymen: 'De aliis autem vocatis clericis extra hunc statum, cum licet eis coniugari ut laicis, non contendo': I have no quarrel concerning other so-called clerics beyond this state, since it is allowed for them to be married just like laymen.[43]

The implications of Lollard interest in this question are, however, interesting and in some respects ambiguous. The chief objection is to the failure of priests, consequent upon their preoccupation with administrative offices in the human kingdom, to fulfil their proper function of evangelism, a failure that is castigated in no uncertain terms. Associated with this are the vices attendant upon the quest for a career: absenteeism, pluralism and the constant exchanging of benefices.[44] Less predictably, the second result is the impoverishment of the laity, not only in spiritual but also in material terms. Salaries are being diverted to the church. Not only are clerks said to occupy posts that could well be filled by laymen, but there is also a suggestion (historically largely inaccurate) that in this they are displacing laymen from positions that traditionally they have filled.[45]

At first sight the claims seem to be those that might be expected of a group that Pecock later characterised as 'þe lay partie'. Coupled with this, however, there is censure of those lords who collude in this diversion – they are equal traitors to God with the clerics they advance. John of Gaunt would obtain no advantage here: instead of being able to pay for the services of his bureaucrats with the benefices in his gift, he would have to pay real money to laymen. Wycliffe faced this problem in *De blasphemia*, but predictably refused to allow that a secular ruler should gain service through the ill-gotten wealth of the church.[46] To him the remedy lay in the reduction of the church to its pristine evangelical poverty, and the consequent ability of the king to raise sufficient revenues from the country to finance a secular administration.[47]

Is this objection to the *ambidexter*, then, a disinterested attempt to restore the clergy to their evangelical role? or can we discern here the mundane voice of any lay faction? There seems little in the specifically Lollard argument to attract the king or the great lord; something perhaps to gain the interest of the lesser gentry, those who might, or whose sons might, fill the offices vacated by the clergy. The desire of Edward III in the early years of his reign for administrators subject to civil law, *justiciables en touz cas* as the 1371 petition more elegantly put it, is apparently absent from the Lollard case. That the most public airing of this case came at a session of parliament may not be accident: the knights of the shire and the other lay representatives are precisely those whose interests might be served by pursuing this line of attack.

Directly, of course, the Lollard petition to parliament had no effect, even if it was ever presented. But for other reasons this particular plea seems to have had later repercussions. Restiveness with the secular preoccupations of the clergy was not solely a heterodox feeling: John Gower, no friend to Lollardy, voices similar disquiet.[48] Probably around the time of the conclusions there was complaint from the cathedral chapter of Hereford about the damage done to the church by the long absence of the dean John Prophete, caused by his work in the office of the privy seal, work that was recognised in 1392 by the title of 'clerk of the Council'. Doubtless the tasks the chapter felt Prophete should have been doing did not include preaching, but any recall from secular to ecclesiastical administration would have effected part of the Lollard remedy.[49] One factor in the decline in clerical recruitment in the early fifteenth century, it has been argued, lies in the preference of those seeking advancement in secular administration for lay status, and that preference may reflect the longstanding criticism of ambidextrous clerks.[50] It is ironic that the deposition articles and associated documents in 1399 suggested that Richard II had acted against the interests of the church, when, at least in regard to his administration, his use of episcopal servants had been so extensive.[51] But then those documents, like the 1395 *Twelve Conclusions*, were pieces of political propaganda, not impartial reports. Both, however, reveal much about the issues, often conflicting and even contradictory, that excited contemporaries.

Notes

[1] All quotations from Wycliffe's works are from the editions of WS, by page and line numbers; here *De blasphemia*, p. 194, l. 16.

[2] Thomas Walsingham, *Historia Anglicana*, ed. H.T. Riley (RS, 1863–4), ii, pp. 32–3, largely replicated in *Chronicon Angliae*, ed. E.M. Thompson (RS, 1874), pp. 321–2.

[3] See, for instance, *De ecclesia*, p. 291, ll. 17ff, *De officio regis*, p. 28, ll. 16ff and p. 154, ll. 23ff.

[4] Text quoted from Hudson, *Selections*, no. 3, ll. 63–72. See below, p. 58 for the whole conclusion.

[5] *De blasphemia*, p. 261, ll. 29, 35; p. 263, l. 24; p. 262, l. 28.

[6] *De blasphemia*, p. 261, l. 28; p. 265, l. 22; a quotation, as Wycliffe notes, from Augustine.

[7] *De blasphemia*, p. 271, l. 17; although the others do not directly address the question, the implications of this demand for clerical residence in their cures is spelt out in the third. The petitions seem to have gained independent circulation; see Walsingham, *Historia Anglicana*, ii, pp. 51–2, Thompson (ed.) *Chronicon Angliae*, pp. 336–7.

[8] *De officio regis*, p. 28, ll. 16ff., cf *De civili dominio*, iv, p. 436, ll. 5ff for the separation of offices according to Aristotle.

[9] *Dymmok*, pp. 146–59. For further comments see Fiona Somerset's paper below, pp. 58–61.

[10] Respectively, pp. 146, l. 1–147, l. 22; pp. 148, l. 15–149, l. 17, p. 149, ll. 22–32, pp. 155, l. 30–156, l. 37.

[11] *Dymmok*, pp. 147, l. 23–148, l. 14; a sixteenth-century interlinear note in the Cambridge manuscript suggests the reference is to Ethelwulf, died 858.

[12] *Chroniques de London*, ed. G.J. Aungier (Camden Society 28, 1844), p. 86. For recent summaries of the crisis, with references to the extensive earlier literature, see R.M. Haines, *Archbishop John Stratford, Political Revolutionary and Champion of the Liberties of the English Church ca. 1275/80–1348* (Studies and Texts 76, Pontifical Institute of Medieval Studies, Toronto, 1986), pp. 278–327; W.M. Ormrod, *The Reign of Edward III* (New Haven and London, 1990), pp. 81–6; S.L. Waugh, *England in the Reign of Edward III* (Cambridge, 1991), pp. 213–19.

[13] E.B. Fryde, D.E. Greenway, S. Porter and I. Roy (eds), *Handbook of British Chronology* (London, 3rd edn, 1986), pp. 86, 105.

[14] *Rot. Parl.* ii, p. 304; B. Wilkinson, *The Chancery under Edward III* (Manchester, 1929), pp. 124–7, suggested that the petition originated with the lords rather than the commons.

[15] See M. Aston, '"Caim's Castles": Poverty, Politics and Disendowment', in Aston, *FF*, pp. 95–131, at p. 105, and references there.

[16] See the lists provided in Fryde *et al.* (eds) *Handbook* (above, n. 13), pp. 86, 105, 94 respectively.

[17] Details here derived again from the dates given in Fryde *et al.* (eds) *Handbook*, pp. 78–106 and, for the tenure of bishoprics, pp. 225–84.

[18] R. Somerville, *History of the Duchy of Lancaster*, i, 1265–1603 (London, 1953), p. 366.

[19] See J.R.L. Highfield, 'The English hierarchy in the reign of Edward III', *TRHS*, 5th series 6 (1956), pp. 115–38 at pp. 121–2.

[20] See M. Aston, 'The Impeachment of Bishop Despenser', *BIHR*, 38 (1965), pp. 127–48 and references there.

[21] C. Given-Wilson, *The Royal Household and the King's Affinity* (New Haven and London, 1986), p. 182; he notes, pp. 175–83, the increase in the number and importance of powerful clerks in the 1380s and later in the 1390s.

[22] See, for instance, *Lollard Sermons*, ed. G. Cigman (EETS, 294, 1989), no. 2, l. 438, or unprinted texts in BL, MS Egerton 2820, f. 49v, and Oxford Bodleian Library MS Eng. th. f. 39, f. 41.

[23] *Thirty-Seven Conclusions of the Lollards*, printed under the title *Remonstrance against Romish Corruptions*, ed. J. Forshall (London, 1851), p. 2; the shorter Latin version printed by H.F.B. Compston, *EHR*, 26 (1911), p. 742, is closer to the 1371 wording: 'Prelati, sacerdotes, vel diaconi non habebunt officia secularia, ut puta Cancellariam, Thesaurariam, cum secreto sigillo et aliis in curia secularium dominorum': Prelates, priests and deacons should not hold secular office, offices such as those of chancellor, treasurer, with the privy seal and other (seals) in the court of lay lords. (The manuscript is now BL Add. 38510 section O – information I owe to the kindness of Dr Nigel Ramsay.)

[24] Arnold, *SEW*, iii, p. 215, l. 16; Matthew, *EWW*, p. 168, l. 17, p. 246, l. 13.

[25] Unprinted dialogue in Durham University Library, MS Cosin III.6, f. 15.

[26] Egerton 2820, f. 49r–v.

[27] Arnold, *SEW*, iii, p. 215, ll. 5ff.

[28] Matthew, *EWW*, p. 195, l. 25 (and *cf.* p. 149, l. 10); Arnold, *SEW*, iii, p. 335, l. 20.

[29] *Remonstrance*, ed. Forshall, p. 153.

[30] Matthew, *EWW*, p. 13, l. 10; cf *Thirty-Seven Conclusions*, p. 2, 'most whil seculer men ben sufficient to do suche seculer officis' (not found in the Latin version).

[31] Hudson and Gradon, *EWS*, iii, p. 320, Appendix l. 50, derived from Wycliffe, *Sermones*, iv, p. 503, l. 20; Matthew, *EWW*, p. 168, l. 14 and see also p. 22, l. 13.

[32] Matthew, *EWW*, p. 246, l. 13, p. 247, l. 3.

[33] Matthew, *EWW*, p. 277, l. 2, and cf. p. 394, l. 9.

[34] Published in C.H. Clough (ed.), *Profession, vocation and culture in later medieval England: essays dedicated to the memory of A.R. Myers* (Liverpool, 1982), pp. 90–129; see earlier M. Hastings, *The Court of Common Pleas in Fifteenth-Century England* (Ithaca, 1947), p. 61, though compare her list of the keepers of writs and chirographers (pp. 271–82) where the majority of holders of these offices are shown to be clerics.

[35] Details from Fryde *et al.* (eds) *Handbook*, pp. 85–7; see also the comments and references in R.N. Swanson, *Church and Society in Late Medieval England* (Oxford, 1989), pp. 103–8, and the comments of Wilkinson in *Chancery under Edward III*, pp. 116–23 on Edward III's return to a clerical chancellor in 1343 up to 1371.

[36] Fryde *et al.* (eds) *Handbook*, pp. 103–6.

[37] *Ibid.*, pp. 78, 80–1; cf T.F. Tout, *Chapters in the Administrative History of Mediaeval England*, v, (Manchester, 1930), p. 79.

[38] Fryde *et al.* (eds) *Handbook*, pp. 94–5.

[39] Somerville, *Duchy of Lancaster*, pp. 115, 364–9.

[40] W.A. Pantin, *The English Church in the Fourteenth Century* (Cambridge, 1955), pp. 11–14.

[41] See my discussion of the case in Biller and Hudson (eds), *Heresy and Literacy*, pp. 222–36.

[42] C.R. Cheney, *Notaries Public in England in the Thirteenth and Fourteenth Centuries* (Oxford, 1972), pp. 78–80, where the ambivalence of ecclesiastical regard for this office is noted (Innocent III's prohibition on clerics in it, 'ne clerici vel monachi secularibus negotiis se immisceant' (*PL*, 216, cols. 486–7), modified by later qualification to exclude married men).

[43] *De blasphemia*, p. 261, l. 25.

[44] For the factual background to the Lollard claims see W.R. Jones, 'Patronage and Administration: the King's Free Chapel in Medieval England', *Journal of British Studies* (1969–70), pp. 1–23 at pp. 1, 7–8, 12, the contributions of R.L. Storey, 'Ecclesiastical Causes in Chancery', pp. 236–59 at pp. 244–6, and of A.L. Brown, 'The Privy Seal Clerks in the Early Fifteenth Century', pp. 260–81 at pp. 277–8, in D.A. Bullough and R.L. Storey (eds), *The Study of Medieval Records presented to Kathleen Major* (Oxford, 1971).

[45] Cf Wycliffe's *De symonia*, p. 97, l. 15.

[46] *De blasphemia*, p. 264, l. 6; cf *De veritate sacre scripture*, iii, p. 82, l. 21.

[47] *De blasphemia*, p. 265, l. 20.

[48] *The Complete Works of John Gower*, ed. G.C. Macaulay (Oxford, 1899–1902), *Vox clamantis* iii, ll. 137–42, note especially ll. 141–2 'Clauiger ethereus Petrus extitit, isteque poscit/ Claues thesauri regis habere sibi': Peter was the bearer of the keys to heaven, but this fellow demands the keys to a king's treasure for himself (tr. by E.W. Stockton, *The Major Latin Works of John Gower* (Seattle, 1961), p. 120), *Mirour de l'Omme*, 19489–500, 22261–72.

[49] The case is reviewed by Brown, 'The Privy Seal Clerks' (1971), pp. 276–81; Brown convincingly argues that the complaint, which exists only in undated and unlocalised draft, relates to Hereford and not to Prophete's later position as dean of York.

[50] R.L. Storey, 'Recruitment of English Clergy in the Period of the Conciliar Movement', *Annuarium Historiae Conciliorum*, 7, (1975), pp. 290–313 at pp. 309–10.

[51] See R.L. Storey, 'Clergy and common law in the reign of Henry IV' in R.F. Hunnisett and J.B. Post (eds), *Medieval Legal Records: Essays in memoriam C.A.F. Meekings* (London, 1978), p. 342; for the documents see C. Given-Wilson, *Chronicles of the Revolution 1397–1400* (Manchester, 1993), especially pp. 172–84.

3

ANSWERING THE *TWELVE CONCLUSIONS*: DYMMOK'S HALFHEARTED GESTURES TOWARDS PUBLICATION

Fiona Somerset

The writers of the *Twelve Conclusions* set themselves apart from the institutional clergy. They strongly disapprove of clerical involvement in secular administration, calling the 'men of duble astate' who engage in it 'hermofodrita', and they censure the clergy's corrupt spiritual activities by linking them with dubious secular practices: bishops who ordain priests are giving out the livery of Antichrist; sellers of letters of fraternity are selling the bliss of heaven 'be chartre of clause of warantise'; the pope by the logic of his claim to be able to grant pardons for sin is the treasurer furthest from charity. However, while the writers distance themselves from the sort of involvement with secular affairs they think typical of the corrupt clergy, contrasting themselves with the pope – if he is the worst sort of treasurer, they are the best; poor men and treasurers of Christ, holders of genuine spiritual rather than bogus salvific capital – they leave obscure whether they themselves are clerics or laymen. Patently they have had considerable access to clerical learning: they correctly use a distinction between 'latria' and 'dulia' worship and cite Wycliffe's *Trialogus* in Latin. But they also make a bid for a role in public affairs that they would surely characterise as secular: as 'procuratouris' with an 'ambaciat', 'pursuing' a 'cause', before parliament – even if they look beyond parliament as well, petitioning God rather than (as a petition presented in parliament typically would) the king or the commons,[1] and laying stress on their wish to see their ideas not only reach the lords and commons in parliament, but be 'communid' 'in oure langage' to all true Christian men.[2]

Were those responsible for writing and 'publishing' the *Twelve Conclusions* laymen, then, or were they clerics? Or was a mixed group involved? In contrast to Walsingham, who reports that clerical 'Lollardi' worked in close collusion with a group of noble and knightly supporters who were certainly involved in the posting of the conclusions even if not in drawing them up, Roger Dymmok gives no credence to the efforts of the authors of the *Twelve Conclusions* to associate themselves with lay as well as clerical authority.[3] He ascribes the writing and publication of the *Twelve Conclusions* solely to clerics, disparaging their address to the laity as evidence of ingratitude to the church that has educated them, and their use of English as revealing how little they had gained from that education.[4] Any members of the laity who may be convinced count for Dymmok as audience, not participants. And the manner of the *Twelve Conclusions'* publication counts for him as an unauthorised assumption of a kind of public role to which their writers are not entitled; he terms it their

> publicacione libelli famosi et eiusdem expansione apud Westmonasterium in ostio Aule Regalis, in pleno parliamento, in conspectu omnium prelatorum, procerum, nobilium et huius regni populi uniuersi (*Dymmok*, p. 15, ll. 23–7): publication of an infamous *libellus*, and display of that same *libellus* at Westminster, on the door of the Regal Chamber in full parliament, in the sight of all prelates, dukes, nobles, and the whole of the people of this realm.

Publicacio is the term used to describe public preaching, proclamation, and the promulgation of statutes; *libellus* is used to describe short legal documents such as deeds, writs, and bills as well as books; while *expansio* elsewhere describes, in a gesture reminiscent of the unrolling and display of the *Conclusions*, how the banners of kings are unfurled on the battlefield.[5] For Dymmok this unprecedented bid for the attention of the highest as well as potentially the broadest of publics is an untoward usurpation by clerics of status not so much (as in the *Twelve Conclusions* writers' complaints about the clergy) as laymen – for as we will see Dymmok will defend in the strongest terms the holding of secular office by ecclesiastics – but as what he calls 'public persons'.

Dymmok's category of 'public persons' includes influential figures in the secular and ecclesiastical hierarchies: kings, dukes, bishops, and scholastic doctors. Dymmok includes himself among this group, by virtue of his doctorate, but excludes the Lollards.[6] This representation is, of course, skewed, and in at least two directions. For one thing, doctors rank with kings, dukes, and bishops only by an extraordinary kind of special pleading. Even Dymmok's inclusion of bishops and dukes is rather unusual: Aquinas, who is probably Dymmok's most immediate source on this as on many other matters, calls only kings, princes, and other rulers 'public persons'.[7] For another thing, status as 'public persons' by Dymmok's definition is not what the Lollards are claiming. Instead, the secular roles they mention, those of ambassadors, procurators, or treasurers, are of just the kind occupied not by 'public persons', but by the clerics or gentry in their service who represent them in particular capacities – even if the 'public person' the Lollards claim to represent is Christ.[8] Dymmok is not prepared to accept the Lollard claim of direct service to Christ,[9] but neither is he comfortable with the notion that the Lollards have the support of some more tangible 'public person' or persons; he invokes national pride against the mere possibility: 'Per hunc enim modum faciendi ceteris nacionibus dare possent intelligere regem uel alias personas publicas et potentes regni ipsis fauorem . . . prebuisse . . .' (*Dymmok*, p. 27, ll. 6–10): 'such behaviour might lead other nations to conclude that the king, or other public persons powerful in the realm, had shown favour to these'. Clerical service to 'public persons' is something Dymmok is concerned to defend, not decry – and I would suggest that despite his claim to be a public person in his own right, this defence operates very much for his own benefit.

The status of Dymmok's family, who were Lincolnshire gentry of some importance, might well have disposed him toward the position he takes.[10] Sir John Dymmok, his father, was a retainer of John of Gaunt and member of parliament in 1372, 1373, and 1377. He held in addition a position of considerable if largely ceremonial importance, acting as Champion of England at Richard II's coronation. After Sir John's death in 1381 the position of Champion would have been Roger Dymmok's by hereditary right had it not been for his ecclesiastical status; indeed, in 1399 and again in 1413, it fell to his younger brother Sir Thomas Dymmok.[11] Roger Dymmok himself, however, although he did become a doctor of theology and thus by his own definition counts as a 'public person', seems never to have succeeded in gaining any important secular office. He was prior of the Boston Dominican house from 1379 onward and regent of the London house after 1396, but these offices involved him in purely ecclesiastical duties rather than in public affairs. He does not seem to have been offered any other opportunity to engage in affairs of state, and although he apparently preached a sermon before Richard II in 1391, there is no sign that he was ever in favour at court. Rather to the contrary: in the *Calendar of Close Rolls* there is an entry directed to the keepers of the passage at London, Dover, and Sandwich asking them to permit Dymmok passage; although previously, on account of information that he planned to pass to foreign parts in order to prosecute suits to the prejudice of the king and many of the people, he had been forbidden passage, now Dymmok has promised 1) not to go abroad without special licence from the king; 2) not to make any suit or attempt that might tend to contempt or prejudice of the king, or to hurt his people, or to impair the laws, customs, ordinances, or statutes of the realm; 3) not to send anyone else to make such a suit.[12] While the machinations behind this document are unclear, it is evident that Dymmok was not among the king's trusted servants.

In answering the *Twelve Conclusions*, then, Dymmok has no more ready access to sanctioned channels of broad public communication, available to ecclesiastic and secular 'public persons' and those in their service in the late fourteenth century, than his opponents had – an easy explanation for why his answer to them exploits none of those channels. His answer was not presented to parliament, whether as the sort of parliamentary sermon the chancellor might have addressed to the assembly or as a petition produced or advocated by members of parliament.[13] Still less did it become the more widely promulgated statute that might result from a parliamentary petition. It was not issued as a writ from Chancery to the bishops, requiring them to ask the lower clergy to instruct the broadest possible public by means of sermons and of special prayers, masses, and processions.[14] Nor, even though it would have been perfectly legitimate for a licensed or invited preacher to address the public in this way and presumably Dymmok could have arranged such an occasion if he had wanted to, was his reply a public vernacular sermon given in London or Oxford and perhaps subsequently disseminated in written form.

Instead, Dymmok produces a voluminous treatise which discusses in detail and refutes in turn every point of each of the Lollard conclusions, and indeed argues over their heads, so to speak, with related issues raised by Wycliffe and earlier polemicists.[15] The scholastic format and mode of proceeding of his text is just what we would expect from a man with Dymmok's training; these, after all, are the weapons he has been trained to wield. But Dymmok attempts to move beyond the extremely narrow audience of educated clerics we would expect for a treatise like his; he addresses himself to the king, and through and beyond him to the widest possible public:

> Scire etiam dignetur uestra precellentissima celsitudo, mei propositi non esse nimium subtilia et scolastica argumenta in presenti opusculo adducere, set talia que intelligi ualent ab omnibus, sicud omnibus supradicti ueritatis adversarii haurienda venenosa pocula doctrine infuderunt, ita ut et omnibus peruenire ualeat hoc antidotum catholice ueritatis, ut ex eo pateat uniuersis quam periculosum fuerit eorum documentum et quod nullum protulerunt pro sua assercione ualidum argumentum. (*Dymmok*, pp. 9, l. 38–10, l. 7):
>
> May it be worthy of the notice of your most excellent highness that my purpose in the present small work is not to adduce overly subtle and scholastic arguments, but arguments of a sort that may be understood by everyone – in the same way that the previously mentioned enemies of truth have poured out their venomous doses in such a way that everyone may drink them – so that this antidote of catholic truth may also reach everyone, with the result that it will be clear to absolutely everyone how dangerous their document is, and that they offer no valid argument for their assertion.

Dymmok claims to offer in his book a *universal* antidote; one that will make clear to *everyone* who might encounter the *Twelve Conclusions* the invalidity of the Lollard arguments and the danger of their document. One motive for referring to a universal audience here is perhaps to avoid telling the king that the work has been written simply enough for *him* to understand. But Dymmok does not have to appeal to the assent of *everyone* to his simplified argument in order to avoid insulting the king. Rather, he is seeking not just the highest, but the widest ratification possible, in a bid for a public role designed directly to counter that assumed by the Lollards.

If part of what Dymmok intends in providing a self-styled public antidote to the *Twelve Conclusions* is to advertise his worthiness for office through a symbolic display – similar perhaps to that proffered by the Champion at a coronation? – of his would-be royalism, then it does not seem to have worked. Dymmok did become regent of the London convent after writing the *Twelve Conclusions*, but he seems to have incurred suspicion shortly thereafter. However, Dymmok's ostensible purpose of convincing a universal audience could not have been accomplished either, for the actual physical dissemination of his text was very limited. Along with the presentation copy presented to the king there are records of only four other manuscripts that include his text. None of them is pitched much lower than the one presented to the king; only one of them, indeed, a devotional volume of the sort typically owned by those in the upper reaches of the nobility, seems to have been owned by someone outside the narrow scholastic audience writing of this sort normally had.[16] Of the other three, one was first owned by two bishops, then given to the Cambridge University library; a second, evidently a Dominican product, was owned by a master John Arnold, perhaps of Merton, in 1439; and the third, possibly produced for consultation in scholastic argument and most probably owned by a monastery, is composed of anti-Wycliffite materials by Woodford and Dymmok.[17]

There is, nonetheless, one at least somewhat wider audience that Dymmok could realistically have hoped to reach even by means of the presentation copy alone, and one with whose concerns we might expect him, by reason of his family connections, to be especially familiar: that of lesser nobility and gentry in service at court. Although we need not believe that all books presented to Richard were read by the royal household (or indeed in some cases that he read them himself), it seems entirely possible that some courtiers literate in Latin could have read Dymmok's text, and others could have been told about it.[18] Much though Dymmok attempts to play down as far as possible the notion that the Lollards had supporters and even collaborators at court, Walsingham's account tells a different story – as, indeed, do modern investigations of the 'Lollard knights'. And interest in the *Twelve Conclusions* need not even have been confined to knights and gentry who might be described as Lollards: the *Conclusions* contain much that would surely have appealed to anticlerical sentiments common among this class and at court.[19] Interest at court in the proposals put forth in the *Twelve Conclusions* might incline nobles and gentry to consider Dymmok's reply, even if only as a prelude to dismissing its arguments: if Dymmok knew about such interest, it might dispose him all the more towards attempting to appeal to nobles and gentry at court – at least insofar as such an appeal would not obstruct his address to the king.

What evidence is there that Dymmok makes any attempt to pitch his text to this audience at court or indeed any wider audience? On most occasions where

Dymmok differentiates the membership of his audience rather than addressing an amorphous 'omnibus', he shows a bias towards its upper end. Typically an *ad status* address invokes the public good and advises representative groups at all levels of society about how they should behave in order to maintain it, whether by discussing members of the three estates in turn or by anatomising society according to the extended metaphor of a body, building, boat, or what-have-you.[20] But when Dymmok explains how each person should behave in accordance with his status, when he tells 'unusquisque . . . in gradu suo' how to combat the heretics, for example, it is those he classifies as pastors who concern him, not their sheep: doctors, kings, and princes, not the 'simplices', the 'Christianum populum', that they protect:

> . . . contra quos [aduersarios] ecclesie diligencia pastorum inuigilet, ne gregem dispersum morsibus uenenosis interimant. Sancti doctores eosdem suis predicacionibus ac disputacionibus compescant, ne simplices seducant per apparenciam ueritatis. Reges uero et principes accincti armis contra ipsos insurgant, ne uiolent[a][21] adunacione peruersorum nouiter insurgencium Christianum populum opprimant . . .
>   . . . unusquisque prompto animo eidem in gradu suo respondeat illud Ysaie VI: 'Ecce ego, mitte me,' ut debita cooperacione omnium fidelium sancta mater ecclesia ab istorum malignancium defendatur . . . (*Dymmok*, pp. 314, l. 32–315, l. 7):
> . . . against which [adversaries] let the diligence of shepherds of the church keep watch, lest they should destroy the scattered flock with their venomous bites. Let holy doctors suppress them with their preaching and disputation, lest they should seduce the simple with the appearance of truth. Let kings and princes girded with arms rise up against them, lest the raging throng of their perverse insurgencies should oppress the Christian people.
> . . . Let each in his degree with a ready mind reply to Him as in Isaiah 6: 'Here I am, send me', so that with the due cooperation of all the faithful, holy mother church may be defended from their malignance.

The way Dymmok demarcates pastors from the 'simplices', the undifferentiated remainder of the 'Christianum populum' whom those pastors protect from seduction, is unusual. Normally the church's metaphorical shepherds are those clerics at whatever level who are engaged in duties typically regarded as pastoral: preaching, teaching, administering sacraments, and so on. Here, however, Dymmok picks out as his pastors a mixed group of important laymen and clerics from among that group he has defined as 'public persons': scholastic doctors who engage in disputations as much as preaching, and kings and princes whose martial role can be viewed as pastoral only by a sort of blinkered extension. Much though Dymmok calls on the 'debita cooperacione omnium fidelium', the undifferentiated *simplices* these pastors protect can hardly be said to contribute, except perhaps in demonstrating the dangers of Lollard publication: they are fragile in their virtue, ready to be led astray by the slightest intellectual temptation.[22]

But are only scholastic doctors, kings, and princes (as this passage seems to imply), excluded from the ranks of the simple, and capable of the required 'cooperacio'? If the lesser nobility and gentry are granted pastoral capacities anywhere, it seems likely that it will be where Dymmok (adapting the method anticlerical writers so often employ) attempts to show his audience that his interests coincide with theirs. While other examples might be considered, nowhere does Dymmok's approach stand out better as a counter to anticlerical appeals to knights and nobles, on the basis of common interest, than in his response to conclusion six, where he defends the capacity of clerics to hold secular office.

The anticlerical complaint that the clergy ought not to have temporal jurisdiction had featured for some time in ongoing conflicts over the respective powers of ecclesiastical and secular government. In the more traditional version of this argument, secular authorities are typically exhorted to reform some section of the clergy by forcing them to attend to their proper spiritual jurisdiction and their pastoral duties. At the same time, the exercise of secular power is itself often represented as a pastoral activity; in the pseudo-Ockham *Dialogus inter militem et clericem*, for example, *Miles* suggests that the king's role as defender of the realm is a pastoral one, whereas clerics who neglect to support him through taxation are delinquent in their pastoral obligations. Secular power may even be encouraged to take over activities associated with the clergy's pastoral ministry but inadequately performed by them, as when an annotation in Trevisa's *Polychronicon* translation asks that lords should remove the superfluous possessions of monks and take over the neglected monastic duty of administering alms to the poor.[23]

Conclusion six puts forth an elaboration of this argument characteristic of Wycliffe and his followers:

> þe sexte conclusium þat mayntenith michil pride is þat a kyng and a bisschop al in o persone, a prelat and a iustise in temperel cause, a curat and an officer in wordly seruise, makin euery reme out of god reule. þis conclusiun is opinly schewid, for temperelte and spirituelte ben to partys of holi chirche, and þerfore he þat hath takin him to þe ton schulde nout medlin him with þe toþir, *quia nemo potest duobus dominis seruire*. Us thinkith þat hermofodrita or ambidexter were a god name to sich manere of men of duble astate. þe correlari is þat we, procuratouris of God in þis cause, pursue to þis parlement þat alle manere of curatis boþe heye and lowe ben fulli excusid of temperel office, and occupie hem with here cure and nout ellis. (Hudson, *Selections*, p. 26, ll. 62–72).

Not only should ecclesiastical government be denied any secular role, but individual members of the clergy ought not to hold positions in the secular hierarchy. Secular authorities ought to secure pastoral benefits for the people by forcing not just the church administration to attend to its proper pastoral duties, but also each one of the church's clerical members.[24] Dymmok's inference that an argument based on Hugh of St Victor's *De sacramentis* II, ii, 3 lies behind the Lollard conclusion and its corollary is characteristic of the way he argues over the heads of the *Twelve Conclusions*; here he is very likely thinking of Wycliffe, who frequently cites *De sacramentis* II, ii when arguing for strict limits on the powers and activities of clerics.[25] In *De Ecclesia*, for example, Wycliffe uses *De sacramentis* II, ii, 3 to assert that clergy should have no secular jurisdiction, that they are not entitled to own but only to use what they hold, and that they must employ lay officials not only to fight for them (as even Dymmok concedes), but even to pursue justice on their behalf.[26]

Both the sixth conclusion and the argument from Wycliffe upon which Dymmok seems to be drawing demonstrate a detailed awareness of the extent to which 'secular' and 'spiritual' powers and personnel interpenetrate one another in fourteenth-century England – in company with the impossibly idealistic notion that it might be possible to disentangle them at every level, removing 'curates' from secular offices ranging from the king's council to the judiciary to clerkships on the one hand, and handing over secular tasks involved in church administration to laymen on the other. But whereas the more traditional version of the argument is straightforward in its offer to secular power of an increased sphere of influence that the pope, or the particular order being criticised, would wish to deny, both the Wycliffite version and Dymmok's attempt to counter it are obliged to develop a more nuanced approach. Both want to cast themselves as royalists supportive of the claims of secular power, but both on the other hand also want to criticise some of the practices of secular rule.

Elsewhere, as we have already seen, Dymmok attributes pastoral roles to kings and princes as well as scholastic doctors: he is no less willing than anticlerical polemicists to suggest that figures at the very top of the secular hierarchy, at least, may share spiritual power of a sort with clerics. In his reply to conclusion six, however, Dymmok counters its restriction of clerical roles on pastoral grounds with a new alternative theoretical justification, also based on pastoral grounds, for clerical involvement in secular affairs.

Dymmok suggests that on many occasions curates can best help the souls under their care, not by residing in their parishes, but by serving their lord in some temporal capacity, for they will then be able to direct the lord about how best to administer his goods for the good of his subjects:

Nonne talis meritorie ageret licitum ministerium tali domino inpendere ad sui correctionem, et omnium subditorum ipsius domini alleuiacionem et solacium, et malorum exemplorum extinctionem? Immo certe. . . . de licencia sui prelati domino certo ministraret sua temporalia bona ministrando, cuius industria dominus suus de multis malis se corrigeret . . . (*Dymmok*, p. 153, ll. 20–8, 25–9, 20–2):

May it not be meritorious for some curate licitly to devote his ministry to a lord, for that lord's correction, and the relief and solace of his subjects, and the removal of bad examples? Indeed, certainly. . . . with licence from his prelate, the curate may assuredly minister to the lord by administering his temporal goods; and by his labour, his lord may correct himself from many evils . . .

This moral and indeed fiscal advisory power will enable curates to curb all manner of abuses: 'puta de extorsionibus falsis, decimacionibus, adulteriis et huiusmodi, quorum exemplum pestiferum patriam infecerat uniuersam' (Dymmok, p. 153, ll. 22–5): 'as for example false extortions, tithes, adulteries, and suchlike, the pestiferous example of which infects the whole country'. By transferring the accepted method by which clerics offer spiritual guidance into the secular sphere, Dymmok offers a new sort of justification for clerical activities that most at best try to ignore; one that bolsters the moral authority of clerics over the lords they serve and dignifies the kind of service they offer. Far from there being a need for nobility and gentry to ensure that the clergy carry out their pastoral role, the work clerics are doing in the secular sphere is already a kind of pastoral work that ensures that lords fulfil their secular role.

But Dymmok does not simply want to suggest, in counterposition to the Lollards, that clerics should take over or at the very least supervise secular governance: that would be no way to persuade a secular audience. Instead, he goes on to propose an ethical ideal for both gentry and clerics. While he unsurprisingly makes no attempt to rehabilitate the term 'hermofodrita', Dymmok redefines its companion epithet 'ambidexter' into an ideal to be aspired to by any holder of 'pastoral office', gentry or cleric:

Debet igitur mens hominis non esse mollis, ad modum cere mutabilis ad cuiuslibet sigilli inpressionem, set dura, quasi adamas inflexibilis et totam fortunam mundi in sui conuertere qualitatem, et sic uere fortis esset eo quod aduersa sicud et prospera equanimiter portaret, nec ex illis deiectus, nec ex aliis elatus, et talis solus maxime dignus esset pastorali officio insigniri eo quod uerisimile est talem nec auaricia nimia uel ambicione laxatum prosequi mundialem fauorem, nec ex alio latere propter metum mortis uelle gregem deserere, uel recedere a iusticie rigore, de quibus dicit Christus (Iohannis x): 'Pastor bonus animam suam ponit pro ouibus suis, set mercenarius fugit, si uiderit uenientem lupum, quia mercenarius est et non pertinet ad eum de ouibus'. (*Dymmok*, p. 156, ll. 20–34, punctuation modified):

Therefore a man's mind should not be soft and changeable as is wax at the imprint of any seal, but hard, inflexible as adamant, able to convert any worldly fortune to its own quality, and in this way truly strong, so that it may bear both adversity and prosperity with equanimity, neither dejected by one nor elated by the other. Only a man of this sort is most worthy to be marked out for pastoral office, because it is unlikely that such a one, made slack by excessive avarice or ambition, will seek worldly favour, or on the other hand that he will wish to desert his flock for fear of death, or depart from the full rigour of justice. Christ speaks of such men in John 10: 'The good shepherd lays down his life for his sheep, but the hireling flees if he sees a wolf coming, because he is a hireling, and the sheep do not belong to him'.

The ideal Dymmok holds up here is typical – until its fifth line, at least – of the sort of Boethian advice offered in courtly literature in the exemplary fall-of-princes mode. As always, the advice about fortitude in the face of changing fortunes this sort of writing offers is meant at least as much for those in service to royalty and subject to its whims as it is meant for the king or prince subject to changes of fortune. But not content merely to desanctify the ambidextrous ideal he has set up so as to extend it to laymen as well as clerics, Dymmok goes on, quoting the passage from John 10 most frequently used in describing the ideal of pastoral service by clerics, to dignify all those who embody the ambidextrous ideal as being worthy of an office designated as pastoral: 'talis solus maxime dignus esset pastorali officio insigniri'. By the end of his arguments for why clerics should hold secular office, Dymmok has dignified as pastoral and endowed with moral authority not only the secular activities of clerics, but even those of knights and gentry.

While Dymmok assumes the pastoral role for clerics who hold secular office that he defends in conclusion six and while he attempts to cast himself as a pastoral adviser to the king, it is rather more difficult for him to stake out common ground with the gentry. Both in his reply to the corollary to conclusion ten and in his reply to conclusion twelve (*Dymmok*, pp. 260–71, 292–304), Dymmok slips from a more generally focused discussion, applicable to nobility and gentry as well as the king, to a defence of regal magnificence by reference to the example of Solomon. Kings who tax heavily and spend lavishly on external display, as Solomon did, impress neighbouring kings into maintaining peaceful relations, and intimidate their subjects into obedient compliance. The special appeal of these arguments for Richard II, never much of a fighter but a lover of magnificent display, is obvious: equally obvious is that Dymmok's shift to discussing the king alone, and especially the kinds of regal behaviour he approves in these passages, might badly damage any wider appeal.

Still, although it has been argued that Dymmok's defence of magnificence wholeheartedly endorses Richard's policies or, as Eberle puts it, is a 'sympathetic presentation of Richard's own point of view', it must be noted that along with upholding the king's entitlement to heavy taxation and the ostentatious display of wealth, Dymmok also holds himself up as an adviser to the king by including, in however muted and cautious a fashion, recommendations about the limits that even kings ought to observe.[27] Might the qualifications to Dymmok's approbation also salvage his wider appeal?

Directly after the defence of regal magnificence in conclusion twelve, which follows his more general argument that need is commensurate with status rather than absolute, Dymmok devotes a chapter to five abuses of clothing. Included among them is his only other reference to *mollicia*, the vice that his ethical ideal of pastorship, in his reply to conclusion six, had pointedly excluded. Even if Dymmok attributes this list of five abuses to Aquinas and interleaves them with repeated reassurances that it is always proper to make use of the clothing commensurate with one's status, the terms in which these abuses are described have acquired a new polemic volatility in late medieval England. The reassurances Dymmok interposes before and after Aquinas's description of two defects of proper attention to clothing cannot neutralise Aquinas's examples:

Cum quibus omnibus stat quantumcunque solempnis apparatus uestium conueniens statui hominis debitis circumstanciis usitatus absque peccato. *Alio modo ex parte defectus potest esse duplex deordinacio secundum affectum; uno modo ex necligencia hominis, qui non adhibet studium uel diligenciam ad hoc, quod exteriori cultu utatur, sicud oportet. Unde dicit Philosphus (VII Etichorum) quod ad molliciem pertinet, quod aliquis trahat uestimentum per terram, ut non laboret eleuando ipsum; alio modo, secundum quod defectum ipsum uestium ordinat ad gloriam. Unde Augustinus (in libro De Sermone Domini in Monte) dicit: 'Non solum in rerum corporearum nitore atque pompa, set eciam in ipsis sordibus luctuosis esse posse iactanciam, et eo periculosiorem, quo sub nomine seruitutis Dei decidit;' et Philosphus dicit (X Etichorum), quod superabundancia inordinatus defectus ad iactanciam pertinet.* Et sicud homines se possunt licite secundum sui status congruenciam ornare sumptuose et artificiose, ita artifices talium ornamentorum licite possunt suas artes exercere, et tales artifices non sunt destruendi set permittendi et fouendi, ut necessarii coadiutores hominum in conuersacione eorum politica et ciuili.[28] (*Dymmok*, pp. 296, l. 24–297, l. 9):

With all of this it remains consistent that a show of clothing, if fitting to the status of a man and used in the appropriate circumstances, however solemn it may be, can be used without sin. 'In another way, on the side of lack or defect, there can be a disorder of affect in two ways. In one way from the negligence of a man who does not give proper attention or diligence to his attire. And thus the Philosopher says (*Nicomachean Ethics* book 7) that it pertains to softness, that someone drags his clothing on the ground to avoid the labour of lifting it. In another way, as that defect of clothing is ordered towards vainglory. And thus Augustine (in his book about the Sermon of our Lord on the Mount) says "Not only in the elegance and pomp of bodily things, but also in those that are sordid and muddy, there can be boastfulness, and the second is more dangerous in that it goes by the name of service to God", and the Philosopher says (*Nicomachean Ethics* book 10) the overabundance of a lack is a kind of boastfulness.' And just as men can licitly ornament themselves sumptuously and with artifice, in a manner fitting to their status, so the artificers of such ornaments may licitly exercise their artistry; and such artificers are not to be abolished, but permitted and even cherished, as necessary to men's political and civil life.

From the mid-1380s onward in England the most frequent referents for the second abuse of boastful insufficiency are the Lollards: Dymmok himself elsewhere comments on the Lollards' 'apparenciam humilitatis . . . in uestimentorum deiectione': 'appearance of humility . . . in the lowliness of their clothing'.[29] But *mollicia* and its association with the dragging of clothing, were in late medieval England acquiring a new set of associations in court satire. These associations are perhaps rather less compatible with Dymmok's supposedly wholehearted approval of unlimited regal magnificence – and even with his attempts at wider appeal.

Aquinas himself, in his commentary on the passage from the *Ethics* that he cites in describing the first abuse, commented that dragging one's clothing creates as much work as it saves: 'Et licet imitetur laborantem in hoc quod vestimenta trahit, et per hoc videtur non esse miser, habet tamen similitudinem cum misero inquantum fugiens laborem sustinet laborem': 'And although he acts like a labourer in that he drags his clothing, and in this he seems not to be wretched, he nonetheless resembles the wretch in that while fleeing labour he undergoes it'.[30] Late medieval English court satiric examples similarly focus on the misdirection of effort that dragging one's clothing betokens, even if they generally associate this misdirection with excessive rather than defective concern. *Richard the Redeles*, for example, describes courtiers' preoccupation with the design of their clothing in these terms:[31]

> And, but if the slevis slide on the erthe,
> Thei woll be wroth as the wynde and warie hem that it made;
> And [but] yif it were elbowis adoun to the helis
> Or passinge the knee it was not accounted. (III, ll. 153–6).

And Hoccleve in his *De Regimine Principum* suggests that the dragging sleeves require so much effort that courtiers who sport them cannot defend their lord as they ought.[32] The implication is the same later in *Richard the Redeles*, when 'the sleeves' say 'Let sle him', '*have* him slain', but then rather than carrying out the action they have urged, merely mock Wisdom's clothing – though this may be a fate worse than death in their view.[33] If, as seems likely, the association of *mollicia* with dragging clothing (as here in Dymmok's reply to conclusion twelve) and unworthy service to one's lord (as in Dymmok's reply to conclusion six) already in the 1390s evokes the sort of early fifteenth-century court satire in which these associations are combined, then Dymmok's quotation of Aquinas implies a rather more critical attitude to Richard's household: it is significant too that Dymmok omits from his description of Solomon's household in the previous chapter any mention of the detailed description in 3 Kings 10:5 of the possessions and clothing of Solomon's household as well as Solomon himself. While Dymmok's muted criticism might, like later satire against courtiers, appeal to a wider gentry audience, it is not clear whether those within the king's household, or aspiring to enter it, would be equally appreciative.

If this example of Dymmok's criticisms of the king and court's expenditure is circumspect even to the point of non-existence, then within Dymmok's defence of taxation in part ten there is a much more overt example, however strongly undercut by Dymmok's subsequent blaming of women, and however couched in quotation from authorities. In the midst of his defence of taxation and expenditure by the king especially for defence of the country, but equally appropriately for the display for his majesty, Dymmok mentions the possibility of abuse:

Set cum secundum Philosphum (in *Politicis*) regem oporteat copiam habere diuiciarum et possessionum ad sui et suorum defensionem, cauere summo opere debent reges et domini temporales, ne bona sua indiscrete consumant in expensis excessiuis aut suas possessiones notabiliter diminuant eas aliis indebite conferendo et sic semetipsos impotentes efficiant maliciis aduersariorum resistere aut honorem regium in necessariis sumptibus conseruare, ne populum sibi subiectum in sui defectum in taxis et aliis exactionibus onerosis compellantur, plusquam necesse fuerit, onerare. In cuius rei evidenciam (Deut XVII) mandauit Dominus regibus uniuersis, ut haberent tam in expensis et sumptuosis negociis, quam in exactionibus in populo faciendis, moderamen debitum et mensuram, dicens: 'Cum rex fuerit constitutus, non multiplicabit sibi equos, ne reducat populum in Egiptum', id est, pristinam Egipciacam seruitutem, 'equitatus numero subleuatus; non habebit uxores plurimas, que illicitant animam eius, neque argenti et auri immensa pondera', scilicet a populo suo talia exigendo. Cui precepto rex Salomon contraueniendo secundum Magistrum in Historiis diuinam incurrit offensam et sui regni demeruit diuisionem et scissuram perpetuis temporibus duraturam. (*Dymmok*, p. 264, ll. 3–27):

But since according to the Philosopher (in the *Politics*) the king should have an ample store of riches and possessions in order to defend himself and his realm, kings and temporal lords should take great care, lest they should indiscreetly consume their goods through excessive expenditure, or significantly diminish their possessions through unduly bestowing them on others, and in this way render themselves incapable of resisting the malice of their enemies or maintaining their regal honour with regard to necessary expenditures; and lest they should be compelled to make up the lack by burdening the people subject to them with taxes and other onerous exactions more than is necessary. As evidence of this, the Lord (Deuteronomy 17) ordered all kings to maintain, both in expenditures and in exactions from the people, the proper moderation and measure, saying, 'when he is made king, he shall not increase the number of his horses, nor lead back the people into Egypt' – that is, their former Egyptian servitude – 'he shall not increase the number of his knights, nor have many wives, who would lead him into licentiousness, nor an immense weight of gold and silver' – requiring these things from his people, that is. According to the Master of Histories, king Solomon by contravening these precepts incurred divine anger and brought upon his realm everlasting divisions and factions.

The statement Dymmok attributes to the 'Magistrum in Historiis' here makes explicit a danger in Dymmok's defence of Richard as a type of Solomon, latent in his replies to conclusions ten and twelve. Even if after coming to the throne in his youth Solomon ruled for a time with exemplary wisdom, so that the comparison might flatter Richard II, Solomon later became what Richard is in 1395 coming to resemble all too closely, a tyrant. The implication of the cautious and authority-hedged limitations suggested here is that Solomon's tyranny was linked to his taxation and expenditure. When we consider how frequent complaints about excessive taxation and irresponsible expenditure were throughout Richard's reign, Dymmok's argument seems perilously strong. Even Dymmok's protests two chapters later that Solomon degenerated into tyranny not because he exacted huge taxes, but because he took foreign wives, may not do much to soften his implied criticism: while Dymmok might not yet have known it, Richard was soon to cement a controversial treaty with France by means of a marriage with Isabella of France. Dymmok may have done a better job of reconciling his advisorial pose with his efforts to appeal to an audience of nobility and gentry here, but he has also put himself at a greater risk that his advice will offend the king.

If we accept what circumstantial and internal evidence suggests, that addressing a court audience is at least part of Dymmok's concern, then could his book have shown even this more restricted audience what he promises in his address to the king to show everyone? If the lowest common denominator Dymmok aims for is not an average villager but a regionally influential member of the gentry resident at court, then how does the content of his book measure up to the project of convincing his public that the Lollard document is dangerous and contains no valid arguments?

In massively expanding each Lollard conclusion into a set of three to ten opposing conclusions, Dymmok makes plenty of room for showing the dangers of the Lollard document as well as the invalidity of its arguments. Along with presenting the manner of its publication as a usurpation upon the proper domain of public persons, Dymmok builds up a frightening picture of the implications that might logically, or else through 'vulgar understanding', be adduced from Lollard beliefs. He sums them up here:

> . . . isti se fingunt Christi thesaurarios et nuncios et tamen contrarium dicunt et faciunt euangelice ueritati . . . (*Dymmok*, p. 311, ll. 26–8)
>
> Docent namque mulieres *nulli petenti* ex caritate *negare* corpora sua, que doctrina, si licita credatur, aufert uerecundiam de fornicacione. Asserunt insuper *titulo* caritatis, quemlibet omnia temporalia possidere, quod si uerum sit, ad intellectum uulgarem populi quilibet posset bona cuiuscuncque sibi assumere, et tunc nullus de furto uerecundaretur, cum nullus homo nisi propria accipere posset. Dicunt insuper nullum peccato mortali innodatum aliquid *iusto titulo possidere*, ex qua doctrina nichil aliud restat, nisi ut quilibet contra alium peccatum mortale obiciat, et eius bona auferat per uiolenciam, si eo sit forcior, et sic rapina ducetur in consuetudinem et putabitur satis licite exerceri, et sic suis peruersis doctrinis licenciam tribuunt, uiciis uirtutibus conculcatis. (*Dymmok*, pp. 311, l. 36–312, l. 13; my emphases):
>
> These pretend to be treasurers and messengers of Christ, but speak and do the opposite of gospel truth . . .
>
> For they teach women for the sake of charity to deny their bodies to no petitioner; which teaching, were it believed licit, would remove the shame from fornication. They assert, moreover, that each person possesses all temporal goods by title of charity. If this were true, then according to the vulgar understanding of the people anyone could take for himself the goods of anyone, and no one would be ashamed of theft, since no man could take what was not his own. They say, furthermore, that no one snared in mortal sin can possess anything by just title. From this teaching it would come about that anyone might accuse another of mortal sin and take his goods by violence, if he were stronger than him; and thus seizure would become customary and be thought licit. Thus their perverse teaching give licence that vices should tread virtues underfoot.

Through an echo of their initial self-description as 'tresoreris of Cryst', through quasi-legal terminology, Dymmok hints once again at the presumption of the Lollards' manner of publication. But in addition, here he moves furthest from the meticulous if fastidious quotation of what the Lollards have actually written that characterises his refutations. In tarring the Lollards with the brush of the *reductiones* that he has drawn out from their views, he produces three conclusions guaranteed to horrify anyone threatened by the 'vulgar understanding', the *intellectum vulgarem* he mentions.

While any property owner will see the force of Dymmok's assessment of the dangers of the *Twelve Conclusions*, however, how many of his audience will be able to assess his arguments and judge whether they are better than those the Lollards supply? In his initial promise, as we saw, Dymmok places the burden of sufficient explanation squarely upon his own shoulders: he commits himself to using 'talia [argumenta] que intelligi ualent ab *omnibus* . . . ut ex eo pateat *uniuersis* quam periculosum fuerit eorum documentum et quod nullum protulerunt pro sua assercione ualidum argumentum'. He attributes to *everyone* the capacity to give an informed assent to his side of the case, and what is more, he represents that capacity here as an academic one: it is specifically the superiority of his arguments that his universal audience is expected to recognise. We have already noted that in practice Dymmok denies the *simplices* the capacity to make an informed judgement. But the boundaries of this group are not clear. Will only kings, princes, and doctors be allowed to weigh Dymmok's arguments? Or at the other extreme, will only those for whom the *intellectum vulgarem* of Dymmok's *reductiones* is attractive be excluded?

Since none of his other works is extant it is impossible to determine whether Dymmok has, as he claims, written in a more straightforward style than usual. But he does seem to have made some effort to pitch his text to a non-academic audience. He anticipates the need to explain more fully than usual argumentational techniques and concepts from grammar, logic, biblical interpretation, and natural science.[34] He makes use of the conventions of academic genres such as the determination, lecture, and disputation, proceeding by demonstrative argument and embedding arguments staged in dialogue form[35] and discussions in *quaestio* form[36] in his prose, but he is more clear about his procedure than scholastic treatises often are: he spells out what he is doing step by step rather than using the scholarly abbreviations and 'therefore etc's' frequently found in university lecture notes or records of disputations.[37] Though on many occasions he loads his prose down with the machinery of argumentation, typically such machinery is non-functional, intended for display, and his meaning readily apparent despite it.[38]

Still, the methods Dymmok uses to make his text accessible reveal other motives than comprehensibility. Other motives are particularly conspicuous where he uses that hallowed technique of lay instruction, the analogy. In replying to conclusion five, for example, when explaining how material things gain supernatural power without being altered in any way apparent to the senses, Dymmok makes an analogy with the way in which a mayor, or similarly a temporal or spiritual lord, acquires a new power of governing without sensing any change in himself:

... sicud maior ciuitatis nullam sensibilem mutacionem in se sentit nec habet, quam prius non habuit, et tamen potestatem habet nouiter sibi commissam uirtute officii a rege totam ciuitatem gubernandi et nociua illi ciuitati compescendi. Similiter, cum homo de nouo adquirit dominium uel dignitatem siue temporalem, ut regiam dignitatem, siue spiritualem, ut papatum uel episcopatum, nulla in eo fit mutacio sensibilis, et tamen uirtutem magnam spiritualem recipit, quam prius non habuit, ex diuina ordinacione ad talem populum gubernandum, et populus a Deo inclinacionem accipit, ut eidem obediat et ipsum timeat ceteraque faciat ad eius imperium, que suo regimini conueniunt. (*Dymmok*, p. 128, ll. 18–30):

... just as when he takes office the mayor of a city neither feels nor undergoes any sensible change, but nonetheless has a power for governing the whole city and preventing harm to it newly committed to him in virtue of his office by the king. Similarly, when a man newly acquires lordship or honour or temporal possessions, as for example regal dignity, or spiritual dignity (such as the papacy or an episcopate), no sensible change is made in him, but nonetheless he receives by divine ordination a great spiritual power that he did not have before for governing that people, and the people are inclined by God to obey him and fear him and do whatever else befits his reign.

What is startling about Dymmok's analogy is that it advances his theory of governance so boldly and, as it were, offhandedly. Contrary to the writers of the *Twelve Conclusions*' implicit theory that all power is held directly from God, Dymmok here claims that all offices below those of king and pope or bishop are held through those authorities rather than directly. Furthermore, unlike the more usual sort of royalist argument, here Dymmok attributes divinely ordained and popularly accepted regal power not only to the king, but to the pope and his bishops as well.[39]

Some of Dymmok's analogies, too, show quite clearly the sort of audience for whom he hopes to elucidate his point. When he compares the case of a corrupt order which, he argues, ought not to be disendowed but instead reformed, with a case where the laws of inheritance would dictate that a traitor's lands should be kept for his son, the special appeal to landowners is blatant, especially in the late 1390s when Richard's attempts to take to himself the inheritance of traitors' lands were highly controversial (*Dymmok*, p. 176, ll. 17–25).[40] Similarly, where Dymmok likens the behaviour of pilgrims to the outward signs of secular love, it seems obvious that he hopes to appeal to the sort of audience that is familiar with courtly love poetry (*Dymmok*, p. 193, ll. 18–32).

Still, even if these analogies carry heavy ideological freight, not all Dymmok's analogies are as helpful; some seem deliberately intimidating. In countering conclusion two, for example, where the Lollards began to use scholastic terminology in earnest, Dymmok deploys prolonged digressions on logic and

natural science in which, as in the examples just examined, the material has little
or nothing to do with the matter at hand beyond the analogy it offers.[41] Unlike
the previous examples, however, here Dymmok chooses not familiar examples
that illuminate the concept to be explained, but unfamiliar and probably
daunting material. In this case his concern seems rather to show that he knows
more than the Lollards than to make sure that his readers understand why his
argument is better.

But this temporary lapse into obscurantism is not as telling an index to the
authenticity of Dymmok's desire to submit his arguments for public judgement as
are the final few pages of his text, where he returns to his initial promise and
devotes his full attention to explaining how his audience should be able to
distinguish the Lollards' semblance of holiness from the authentic sanctity of
legitimate preachers and teachers. As Dymmok has been emphasising from the
beginning, not everyone has the information and abilities they would need to tell
a good argument from a bad one; here it finally becomes clear just who it is that
he views as irremediably incapable of informed judgement. Dymmok exhorts all
the faithful not to believe the Lollards, giving the specious impression that he has
reached a logical conclusion by introducing his recommendation 'Igitur a multo
forciori,

> nullus fidelis debet eis prebere *assensum*, cum *constat* eos directissime *contraria*
> sentire euangelice *ueritati* et nullum *signum* ostendunt in sue *assercionis euidenciam*,
> nec in uita aut in moribus sanctorum *congruunt* disciplinis. (*Dymmok*, p. 307,
> ll. 7–12; my emphases):
>
> Therefore, all the more ought no faithful man to offer them assent, since it has
> been established that their meaning is most directly contrary to gospel truth,
> and that they show no evidence for their assertion, nor do their teachings
> correspond to the life and mores of the saints.

The impression that the skill required will be clerical and the decision based on
academic criteria is intensified by the density of terminology of argument packed
into this directive: one might think Dymmok was telling his readers how to test
whether a proposition is well formed. But as the more specific condemnation that
immediately follows reveals, the process of discrimination is not so clear-cut:

> Nichil amplius habent, nisi quandam apparenciam humilitatis in gestu, in
> capitis demissione, in uestimentorum deiectione et ieiunii simulacione,
> simplicitatem pretendunt in uerbis, caritate Dei et proximi se feruere
> affirmant, cuius feruore excitati se continere non posse pretendunt a doctrina
> pestifera prius dicta, dicentes se non timere quantumcunque mundi aduersa
> aut mortem subire, si oporteat, pro defensione sui erroris. (*Dymmok*, p. 307,
> ll. 12–19):

They have nothing more than a kind of appearance of humility in their demeanour, their lowly clothing, and their simulated fasting. They pretend simplicity in their words, they affirm fervently that they live in charity as regards God and their neighbours. Excited by that charity, they pretend they cannot contain themselves from the pestiferous teaching mentioned before; they say that they do not fear to undergo however much worldly adversity or even death, if it should be necessary, in defence of their error.

The problem is that every aspect of the *appearance* Dymmok describes is associated with the outward aspect of Christian virtue as much as with hypocrisy. If the Lollards are hypocrites as accomplished as he claims, if every aspect of their *appearance* is good, then Dymmok can offer no experiential proof that this appearance is a false front, and no method by which his readers can tell the difference.

Dymmok tries to suggest that the difficulty of telling whether someone follows Christ is as easy as telling an ape from a man:

Simia quidem omnia membra hominis habet et per omnia hominem imitatur – Numquid propterea dicendus est homo? Sic eciam heresis omnia misteria ecclesie habet et imitatur, set non sunt ecclesie . . . (*Dymmok*, p. 308, ll. 4–7):

An ape has all the members of a man, and imitates a man in all things. Should it on that account be called a man? So too heretics have and imitate all the mysteries of the church. But they do not belong to the church . . .

but then he swings to the opposite extreme, to warn that careful attention is required:

Non dixit 'aspicite' set 'attendite;' 'aspicere' enim est simpliciter uidere, 'attendere' autem est caute considerare, ubi enim certa est et indubitabilis, aspicitur, ubi incerta et dubitabilis, attenditur. Quia igitur in illis aliud pro alio uidetur, aliud desuper positum, aliud intus inclusum, ideo dixit 'attendite', ut scias, quia non corporali aspectu attendendum est set uigilancia spirituali. Attendendum igitur est per opera bona. (*Dymmok*, p. 308, ll. 8–15):

He did not say 'look' but 'attend'; for 'look' means simply to see, but 'attend' means to consider carefully. Where something is certain and not subject to doubt, one looks at it; where it is uncertain and doubtful, one attends to it. Because therefore in these matters one thing seems like something else, one obvious and the other concealed, therefore he said 'attend', so that you would know; because one does not attend by means of corporeal looking, but by spiritual vigilance. One should attend, therefore, through good works.

Even at this point the mental effort required for discerning good from apparent good seems within any conscientious person's capacity; and if the project of maintaining spiritual vigilance is a bit hazy, the explanation that one 'attends' by doing good works gives a concrete recommendation. But in what follows it turns out that the judgement upon the reader's powers of discernment and his probity is to be made in reverse order, and retrospectively:

> Ipsa res facit errare, que facit alterius errorem non cognoscere; qui autem non cognoscit mendacium alterius, non cognoscit eius ueritatem. Sicud, quamdiu facimus opera bona, ipsum lumen iusticie ante oculos nostros adaperit ueritatem, sic et peccata peccancium sensus tenebrescere faciunt, ut non uidentes mendacium cadant in illud. (*Dymmok*, p. 308, ll. 15–21):
> This same thing makes him err, which causes him not to recognise another's error. In the same way that as long as we do good works, the light of justice before our eyes adapts itself to truth, so also the sins of sinners make that sense become dark, so that not seeing the lie, they fall into it.

Not only must Dymmok's readers do good in order to discern apparent from authentic good. If they disagree with Dymmok, then that shows, not that he might be wrong, but that they have erred; and, further, that they were not doing good after all. For they could only have made their mistake because they were sinners already: 'non possunt errores preualere in homines, nisi precesserint peccata, prius enim peccatis plurimis excecatur homo, et sic Diaboli seductione cadit in errorem' (*Dymmok*, p. 308, ll. 24–7): 'errors cannot prevail in men unless sins have gone before them, for first many sins blind a man, and thus by diabolic seduction he falls into error'.

Despite his numerous appeals to it, therefore, it is clear finally that Dymmok has little interest in exposing himself to any broader public judgement. He shifts the boundary between pastors and *simplices* as it suits his need to exact assent. Even if gentry and clerics alike are dignified as pastors in his reply to conclusion six, only the highest public persons qualify as pastors when he addresses 'unusquisque in gradu suo', and in the end only those who agree with him count as undeceived. Although Dymmok may win a rhetorical victory over his adversaries by limiting the availability of his text to those he might be prepared to regard as fellow pastors, his then proceeding to classify any of this group who may disagree with him *simplices*, renders that victory a hollow one.

Notes

[1] On the procedure of presenting petitions in parliament see J.S. Roskell, Linda Clark and Carole Rawcliffe (eds), *The History of Parliament. The House of Commons 1386–1421*, 4 vols (Stroud, 1993), i: pp. 76–103.

[2] Admittedly 'true men' is one of the Lollards' 'coded' self-descriptions; it could be argued that the still wider audience the writers mean to reach will be made up of Lollards. (See A. Hudson, 'A Lollard Sect Vocabulary?', in M. Benskin and M.L. Samuels (eds), *So meny people longages and tonges: Philological Essays in Scots and Medieval English presented to Angus McIntosh* (Edinburgh, 1981), pp. 15–30 for discussion of 'true men' and several other characteristic Lollard terms.) But even in the confined sense, the group 'alle trew cristene men' has the potential to include all who come in contact with the *Twelve Conclusions* and find they agree with them. The *Twelve Conclusions* are most conveniently available in Hudson, *Selections*, pp. 24–9, 150–5.

[3] I cite Walsingham's *Chronica Maiora* in *Johannis de Trokelowe et . . . Annales*, ed. H.T. Riley *(RS, 1866)*. Walsingham claims the Lollards put together the list 'animati . . . favore quorundam procerum, et instigatione militum aulicorum': 'encouraged by the favour of certain nobles, and at the instigation of chamber knights'; and that chamber knights were responsible certainly for posting the poem appended to the *Conclusions* and bringing to them a tone of occluded menace, and perhaps for posting the *Conclusions* as well. As usual stressing Richard's defence of the church, Walsingham claims the group were taking advantage of Richard's absence in Ireland to express their hostility to the church establishment, and that when at the request of worried bishops Richard returned, he dealt severely with the chamber knights involved *(Johannis de Trokelowe et . . . Annales*, pp. 174–83, p. 174, ll 9–10). None of the other chroniclers mentions the incident; in his *Historica Anglicana* Walsingham adds that the *Conclusions* were also affixed to the door of St Paul's. (*Historica Anglicana*, ed. H.T. Riley, 2 vols, (RS, 1863–4), ii, p. 216). *Fasc. Ziz.* (*c.* 1439) claims in introducing them that the conclusions were 'in quodam libello porrectae pleno parliamento regis [or 'regni'] angliae': 'displayed in the form of a bill in the full parliament of the king [or 'realm'] of England' (*Fasc. Ziz.*, p. 360), while Netter (1426–30), see for example, T. Netter, *Thomae Waldensis Doctrinale Fidei Catholicae*, ed. F.B. Blanciotti, 3 vols (Farnborough, 1967, Venice, 1757), iii, 404a, 681 bc, a pamphlet on the Schism in Oxford, Bodleian Library, MS Digby 188, f. 66^r–v (1395–8; see discussion by M. Harvey, *Solutions to the Schism: A study of some English attitudes 1378 to 1409* (St Ottilien, 1983), pp. 68–9 and 74–6), and the condemnation of five of the articles in a letter from Pope Boniface IX to the archbishops of Canterbury and York in September 1395 (*CPapReg, 1362–1404*, pp. 515–16) draw upon the conclusions without mentioning the manner of their publication. On reactions to the *Twelve Conclusions* see as well M. Aston, 'Lollardy and Sedition, 1381–1431', in Aston, *LR*, pp. 1–47, at 21–3, and 'Caim's Castles', in Aston, *FF*, pp. 95–131, at 109–14; and Hudson, *PR*, esp. pp. 92–3.

[4] On their ingratitude, see *Dymmok*, p. 13, ll. 31–8; on their lack of eloquence, see *ibid.*, p. 25, ll. 10–11. Boniface's letter also makes a point of the Lollards' ingratitude, while (in a way that would seem to weaken that accusation?) also suggesting that laymen as well as clerics are Lollards. (*CPapReg, 1362–1404*, p. 515)

[5] See R.E. Latham, *Revised Medieval Latin Word-List from British and Irish Sources* (London, 1965), s.vv. 'libellus' and 'publicatio' for the senses mentioned here. See D.R. Howlett *et al.*, *Dictionary of Medieval Latin from British Sources* (Oxford, 1975–) s.vv. 'expansio', 'expandere' for king's banners. Knighton, for example, uses the verb 'expandere' to describe how Robert de Vere at Radcot bridge, seeing Henry of Derby approach, 'Statim pedem fixit, uexillum regis quod ibi paratum habuerat expandere iussit, et super lanceam erigere' (*HK*, pp. 420–1): 'At once he stood his ground, ordered the king's banner, which he had ready, to be unfurled and raised upon a lance', before running away.

[6] Dymmok specifies the membership of the group in most detail in this explanation of why public persons have an obligation to exemplary rather than eccentric conduct: '. . . quamuis forte persone priuate sine inconuenienti illud ieiunium possunt obseruare, tamen mihi uidetur quod

persone publice hoc non facerent, sicud sunt reges, episcopi, doctores, duces et tales, qui magnum regimen in populo sorciuntur, ne per hoc factum nouam inducant in ecclesiam consuetudinem' (*Dymmok*, p. 122, ll. 32–7): 'although perhaps private persons may fittingly observe that fast, nonetheless it seems to me that public persons, that is, kings, bishops, doctors, dukes, and suchlike, who are allotted an important role in government of the people, should not do so, lest by so doing they should bring in a new custom in the church'.

[7] For Dymmok's citation of one of Aquinas's references to private (as opposed to public) persons as those persons not qualified by their status to wage war or (significantly) raise up a multitude of people in any way, see p. 262. All Aquinas's references to public persons refer to rulers qualified to make laws and wage war: see the references listed in R. Busa *et al.* (eds), *Index Thomisticus Sancti Thomae Aquinatis Operum Omnium indices et concordantiae* (Italy, 1975), vol. xviii.

[8] The Lollards may be drawing on Wycliffe's theory, expressed for example in *De potestate pape*, ed. J. Loserth (London, 1907), pp. 7–21, that power does not exist absolutely *per se*, and is conferred directly by God rather than through human intermediaries.

[9] Instead, he dismisses their claims as presumptuous (*Dymmok*, pp. 157–9), and defends the orthodox theory of ordination (pp. 53–70 *passim*; but especially pp. 65–6, and 146–7).

[10] For records relating to Dymmok's life see H.S. Cronin's introduction to the *Liber*, pp. xi–xv; and the entries for Roger Dymmok in Emden, *BRUO*, ii, and *DNB*, vi. My thanks to Anne Hudson for discussing with me the new entry on Dymmok she is preparing for the revised *DNB*.

[11] It seems most likely that Roger was the eldest of Sir John's sons; however, the very fact that Roger became an ecclesiastic may indicate that there were other obstacles, such as bastardy perhaps, to his inheritance. That there may have been other reasons why Roger did not inherit from Sir John does not of course stand in the way of my suggestion that Roger may have wanted the sort of public position others in his family held.

[12] *CCR*, membrane 23, no date or place given, but included among entries for autumn 1397; summarized in *CCR, 1396–99*, p. 150. Cronin discusses the affair: see *Dymmok*, pp. xiii–xiv.

[13] On parliamentary sermons see R.N. Swanson, *Church and Society* in *Late Medieval England* (Oxford, 1989), pp. 93–4; on who could present various kinds of parliamentary petition and how they were dealt with see Roskell's discussion cited in n. 1.

[14] This method of disseminating carefully doctored information, in particular about current foreign policy, appears to have been used frequently during the war with France. On its general mechanisms see W.R. Jones, 'The English Church and Royal Propaganda During the Hundred Years War', *Journal of British Studies*, 19:1 (1979), pp. 18–30, esp. 21 and 29. For a valuable survey of its use in the diocese of Lincoln see A.K. McHardy, 'Liturgy and Propaganda in the Diocese of Lincoln during the Hundred Years War', *SCH*, 18 (1981), pp. 215–27.

[15] Margaret Aston has pointed out ('Caim's Castles', see n. 3, p. 113 n. 56) that Dymmok argues over the heads of the *Conclusions* in more than just the obvious example of the fourth conclusion, where the Lollards quote Wycliffe's *Trialogus* and Dymmok in reply cites copiously from the history of the eucharistic controversy. I will briefly examine another example below, pp. 58–61.

[16] The manuscript, now Cambridge, Trinity Hall 17, is apparently the presentation copy that was given to the king: this is a very high quality volume, well-written and ornamented throughout, with four illustrations; M.R. James dates it late fourteenth century. London, BL, MS Cotton Otho C.xvi is the collection reflecting noble tastes; Dymmok's text, listed in the table long with seven saints' lives and two histories, has not survived. Catalogue descriptions of the manuscripts known to Cronin are conveniently reproduced in his introduction: see *Dymmok*, pp. xvi–xxv.

[17] Cambridge University Library, MS Ii.4.3, fifteenth century, belonged first to a bishop of Ely, then to Thomas Rotherham, bishop of Rochester, archbishop of York and chancellor of England as well as of Cambridge, who gave it to the library in 1480. Oxford, Bodleian Library, MS Lat. th. e. 30, *c.* 1400, includes three Dominican letters of fraternity in its flyleaves and the note (f. 150ᵛ) that it belonged to master John Arnold – perhaps the same master John Arnold of Merton who owned the manuscript of meditations now Oxford, Jesus College 36, in 1440, Paris, Bibliothèque Nationale,

fonds lat. 3381, early fifteenth century, includes as well as Dymmok's text a letter and a treatise against Wycliffe's *Trialogus* by Woodford. While it cannot be conclusively identified with any of the five known copies, we do in addition have one further record of ownership: John Carpenter, common clerk to the city of London and noted bibliophile, mentions a copy in his 1442 will; it may have been one of the books his executors Reginald Pecock and his relative, master John Carpenter, later bishop of Worcester, selected for inclusion in the Guildhall Library. As a book collector with bishops among his close relatives and friends, John Carpenter may not be an entirely typical representative of the literate gentry of his day. Still his ownership and the possible further dissemination through his bequest of a copy of Dymmok's treatise fulfil, somewhat after the fact, the potential for reaching a wider readership that Dymmok seems to have made little effort to achieve. (On Carpenter see M. Aston, 'Bishops and Heresy: The Defence of the Faith', in *FF*, pp. 73–93, at 90–1.)

[18] N. Orme has investigated how courts and monasteries, universities, and the households of bishops and nobles were centres for the education of at least a few members of the nobility and the gentry ('The Education of the Courtier', in V.J. Scattergood and J.W. Sherborne (eds), *English Court Culture in the Later Middle Ages* (London, 1983) pp. 63–85). Even members of the household who did not have sufficient skill in reading Latin would presumably have had access to tutors, confessors, and other educated clerics in the household who would be entirely competent to read a book like Dymmok's and retail it to whomever they saw fit. Fellow Dominicans in the royal household might have been especially eager to pass on the content of Dymmok's text; Richard's confessor in 1395, John Burghill, was for example a Dominican. (On clerks in the royal household see C. Given-Wilson, *The Royal Household and the King's Affinity: Service, Politics and Finance in England 1360–1413* (London, 1986), pp. 175–83.)

[19] A number of studies since K.B. McFarlane's rehabilitation of the evidence (McFarlane, *LK*) have investigated Lollardy, support for Lollards, and/or sympathy with Lollard views among the nobility and gentry. See for example M. Wilks, 'Royal Priesthood: The Origins of Lollardy', in *The Church in a Changing Society* (Proceedings of 1977 CIHEC Conference; Uppsala, 1978), pp. 63–70; J.A. Tuck, 'Carthusian Monks and Lollard Knights: Religious Attitude at the Court of Richard II', in *Studies in the Age of Chaucer, Proceedings*, 1 (1984), pp. 149–61; P. McNiven, *Heresy and Politics in the Reign of Henry IV: The Burning of John Badby* (Woodbridge, 1987); and Hudson, *PR*, pp. 110–19. See also n. 23 below.

[20] On estates literature in general, the most illuminating survey is Jill Mann, *Chaucer and Medieval Estates Satire* (Cambridge, 1973); appendix A lists estates included in a number of texts which aim at a comprehensive address to all of society, and will give the reader an idea of the more usual breadth of address. While Mann concentrates mainly on literary texts rather than sermons, Alan J. Fletcher's 'The Social Trinity in Piers Plowman' places the use of *ad status* address in *Piers Plowman* in the context of uses of these conventions in contemporary sermons (*RES* n.s. 44 (1993), pp. 343–61). For other examples of this sort of address not included in Mann or mentioned by Fletcher, see *Lollard Sermons*, ed. G. Cigman (EETS, 294, 1989) expansion to sermon 11, pp. 137–9, ll. 202–300, and *Sermon of Dead Men*, pp. 222, l. 524–224, l. 618. On vernacular sermons *ad status* see also H.L. Spencer, *English Preaching in the Late Middle Ages* (Oxford, 1993), pp. 65–8.

[21] Emending Cronin's misprint 'uiolent'.

[22] Dymmok does allow the *simplices* virtue: 'contingit simplices, nullam uel paruam potestatem habentes, maiores esse et meliores quoad Deum illis, qui regali uel episcopali fulserant dignitate' (*Dymmok*, p. 61, ll. 14–17): 'on some occasions the simple, having no power or little, are greater and better in God than those who shine out with regal or episcopal dignities'. See also *ibid.*, p. 44, ll. 13–24, p. 45, ll. 14–18, and p. 80, ll. 20–2. But he also remarks frequently on its fragility: see *ibid*, p. 13, ll. 2–15, p. 14, ll. 16–19, p. 15, ll. 4–8, p. 251, ll. 8–13, and pp. 274, l. 35–275, l. 29, as well as the *ad status* address just quoted in the text.

[23] I pick out these examples from an extensive tradition of interclerical and anticlerical polemic because they were probably available in English in London in *c.* 1395. The issues they treat, taxation and disendowment of the clergy, are longstanding, but seem to have been especial concerns for the

nobility and gentry and keen preoccupations of Parliament in the late fourteenth century. On late fourteenth- and fifteenth-century interest in disendowment see Aston's survey in 'Caim's Castles' in Aston, *FF.*

[24] Hudson, *PR*, p. 346, mentions this argument as the last of three on the temporal power of the church characteristic of the Lollards, and gives several examples of its use in Lollard texts. Wycliffe's most extensive and specific comments on the holding of particular secular offices by clerics are in *De blasphemia*, ed. M.H. Dziewicki (London, 1893). See especially his comment on the chancellor: 'Quid, rogo, pertinet ad archiepiscopum occupare cancellarium regis, que est secularissimum regni officium?' (*op. cit.*, p. 194, l. 16): 'How, I ask, can it be appropriate for the archbishop to occupy the post of chancellor of the king, which is the most secular office in the realm?'; and his list of numerous secular offices that the lower clergy ought not to occupy (pp. 261, l. 3–264, l. 5). For Wycliffe's theoretical justification of this position see below, n. 26.

[25] The nine chapters of Hugh of St Victor's 'De Unitate Ecclesiae', book ii, part ii, of his *De sacramentis Christianae fidei*, appear in *PL*, clxxvi, cols. 173–618 at cols. 415–22.

[26] Dymmok's concession that clergy should hire others to fight for them appears on *Dymmok*, pp. 148–9. Wycliffe uses Hugh's *De sacramentis*, ii, 3 in *De Ecclesia*, ed. J. Loserth (London, 1886), pp. 316, l. 11–318, l. 26, and pp. 378, l. 29–380, l. 5. See also 'Determinacio ad argumenta Wilhelmi Vyrinham', *Opera Minora*, ed. J. Loserth (London, 1913), pp. 415–30, at p. 422, where Wycliffe cites Hugh in arguing that secular lords cannot grant to clergy regal prerogative, secular lordship, or capital dominion; and *De Potestate Pape*, ed. J. Loserth (London, 1907), pp. 7–21, where to launch a complex discussion of the nature and sources of secular and spiritual power of Wycliffe counterposes Hugh's demarcation of the two powers with the observation that 'clerici nostri videntur habere potestatem secularem concessam eis a regibus': 'our clerics would seem to have secular power granted to them by kings' (p. 8, ll. 4–5).

[27] P.J. Eberle, 'The Politics of Courtly Style at the Court of Richard II', in G.S. Burgess *et al.* (eds), *The Spirit of the Court* (Dover, NH, 1985), pp. 168–78, at 173.

[28] My italics: Cronin, who uses italics to demarcate Dymmok's quotations from authorities from Dymmok's own commentary and exposition, does not notice the resumption of quotation from Aquinas here.

[29] *Dymmok*, p. 307, ll. 12–14; see discussion of the surrounding passage on pp. 69–70 below. See also Hudson, *PR*, pp. 145–7, for various other discussions of clothing by Lollards and their opponents, and W. Scase, '*Piers Plowman' and the New Anticlericalism* (Cambridge, 1989), p. 168, n. 18, for the wider tradition in antifraternal satire and criticism of Beguines.

[30] St Thomas Aquinas, *S. Tho super Ethica Sancti doctoris Thome de aquino in decem libros ethicorum Aristotelis profundissima commentaria cum triplici textus translatione antiqua videlicet Leonardi aretini nec non J. argyropili* (Venice, 1539), f. iii^v, col. ii, ll. 11–13; abbreviations silently expanded. In the standard modern reference, the passage under discussion is *Nicomachean Ethics* 1150b, book 7, chapter 7.

[31] Quoted from the edition of the text in H. Barr (ed.), *The Piers Plowman Tradition* (London, 1993), pp. 101–33 at 121–2.

[32] See Hoccleve, *Regement of Princes*, ed. F.J. Furnivall (London, 1897), ll. 463–9, and also 421–7, 533–6.

[33] See *Richard the Redeles*, III, ll. 234–8; H. Barr (ed.), *The Piers Plowman Tradition* (London, 1993), p. 125.

[34] One example of each for the reader to consult, though there are many more of each sort: *Dymmok*, p. 54, ll. 7–9, p. 30, ll. 15–16, p. 48, ll. 8–10, p. 147, ll. 5–11, pp. 98, l. 32–99, l. 3.

[35] See the reply to the Lollard's question posed to a posited pilgrim (*Dymmok*, p. 195, ll. 18–30); and for a lengthier exchange, Dymmok's demonstration of how Behemoth attempts to tempt people (*ibid.*, pp. 273, l. 28–274, l. 30).

[36] Chapter four of the seventh part is in *quaestio* form, built around a passage from Aquinas which reconciles two views (*ibid.*, pp. 167–9).

[37] For example, Maidstone's *Determinacio*, dated by Edden to between 1384 and 1392 and

probably before 1390, and produced solely for a clerical audience in opposition to Ashwardby's sermons given before mixed audiences, contains this rather obscure passage: 'Et ideo ad argumentum. Cum arguitur: doctor ille dicit sic, ergo sic est; dicitur negando contrariam': 'And so to the argument. When it is argued "that doctor says so, therefore it is so", it is said by denying the contrary'; or to amplify, 'And so, let us move on to consider our adversary's argument. Where he argues "that doctor says so, therefore it is so", we can show that the argument is false by denying that its contrary [that doctor says not, therefore it is not so] is true' (V. Edden, 'The Debate Between Maidstone and Ashwardby', *Carmelus*, 34 (1987), pp. 113–34, at 121, ll. 1–2). (See pp. 114–15 on the dating.) Maidstone's argument is not ill-formed, but it does in places employ a cryptic academic shorthand characteristic of university-produced prose.

[38] See, for example, the passage quoted at p. 69, below, or *Dymmok*, pp. 274, l. 35–275, l. 29.

[39] Paul Strohm explores the ideological implications of another of Dymmok's explanations of imperceptible change: see P. Strohm, 'Chaucer's Lollard Joke: History and the Textual Unconscious', *Studies in the Age of Chaucer*, 17 (1995), pp. 40–1.

[40] On the development of penalties of forfeiture for treason see J.G. Bellamy, *The Law of Treason in England in the Later Middle Ages* (Cambridge, 1970), *passim*. C.D. Ross suggests that Richard's attempts in 1397 to impose the strictest possible penalties of forfeiture on traitors, even disinheriting their heirs, was one important cause of his deposition (C.D. Ross, 'Forfeiture for Treason in the Reign of Richard II', *EHR*, 71 (1956), pp. 560–75).

[41] See especially p. 54, ll. 11–32, pp. 57, l. 34–58, l. 4, p. 58, ll. 11–30; Dymmok uses analogies of the hierarchy of powers in the human soul and of the 'propagation of species' which was thought to be involved in vision (for a lucid introduction to which see K.H. Tachau, *Vision and Certitude in the Age of Ockham: Optics, Epistemology, and the Foundations of Semantics, 1250–1345* (Leiden, 1988)) in order to justify his assertion that priests accept from Christ a higher power than that of the angels.

4

PIERCE THE PLOUGHMAN'S CREDE: LOLLARDY AND TEXTS

John Scattergood

Christianity is a religion of the book . . .[1]

P ierce the Ploughman's Crede is one of the earliest imitations of Piers Plowman
and it is concerned, like its predecessor, with political and religious issues.
Like Langland, its narrator wanders through a world which is
recognisably that of late medieval England: he sees things to which he reacts with
anger, scorn and pity; he meets people with whom he argues. Like Langland, he
is engaged in a quest for knowledge, but in his case it is knowledge of a very
precise and simple kind. Mindful of his Christian duty, the narrator seeks
somebody who will teach him his creed, the basic official summary of his
religious belief, lest his parish priest give him a penance if he fails to learn it by
Easter:

> Whan y schal schewen myn schrift schent mote y worthen,
> The prest wil me punyche and penaunce enioyne.[2]
>
> (ll. 9–10)

His parish priest is obviously one who takes seriously his duty to examine
parishioners in the matter of their belief. But writers like Mirk, for example, also
stipulate, amongst other things, that the parish priest should teach the rudiments
of belief – the paternoster and creed, twice or thrice a year.[3] Why the narrator
has not benefited from this sort of instruction is never revealed: perhaps the
reader is meant to assume that it was never properly given, or alternatively that
the narrator never attended to it and is now trying to make up for his earlier
neglect. But this issue is not raised in the poem, which assumes that the
individual Christian is responsible for seeking out his own instructor.

The form of the poem is a partial enactment of its meaning. The narrator is a
layman, though not unlearned: he has mastered some of the basic rudiments of
Christian knowledge, and can even quote some texts from the Bible (ll. 140–5,
149–51, 259–65). But he is poor and cannot afford to pay for the instruction he
needs: if somebody teaches him it will have to be 'for Cristes loue' (l. 37).
Because the friars have told him that 'all the frute of the fayth was in here foure
ordres' (l. 29), he goes to them, to each order in turn; but they will not teach him

unless he pays them. As a Carmelite tells him: 'Oure power lasteth nought so feer but we some peny fongen' (l. 407). Instead, they criticise each other and devote themselves to more financially profitable things. In a gesture which is at once physical and spiritual, he leaves them:

> Thanne turned y me forthe and talked to my-selue
> Of the falshede of this folk – whou feithles they weren.
>
> (ll. 418–19)

Help comes from Pierce the Ploughman – a layman like the narrator, and poor, but better educated – who discusses the iniquities of the friars with the narrator and eventually teaches him the creed. Though the narrator is, so far as one can tell, orthodox in his religious attitudes, the ploughman is a Lollard, and this colours both his attitudes to the friars and his version of the creed.[4] The author of the poem also appears to be a Lollard (though, interestingly, he is not against confession), and the work enacts the related Wycliffite beliefs that the clergy, particularly if they are corrupt, are neither fitting nor necessary for the promulgation of Christian doctrine, and that any right-thinking layman, if of good life, even if he is not formally trained, may teach the word of God and Christian belief.

Most who have written on the poem have assumed that its main impulse is satiric, that it attacks the friars by means of a 'subtle and oblique approach': 'The evils of the friars are seen through the eyes of an unbiased and naive narrator and heard from the lips of the friars themselves'.[5] He exploits the charge frequently made by Wycliffites that the four major orders were prone to disparaging each other:

> . . . yif men askeden of thise foure sectis whether alle thise ordris ben euene goode, thei wolen seye anon: 'nay, but oon is betere then an other;' & thus bi here owen speche they tellen that they leuen the betere and louen persones of here ordre not euene aftir that thei ben goode, & so this diuision of freris bi thise ordris that ben not groundid makith a priue enuye and puttith out loue of god . . .[6]

And what they say in opposition to each other through this 'priue enuye' is augmented by criticisms made by Pierce the Ploughman himself.

There is much to be said for this view of the poem. The criticism of the friars is unsystematic and frequently repetitious, but it adds up to a list of fairly traditional jibes, some of which go back as far as William of St Amour,[7] and many of which reappear in Wycliffite diatribes: friars are described as being the devil's agents (l. 460) and 'of the kynrede of Caym' (l. 486), alluding to the well-known acrostic CAIM (Carmelites, Austins, Jacobins, Minorites) on the initials of the four orders; they are 'founded . . . on Farysens feyned for gode' (l. 487, cf. 547); they are like false prophets (ll. 457–9); they usurp the privileges and functions of other areas of the clergy and sell the sacraments (ll. 468–9, 702–18); they are greedy and lack charity (ll. 67–9) even towards their own brothers; they hunt legacies from the dying (ll. 408–17); they are lecherous (ll. 44, 59, 83–5), gluttonous (ll. 760–5), and slothful. They have fallen away from the ideals of their founders (ll. 464–6, 775–8). This is most striking in the descriptions of the huge wealth of the orders (which were founded as attempts to recreate the virtues of apostolic poverty) as manifested in the splendour of their buildings, the opulence of their dress, and the delicacy and quantity of their food. The rich Dominican convent[8] would have required 'the tax of ten yer . . . trewly y-gadered' (l. 189) in order to finance it, and it is there that the narrator finds, significantly in the refectory, a well-dressed and overfed representative of this proud order:

> Thanne turned y agen when y hadde all y-toted,
> And fond in a freitour a frere on a benche,
> A greet cherl and a grym, growen as a tonne,
> With a face as fat as a full bledder
> Blowen bretfull of breth and as a bagge honged
> On bothen his chekes, and his chyn with a chol lollede,
> As greet as a gos eye growen all of grece;
> That all wagged his fleche as a quyk myre.
> His cope that biclypped him wel clene was it folden,
> Of double worstede y-dyght doun to the hele;
> His kyrtel of clene whijt clenlyche y-sewed;
> Hyt was good y-now of ground greyn for to beren.
>
> (ll. 219–30)

As often in this work, the comparisons in part carry the argument – the wine or beer cask ('tonne'), the pig's or sheep's bladder, the goose egg, the corn ('greyn') all connote food. And all this contrasts with the poverty of the narrator and, when he appears, the ill-clad Pierce the Ploughman who, with his equally poorly dressed wife and his four thin and 'feble' oxen, works the fields in a wet and icy landscape, while his hungry children cry 'at the londes ende':

> His cote was of a cloute that cary was y-called,
> His hod was full of holes and his heer oute,
> With his knopped schon clouted full thykke;
> His ton toteden out as he the londe treddede,
> His hosen ouerhonged his hokschynes on eueriche a side,
> Al beslombred in fen as he the plow folwede . . .
>
> (ll. 422–7)

This may be precise in a harrowingly graphic way, but it is not simply descriptive: the allusion to the hair growing through the holes in a hood makes this figure into a proverbial embodiment of poverty and indigence.[9] Yet it is not from the friars but from this Lollard representative of the labouring agrarian poor that the narrator receives generous friendship, an offer of food, and intellectual enlightenment.

To see the poem as a satire on the friars is, therefore, obviously valid to some degree. And, indeed, it ends with a prayer for the salvation of all those friars 'that faithfully lybben', and adds that 'alle tho that ben fals fayre hem amende' so that they too may attain eternal life (ll. 846–50). But there may be more to it than this, a subtext which addresses, in a sporadic and unsystematic way, a set of related problems which not only divided Lollards from the established church and the clergy, but divided one Lollard from another. By whom and by what means are the laity to be instructed; who shall teach and how? In a movement dominated by the book and written texts, what are the texts by means of which instruction can best be given? This is very much a poem that tries to distinguish between those texts which mislead and those which can be trusted.

There are several indications in the poem that this may be something which centrally concerned the author. The first emerges from the contemporary allusions to John Wycliffe and Walter Brute – both of whom are mentioned ostensibly as examples ('Wytnesse . . .' 'Byhold . . .') of men who were resentfully persecuted by the friars because they had, rightly in the view of the ploughman, pointed out the shortcomings of the by now decadent orders:

> Wytnesse on Wycliff that warned hem with trewth;
> For he in goodnesse of gost graythliche hem warned
> To wayuen her wikednesse and werkes of synne.
> Whou sone this sori men seweden his soule,
> And oueral lollede him with heretykes werkes.
>
> (ll. 528–32)

> Byhold open Wat Brut whou bisiliche thei pursueden
> For he seyde hem the sothe and yet, syre, ferthere,
> Hy may no more marren hym but men telleth
> That he is an heretike and yuele byleueth,
> And prechith it in pulpit to blenden the puple.
> And wolden awyrien that wight for his well dedes . . .
>
> (ll. 657–62)

Wycliffe and Walter Brute, however, did not attract the disapproval of the ecclesiastical and civil authorities principally because of their disputes with the friars – though Wycliffe's were extensive, and though William Woodford, a

Franciscan, wrote against his beliefs and against Brute's – but because of their function as teachers and spreaders of heresy, Wycliffe mainly in lectures at Oxford university and Brute largely in the west of England. The accusations against Brute, when he was examined before John Trefnant, bishop of Hereford in 1391–3, stress this.[10] He is described generally as 'laycum literatum' (a literate layman) who has seduced the people of the diocese 'de die in diem informando et dogmatizando private et occulte tam nobiles quam plebeios in nonnullis conclusionibus hereticis' (from day to day informing and teaching privately and secretly as well nobles as commoners in several heretical conclusions). And the individual accusations refer to a variety of articles against the faith 'per ipsum assertis ac palam et publice dogmatizatis' (declared and taught by him openly and publicly). Here lines 660–1 look like an echo of these accusations. In a lengthy written defence of his views, in Latin, Brute describes himself as 'peccator, laycus, agricola, cristianus' (a sinner, a layman, a farmer, a Christian) and stresses his Welsh parentage. Like Sir John Oldcastle he seems to have been much influenced by the preaching of William Swinderby and, like Oldcastle, he appears to have been a highly educated member of the gentry class. He was an esquire who owned some property in Herefordshire and who took his duties as a religious instructor as seriously as Wycliffe would have wished. He argued, amongst other things, that laymen should hold the power to grant absolution in just same way as priests, and that women equally should have the power to preach, consecrate the eucharist and absolve. Clearly Brute's activities as a layman who disseminated Wycliffite religious ideas were of interest to a poet whose ploughman-hero does precisely the same thing.

A second indication of the importance of teaching in the poem is clear from the way in which it is physically set out: its opening and closure depend on the format of the primer – a book of devotions which also served as an elementary schoolbook, designed for the laity, which taught both the rudiments of Christian belief and literacy.[11] Though they vary a little from one to another, primers, which were produced in great numbers in Latin, and increasingly in English from the thirteenth century onwards, sometimes begin with the alphabet, preceded by the sign of the cross. The alphabet (which was sometimes known as the 'cross-row' from its prefatory symbol, or 'abc' or 'abece' from its first three letters) began with a capital 'A' followed by the letters in miniscule script (including 'a'), the abbreviations for *et* and *con*, then three dots or tittles, and finally the words *est amen*. This is normally followed by the basic prayers – the *paternoster* and *ave* – and the creed. Then come the matins and hours of the Virgin and the articles of the faith, and sometimes a variety of other items. A manuscript in the library of Trinity College, Dublin (MS 70) contains just such a collection of material preceded interestingly by Wycliffite texts (Later Version) of the Psalms and Canticles.[12] The opening of *Pierce the Ploughman's Crede* reads 'Cros, and Curteis Crist this begynnynge spede' (l. 1) – of which the poem's latest editor

Alphabet preceding *Paternoster, Ave* and the Creed in Trinity College, Dublin, MS 70, f. 174ʳ. (By permission of The Board of Trinity College, Dublin) writes, 'Cross is both the cross on which Christ was crucified and the cruciform mark often placed at the beginning of a piece of writing . . .'.[13] It is more likely, however, that the poet had in mind the primer here, as a few lines later he writes:

> A. and all myn A. b. c. after haue y lerned,
> And patred in my pater-noster iche poynt after other,
> And after all myn Aue-marie almost to the ende;
> But all my kare is to comen for y can nohght my Crede.
>
> (ll. 5–8)

He imitates the layout of the alphabet as it appears in the primer, a capital 'A' followed by all the letters, and then mentions the prayers in the order in which they occur – *paternoster* and *ave*. But this, in the fiction of the poem, is as far as the narrator has got: he is stuck at the creed, and would have remained uninstructed and unenlightened beyond the *ave* had the Lollard ploughman not taught him the next item. The poem ends with the text of the creed, marked off as CREDO, which is recited, with a certain amount of commentary, to the narrator. Belatedly, the literate layman, who wants to advance his Christian education, acquires instruction, and his knowledge of the rudiments of the Christian faith advances one small but important step. The poem is framed by reference to a specific teaching book and by a precisely ordered process of learning.

The poem, however, is interspersed with references to methods, suggested by the friars, of acquiring salvation and avoiding penance, which do not involve learning the creed. A Carmelite promises the narrator to take 'all thy penance in peril of my soule' and to absolve him completely 'though thou conne nought thy crede' – but only if 'thou mowe amenden our hous with money other elles . . .' (ll. 393–7). Earlier, in a passage reminiscent of the offer made by the 'confessour i-copet ass a frere' to Lady Meed in *Piers Plowman* A. iii ll. 36–66, the Minorite promises the narrator, in return for money, that St Francis would intercede for his salvation, that the friar himself would be responsible for absolving him even though he did not know his creed, and that his name would be inscribed in the 'wide windowe westwarde' of the convent:

> Thi name schall noblich ben wryten and wrought for the nones,
> And, in remembrance of the y-rade ther for euer.
> And, brother, be though nought aferd; bythenk in thyn herte,
> Though thou conne nought thi Crede, kare thou no more.
>
> (ll. 128–31)

Like Langland, this narrator is not impressed by the offer: in his view, to be written into part of the text of a window will not serve for salvation. Nor is he persuaded by a similar offer he receives later. The Austin friar proposes that, in

return for money or gifts of other kinds, he could seek to purchase a letter of confraternity entitling him to belong to a lay penitential association run by the order:

> Thou schalt ben brother of our hous and a boke habben
> At the next chapitre chereliche ensealed;
> And thanne oure prouinciall hath power to assoilen
> Alle sustren and bretheren that beth of our order.
> And though thou conne nought thi Crede knele downe here;
> My soule y sette for thyn to asoile the clene,
> In couenaunt that thou come againe and katell vs bringe.
>
> (ll. 326–32)

What is interesting here is that the 'boke' is not something from which one can
learn the rudiments of Christian doctrine, like the primer, but a document
designed to give authority, to look official with its seal, like the 'bulle with
bisshopes seles' used by Langland's Pardoner to impress 'lewde men' (*Piers
Plowman* A. Prol. ll. 66–76) and to obtain money. As he meditates on this proposal
a few lines later, it occurs to the narrator that the simple texts containing the
elements of the faith have been subverted by sinfulness, by ostentation and greed:

> Heere pride is the pater-noster in preyinge of synne;
> Here Crede is coueytise . . .
>
> (ll. 336–7)

Letters of confraternity and this kind of absolution were frequently criticised by
Wycliffites.[14] Like the inscription of names in windows, they involve the
fraudulent use of writing and promised short-cuts to salvation, which to this way
of thinking were ineffective. As texts they were useless. Here they are invoked
only to be rejected.

Nor, in the view of this poet, was it possible to be instructed by way of images,
though this was held to be for most, particularly the unlearned or illiterate, a
perfectly respectable and acceptable way of acquiring the rudiments of
Christianity. The classic statement on this matter was by Gregory in a letter
reproving the iconoclast Bishop Serenus of Marseilles for his actions: what a book
('scriptura') is to the learned who can read, he argues, an image ('pictura') is to
those who cannot read: a picture serves as reading for the people.[15] In the later
Middle Ages this position was modified and elaborated in a number of ways.
According to Aquinas, images and pictures were useful for three reasons – for
teaching, as through a book, for implanting information in the memory in an
effective way, and for arousing feelings of devotion.[16] There were even those, like
Durandus, who felt that images and pictures were more likely to move the
emotions than books: 'Pictura namque plus videtur movere animum, quam

scriptura.'[17] Wycliffe was not wholly opposed to the church's standard teaching on images. In his *Tractatus de Mandatis Divinis* he quotes Gregory's letter and makes a distinction between the proper and improper use of pictorial representation: 'It is evident that images may be made both well and ill: well in order to rouse, assist and kindle the minds of the faithful to love God more devoutly; and ill when by reason of images there is deviation from the true faith, as when the image is worshipped with *latria* or *dulia* or unduly delighted in for its beauty, costliness, or attachment to irrelevant circumstances.'[18] Because of their power on the human senses (and sight was held to be the dominant sense) images, if wrongly used, could lead people astray. When he speaks about the rich ornamentation of friary churches the Lollard ploughman in this poem adopts a fairly orthodox moderate Wycliffite position:

> ... though a man in her mynster a masse wolde heren,
> His sight schal so be set on sundrye werkes,
> The penounes and the pomels and poyntes of scheldes
> With-drawn his deuocion and dusken his herte;
> I likne it to a lym-yerde to drawen men to hell,
> And to worchipe of the fend to wraththen the soules.
>
> (ll. 560–5)

Here the inappropriate splendour of essentially non-religious ornamentation distracts the would-be worshipper from his devotions through the powerful sense of sight. The colourful decoration does not illuminate but darkens ('dusken') his heart, not helping to save his soul but enticing it to damnation. Earlier, the narrator had been similarly offended by the ostentatious secular additions to the stained-glass windows of the Dominican convent – the engraved names, the armorials of noble benefactors, and the marks of merchants:

> Wyde wyndowes y-wrought y-written full thikke,
> Schynen with schapen scheldes to schewen aboute,
> With merkes of merchauntes y-medled bytwene,
> Mo than twenty and two twyes y-noumbred.
> Ther is none heraud that hath half swich a rolle,
> Right as a rageman hath rekned hem newe.
>
> (ll. 175–80)

Again the comparison with texts is significant and implicitly carries with it a condemnatory argument. The documents mentioned – the herald's roll which usually contained pictures of coats of arms, and the 'ragman', a justice's roll with the seals of witnesses attached – were characteristically of showy appearance and connoted authority in the secular world of chivalry and law. What is represented in these windows, what is written in this surrogate book, cannot provide the poor layman with instruction and enlightenment, and, indeed, may distract him from his proper feelings of devotion.

Texts of a more conventional sort are also mentioned in the poem, but dismissively, in typical Lollard fashion. The narrator asks an Austin friar if he knows any 'creatour on erthe' who can 'teche and treweliche enfourme' him about his creed, who will do it without 'flaterynge fare' and who will 'feyne' nothing, 'That folweth fulliche the feith and none other fables' (ll. 270–4). The opposition behind these lines, between the truth of scripture and the falsehood of 'fables', is often made in controversial Lollard tracts, where friars (and sometimes curates) are accused of using inappropriate texts in order, amongst other things, to deceive the people, to distract from the harshness of doctrine, to prevent the offence which might be caused by direct criticism, or to win money by entertaining. In *On the Leaven of the Pharisees*, for example, appears the accusation:

> . . . thei [friars] techen opynly fablys, cronyklis and lesyngis and leuen cristis gospel and the maundementis of god, and yit don thei this principaly for wordly wynnynge, frendschipe or veyn name thei don ayenst the chifwork of gostly mercy . . .[19]

In fact the collocation of 'fablys, cronyklis and lesyngis' in opposition to the truth of scripture is fairly habitual, almost a Lollard formula. By 'fablys' are evidently meant moral anecdotes used conventionally by preachers to make ethical points memorable. The 'cronyklis' which incurred so much displeasure are specified in greater detail elsewhere: 'thei shulden not preche cronyclis of tho world, as tho batel of Troye, ne other nyse fablis, ne monnis lawes founden to wynne hom tho money' – evidently material from classical history is meant, which is not only of dubious truthfulness, but is non-Christian as well.[20] In *Pierce the Ploughman's Crede*, the Minorite makes much the same point against the Carmelites, who are described as 'yugulers and iapers by kynde' who 'byiapeth the folke with gestes of Rome' (ll. 43–6) – here referring to the *Gesta Romanorum*, a collection of stories which was drawn on extensively for moral *exempla* by generations of medieval sermonists. It is one testimony to the solidity of the movement that Lollard preachers accepted this severe curtailment of the textual material available to them. According to Anne Hudson, 'no Lollard sermon contains any story material from outside the Bible – no classical anecdote, no pious saint's life story, no moral exemplum.'[21]

But some Christian texts are also set aside as unsuitable and misleading. In *Pierce the Ploughman's Crede* the Minorite twice accuses the Carmelites, who were often called the Order of Our Lady of Mount Carmel, of deceiving women 'with glauerynge wordes' (l. 51) and by telling many lying stories about Mary:

Thei maketh hem Maries men (so thei men tellen),
And lieth on our Ladie many a longe tale.

(ll. 48–9)

And at the lulling of oure Ladye the wymmen to lyken,
And miracles of mydwyves and maken wymmen to wenen
That the lace of oure ladie smok lighteth hem of children.

(ll. 77–9)

The use of the word 'lulling' here suggests a disapproval of the many lullabies extant, often in carol form, in which Mary sings to the infant Jesus. Lullabies of this sort are often to be associated with the friars (though not exclusively with the Carmelites): MS Harley 913 in the British Library, which was perhaps compiled by the Franciscan Michael of Kildare in the early fourteenth century, contains the famous 'Lollai, lollai, liteil child, whi wepistou so sore . . .'; and the commonplace book of another Franciscan, Friar John of Grimstone, now MS Advocates 18. 7. 21 in the National Library of Scotland, preserves several others.[22] The use of 'talis' and 'miracles', however, suggest that this author may also have had in mind as a category the so-called 'miracles of the Virgin' – tales of wonders attributed to the intercession of Mary, many of them folkloric in origin and appearing to come from the eastern Mediterranean. These highly fanciful stories became immensely popular in England: both Bede in the eighth century and Aelfric in the tenth and eleventh used them in religious writings 'to illustrate an incident in the life of a holy person or to point a moral'; and in the later Middle Ages extensive collections, usually called *mariales*, grew up, which came to be used, amongst other things, as source books for *exempla* and moral anecdotes in sermons.[23] The specific miracle of 'mydwyves' referred to, however, occurs in one form in nothing more esoteric than the *Legenda Aurea*, which contains two readings for 25 December: one deals with the nativity of Christ in which appears the story of the midwife Salome, who doubted the virginity of Mary and whose hands withered on touching Mary, but were restored to wholeness through contact with Christ; the second deals with St Anastasia. A Lollard sermonist, speaking scornfully of belief in this 'miracle', appears to have run the two readings together:

For riht as the sunne cometh thorough glas, riht so the Hooli Gost wroughte bothe the conceyuynge and the birthe of this blesside chylde, withoute wem of bodi or any desese of the worthi maydenes bodi, his mother. And this proueth also wel that her nedide at that tyme no midwyues, ne non helpe to that birthe, as othere wymmen neden. And so thei dremen that seien that Anastase, with creuen hoondes, was Oure Ladi midewyif, and at that tyme sche was helid of her hondes.[24]

He offers a 'factual' rebuttal: Anastasia was born long after Christ died, and is celebrated on Christmas Day only because she died on 25 December. It is fairly clear from statements such as this that Lollards objected to 'miracles of the Virgin' because there was no biblical evidence to support them. Like lullabies, they are texts not to be trusted.

Helen Barr, the latest editor of *Pierce the Ploughman's Crede*, thinks that the 'miracles of mydwyves' in this context refer to miracle plays, such as the *Birth of Christ* play from the N-Town cycle where a slightly different version of the incident is staged (see ll. 137–320).[25] It is difficult to be sure, but the context here may be preaching (see 'prechen', l. 80). However, the Minorite does mention 'myracles' (l. 107) in a later passage where plays are almost certainly meant, and these are another sort of text which Lollards distrusted. Plays were generally regarded by Lollards as unsuitable and inappropriate vehicles for religious subjects. The author of a tract on the *Ave Maria* approaches the topic by saying that once, in the past, there had been a decorous way of using dances and songs to celebrate religious festivals, but that modern practices had fallen away from the old standards:

> . . . but nowe he that kan best plaie a pagyn of the deuyl, syngynge songis of lecherie, of batailes and of lesyngis, & crie as a wood man & dispise goddis maieste & swere bi herte, bonys & alle membirs of crist, is holden most meri mon & schal haue most thank of pore & riche; & this is clepid worschipe of the grete solempnyte of cristismasse . . ..[26]

The justification for religious plays rested on much the same arguments as those which were adduced to support the use of pictures – that they were especially useful for the instruction of the unlettered Christian and could move him to devotion by presenting memorable images to his sight. Indeed, it was sometimes urged that plays were more effective than pictures since they were more lifelike, because of the movements and speeches they embodied.[27] The *Tretise of Miraclis Pleyinge*, which is probably of Lollard origin, rehearses a series of closely argued points against the dramatic representation of Biblical stories, including a refutation of the idea that they served as lifelike pictures:

> we seyn that peinture, yif it be verry withoute mengyng of lesyngis, and not to curious, to myche fedynge mennus wittis, and not occasion of maumetrie to the puple, thei ben but as nakyd lettris to a clerk to riden the treuthe. But so ben not myraclis pleyinge that ben made more to deliten men bodily than to ben bokis to lewid men. And therfore, yif thei ben quike bookis, thei ben quike bookis to schrewidenesse more than to godenesse.[28]

Implicit here are all the Lollard suspicions that such dramatic representations are falsely misleading, idolatrous, conducive to wickedness and indecorous: but what is particularly interesting for the present argument is that plays are presented as books which fail to deliver religious truths.

The text that, in the Lollard view, could be infallibly relied on was the Bible, but even the use of this was problematical for some of the sect, among whom, it appears, the author of *Pierce the Ploughman's Crede* was numbered. Among Lollards there was a widespread distrust of the 'gloss' to the Bible, and the way that it had been, and was still interpreted by the friars. The term 'glose', with its derivatives, was one frequently used by Lollards: it sometimes meant 'to flatter' as here at line 367; and sometimes it refers primarily to the corpus of written interpretations of passages of the Bible, culled from the fathers, which frequently accompanied, and sometimes swamped, the text, something hinted at in, 'But now the glose is so greit in gladding tales . . .' (l. 515).[29] But the two senses, witness the second of these instances, were frequently run into each other, as in the following passage accusing the friars of enriching themselves by providing easy penances for the wealthy and powerful through the misinterpretation and distortion of the Bible:

> Weren her confessiones clenli destrued,
> Hy schulde nought beren hem so bragg ne belden so heyghe,
> For the fallynge of synne socoureth tho foles,
> And bigileth the grete with glauerynge words,
> With glosinge of godspells thei Gods worde turneth,
> And pasen all the pryuylege that Petur after vsed.
>
> (ll. 705–10)

Few Lollards would have disagreed with the proposition that the Bible as a text glossed by the friars was something not to be trusted. But there was a difference of opinion in the movement about whether the gloss was of any value at all, irrespective of who used it. The early academic Lollards, particularly those who produced the translations of the Bible, used the standard glosses – the *Glossa Ordinaria*, Lyre, and others – as aids to elucidation. So too did those who produced the Glossed Gospels and the Psalter commentaries. And many Lollard sermons quote or make reference to the works of the fathers.[30] Of the nineteen books John Purvey possessed at his death in Newgate prison, London in 1414 appear works by Chrysostom, Augustine, Jerome, Gregory, the glosses of Nicholas of Lyre, Peraldus, and others.[31] But though Wycliffe himself may not have been as much a believer in *sola scriptura* as those who accused him maintained, the belief that the Bible alone was sufficient to provide the good Christian with all the doctrine he needed was prevalent among his followers. As Thomas Garenter affirmed to Archbishop Chichele in 1428: 'I holde noo scripture catholyk ner holy but oonly that ys contened in the bible.'[32] There is more than a hint of this view in *Pierce the Ploughman's Crede*. The narrator asks the Austin friar to direct him to somebody who will teach him 'With-outen gabbynge

of glose as the godspelles telleth' (l. 275), and puts a similar request to the
Carmelites for somebody who 'gloseth nought the godspell but halt Godes hestes'
– as if the gloss axiomatically subverted God's words and overturned his
commandments. He trusts the Bible as a text, but not the text which
accompanied and was supposed to interpret it.

The position which is being defined in this poem is essentially an anti-
intellectual and anti-academic one. The useless and misleading paraphernalia of
accumulated information, interpretation and opinion associated with scholastic
traditions of learning, in which friars were expert, is rejected, along with other
texts more or less distracting. The Bible and a book of devotions which served as
an elementary schoolbook – the primer – from which one might learn literacy
and the elements of the faith are, it seems, all that the right-thinking Christian
needs. And Pierce is very explicit, in relation to the friars, that elaborate learning
represents an aspect of their deviation from the morally sound principles of their
founders. Neither Francis nor Dominic, he says, ordained that their followers
should acquire doctorates or become 'Masters of dyvinite' (ll. 579–81). But now,
he continues, learning is sought for and the simple text is subverted:

> Swiche a gome godes wordes grysliche gloseth;
> Y trowe, he toucheth nought the text but taketh it for a tale.
> God forbad to his folke and fullyche defended
> They schulden nought stodyen biforn ne sturen her wittes,
> But sodenlie the same word with her mowth schewe
> That weren yeuen hem of God thorugh gost of him-selue.
> Now mot a frere studyen and stumblen in tales,
> And leuen his matynes and no masse singen,
> And loken hem lesynges that liketh the puple . . .
>
> (ll. 585–93)

And the ploughman returns to this issue when he is instructing the narrator in his
creed. Many masters of divinity, he says, 'Folwen nought fully the feith as fele as
the lewede' (ll. 826–7), and further, he doubts whether a man's intelligence is
sufficiently powerful to know the secrets ('pryuite') of Christ (ll. 828–9). The ideal
preacher and teacher is not a learned man, but a man of 'perfect life':

> It mot ben a man of also mek an herte,
> That myghte with his good lijf that Holly Gost fongen;
> And thanne nedeth him nought neuer for to studyen,
> He mighte no maistre ben kald, for Crist it defended,
> Ne puten no pylion on his piled pate;
> But prechen in parfite lijf and no pride vsen.
>
> (ll. 830–5)

In the face of this attitude – which sets aside theological and philosophical speculation and relies entirely on the inspiration of the holy spirit – all difficulties tend to disappear, even in relation to something as intellectually tricky and contentious as the sacrament of the altar. Pierce disparages the friars for concerning themselves with this issue (though it was Wycliffe who raised it initially): they become more confused ('masedere'), he says, the more it is discussed (ll. 817–21).[33] He advises that such arguments ought to be ignored because the 'trewthe' is plainly apparent from a biblical text:

> Therfore studye thou nought theron, ne stere thi wittes,
> It is his blissed body, so bad he vs beleuen.
>
> (ll. 825–6)

Because Christ said 'Hoc est corpus meum' (Luke 22:19) all philosophical and doctrinal problems disappear. In the presence of this sort of reductiveness it is hard to see what all the fuss was about. But, of course, this is a grotesque oversimplification of what was a complex issue. And elsewhere in this work the citation of a biblical text is regarded as proof sufficient to overcome an opponent in a dispute, without further argument or analysis of the question. The narrator and Pierce seem well on the way to becoming simple 'Bible men'.

In the last twenty years or so of the fourteenth century, anti-intellectual sentiments are not hard to find in English writing (though they are not confined to England), especially in relation to what may have been perceived as the quibbling and over-refined nature of much theological dispute. Langland, Chaucer, and the author of the British Library, Vernon MS lyric 'This World Fares as a Fantasy' all advert to this issue in different ways.[34] In part Lollard reservations about the effectiveness of intellectual enquiry draw energy from this general dissatisfaction. But equally, some Lollards, mainly those from academic backgrounds, could themselves be accused of an over-zealous attention to the minutiae of doctrine. When Chaucer's Shipman forms the idea that the Parson may be a Lollard, he is perturbed and says, 'He schal no gospel glosen here ne teche' (*Canterbury Tales*, II. [B1] 1180) – fearful of the intricacy of what may turn out to be a heretical sermon. And Thomas Hoccleve, writing in 1415 against Oldcastle, parodies the intellectual and textual questioning he associates with the movement:

> 'Why stant this word heere?' / and 'why this word there?'
> 'Why spake god thus / and seith thus elleswhere?'[35]
>
> (ll. 158–9)

The criticisms of the over-intricacy of learning in *Pierce the Ploughman's Crede* are all directed at the friars and are made on behalf of relatively uneducated members of the movement – a narrator who has the bare literacy to get him through the first few pages of his primer, and a ploughman who describes himself modestly as 'a lewed man' who may 'in some poynt erren' and who submits himself to the correction of his readers: 'Iche a word by him-self and all, yif it nedeth' (ll. 840–5). *The General Prologue* to the Lollard Bible had taught that 'God bothe can and may . . . speede symple men out of the vniuersitie, in myche to kunne hooly writ as maistris in the vniuersitie.'[36] And texts like *The Lanterne of Light* made clear that, 'The apostlis of Crist and othir seintis weren not graduat men in scolis, but the Holi Goost sodenli enspired hem, and maden hem plenteuous of heuenli loore.'[37] A similar claim is made in *Pierce the Ploughman's Crede* in lines 587–90 where Pierce says that study is not necessary, but that men should spontaneously ('sodenlie') speak the 'same word' with their mouths that God gave them through his spirit ('gost of him-selve'). Though in this poem the narrator is seeking knowledge, it is knowledge of a severely constrained order – enough to enable him to understand the rudiments of the faith and the Bible, texts to be trusted, and for the rest a simple faith in God appears to be sufficient for him.

Writing about the Lollard movement some years later in *The Reule of Cristen Religion*, Pecock sought to distinguish two strands of opinion in relation to the use of texts. On the one hand there were those who argued that the Bible in the vernacular should be studied carefully, and nothing else, because that text alone had status and authenticity as God's word. But there was also a view held by others that 'vnsauery bokis' in the vernacular which were not biblical were also of value:

> . . . that tho now seid bookis had among hem in her modiris langage bisidis the bible, ben noble and wirthi and profitable bookis to alle cristen mennes leernyng and rewling, and ben as riche jewelis to be dertheworthly biclipped, loued and multiplied abroad of alle cristen peple.[38]

So far as is known there was never any great debate on this issue in the Lollard movement, but that does not mean that the divisions which Pecock perceived did not exist or that the divisions were not important: it may be that the movement was not as solid and univocal as its detractors said.[39] *Pierce the Ploughman's Crede* is, as scholars have long recognised, an attack on the friars, but what needs to be stressed is that it represents not the Lollard movement as a whole, but a particular strand of opinion in the Lollard movement: it is written from the fundamentalist, *sola scriptura*, anti-intellectual wing, which sought truth in radical simplification and a deliberate narrowing of focus. The base of the movement was literary – wisdom came from books – but that base was narrowly circumscribed by people such as this author, who never, though, appears to question his own use of a poetic medium for his polemical diatribe. Low-church English Christianity is beginning to ally itself with philistinism. In the impatient, self-righteous, and rather intolerant words of this poet one can hear not too far off the breaking of stained glass, the closing of the doors of theatres, and the crackle of burning books.

Notes

[1] See Aston, *LR*, p. 105.

[2] *Pierce the Ploughman's Crede* is quoted from the edition by Helen Barr in *The Piers Plowman Tradition* (London, 1993), pp. 57–97.

[3] See *John Mirk's Instructions for Parish Priests*, ed. G. Kristensson (Lund Studies in English 49, Lund, 1974), pp. 71ff.

[4] For the complex relationships between Lollardy, Langland and *Pierce the Ploughman's Crede* see particularly David Lawton, 'Lollardy and the *Piers Plowman* Tradition', *Modern Language Review*, 76 (1981), pp. 780–93; and Christina von Nolcken, '*Piers Plowman*, the Wycliffites and *Pierce the Ploughman's Crede*', *Yearbook of Langland Studies*, 2 (1988), pp. 71–102.

[5] See Thorlac Turville-Petre, *The Alliterative Revival* (Cambridge, 1977), p. 112. For a fine reading of the poem from this point of view see David Lampe, 'The Satiric Strategy of *Peres the Ploughman's Crede*', in B.S. Levy and Paul Szarmach (eds), *The Alliterative Tradition in the Fourteenth Century* (Ohio, 1981), pp. 69–80. See also the incisive though brief comments of Russell A. Peck, 'Social Conscience and the Poets', in F.X. Newman (ed.), *Social Unrest in the Late Middle Ages* (Medieval and Renaissance Texts and Studies, 39, 1986), pp. 113–48, especially 129–33.

[6] From *Tractatus de Pseudo-Freris* in Matthew, *EWW*, p. 310.

[7] For these ideas see Penn R. Szittya, *The Antifraternal Tradition in Medieval Literature* (Princeton, NJ, 1986), especially pp. 197–230.

[8] For the suggestion that this description may be of the London Blackfriars see A.I. Doyle, 'An Unrecognised Piece of *Pierce the Ploughman's Crede* and other Work by its Scribe', *Speculum*, 34 (1959), pp. 428–36.

[9] See B.J. and H.W. Whiting, *Proverbs, Sentences and Proverbial Phrases from English Writing Mainly before 1500* (Cambridge, Mass., 1968), H 22 – though this instance is earlier than any cited there.

[10] For Walter Brute's examination see *Registrum Johannis Trefnant Episcopi Herefordensis*, ed. W.W. Capes (Canterbury and York Society, 20, 1916), pp. 278–365. For Brute's ideas on women priests see Aston, *LR*, pp. 55–9; and for his ideas in general see Hudson, pp. 47–8, 99, 274, 295, 298–9, 307–8.

[11] See Edgar Haskins, *Horae Beatae Mariae Virginis or Sarum and York Primers* (London, 1901) for an account of late medieval English primers. See also Nicholas Orme, *English Schools in the Middle Ages* (London, 1973), pp. 60–2 for the place of the primer in the educational system. And see especially Aston, *LR*, pp. 123–5 for the importance of the primer in relation to devotional literacy. She writes, 'The widespread dissemination of primers in the later middle ages makes it likely that this use of the text to learn letters as well as devotion, was spreading long before sixteenth-century reformers gave it such a tremendous boost'; p. 123.

[12] TCD, MS 70, ff. 174ʳ et seq. See p. 82. For a fine account of the devotional importance of orthodox primers see Eamon Duffy, *The Stripping of the Altars: Traditional Religion in England c. 1400–1580* (New Haven and London, 1992), pp. 233–65.

[13] Helen Barr, *The Piers Plowman Tradition*, p. 213.

[14] See, for example, the Wycliffite text *The Church and its Members* in Arnold, *SEW*, pp. 377–8.

[15] See *PL*, 77, col. 1128.

[16] *Scriptum super Libros Sententiarum*, ed. P. Madonnet and M.F. Moos (Paris, 1933), III, ix, Solutio 2 (p. 312).

[17] *Rationale de Divinis Officiis* (Naples, 1859), p. 24.

[18] *Tractatus de Mandatis Divinis*, ed. J. Loserth and F.D. Matthews (WS, London, 1922), p. 156. On this whole question see Aston, *LR*, pp. 135–92.

[19] See Matthew, *EWW*, p. 16; and for other examples of the same idea p. 153 (*The Office of Curates*); p. 50 (*Comment on the Testament of St Francis*), and pp. 59, 73, 105 (*Of Prelates*).

[20] See Arnold, *SEW*, iii, p. 180.

[21] Hudson, *PR*, p. 270.

[22] For Harley MS 913 see W. Heuser, *Die Kildare-Gedichte* (Bonn, 1904); and for Advocates MS 18. 7. 21. see Edward Wilson, *A Descriptive Index of the English Lyrics in John of Grimestone's Preaching Book*, (Medium Aevum Monographs, New Series ii, 1973).

[23] For the *mariales* and England see Beverly Boyd, *The Middle English Miracles of the Virgin* (San Marino, CA, 1964); and Ruth W. Tryon, 'Miracles of Our Lady in Middle English Verse', *Publications of the Modern Language Association of America* 38 (1923), pp. 308–88.

[24] See *Lollard Sermons*, ed. G. Cigman (EETS, 294, 1989), p. 59. See also the account of this same 'miracle' in G.R. Owst, *Literature and Pulpit in Medieval England* (Cambridge, 1933), pp. 497–502.

[25] For this play see Peter Happe (ed.), *English Mystery Plays* (Harmondsworth, 1975), pp. 236–43. For a similar incident see *The Chester Mystery Cycle*, ed. R.M. Lumiansky and David Mills (EETS, SS 3, 1974), pp. 115–18, ll. 477–563). For Helen Barr's comment see *The Piers Plowman Tradition*, p. 217.

[26] See Matthew, *EWW*, p. 206.

[27] For this whole question see Rosemary Woolf, *The English Mystery Plays* (Berkeley and Los Angeles, 1972), pp. 77–101.

[28] Quoted from Hudson, *Selections*, pp. 103–4, ll. 265–271. For the whole text see Thomas Wright (ed.), *Reliquiae Antiquae*, ii (London, 1843), pp. 42–57.

[29] On this see the interesting comments of Wendy Scase, *'Piers Plowman' and the New Anticlericalism* (Cambridge, 1988), pp. 78–83; and Helen Barr, *Signes and Sothe: Language in the Piers Plowman Tradition* (Cambridge, 1994), pp. 90–1.

[30] See Hudson, *PR*, pp. 209–17, 238–77.

[31] See Maureen Jurkowski, 'New Light on John Purvey', *EHR* 110 (1995), pp. 1180–90, which establishes the date and circumstances of Purvey's death and includes a list of his forfeited books from PRO, E153/1066.

[32] Quoted from *Reg. Chichele*, iii, p. 206, by Hudson, *PR*, p. 228.

[33] For an attempted explanation of this passage see Russell A. Peck, 'Social Conscience and the Poets': 'Perhaps his accusation that friars are the guilty ones for denying the living presence in the Eucharist is deliberately perverse (that being the charge usually brought in more recent times against Wyclif). But it may well be that the Wyclif we know, with all his writings conveniently available in our libraries, is not the Wyclif the poet knew. The fact that the poet so strongly defends the Eucharist may simply be proof that there was considerable latitude of thought among Wycliffites in the 1390s and that many of them – men like Clanvowe and probably others of the so-called Lollard knights – were for the most part quite orthodox in matters of the sacraments'; p. 133.

[34] For this aspect of Langland see Scase, *'Piers Plowman' and the New Anticlericalism*, especially pp. 40–6; for Chaucer see below; and for the lyric see Carleton Brown (ed.), *Religious Lyrics of the Fourteenth Century*, 2nd edn. rev. by G.V. Smithers (Oxford, 1957), No. 106, pp. 160–4. For hostility to learning among Lollards see Hudson, *PR*, pp. 224–7.

[35] See *Hoccleve's Works: The Minor Poems*, ed. F.J. Furnivall and I. Gollancz (EETS, ES 61, 73, 1892–1925; rev. single vol. edn by Jerome Mitchell and A.I. Doyle, 1970), no. ii, pp. 8–24.

[36] Forshall & Madden, *HB*, i, p. 52.

[37] *The Lanterne of Liȝt*, ed. L.M. Swinburn (EETS, OS 151, 1917), p. 516.

[38] *Pecock's Reule of Crysten Religioun*, ed. W.C. Greet (EETS, OS 171, 1927), pp. 17–18.

[39] For some brief comments on this division in Lollard attitudes to non-biblical books see Aston, *LR*, p. 206.

5

KNIGHTLY PIETY AND THE
MARGINS OF LOLLARDY

J.A.F. Thomson

Modern studies of the development of Lollardy have followed two main approaches: the analysis of Lollard manuscripts, and prosopographical studies of individuals whom either contemporary chroniclers or later historians have identified as sympathisers with heresy. The former is best exemplified in the work of Professor Anne Hudson, who has set out her views in a series of influential papers, many of the earlier of which were collected in the volume *Lollards and their Books*, and in her major work of synthesis, *The Premature Reformation*.[1] The most famous exponent of the latter approach was the late K.B. McFarlane in his posthumously published study of the Lollard knights.[2] These two approaches are mutually complementary, because Lollardy had many different aspects: on the one hand there was the scholastic inheritance from Wycliffe, which led to continuing philosophical debate over theological ideas, while on the other hand there was the popular movement, given a stimulus at the start by the support afforded it by a number of influential laymen, who were willing to offer protection and patronage to academic dissent. But although the lay supporters may have sympathised with some of the scholars' basic ideas, they themselves were not trained in the intellectual subtleties of the schools, but were subject to other influences than academic ones. They were affected also by current modes of piety and by current prejudices and political interests.

One of the most crucial forms of evidence which McFarlane used in his examination of the knights' piety was in the language of their wills, where certain sentiments were expressed in recurrent formulae, such as contemptuous language towards their physical remains and requests for burial to take a humble form. This language was found in the wills of individuals who were identified by contemporary chroniclers as supporters of Lollardy, of others who, although not so identified, can be shown to have had family, social and political connections with those who were, and of others again who fall into neither of these categories. The range of individuals who used such language raises problems of methodology, and has led to some criticisms of McFarlane's approach. Because one sees a variety of people employing this terminology, it would be dangerous, indeed erroneous, to assume that those who did so were necessarily Lollard sympathisers, and it is more accurate to assume that it reflected a fashionable trend of pious expression at the time, one indeed which is found on the continent as well as in England – in fact it has been pointed out that there is less contempt for the body in England than there is on the continent at this period.[3] Nevertheless, it is worth re-examining the careers of some of the individuals whom McFarlane noted as having identifiable connections with the alleged Lollard knights, and who employed this language in their wills, not least because a fuller consideration of both their testamentary dispositions, and in some cases their actions during their lives, gives a fuller and more complex view of their religious outlook.

McFarlane did not have time, before his premature death, to pursue his investigations into their careers and outlook as fully as he would doubtless have wished to do, and such enquiries might well have led him to modify the opinions which were expressed in his posthumously published study. Although some of the conclusions reached later will be contrary to his, the method of approach which he employed can certainly still yield fruitful dividends. It is possible to extend the picture of a network of social and personal contacts which embraced not only the chroniclers' named suspects, but also those who used similar language in their testamentary dispositions. It is the careers of these persons, Sir Brian Stapleton, Sir William Stourton, Dame Alice Sturry, Edward Cheyne, the two Sir Thomas Brokes, and Sir Gerard Braybroke, which provide the core of the evidence considered in this paper. To these I have added one further relevant case, that of Lady Perrin Clanvow, which McFarlane did not mention but which provides close parallels to the others. There is indeed a wider value in examining the careers and outlook of this group, because quite apart from the question of alleged Lollard sympathies in the wills, the testamentary and career evidence illuminates the spiritual concerns of an influential class at this period. It also raises a further question, of how possible dissidents were able to survive ecclesiastical sanctions for so long.

The piety of these individuals showed considerable variety. They cannot be seen as a sect, but rather as a group of individuals, whose doctrinal views were by no means homogeneous. Personal associations among them undoubtedly existed, which may well have led to similarities in their views, but it would be erroneous to see these as identical. Even more important is the fact that some of these views might be radical but were not necessarily heretical, for the margin between orthodoxy and heresy was by no means clear-cut, and individuals who held some unorthodox views were not necessarily opposed to the church's teaching in every respect. Indeed it is often by no means certain what precisely all their views were, for much of the evidence which has survived is purely circumstantial.

We have the trial record of only one Lollard knight, Sir John Oldcastle in 1414, who had to answer for his beliefs in a church court. His opinions may be clear, for there is no reason to assume that the material in the archbishop's register has been misrecorded, but the beliefs of other suspects can only be inferred from indirect evidence. The clerical chroniclers who made allegations of

Lollardy against particular knights might well blur distinctions between doctrinal deviance and anti-clerical sentiment among men who wished to secularise ecclesiastical property to finance the king's needs, or who were critical of papal power: it is worth remembering that the second Statute of Provisors and the third Statute of Praemunire were approved by Parliament at the time that alleged Lollardy was emerging in the English knightly class, but the earlier statutes on these matters long antedate the teachings of Wycliffe. The church authorities undoubtedly deplored the radical nature of such views on their property and, at least to some extent, the restrictions on papal power, but these could be advocated by individuals who did not question the fundamental doctrines of the church. More seriously, only a narrow line existed between evangelical piety and heresy, and some of the sentiments expressed in the wills of men accused of Lollardy can be found elsewhere, among men even within both the ecclesiastical and the secular establishment. Because close personal ties existed among the alleged Lollard knights, the links of some of them with intellectual heresy and with known heretics have given rise to a belief in guilt by association. Such evidence, however, does not prove that they all held identical views, nor that their views were totally unorthodox.

There is no doubt that within the landed class of the late fourteenth and early fifteenth centuries, there were men who were attracted to an evangelical style of religion and who were concerned with the pursuit of personal salvation by means beyond the routine practices of confession and regular receipt of the sacraments which the church required. There was always a danger that such a do-it-yourself religion might slip out of the authorities' control. Some such men may have been heretical in outlook, but others may have been more eclectic in their beliefs, combining characteristics which can be identified in the Lollard knights with other more orthodox forms of piety. Among the men whom McFarlane identified as being on the fringes of Lollardy one can see expressions of such an attitude in the language of their wills. Among the common features of these one finds requests for a simple burial and contemptuous language about their future physical remains, which were described in such formulae as 'stinking carrion' or 'my wretched body'. This attitude of self-contempt closely parallels the moral and spiritual sentiments expressed in the treatise *The Two Ways* written by Sir John Clanvow, who not only was accused of heresy by the St Albans chronicler Thomas Walsingham, but also was willing in the work to identify himself with the despised sect.[4] So far the arguments for a common form of religiosity hold good, but do they point towards a dissident *group*? When one looks at other individuals whose wills employ similar language, it is clear that they were not unique, and so the legitimacy of supposing that they were also Lollard sympathisers becomes harder to assess. In some cases they may well have had contacts with religious dissidence, and it certainly is possible to establish social contacts between some of these fringe evangelicals and the men accused of Lollardy. In other cases it is equally clear that they were unsympathetic to heresy; indeed one man who used the same terminology was Archbishop Thomas Arundel, the most determined opponent of heresy in the early fifteenth century.

The wills and the careers of some of these suspected 'sympathisers' provide a fuller and perhaps more complex picture of the ambience of knightly piety in this age than simply evidence of emerging heresy. It is necessary to examine the individual cases in detail before trying to reach general conclusions, and the simplest method is to follow McFarlane in treating them in chronological order. The earliest one which used the terminology found in the wills of the Lollard knights was Sir Brian Stapleton's, which dated from 1394.[5] Unlike the other wills, it is in French, reflecting the fact that in the testator's generation English had not yet become the normal language of upper-class society. But the fact that it was in the vernacular rather than in Latin parallels those of the later Lollard knights.

Stapleton was one of two brothers who played a prominent part in the Hundred Years War; his brother Miles, who died about 1365, was one of the founder knights of the Garter, and he himself was admitted to the order in 1381, when he was probably in his mid-fifties.[6] Even then, however, he was active in royal service, for he was appointed as captain of the castle of Guines a year later.[7] He had connections with two men whom the chroniclers suspected of heresy; he was closely associated with William Montagu, earl of Salisbury, the uncle of the alleged Lollard knight Sir John Montagu, and he was the father-in-law of another, Sir William Neville. In 1354 Stapleton witnessed one of the earl's charters, and when in 1363 the Black Prince gave leave to the earl to make an enfeoffment to uses of Hawarden Castle, Stapleton was one of the feoffees.[8] By that time Sir Brian had probably served in France, for in 1363, 1365 and 1368, he appointed attorneys to safeguard his interests in England before going overseas; in the previous years he had served his brother Miles in the same capacity, so he had presumably remained at home then.[9] He must have acquired some prominence in the wars, because on two occasions he is mentioned in Froissart's *Chronicles*. In 1369 he is named as a member of the force that went to Aquitaine with the earls of Cambridge and Pembroke, and in 1373 it was in the company of his old patron, the earl of Salisbury, that he served in Brittany, when he may have been one of the men whom Froissart described as being of great prudence.[10] It is perhaps worth noting that Sir William Neville was another member of that force.

Even before Stapleton's campaigns in France, he had received various appointments to public office in England. He was a commissioner of oyer and terminer in Yorkshire in 1358, and in the 1360s and 1370s he was a member of the commission of the peace in the West Riding. On the earlier of these occasions one of the other commissioners was the most famous pious layman of the mid-fourteenth century, Henry of Grosmont, duke of Lancaster.[11] It is perhaps doubtful if Duke Henry ever actually served in person, because records of sessions of the peace suggest that the membership of it did not necessarily involve actual service, and because Henry died some two months after his appointment. But the duke's northern interests, and his membership of a select order of knighthood of which Sir Brian's brother was also a member, makes it almost certain that Stapleton met him at some time. Such a contact might possibly have affected the pattern of Sir Brian's own piety, which is best demonstrated in his will. At all events one knows that he moved in circles which practised an active piety even while living in the world and being engaged in royal service, something which mirrors the outlook of some at least of the Lollard knights. His actions as a manorial lord, furthermore, show that he was concerned to look after the spiritual interests of his dependants. The papal registers note that in April 1391 he petitioned for an indult that the inhabitants of the town of Carleton should have permission to bury their dead in a cemetery by a chapel in the town, because they could not reach their parish church if the River Aire was in flood. Three months later an indulgence in aid of the chapel noted that Stapleton had built an oratory of the Holy Trinity in the chapel there.[12]

There is, however, nothing in Stapleton's will to suggest that his own religious views were in any way unorthodox or that he was hostile to the church establishment. His funeral torches were left to various churches, he made bequests to houses of both friars and nuns, various possessions mentioned in his will show imagery of the Virgin Mary, and the supervisor of his will was Richard Scrope, the future archbishop of York. One of his books was noted as having belonged to the hermit of Hampole, namely Richard Rolle, a clear indication that he was attracted to the teachings of the English devotional writers of the period. Indeed Rolle had benefited from the patronage of various Richmondshire families who lived in the neighbourhood of Hampole, including the Stapletons. While it is true that four manuscripts of Rolle's commentary on the Psalter have had Wycliffite commentaries on the canticles appended to them,[13] there is no reason to believe that Stapleton's book had been altered in any way. His beliefs appear to be completely conventional, and in the circumstances the instructions he gives for the burial of his caitiff body (*mon chautiffe corps*) cannot be taken to indicate anything more than a firm, but orthodox, piety. And even despite the request for a humble burial, his best armour was paraded in his funeral procession, and presented at the altar when the priest was offering mass.[14]

Stapleton belonged to an older generation than the Lollard knights, although he outlived at least two of them, including his son-in-law, Sir William Neville. But the request for a humble burial was not uncharacteristic at the time. In 1390 John Dauntsey, a gentleman from Wiltshire, asked to be buried 'ryghnaked as I came in to the herthe' and requested a modest funeral.[15] His will did not use the same contemptuous language about the body which is found in Stapleton's will, in those of the Lollard knights and in a number of others which will be considered later, but the stipulations for his funeral arrangements are not dissimilar. The parallels are sufficiently close to suggest that requests couched in such language were fashionable at the time. One does, however, find this expressed contempt for his physical remains in the will of Sir William Stourton, but its other details suggest that his views resembled Stapleton's, namely radical but still within the bounds of orthodoxy. The fact that his associates included some of the Lollard knights, however, suggests that he moved within a social circle and perhaps also a spiritual ambience which was acceptable to both orthodox and heretics. In January and February 1400 Stourton appears as a feoffee to uses in the company of Sir Thomas Latimer and Sir John Cheyne, and of Sir Philip de la Vache, the son-in-law of Sir Lewis Clifford, and he also was a tenant of Sir John Montagu for land in Somerset. Later, in 1408, he is named as a co-attorney for Sir John Grey, with another former Lollard suspect, Thomas Compworth.[16] Another of his acquaintances was Sir Thomas Broke, who likewise had close connections with suspect heretics and whose career will be noted later.

Stourton was a lawyer by training and was involved in public affairs in the southwest throughout the reigns of Richard II and Henry IV. He was first appointed to the Wiltshire commission of the peace in 1382, and was granted the keepership of the castle in Mere in the same shire in 1386.[17] From 1389 onwards he was frequently appointed to the commission of the peace in both Wiltshire and Dorset, and was also appointed to various *ad hoc* commissions in the same shires.[18] The revolution of 1399 and the usurpation of Henry IV did not interrupt his career as a public servant. Indeed, his involvement in public life became more marked from 1401 onwards, when he was first elected to parliament as a knight of the shire for Somerset. He was returned again for the same shire in 1402 and 1404, was elected for Wiltshire in 1407, and for Dorset in 1410 and 1413. In his parliamentary activity he was closely linked with the Broke family: the elder Sir Thomas, who had already been an MP in Richard II's reign, was his colleague for Somerset in 1402 and 1404, and the younger Sir Thomas was his fellow-member for Dorset in 1413. Stourton's prominence is reflected in the fact that in 1413 he was elected Speaker, although he resigned the office, probably on health grounds, for he died shortly afterwards.[19]

His will showed some of the signs of austerity which are often associated with Lollardy. In his burial instructions he left 'his putrid body, naked as it came into the world except for a linen cloth', but although he asked for a simple funeral, he certainly expected it to be traditional, with the normal masses to be said at it. Even more significant was the intended place of burial, the Carthusian monastery of Witham, with which he had had long-standing connections – in 1392 he had received two licences to alienate land to it in mortmain.[20] The beneficiaries of the will included the prior and convent, and he also bequeathed a gold cup to Archbishop Arundel of Canterbury. As Stourton drew up his will in 1410, at a date when Arundel had already shown not only hostility to heresy but also a positive determination to suppress it, it is hard to believe that he can have been particularly sympathetic to religious dissent. His career suggests that he was well-disposed to the church, for he served as legal adviser to both the abbot of Glastonbury and the dean and chapter of Wells, as well as making gifts to Witham. It probably reflects the austerity of his religion that he wished to be buried in a house of the Carthusians, the most consistently austere of the religious orders. His personal piety is also indicated by the possession of four service books, one of which he had received from his father, and a vernacular book of the Legends of the Saints. It perhaps reflects the importance which he attached to these books that they were specifically named among his bequests to his son.[21] His will does not make any reference to possession of any vernacular text of the Scriptures, but a rather earlier one of another lawyer, John Bount of Bristol, drawn up in August 1404 and proved in February 1405, states that Stourton then had temporary possession of Bount's copy of the English Scriptures, which he was wishing to leave to a certain John Canterbury.[22] Possibly at this date, before the intensification of Arundel's proceedings, neither ownership nor temporary possession of vernacular Scriptures was regarded with the suspicion which it would have incurred later. One may assume a high level of piety in the owners or custodians of such works, but one certainly cannot take it as a proof of heresy. The only aspect of Stourton's career which may give rise to suspicion lies in the contacts of some of his associates: Thomas Broke was to be associated with Oldcastle, and the Derbyshire lawyer Thomas Tykhill, who protected Lollard preachers and was temporarily held in custody after the Oldcastle rebellion, was a colleague of Stourton in the service of Henry, Prince of Wales. Stourton was the prince's chief steward for his southern estates, while Tykhill held the equivalent position for the northern ones.[23]

The next comparable will in chronological order which was noted by McFarlane was that of Dame Alice, widow of the Lollard knight Sir Richard Sturry, made in May 1414 and proved in the following November.[24] Like Stapleton's, it was in French. How close her religious views were to those of her late husband is hard to say, for although she did not stipulate any great ceremony for her funeral, she commended her soul to Jesus, the Virgin Mary and all the saints in a completely conventional manner, and made bequests to the friars and to various religious houses. She made provision for masses for her soul, including a trental of St Gregory. Her actions during her life also demonstrate a perfectly orthodox piety. In 1407 she took steps to found a chantry of two chaplains in the chapel of St Anne in the parish church of Hampton Lovett, and in 1412 made an additional grant of land to it. The chaplains were to celebrate for her soul and for those of her ancestors, but it may be significant that no mention was made of spiritual provision for that of her late husband. Was Dame Alice aware of his religious views and consciously repudiating them?[25] If this was the case, she was not the only widow of a Lollard knight to do so; in April 1421 Lady Cobham, Oldcastle's widow, received a papal indult to choose her own confessor, but in this she was described as Joan Pole, *alias* Braybroke, in other words by her maiden name and by that of an earlier and, as far as is known, orthodox husband.[26]

The will of Edward Cheyne, son of the Lollard knight Sir John Cheyne of Beckford (made in July and proved in October 1415), certainly contained some of the elements which McFarlane highlighted as 'Lollard', notably the testator's bewailing of his personal sinfulness and his description of his body as stinking carrion.[27] But some of the other religious provisions in the will were fairly traditional. Torches were left to burn in the church from Good Friday to Easter, the sum of 40s was left to church repairs, and there was a bequest of an altar cloth and a frontal. One hundred shillings were bequeathed to support a priest to celebrate for a year for his father's soul and his own, so clearly he did not doubt the value of traditional intercessory practices. He also left 100s for alms for his and his father's souls. The most interesting provisions in the will, however, relate to his books, because these illuminate both his own religious outlook and that of his family. These included a mass book, a 'Psalter of Richard Ermyte', and a French Bible in two volumes. The last two items were especially treasured, for they were bequeathed on the same terms that his father had left them to Edward's older brother John, who had died intestate.[28] The elder Sir John had charged his son that these should pass to the next male of the family bearing the name of Cheyne, (along with a sword and a cup), so they were clearly regarded as important heirlooms. The French Bible is probably that, with Sir John Cheyne's partially erased name in it, which is now in the Bibliothèque Nationale in Paris.[29] The elder Cheyne could have had various opportunities to purchase a French manuscript, for he had served the crown in diplomatic negotiations with France, the empire and the papacy, and of course many members of the landed class were still probably almost as fluent in French as in English.[30] The English Psalter, in the translation by Richard Rolle, which antedated the Wycliffite version, might have been glossed in a heretical form, but this certainly cannot be assumed.[31] The ownership of such works reflects the piety of the family rather than its unorthodoxy. The Cheynes of Beckford, however, were a cadet branch of a family which had undoubted Lollard connections, the Cheynes of Drayton Beauchamp in Buckinghamshire, which gave patronage to heretical churchmen in the early fifteenth century, and some members of which may have participated in Oldcastle's rebellion.[32] But in Edward's case, the indistinctiveness of the dividing line between heresy and orthodoxy makes it hard for the historian to reach any definite conclusions. McFarlane commented that he clearly shared all his father's views,[33] but this still begs the question of what exactly these views were.

Of all the knights on the fringes of Lollardy the two Sir Thomas Brokes, father and son, are perhaps those who are most vulnerable to suspicion, not least because of their associations with Oldcastle, whose step-daughter married the son. The father, however, had earlier connections with Lollard suspects, for in 1395 Sir Philip de la Vache, Sir Lewis Clifford's son-in-law, named Broke, along with Sir Richard Sturry, as his attorneys while he was going to Ireland on the king's service.[34] In the same year Broke was knight of the shire for Somerset in a parliament which may have been petitioned by the Lollards.[35] His first encounter with Oldcastle may have been in 1405, when he was serving in South Wales, and the father arranged his son's marriage in 1410.[36] The son incurred sufficient suspicion of heresy to be taken into custody and held in irons after the 1414 rebellion, until he obtained sureties in February that he would not attempt to escape. He must, however, have been released by October, when he was enfeoffed with certain of the Cobham lands, to be held to the use of his mother-in-law.[37]

The devotional attitudes of both men, as reflected in their wills, show characteristics similar to those of the Lollard knights.[38] The elder Sir Thomas's was drawn up in 1415 and proved in 1418. It is noteworthy not only for a lengthy preamble, in which he described himself as a wretched sinner and prayed for his unclean soul to be saved from damnation through the merits of Christ, and asked to be buried where men might step on his body as they went into church, but also for the absence of gifts to the clergy. If he sought intercessions for his soul, it was from the poor; he stipulated that three hundred of them should have meat and drink at his funeral, at which there were to be three masses, and each of them should receive 3d. If he could also have three hundred children there, each of them was to be given 1d. Thirteen poor men in russet, who were to be present, were to receive the larger sum of 8d each. Quite apart from the funeral doles, he made substantial bequests to his tenants, asking for restitution to be made to any of them who had been wronged, and he left £100 for distribution to the poor and the blind. The only churchmen mentioned in the will were two who were named as his executors.[39] There certainly are similarities between this will and those of some of the Lollard knights which point to radical tendencies in his religious views, but there are also problems in identifying him as a total rebel against the ecclesiastical establishment. In 1403 he and his wife received a papal indult to have a portable altar on which mass could be celebrated for them.[40] He was also a man who was closely bound up with public affairs and with the court, a fact which demonstrates continuity with the earlier Lollard knights. He served on the commission of the peace and on various ad hoc commissions, as well as being a knight of the shire, and from around 1405 he was described as a king's knight.[41]

His son had a similar record of public service. His parliamentary activity began in May 1413, when he sat for Wiltshire, along with Stourton. After his temporary disgrace following his stepfather-in-law's rebellion, he reappeared in the Commons in 1417 as knight for Somerset, and served in this capacity on three occasions during the following decade.[42] He served, at least intermittently, on the commissions of the peace for Somerset and Devon between 1416 and

1438, and was sheriff of Devon in 1424, so he was clearly regarded as a pillar of the establishment.[43] He was not summoned to parliament as Lord Cobham in the right of his wife, as his father-in-law had been, but in documents of 1434 and 1437 he is given the designation of Thomas Broke, lord of Cobham.[44] He still, however, retained an evangelical outlook in religious matters which is reflected in the language of his will, which dates from 1439. In it he bewailed his sins and desired to have grace before he departed from the world, so that he should be received into everlasting bliss. The preamble was more theological in tone than his father's, for it invoked the Holy Trinity and besought its mercy on him, and expressed the hope that he should be saved through the merits of the Blessed Virgin and of the saints in heaven. It is perhaps noteworthy that there were no bequests to the regular clergy, as this may indicate that he shared Lollard distrust of them and doubted the value of their intercessions, but, like his father, he asked for three masses to be said at the time of his burial.[45]

The final member of the landed class whom McFarlane noted as having a will with Lollard characteristics was Sir Gerard Braybroke, who died in 1429. He certainly had heretical connections: his father had been associated with identified Lollard knights, and his brother Sir Reginald had been one of Joan Cobham's earlier husbands, before she married Oldcastle, and was the father of the younger Sir Thomas Broke's wife. Sir Reginald's piety seems to have been fairly conventional: in 1405 he and his wife received two papal indults, one to choose a confessor who could be empowered to grant them plenary remission, and the other to have a portable altar for the celebration of mass.[46] Sir Gerard's will, however, displayed some doctrinal awareness. After an invocation of the Trinity in precise theological terms 'three persones and oo God in Trinite', he referred to his wretched body and sought God's mercy. But although McFarlane says that the will was 'noticeably full of Lollard cant phrases',[47] one should note that other aspects of it were thoroughly orthodox. He asked for conventional services, a dirge and a mass of the Virgin, and a sung Requiem. He made bequests to the prior of Bushmead, Bedfordshire and the Augustinian canons of the house, and left money to his parish priest for tithes and offerings which he had omitted to pay. He had four priests as his executors, and the dean of St Paul's as supervisor of his will. A codicil to the will included bequests of an altar cloth, vestments and service books, and money was left to endow masses. Gifts were made to St Paul's in London, and torches were to be left burning 'in the worship of oure Lady'. Most strikingly non-Lollard was the bequest of £50 to hire three priests to go on pilgrimage, to Jerusalem, Rome and Santiago, as well as to St Michael's Mount in Cornwall.[48] Braybroke's piety is undoubted, but despite his family connections and his contempt for his physical remains, the overall impression from his will is that it was also completely orthodox.

One will which McFarlane did not note perhaps merits as much attention as some of those which he did, for it has many similarities with them. The testatrix was on the fringes of the Lollard group, the will was in the vernacular, and the testamentary provisions include a request for a humble burial. Lady Perrin Clanvow, who drew up her will in 1422, was the widow of Sir Thomas Clanvow, the heir (and probably the nephew) of the self-confessed Lollard knight Sir John. The will shows comparable signs of piety to those seen in wills discussed earlier, and she also possessed various religious books. One of her bequests was of the collection of tracts called *The Pore Caitif*, and she also left four quires of the doctors on St Matthew to her priest Reynold. In some manuscripts of *The Pore Caitif* questionable material has been added to a fundamentally orthodox work,[49] but there is no evidence as to the nature of Lady Perrin's copy. She owned a massbook, a chalice and a vestment which she left to her brother, and she had an aunt who was prioress of the house of Augustinian canonesses of Limebroke, Herefordshire. She also made provision for priests to celebrate for her after her death.[50] On balance, her views reflect evangelical orthodoxy rather than heresy, and although she may have been sympathetic to some aspects of Lollard beliefs, any case against her remains unproven.

After McFarlane had considered the wills of men who might have been in some way connected with the Lollard knights, he raised the problem posed by the existence of similar testamentary provisions in the wills of men who could in no way be associated with heresy, of whom the most notable was Archbishop Thomas Arundel, Lollardy's most determined opponent. The linguistic parallels between his will and those of the Lollard knights are clear, in the references not only to his sins but also in the request for the burial of his 'foetid and putrid cadaver'. McFarlane comments that such forms are unprecedented outside the circle of the Lollard knights.[51] In some ways, this comment is exaggerated, because it is only in the contemptuous language used about his physical remains that Arundel's will comes closer to those of the Lollard knights than to those of other contemporaries. It is worth stressing that he may have inherited a tradition of evangelical piety from his family. His father had asked for a humble burial in 1375, and restricted the numbers of torches to be placed about his body (although the upper limit of five hundred marks which he set for his funeral expenses was still considerable). There were similar stipulations in the will of the archbishop's brother, the Appellant earl. It is not until the generation of his nephew, who died in 1415, that one sees dignity being emphasised more than humility, when he asked his executors to raise a monument over his father's body, and even he left a smaller sum for funeral expenses ($£130$ $6s$ $8d$) than his grandfather had done.[52] More than twenty years after the archbishop's death his niece Joan, the widow of Sir William Beauchamp, (who had been closely associated with some of the Lollard knights in Richard II's household), made a will in which McFarlane saw certain Lollard parallels. She asked for her simple and wretched body to be given a humble burial but the parallels went no further. She asked for five thousand masses to be said for her soul, endowed two priests to pray for her in perpetuity, and made numerous bequests for commemorative services in various places. Her husband, who had died in 1408, had similarly requested a humble burial, but had also asked for ten thousand masses to be said for his soul in all possible haste after his death.[53]

These wills and their makers clearly represent a particular tradition of piety, in which individuals publicly affirmed their unworthiness and penitence and sought the mercy of God. Only occasionally does one see any substantial rejection of some traditional ecclesiastical practices. Yet even those testators who rejected most forms of endowed intercession for their souls still thought in terms of a funeral mass or masses, a fact which makes it clear that they continued to feel that there was a spiritual value in the sacrament of the altar. It gives no indication of *how* they understood it, nor of whether they believed in the church's teaching on transubstantiation, the point at which Wycliffe's theology had diverged from orthodox belief. After all, Oldcastle, under pressure at his trial, was equivocal on the nature of the sacrament, but shortly before it a chaplain who possessed heretical books had admitted to having celebrated mass in Sir John's presence.[54] Nor indeed should one necessarily assume that all of them regarded it in the same way, for some may have held more radical views than others. Similarly, one can see varying views about the structure of the church and the position of the regular clergy. Oldcastle denounced the pope and the friars as the head and tail respectively of Antichrist at his trial,[55] but some of the knights on the fringes of Lollardy, and even some of those explicitly accused of it, were prepared to seek papal graces to choose confessors and possess portable altars.[56] Anti-papalism, moreover, was not confined to theological dissidents – as noted earlier, the later years of the fourteenth century saw the passage of the second statute of Provisors and the third statute of Praemunire, measures which reflect simply a long-standing wish to exclude papal influence from the administration of the English church. Also, in the wills considered in this paper, there were only three in which no bequests were made to the regular clergy, those of Edward Cheyne and of the two Thomas Brokes. Requests for a humble burial can be found in wills of individuals whose orthodoxy cannot be questioned.

Any consideration of the nature of Lollardy, particularly in its earlier years, must accept that the term had a number of different connotations. The modern perception of it, predominantly as a doctrinal movement which owed its origins to the teaching of Wycliffe, is not necessarily the same as the view that was held of it by chroniclers such as Knighton and Walsingham, who denounced various knights as Lollards and enemies of the church. These chroniclers were writing from the particular point of view of the established order in the church, which feared the implications of some of the policies which were being voiced by the landed class, particularly in connection with the church's rights of property-holding. Because they were also hostile to Wycliffe's doctrinal deviations, they may well have been happy to tar both groups of critics with the same brush. The critics were by no means homogeneous in outlook, and the individuals whose outlooks have been considered above should not be seen as subscribing to a coherent theological point of view, such as can be seen in the various post-Reformation sects. Even when personal ties existed among them, these may have been prompted by shared pious sympathies and a general community of outlook, and it is not necessary to assume that they were identical in all their views. Early Lollardy was complex and individualistic, and each supporter of it was probably drawn to favour it for his or her own particular reasons. They blended their own spiritual values with some aspects of the new ideas, but did not regard themselves as being in revolt from the church. For this reason they were often happy to follow some conventional religious practices.

Similarly, it is not necessary to believe that those members of the landed class who extended their patronage to Wycliffite clergy were necessarily aware of the full implications of their more philosophically defined teachings, nor, even if they were, that they accepted such doctrines unreservedly. While they were willing to give support to such dissidents, perhaps in the hope that they could articulate some of their own criticisms, they were not concerned with the subtle definitions of scholastic theology. Equally, the clerical dissidents were only too willing to secure patronage where they could find it. The *Twelve Conclusions* of the Lollards, which were posted at the time of the January 1395 Parliament, may well represent such an attempt to secure support against the ecclesiastical authorities. The conclusions were academically inspired: the whole structure of the document, and the Latin texts quoted in support of the arguments, reveal this and, more specifically, reference is made to Wycliffe's *Trialogus* in the fourth conclusion. Mention is also made of Aquinas having written the liturgy for the feast of Corpus Christi.[57] These are matters on which dissident churchmen were more likely to be informed than the laity, and it is evident that some of the views which they put forward had little appeal to those members of the knightly class who extended their patronage to them. This is best demonstrated in the tenth of the conclusions, which is uncompromisingly pacifist in tone, even in connection with crusades in heathen lands. But two of the earlier Lollard knights, Clanvow and Neville, took part in a crusade to Tunis and died near Constantinople, and a third, Clifford, was a member of the Order of the Passion, the crusading order founded by Philippe de Mezières to repel the growing threat from the Turks. Of the later knights, Oldcastle was no pacifist, fighting for Henry IV in Wales and taking up arms against Henry V in 1414 and, as noted earlier, the elder Thomas Broke was also willing to fight for his king.[58] It is evident that whatever support such men might extend to Lollard clerks, they did not necessarily subscribe to a complete set of heretical teachings. Some may have carried their beliefs beyond the limits of orthodoxy, if one can believe the story told by the late chronicler John Capgrave, in the context of the Coventry parliament of 1404, at which proposals were advanced for church disendowment, that a number of members of the king's household (and we have seen that this description was applied to the elder Broke) refused to do due reverence to the sacrament when it was being carried through the street, but turned their backs on it and did not remove their hoods.[59]

The pattern of social contacts, as McFarlane noted, throws some light on the piety of particular groups, but it would be dangerous to overlook the existence of friendships and political alliances among men on opposite sides in religious disputes. If one accepts (and the assumption is reasonable) that Archbishop Arundel was the Lollards' most vigorous opponent, one might expect that his political friends shared many of his views. But Thomas, duke of Gloucester, is known to have possessed a copy of the early version of the Wycliffe Bible, at a time before the authorities had forbidden the use of vernacular Scriptures, and one Lollard text, in the form of a dialogue between a friar and secular clerk, was addressed to him. It is reasonable to infer from this that in some quarters he was thought to have some sympathy with the kind of personal piety which bypassed the intermediary role of the church, something which the Lollards exemplified. Furthermore, he had at least one known connection with a particular Lollard knight, for one of the lesser men arrested at the time of Richard II's revenge on the Appellants in 1397 was Sir John Cheyne, who had been closely associated with Gloucester, serving him as deputy constable of England.[60] Cheyne's association with one member of the Appellant faction may well explain why he was initially chosen as Speaker in the first parliament of Henry IV, while his religious predilections made him anathema to Arundel and led to his replacement in the post. And, as was shown earlier, the Cheyne family set store by the possession of a vernacular Bible, albeit in French rather than in English.[61] This may be seen as another aspect of knightly piety of the period, which was reflected also in Sir William Stourton's borrowing of an English text of the Scriptures.[62] A desire to read the Bible was not in itself heretical, though the authorities undoubtedly feared that too easy access to the text might open the doors to rash and unauthorised dogmatising by laymen. It was certainly possible for owners of vernacular bibles to remain within the fold of the church, at least in the years close to 1400.

It is clear that however one understands the term 'Lollardy', its development among the landed class took widely heterogeneous forms, and the extent of their unorthodoxy varied considerably. Networks of friendship provided a means of transmitting ideas among such people, but they did not create any rigid structure which could be described as a sect. The fact that some of the individuals concerned were prominent in public affairs, and in some cases had a connection with the court, probably guaranteed them a reasonable chance of immunity from ecclesiastical prosecution. It is impossible to estimate if in fact anyone was ever acknowledged as the leader of a group, at any rate before Oldcastle's revolt in 1414, although his social prominence following his marriage to Lady Cobham, may well have given him particular standing among the evangelical knights. The events of that year, however, demonstrate that the extent of support which even he could raise was very limited and, significantly, that he did not have much active support from his own class, or even from those families with whom he had personal ties. Even those who might share his religious views were not prepared seriously to challenge the authority of the crown, possibly because the social and political background of many of the evangelical knights was one which involved regular service to it. They were king's men first, and religious radicals second. As long as the king was prepared to turn a blind eye to the views of men in his entourage, they could survive and even prosper, but when a king with strong orthodox convictions, such as Henry V, ascended the throne, the ecclesiastical authorities were able to mount an effective counterattack on those who incurred serious suspicion. When Oldcastle was brought to trial and it was evident that the king would not allow old ties of friendship to stand in the way of enforcing orthodoxy, anyone else who was sympathetic to heretical views found that it was safer to demonstrate their loyalty to Henry by refraining from any obvious patronage of churchmen whose beliefs were questionable. This is perhaps the most obvious explanation of why it was that Lollardy lost the patronage of the landed class and came to be increasingly marginalised as a religious movement after 1414.

Notes

[1] Hudson, *LB*; Hudson, *PR*.

[2] McFarlane, *LK*.

[3] R.N. Swanson, *Church and Society in Late Medieval England* (Oxford, 1989), p. 267; R.N. Swanson, *Religion and Devotion in Europe, c. 1215–1515* (Cambridge, 1995), p. 198; C. Richmond, 'Religion', in R. Horrox (ed.), *Fifteenth-Century Attitudes* (Cambridge, 1994), p. 195.

[4] V.J. Scattergood (ed.), *The Works of Sir John Clanvowe* (Cambridge and Ipswich, 1975), p. 70.

[5] *Testamenta Eboracensia*, ed. J. Raine, i, pp. 198–201 (Surtees Society, 4, 1836).

[6] G.F. Beltz, *Memorials of the Most Noble Order of the Garter* (London, 1841), pp. cliii–cliv, 289–91.

[7] *CPR, 1381–85*, p. 215.

[8] *CCR, 1354–60*, p. 58; *Black Prince's Register*, IV, p. 487.

[9] *CPR, 1361–64*, pp. 64, 146, 395; *1364–67*, p. 167; *1367–70*, p. 152.

[10] J. Froissart, *Oeuvres*, ed. K. de Lettenhove, vii, p. 327; viii, pp. 258, 260, 273, 344; xvii, p. 541.

[11] *CPR, 1358–61*, p. 66; *1361–64*, p. 64; *1374–77*, p. 137.

[12] *CPapReg, 1362–1404*, pp. 392, 394.

[13] Hudson, *PR*, p. 424 and n. 149; J. Hughes, *Pastors and Visionaries* (Woodbridge, 1988), p. 87.

[14] Hughes, *Pastors*, p. 32.

[15] A.D. Brown, *Popular Piety in Late Medieval England* (Oxford, 1995), p. 204. Some members of the clergy showed a similar desire to avoid funeral pomp around this period. Like some of the evangelical knights, they made provision for gifts to the poor; M. Aston, 'Death', in R. Horrox (ed.), *Fifteenth-Century Attitudes*, p. 223.

[16] *CPR, 1399–1401*, p. 207; *1405–8*, p. 437; *CCR, 1399–1402*, p. 117. Although the chroniclers do not identify de la Vache as a Lollard sympathiser, his ties with the named knights were close, and he should perhaps be linked with them. McFarlane, *LK*, pp. 171, 174, 215. On Compworth see below, pp. 120, 163–4.

[17] *CPR, 1381–85*, pp. 141, 248; *1385–89*, pp. 109, 159. He had earlier appeared as an attorney in a plea relating to the manor, in November 1381, on behalf of the executor of a former lord, when the manor was being granted to the king's mother. On this occasion it was noted that the king's father, the Black Prince, had conferred two-thirds of the manor on Sir Lewis Clifford. *CCR, 1381–85*, p. 26.

[18] *CPR, 1388–92*, pp. 139, 342; *1391–96*, pp. 81, 291, 439, 587; *1396–99*, pp. 95–6, 160, 230, 372.

[19] *CCR, 1399–1402*, p. 330; *1402–5*, pp. 126, 366; *1405–9*, p. 399; *1413–19*, p. 103. J.S. Roskell, *The Commons and their Speakers* (Manchester, 1965), pp. 154–5, 363–4.

[20] *CPR, 1391–96*, pp. 124, 158.

[21] *Somerset Mediaeval Wills*, ed. F.W. Weaver (Somerset Record Society, 16, 1901), i, pp. 41–2; Roskell, *Commons and Speakers*, p. 363.

[22] *Somerset Mediaeval Wills*, i, pp. 11–14. The religious outlook reflected in Bount's will was perfectly conventional. He made various bequests to churchmen, including all the mendicant houses in Bristol, and individual gifts to a friar and a Carthusian monk. From the profits of the sale of his lands he endowed prayers for his soul, the souls of his parents, and that of William of Wykeham.

[23] See below, M. Jurkowski, 'Lawyers and Lollardy in the Early Fifteenth Century', pp. 157–9.

[24] *Reg. Chichele*, ii, pp. 7–10.

[25] *CPR, 1405–8*, p. 343; *1408–13*, p. 450.

[26] *CPapReg, 1417–31*, p. 330.

[27] *Reg. Chichele*, ii, pp. 45–9.

[28] McFarlane, *LK*, p. 214.

[29] C.R. Sneddon, 'The "Bible du xiiie siècle": its medieval public in the light of its manuscript tradition', in W. Lourdaux and D. Verhelst (eds), *The Bible and Medieval Culture* (Leuven, 1979), p. 140.

[30] There is a good account of Sir John's career in J.S. Roskell, Linda Clark and Carol Rawcliffe (eds), *History of Parliament. The House of Commons 1386–1421*, 4 vols (Stroud, 1993) ii, pp. 549–52.

[31] See above, p. 99.

[32] McFarlane, *LK*, p. 163 and notes. Thomson, *LL*, pp. 53–4, 60. In the light of the arguments of M. Aston, *LR*, p. 46, I should now accept that there is stronger reason to suspect the Cheynes of heresy in 1431 than I originally thought.

[33] McFarlane, *LK*, p. 214.

[34] *CPR, 1391–96*, p. 533.

[35] *CCR, 1392–96*, p. 419. Sir Thomas was shire knight for Somerset thirteen times between 1386 and 1413; Roskell *et al.* (eds), *History of Parliament*, ii, pp. 377–9.

[36] *CCR, 1402–5*, p. 525; *1409–13*, p. 81.

[37] *CCR, 1413–19*, pp. 116, 121; *CPR, 1413–16*, p. 248.

[38] McFarlane, *LK*, p. 216.

[39] *Somerset Mediaeval Wills*, i, pp. 68–9.

[40] *CPapReg, 1396–1404*, p. 571.

[41] *CPR, passim*. In 1402 and 1404 William Stourton was his colleague as knight of the shire for Somerset. *CCR, 1402–5*, pp. 126, 367; C. Given-Wilson, *The Royal Household and the King's Affinity* (New Haven, CT, and London, 1986), p. 288.

[42] Roskell *et al.* (eds), *History of Parliament*, ii, pp. 375–7. This states that in 1413 he was the MP for Dorset, but the writ *de expensis* shows that it was for Wiltshire; *CCR, 1413–19*, p. 103.

[43] *CPR, 1416–22*, p. 459; *1422–29*, p. 569; *1429–36*, pp. 615, 624; *1436–41*, p. 481; *CFR, 1422–30*, p. 88.

[44] *CCR, 1429–35*, p. 309; *1435–41*, p. 178.

[45] *Fifty Earliest English Wills*, ed. F.J. Furnivall (EETS, Original Series 78, 1882), pp. 129–30.

[46] *CPapReg, 1404–15*, pp. 12, 16.

[47] McFarlane, *LK*, p. 217.

[48] *Reg. Chichele*, ii, pp. 409–14.

[49] Hudson, *PR*, p. 425.

[50] *Fifty Earliest English Wills*, pp. 49–51.

[51] McFarlane, *LK*, p. 219; *Sede vacante Wills*, ed. C.E. Woodruff (Kent Archaeological Society Records Branch, iii, 1914), pp. 81–2.

[52] *Testamenta Vetusta*, ed. N.H. Nicolas (London, 1826), i, pp. 94, 129, 186. Such requests for a humble burial can be seen in the wills of other members of the noble class, e.g. Roger de la Warre in 1368, Humphrey de Bohun in 1369, Edmund, earl of March in 1380, Margaret, countess of Devon in 1391, Michael, earl of Suffolk in 1415, and Thomas, earl of Salisbury in 1428. *Ibid.*, i, pp. 66, 75, 110, 127, 189, 215.

[53] McFarlane, *LK*, pp. 214–15; *Reg. Chichele*, ii, pp. 534–9; *Testamenta Vetusta*, i, pp. 171–2.

[54] *St Albans Chronicle, 1406–20,* ed. V.H. Galbraith (Oxford, 1937), p. 74; D. Wilkins, *Concilia* (London, 1737), iii, p. 338.

[55] *St Albans Chronicle, 1406–20*, p. 75; Wilkins, *Concilia*, iii, p. 356.

[56] An example of this is noted above, p. 103. For further cases among the men accused of Lollardy by the chroniclers, see J.A.F. Thomson, 'Orthodox Religion and the Origins of Lollardy', *History*, 74 (1989), pp. 47–8.

[57] Hudson, *Selections*, p. 25.

[58] *Ibid.*, p. 28. Thomson, 'Orthodox Religion', p. 47.

[59] J. Capgrave, *The Chronicle of England*, ed. F.C. Hingeston, (RS, 1858), p. 288.

[60] Hudson, *PR*, p. 12 and n. 29. *The Great Chronicle of London*, ed. A.H. Thomas and I.D. Thornley (London, 1938), p. 48. For Cheyne's role as deputy constable, see *CPR, 1396–99*, pp. 28, 42, 44, 58, 83, 165; *CCR, 1396–99*, p. 363.

[61] Above, p. 102.

[62] Above, p. 101.

6

DE HERETICO COMBURENDO, 1401

A.K. McHardy

The history of secular punishment for spiritual crimes is as old as Christianity itself, for when 'the whole Council, chief priests, elders and scribes . . . bound Jesus and led him away to hand him over to Pilate'[1] they were breaking with ancient tradition. In the Old Testament serious breaches of religious law ('going to serve other gods') were punished by the whole community, and the method used was stoning: 'The first stones are to be thrown by the witnesses and then all the people must follow'.[2] In the story of the state's punishment of religious crime in England the year 1401 is important, for it was the act *De heretico comburendo* passed in that year, under which Lollards were burnt before the Henrician reformation, and protestants after. Though the effects of this act have been discussed at length,[3] and the act is often referred to in passing, detailed discussion of the legislation itself has been much sparser; the fullest account of the act and its background would appear to be in Pollock and Maitland, the second edition of whose *History of English Law* was published in 1898.[4] A century later another close examination of the text of the act and the circumstances of its passing are surely overdue. The need for such a re-examination was expressed by the late Denys Hay, who considered that 'there is something very odd about the Statute', and thought that the circumstances of its passing deserved some consideration.[5]

The first question we have to ask must surely be: Was new legislation necessary? England was, after all, part of Christendom, her two provinces subject to canon law like others throughout western Europe. It is also a truism that England was very late in experiencing a heretical movement, and that not only other civil governments, but the papacy itself, had developed machinery to deal with its suppression.[6] The only real precedent for the measures taken against the Lollards was the campaign waged against the Templars early in the reign of Edward II.[7] On 14 December 1307 the king received the bull *Pastoralis Praeeminentiae* which ordered him to proceed against the Templars, and in the following year a number were arrested. Finally, in 1309, two representatives of the Inquisition came to England and began to gather evidence.

Their work did not meet with the success which Clement V, and Philip IV of France, had hoped for: in June 1310 the Inquisitors complained to Archbishop Winchelsey that they could find no competent torturers in England, and the Canterbury convocation held later that year gave only grudging consent to torture, stipulating that its use was to result in no one being seriously hurt. The

Inquisitors proposed a novel solution to their problem: the entire trial of the English Templars should be moved to the county of Ponthieu, which was within the king of England's lordship yet subject to the legal system of the kingdom of France. Their scheme was enthusiastically endorsed by Clement V, who in December 1310 offered Edward full remission of sins if he would put the plan into operation.[8]

This episode suggests that only the practical problems of carrying out torture prevented the full force of canon law against heretics from being employed in England in the early fourteenth century, so that in the early fifteenth Henry IV had only to see to the carrying out of the orders of Boniface IX for harsher punishment of Lollards in order to introduce new penalties. Sent to England in 1395 but apparently ignored,[9] this papal mandate enjoined the two archbishops to 'make enquiry against all . . . of the same sect, and require them to return to the unity of the catholic faith; and on their refusal, to strip those who are ecclesiastics of all prerogative of their order, and leave them to be punished by the secular power, and leave those who are laymen to be punished by the secular judge'. Here, we could argue, was all the authority which Henry IV, as well as Archbishop Arundel, could require.

Further, there was an English legal tradition by which the crown could issue writs which had the force of statute. In 1286 the writ *Circumspecte agatis*, issued in respect of judicial action against the bishop of Norwich and his clergy, listed the cases which were to be heard by the courts Christian. It defined the borders of royal and ecclesiastical jurisdictions for the rest of the Middle Ages, and put an end to a long period of conflict.[10]

In 1401, therefore, when William Sawtrey was brought before the convocation of Canterbury province as a lapsed heretic and convicted, it was, in theory, sufficient for the crown to issue a writ ordering him to be committed to the flames. Henry IV was following the precedent of the previous reign in which the well-established machinery of proceeding against ecclesiastical malefactors, the writ *De excommunicato capiendo*,[11] had been strengthened, first in 1382 when bishops were empowered to address requests for heretics' capture directly to sheriffs (instead of *via* the chancellor), and second in 1388 when commissions to search for heretical writings were issued, and when the authority of the king's council afforced episcopal powers.[12]

It was apparently well known also that burning was the appropriate punishment for an obdurate or relapsed heretical offender.[13] First practised by Robert II of France at Orleans in 1022, this method of execution received papal approval in 1184 when Lucius III ordered the handing over of obdurate heretics to the secular power, and it was employed by the Inquisition from its earliest days. Legislation by Frederick II in 1231 (for the kingdom of Sicily) and 1238–9 (for the rest of the empire) was, it seems, the basis for Boniface VIII's 1298 recommendation that this be used as a model in all states. In the fourteenth century there was good and up-to-date knowledge of canon law in England,[14] but what is less clear is the influence of the native legal tradition. The related crimes of witchcraft and devil-worship were punished by fines in Anglo-Saxon law,[15] burning as a punishment being virtually unknown.[16]

In post-Conquest law burning was in theory a punishment for arson, and for the crime of petty treason, the plotting of a woman against her husband or a servant against a master; it was, for some reason, thought a peculiarly fitting punishment for women. In practice it seems rarely to have been carried out.[17] However, in fourteenth-century Ireland, which was within the lordship of the English king, there were instances of the burning of witches, notably Alice Kyteler in Kilkenny in 1324.[18] A well-publicised execution by burning for the crime of petty treason took place on 17 April 1388 when a Hampshire woman, who had committed adultery with the family chaplain, was burned 'juxta Bermondsey' for aiding and abetting the priest's murder of her husband.[19]

When William Swinderby, the first Lollard brought to trial, came before Bishop Buckingham of Lincoln in 1382 he fully expected to be burnt; five friars and three lecherous priests, came 'falsly forsworne . . . and cryinge, . . . to gif ye dome upon my, to berne my, and b[r]outen dry wode byfore'.[20] When Swinderby was caught a second time, in Hereford diocese, he wisely conducted most of his defence by correspondence and did not linger to hear the sentence.[21]

The second Lollard to be brought to a second formal trial was William Sawtrey. An unbeneficed chaplain – a class of churchmen which bishops found very difficult to discipline – Sawtrey had first been convicted and had abjured before Bishop Despenser of Norwich in 1399.[22] He then moved to another diocese, a typical Lollard ploy, in this case to London where he became a parochial chaplain. If he was the same William Sawtrey, chaplain, who had been pardoned for 'diver treasons and felonies' on 6 February 1400,[23] he had additional grounds for foreboding, though 'treason' was an imprecise term.[24] More will be said of Sawtrey later, but for now we may note that K.B. McFarlane argued that Sawtrey's flippant demeanour ('quasi ridendo sive deridendo')[25] at his trial was the result of knowing that a statute would shortly be passed condemning lapsed heretics to death. 'Parliament had been sitting for more than a month when the trial began before a provincial council . . . It is therefore likely that the statute against heresy was already decided on.'[26] We can explore this possibility by considering the chronology of the meetings of parliament and the convocation of Canterbury province which took place early in 1401. The two meetings often took place close together, with convocation usually following parliament. In 1401 the connection was more complicated.

Parliament began on Thursday, 20 January, and on the following two days the receivers and triers of petitions were chosen, and a speaker for the Commons presented. On the following Tuesday, 25 January, there was discussion of a grant of taxation. By the next Monday (31 January) when the Commons presented divers requests to the crown,[27] convocation had already begun, on the previous Wednesday, 26 January. Almost at once three emissaries of the king who were present – Henry Percy earl of Northumberland, Thomas Erpingham the king's under-chamberlain, and Thomas Northbury – made what looks like a plea for action against heretics on the king's behalf.[28] Arundel returned thanks for this message and, after consultation with his colleagues, promised that they would take remedial action, in so far as it lay within their power. He then adjourned convocation until Saturday, 12 February, when Sawtrey was brought before the meeting and Arundel's chancellor, Robert Hallum, read the charges against him. The accused having asked for time to prepare his reply, the hearing began again on Thursday, 17 February, and sentence was passed on the following Wednesday (23 February) when the punishment of the church was carried out: Sawtrey was degraded from his orders and became a layman.[29]

Meanwhile, on 21 February parliament was again in session, as it also was on Saturday, 25 February and on Wednesday, 2 March. It was on this last day that, according to the Rolls of Parliament, a writ was sent to the mayor and sheriffs of London enjoining the burning of Sawtrey, though the writ was actually dated on the previous Saturday, 26 February. The authority for the crown's mandate was that heretics so convicted and condemned ought to be burned with fire, according to divine, human, and canonical law.[30] The wording of the writ suggests that the crown was vested with sufficient powers in law to order a specific form of death penalty for this ecclesiastical crime,[31] a belief not challenged by contemporary opinion;[32] and later in the century and beyond, the writ *De heretico comburendo* was sought by bishops as a weapon against members of their flocks.[33]

It is thus by no means certain that a new statute was required to introduce the punishment of death by burning for obdurate and lapsed Lollards. Nor is there any evidence that legislation was discussed before 2 March, the first and indeed, only precisely datable mention of heresy at this meeting of parliament. The parliament rolls, however, do not tell the whole story of this particular session, which is known from other evidence to have been particularly awkward for Henry IV. Just as 1400 had seen a military challenge to his rule, so the start of 1401 saw a political crisis in which, as a result of a Commons petition, a number of key officials were replaced. The king was forced to replace a number of his own appointees by men of greater experience who had served Richard II.[34]

Parliament continued until 10 March, and it was on this last day of business that the Commons, through their Speaker, Sir Arnold Savage, launched into an extended metaphorical speech comparing a meeting of parliament to the celebration of Mass, and describing three circumstances which gave them especial joy.[35] One of these was that the king had made and ordained good and just remedy for the destruction of that sect by which the faith of the church was like to be undone and the realm subverted. Parliament then granted a tenth and fifteenth. It is at this point, after the conclusion of parliamentary business, that a lengthy petition from the clergy about a certain New Sect, is entered in the parliament roll, followed by an equally lengthy reply.[36]

Far less unusual was a Commons petition to the same parliament that when any man or woman, of whatever condition, should be taken and imprisoned for Lollardy, and remaining steadfast in his replies, he should have such judgement as he deserved ('eit tiel juggement com il ad deservie') as an example to others of that bad sect. This received the reply: 'Le Roy le voet'.[37] Was this the 'good and just remedy' which so pleased the commons?

It certainly bore no resemblance to the statute *De heretico comburendo* which was closely based on the clergy's petition, and the response to it. That this statute was unusual is evident as soon as we begin to examine the text. The language is Latin, and that alone makes it distinctive, for since the start of Edward III's personal reign almost all statutes were in Anglo-Norman. All Richard II's statutes had been in French save for a short paragraph at the start of the 1382 measures against heretics, pardons issued in 1382–3 after the Peasants' Revolt, and an act of 1384 regulating the conduct of judges and defining demarcations between the court of Common Pleas and the constable's court; and after 1401 the next Latin statute concerned treason in the palatinate of Chester and was made in 1419.[38] On linguistic grounds alone we may doubt whether *De heretico comburendo* was drafted by those usually responsible for legislation.

Another unusual linguistic feature was the extravagantly high-flown way in which the clergy addressed their petition to Henry IV, calling him 'Excellentissimo ac graciosissimo Principi Domino nostro Regi'. Such language, as Dr Saul points out, was characteristic of petitions addressed to Richard II in the last years of his reign. Though Dr Saul sees the clergy as habitually using more elaborate language when addressing the king, this form of address in Henry's reign was exceptional, for 'The grandiloquent addresses of the 1390s vanish overnight' on Richard's deposition.[39] The possibility must at least be mentioned that this petition had been drafted in Richard's reign, though never presented, and was only now put forward to parliament.

An act which criminalised heresy and added what was virtually a new punishment to the penal code offered its drafters an opportunity to wax eloquent on the subject of spiritual malefactors, lacing their argument with biblical quotations. They did not take it. Scrutiny of the statute's texts reveals no biblical quotations, and no borrowings from either the legislation of Frederick II or of Boniface VIII.

It was a common device to preface important legislation with the assertion that this was enacted at the urging of the political community; in *De heretico comburendo* this practice was taken to extraordinary lengths. The first part of the statute consists of the clergy's petition repeated almost word for word, with one change being from 'your majesty' to 'his majesty'. The only piece of the petition which is omitted, the last few lines, is the request that the king's ministers should receive lapsed or obdurate heretics and do further what was incumbent upon them,[40] but this was made redundant by the response to the petition which specified that such people should be caused to be burnt 'in a high place'. Almost all the petition's response was included in the statute; only the first few lines, which report that the petition was heard in parliament and that the consent of the magnates and others present was given to the reply, were omitted.[41] Considering that the petition was twice as long as the reply, this act was, from the point of view of the government's drafters, a remarkably labour-saving measure. Close similarity between petition and legislation was not unique: the statute of *Praemunire* of 1393 consisted largely of two petitions, one from the Commons, one from the Lords, followed by a short crown response, while the statute against livery and maintenance of 1397 inevitably used very similar vocabulary to that of the petition which provoked it.[42] Nevertheless, the reliance of *De heretico comburendo* upon the clergy's petition is remarkable, and raises the question of whether this legislation was something of a rush job.

If the act was of doubtful necessity why was it framed at all? Why was it apparently rushed through? Was it discussed in parliament or was it actually drawn up after the meeting had dispersed? What was the urgent timetable to which these framers were working? And who were they? It is now time to suggest some answers. The most important element in the political situation in early 1401 was the fragility of the regime. Henry IV had deposed his cousin less than eighteen months before, and had himself been almost dethroned by the revolt of the earls in January 1400, a revolt which had support not only in Richard's palatinate of Chester but in the heart of England.[43] The parliament which met in January 1401 was Henry's first normal parliament, and it began with the king asking for a grant of taxation, thus breaking a promise made at the time of his accession. Armed resistance to his rule was continuing, and most of the public business of this parliament was concerned with a revolt in Wales. The Commons reserved their greatest concern for the continuing rebellion in Wales and the Marches, and its widespread implications for England; the authority of the king's officers was being widely flouted in Bristol and Somerset, members feared a wholesale breakdown of public order, and they pressed the king to provide a remedy for these troubles and to report to the commons:

Sur quoi nostre dit Seigneur le roy ad comandez a ses Justices, de veier si la Ley soit sufficiente en le cas pur punissement des tielx Rebelx. Et si la ley ne soit sufficiente, que les dits Justices mettent leur diligence, et luy facent report de leur advys, aufyn que mesme nostre Seigneur le roy, par conseil et advys des Seigneurs et Communes suis ditz, ent purra ordeigner ceo que meulx leure semblera celle partie.[44]

Our statute could be viewed as a response to this request; heresy was growing in Bristol[45] and the Marches, and it was, of course, associated in the public mind with insurrection.

Such a solution would explain the absence of biblical or canonical quotations, the emphasis on the movement of suspects from place to place, the threat not only to souls, but to the kingdom, and the lack of any definition of heresy. Viewed in this light the act of 1401 was another in the sequence of measures against heresy, begun in 1382 and continued in 1388, each of which followed the breakdown of public order and the disruption of political life.[46] We could argue further that a regime so fragile could not afford to lodge lapsed and obdurate heretics in prison indefinitely, given the notorious insecurity of both episcopal and secular prisons.[47]

On the other hand, the petition to the king was from 'the prelates and clergy of your kingdom of England', its use of Latin rather than Anglo-Norman suggests the work of archiepiscopal rather than chancery clerks, and it complains at length about the activities of preachers, the writing and copying of books, the making of conventicles, and the holding of schools, all matters of ecclesiastical rather than secular concern.[48] The petition did not ask for new punishments, still less for the death penalty, but for 'an opportune remedy', and that the king's ministers should receive the obdurate and lapsed heretics and should do further what was incumbent on them in this matter ('Ministri vestri in Comitatu . . . recipiant, et ulterius agant quod eis incumbit in ea parte'). In that case the petition, and probably the reply, could be viewed as originating in the administration of Archbishop Arundel; its emphasis on public order was designed to appeal to the king, and to parliament. If that were so, the drafters could be found among Arundel's advisers, men like Robert Hallum, bachelor in both civil and canon law, formerly registrar to Archbishop Courtenay and auditor of causes in the court of Arches, who was now Arundel's chancellor, and a man prominent in the trials of both William Sawtrey and John Purvey.[49] Legislation, as opposed to a provincial constitution, offered Arundel the chance to extend his influence, by the uniform punishment of heretics, throughout the country, rather than having it confined to the southern province; it is a matter of regret that we do not know for certain whether or not Archbishop Scrope of York was present at this parliament.[50]

Whoever was behind this act, was it rushed through to legitimise the execution of Sawtrey? It is by no means clear when his burning took place; some have assumed that he was burnt on 2 March, but this is not what the parliament roll says. Several chronicles mention it, and two describe the event as well-attended, but no precise dates are given.[51] The event provoked no unrest, so it was clearly not popularly seen as unlawful. Perhaps the statute was aimed at strengthening the human law under which his death was deserved, a 'belt and braces' approach to the lapsed heretic on the part of a very insecure regime.

A further curious and interesting point may be observed here. The Commons petitions presented to the parliament of 1401 concluded with this one:

Item priont les Communes, que toutz les Estatutz et ordinances faitz ou a faire en cest present Parlement que sont penalx, ne teignent lieu ne force devaunt le feste de Pentecoste [22 May] proschein venant, lesqueles en le mesme temps puissent estre proclamez.
Responsio. Le roy le voet.[52]

This request was unusual, though we have no means of knowing its cause.

It has been conjectured that the passing of *De heretico comburendo* was aimed at securing the death of John Purvey, Wycliffe's former secretary,[53] whose trial, by convocation, followed shortly after Sawtrey's.[54] Purvey, however, despite his notoriety, was technically a first offender in 1401, and he abjured speedily. His trial began on Monday, 28 February, and he recanted on the following Saturday, 5 March, nearly a week before the ending of parliament.[55]

Yet another possibility is that an act was passed, not because authority was needed, but to strengthen the common law. The influence of civil law on the punishment of heretics has already been mentioned; it was considered paramount by Lyndwood,[56] and was clearly important in the punishment of Sawtrey. It was the constable, Northumberland, and the marshal, Erpingham, who urged on the king's behalf that convocation take strong measures against heresy,[57] and it was to the marshal that, according to the *Annales Henrici Quarti*, Sawtrey was originally committed for punishment.[58]

Perhaps the answer may be that William Chatris *alias* Sawtrey had more exalted connections within the Lollard movement than has hitherto been thought. Unlike Swinderby, his first trial was followed, not by flight into a rural fastness, but by migration to London. At the time of his trial Sawtrey was described as parochial chaplain of 'Sancte Sythe virginis London'.[59] By 1401 this was already an old-fashioned name for the parish which was commonly known as St Benet Sherehog. John Stow preserved the earlier name of this small church in Cheap ward, located between Saint Sythes Lane and Needlars Lane, and Richard Newcourt in the early eighteenth century referred to Stow and explained that Syth was a contraction of St Osyth, who was 'a Queen and Martyr'.[60] Later misidentification of this parish by Sir Edward Maunde Thompson has caused considerable confusion.[61]

As parochial chaplain of St Benet Sherehog, Sawtrey was technically in the employment of the incumbent, John Newton. Newton was a long-serving rector, for he had acquired the benefice by exchange in 1396 and he died, still in possession, in the spring of 1427.[62] Early in Henry IV's reign Sawtrey and Newton can be seen acting together in a case which links them both to a Lollard gentry family of an earlier decade. Thomas Compworth may be justly claimed as the first 'Lollard gentleman'. An esquire of Thrupp, a hamlet in the parish of

Kidlington, just to the north of Oxford, he was accused, in the early 1380s, not only of refusing tithes to the appropriator, Osney Abbey, but of inciting others to follow his example.[63] It was not Compworth himself, but apparently his son, with whom Sawtrey and Newton were linked.

On 20 March 1400 'John Neuton clerk' and 'William Sautry chaplain' were among a group of six (the standard number) who appeared in person before the king in Chancery and mainperned for 'Thomas Compeworth junior otherwise called Thomas Compworth son of Thomas Compworth', whom the king had pardoned for a breach of the peace. This is recorded among the Chancery Files: Bills on Special Pardons.[64] Dr Crook, compiler of the standard list of this class (which was formerly C202D), and who has used it extensively, tells me that the mainpernors were not by any means always professional oath-helpers but were often friends and associates of the accused, so that these files are useful in identifying friendship groups and networks. Description of the crimes involved were, however, common form.[65]

It so happens that Compworth junior's crime can be identified: he murdered one Roger Foliot on Saturday, 28 December 1387, and the fact that the deed took place 'apud Throp, apud Charwell' links him beyond all doubt to the family of the heretical squire. Compworth's case was a protracted one. Originally lodged in the Marshalsea, he was later bailed, and was finally pardoned on 12 June 1398.[66] We may be fairly confident that this miscreant was the son of the tithe-refuser: the descriptions of him are always careful to distinguish the lineage of 'Thomas de Compeworth Junior fil' Thome de Compeworth Senioris', as his pardon describes him.

Indeed, the elder Thomas Compworth was still alive and active. On Friday 17 October 1399 he was one of four men who guaranteed the good behaviour of one William Hyham before the court of King's Bench.[67] One of his associates on that occasion was Sir Alan Buxhill, a friend of John of Gaunt, and most famous as the keeper of the Tower of London who led the notorious sanctuary-breaking raid to Westminster Abbey in 1378. This was an episode which Wycliffe himself subsequently defended before parliament.[68]

The guarantors of the younger Compworth's future good behaviour were a less exalted group, but they still deserve some examination. John Newton, the rector of St Benet Sherehog, may fairly be described as an Essex man, for in the course of his career he held no fewer than seven benefices in the county: Feering (?–1381), Hawkwell (?–1382), Bradwell (near Coggeshall, 1381–4), a moiety of Danbury (1382–7), Holland (Magna, ?–1389), Ingatestone (1391–2) and Manuden (1409–?).[69] The pattern of his tenures, and the fact that he was seemingly not licensed to hold benefices in plurality, suggests that he may have been involved in the business of benefice-broking. The business opportunities offered by London, coupled with the reference to concerted action with his parochial chaplain, suggests that St Benet Sherehog was his likeliest place of habitual residence. 'John Newton' was a common name, and it would be unwise to construct a more detailed biography here. William Draper, another of the group, also possessed a common name and nothing further can be said of him. Thomas Leget, though, is probably to be identified with an esquire who saw active service in Ireland, first with the earl of March under Richard II, and again under Henry IV. For this service he was granted an annuity of five marks in, and custody of, the bridge called 'Rodebridge' near Southampton in January 1401.[70]

The remaining two members of the group are each to be found acting as mainpernors on a number of occasions, so that a professional element may have been present. John Morker was on a number of occasions described as a Yorkshireman and could well have taken his name from the hamlet of that name in the North Riding.[71] On one other occasion he is found acting as a guarantor of future good behaviour along with the final member of the group, Thomas Haseley.[72] Described in the case of the younger Compworth as being 'of the county of Hereford', Haseley almost certainly originated from the borders of south Oxfordshire and Berkshire. His appearances in Chancery during the first year of Henry IV's reign came at the start of a career which was to last nearly fifty years, included two elections to parliament, and saw him knighted in 1445. Considering that he was probably the son of a bondman, this was a considerable achievement. There is no suggestion that Haseley had Lollard sympathies; quite the reverse, for in 1419 he apprehended a former councillor of Sir John Oldcastle, and it is likely that the 'great Bible' which he bequeathed to the London Crutched Friars was a Vulgate.[73]

The six mainperners who supported the younger Compworth have few obvious links. Lollardy links him, at one remove, with Sawtrey, and Sawtrey and Newton were connected through their parish church. It is possible that at least some of the others were members of the same parish, with two quasi-professional mainperners, Haseley and Morker, brought in to make up the requisite number. The fact that Sawtrey appeared in Chancery on 20 March 1400 shows that he had not gone into hiding in London. Indeed, another interpretation of the cheerful manner shown by Sawtrey at his trial was that he thought he had nothing to fear. Coolness while under investigation was a feature of more than one Lollard suspect.[74]

Did Sawtrey realise the seriousness of his position, and his accusers know that this case was to be a turning point in the history of heresy? There is actually nothing in the appearance of the record of Sawtrey's second heresy trial in Archbishop Arundel's register to indicate that this was viewed as an episode of particular importance. This register, now in two volumes, was probably bound in the sixteenth century, and there is considerable chronological confusion in both volumes.[75] The record of convocation of 1401 is in volume II and begins on folio 1ᵛ. This is introduced by a heading in the characteristic large, bold hand habitually employed in episcopal chanceries to indicate the start of a new type of business or the commencement of a new episcopal year, and the 'C' of *convocatio* is modestly decorated in the style usually favoured by Arundel's clerks.[76] The first business of convocation was the voting of a grant of taxation to the king. This occupies folios 1ᵛ to 3, but ends some three inches from the foot of that folio. On the *verso* of folio 3 there starts a long entry which is no part of the record of convocation. The record of Sawtrey's trial begins on folio 178ᵛ, which is the start of a new gathering, and it is introduced by a heading in the same enlarged hand, and with a decorated 'C' as before.[77] Thus the records of these two types of business coming before the one meeting are entirely independent, a fact which is not evident from the printed page.[78] It may be that the record of Sawtrey's trial was originally intended to be bound among the *memoranda* section of the register, or even that it was destined for the more ephemeral judicial material. Miss Barber's comment that 'It almost looks as though the record of this trial was bound in as an afterthought', reminds us how easily lost such records were.

Our investigations so far confirm the shrewdness of Professor Hay's observation: the statute *De heretico comburendo* has many unusual, and even odd, features. Its language, diction, the somewhat confused circumstances of its passing, along with the record of William Sawtrey's trial, all suggest that this was not a measured response to a theological problem; it was not the long-planned 'thank you' of Henry IV to Thomas Arundel for his part in effecting the deposition of Richard II, which is sometimes claimed. Indeed, Arundel was to emerge as the scourge of Lollards only later in the reign.[79]

There is, however, no doubt of his commitment to the kingship of Henry IV, and in early 1401 that regime's survival was still in doubt. Any upholder of law and order in the years immediately after Richard II's deposition would surely have looked askance at the Lollards. Had they not been behind the Peasants' Revolt, an episode which not only challenged royal power and all conventions of social status, but unleashed popular hatred against Henry's own father and wrought the destruction of his great London palace of the Savoy?[80] There had been Lollard disturbances in London since then.[81] The document which links William Sawtrey with the son of the Lollard squire Compworth suggests, though it can do no more, that the Lollard network which Oldcastle was later to call on was already coming into being. London had a particularly volatile population; in the spring of 1400 even the youth of the population was getting out of hand, playing violent gang games of a dangerously political nature.[82]

The visit later in that year of the Greek emperor, Manuel II Palaeologus, flattering though it was, only added to Henry IV's difficulties, and his expenses.[83] Manuel arrived in Dover on 11 December, reached London on 21 December, and remained for two months at Eltham palace. The Greeks created a powerful impression. The emperor did not ride, but walked with his men through London; they did not distinguish their ranks by means of dress, but all wore simple white clothes. Above all, their liturgy was remarkable, for it was chanted in the vernacular ('in eorum vulgari'), and all joined in, soldiers as well as priests. Even Adam of Usk was impressed by their devotion.[84] The effect of this visit on those with Lollard leanings was powerful, and it was apparently Lollard agitation in London which prompted parliament to ask for measures to be devised against them.[85] It was small wonder that crown and church cooperated, perhaps in some haste, to enact a law whose declared intention was not reformation, nor retribution, but deterrence.[86]

There is an ironic postscript to this episode. Robert Hallum who, in 1401, as Arundel's chancellor, took part in the trials of both Sawtrey and Purvey, became bishop of Salisbury in 1407, and in 1414 he was commissioned to attend the council of Constance where he became president of the English nation.[87] In 1415 he was to make use of his experience in dealing with heretics when called on to assist with the examinations of John Hus and his follower, Jerome of Prague.[88] Jerome declared himself ready for martyrdom: 'If you want my death, may God's will be done'. To this Hallum answered by quoting Ezekiel 33:11: ' "As I live", says the Lord God, "I have no desire for the death of the wicked. I would rather that the wicked should mend their ways and live".'

Notes

[1] Mark 15:1 (Revised English Bible).

[2] Deuteronomy 17:2, 7 (Revised English Bible). I owe thanks to Professor W.D. McHardy for drawing my attention to this point.

[3] For some of the consequences of the act see Peter McNiven, *Heresy and Politics in the Reign of Henry IV: The Burning of John Badby* (Woodbridge, 1978).

[4] Sir Frederick Pollock and Frederic William Maitland, *The History of English Law before the time of Edward I*, 2 vols, 2nd edn (Cambridge, 1898), II, pp. 543–57.

[5] The opinion was expressed during a tutorial at the University of Edinburgh in the course of the academic year 1964–5. This paper should be viewed as a small and tardy tribute to the late Professor Hay's inspiring teaching.

[6] James A. Brundage, *Medieval Canon Law* (London, 1995), pp. 92–3, 95–6.

[7] For what follows see Malcolm Barber, *The Trial of the Templars* (Cambridge, 1978), pp. 193–204.

[8] *Ibid.*, pp. 198–9.

[9] *CPapReg, 1362–1404*, pp. 515–16; *Registrum Johannis Trefnant Episcopi Herefordensis*, ed. W.W. Capes (CYS, XX, 1916), pp. 405–7.

[10] See Maurice Powicke, *The Thirteenth Century 1216–1307*, 2nd edn (Oxford, 1962), pp. 481–3.

[11] F.D. Logan, *Excommunication and the Secular Arm in Medieval England* (Toronto, 1968) is the standard work on this procedure, which was observable from the early thirteenth century. For the connection between this procedure and the legislation of 1401 see pp. 69–70.

[12] H.G. Richardson, 'Heresy and the Lay Power under Richard II', *EHR*, 51 (1936), pp. 1–28.

[13] For what follows I am grateful to Prof. Bernard Hamilton for allowing me to make use of his manuscript article on 'Burning at the Stake', which he has written for a projected third edition of *The Oxford Dictionary of the Christian Church*.

[14] See Antonia Gransden, 'The Question of the Consecration of St Edmund's Church', in Ian Wood and G.A. Loud (eds), *Church and Chronicle in the Middle Ages: Essays Presented to John Taylor* (London, 1991), pp. 72–5.

[15] *English Historical Documents, Vol. I c. 500–1042*, ed. Dorothy Whitelock (London, 1968), pp. 363 (Wihtred 12), 437 (Law of the Northumbrian Priests, 48). I owe these references to the kindness of Prof. Christine Fell.

[16] Prof. Fell tells me: 'I can find no reference to death by burning as a penalty except a horrid one

in Athelstan IV in which it is the penalty for theft by a female slave (but apparently theft away from the home estate) and other female slaves have to participate in the execution. The equivalent penalty for a male slave is death by stoning.'

17 Pollock and Maitland, *History of English Law*, ii, pp. 493, 504 and n. 2, p. 511.

18 *A Contemporary Narrative of the Proceedings against Dame Alice Kyteler, prosecuted for sorcery in 1324*, ed. Thomas Wright (Camden Society, Old Series, 24, 1843). Dr Dorothy Johnston kindly drew my attention to this case.

19 *The Westminster Chronicle*, ed. and trans. L.C. Hector and Barbara F. Harvey (Oxford, 1982), pp. 322–3 and n. 7. We are asked to believe that the woman's name was Elizabeth Wanton, surely a medieval joke. For a full discussion of this case in the context of the treason laws see Paul Strohm, *Hochon's Arrow: The Social Imagination of Fourteenth-Century Texts* (Princeton NJ, 1992), pp. 121–44. The crime of petty treason is discussed by J.G. Bellamy, *The Law of Treason in England in the Later Middle Ages* (Cambridge, 1970), Appendix 2, pp. 225–31.

20 *Registrum Johannis Trefnant*, pp. 238–9. Thanks are due to Prof. Anne Hudson for this reference.

21 McFarlane, *JW* (London, 1952), pp. 130–4.

22 *Ibid.*, pp. 150–1.

23 *CPR, 1399–1401*, p. 190.

24 Bellamy, *Law of Treason in England*, pp. 13–14; Nigel Saul, 'Richard II and the Vocabulary of Kingship', *EHR*, 110 (1995), p. 865.

25 D. Wilkins, *Concilia Magnae Britanniae et Hiberniae* (London, 1737), iii, p. 258.

26 *Ibid.*, p. 151.

27 *Rot. Parl.*, iii, pp. 454–8.

28 The representatives, Henry Percy, earl of Northumberland, Thomas Erpingham the king's under-chamberlain, and Thomas Northbury, spoke on behalf of the king and the nobles of parliament warning of the imminent destruction of the .catholic faith unless it received speedy succour and a remedy was put in place; Wilkins, *Concilia*, iii, p. 254.

29 *Ibid.*, pp. 254–60.

30 *Rot. Parl.*, iii, p. 459; calendared in *CCR, 1399–1402*, p. 265.

31 James Stephen, *A History of the Criminal Law in England* (London, 1883), ii, p. 449.

32 The writ was used for the first time on this occasion, but 'Lyndwood thought that the writ *De heretico comburendo* was one which the king could use at his discretion', *ibid.*, pp. 446, 448.

33 Logan, *Excommunication and the Secular Arm*, pp. 69–71, for the legal weakness of the writ, and its use, pp. 191–3.

34 A. Rogers, 'The Political Crisis of 1401', *Nottingham Mediaeval Studies* 12 (1968), pp. 85–96. For example, John Scarle, the long-standing Lancastrian retainer, was replaced as chancellor on 9 March by Edmund Stafford, bishop of Exeter.

35 This section of the parliament roll, PRO, C65.64 m. 10, is reproduced as the frontispiece to volume iii of J.S. Roskell, Linda Clark and Carol Rawcliffe (eds), *The History of Parliament. The House of Commons 1386–1421*, 4 vols (Stroud, 1993).

36 *Rot. Parl.*, iii, pp. 466–7.

37 *Ibid.*, iii, p. 473.

38 *Statutes of the Realm* (Record Commission, 1810–28), vols. i, ii.

39 Saul, 'Vocabulary of Kingship', *EHR*, 110 (1995), pp. 854–77, esp. p. 877, n. 1.

40 *Rot. Parl.*, iii, p. 467.

41 The petition and reply are printed in *Rot. Parl.* iii, pp. 466–7, and the statute in *Statutes of the Realm* (Record Commission, 1810), ii, pp. 125–8.

42 *Statutes of the Realm*, ii, pp. 84–6, 93; *Rot. Parl.*, iii, p. 339.

43 David Crook, 'Central England and the Revolt of the Earls, January 1400', *Historical Research*, 64 (1991), pp. 403–10.

44 *Rot. Parl.*, iii, p. 457.

45 See the mandate of 1397 for the production of two Bristol Lollards, John Mountford and

Thomas Craft, before the council, in H.G. Richardson, 'Heresy and the Lay Power', *EHR*, 57 (1936), p. 28; for Swinderby and Purvey in Bristol and the Marches see McFarlane, *JW*, pp. 127, 154.

⁴⁶ H.G. Richardson, 'Heresy and the Lay Power', p. 10.

⁴⁷ For examples of escapes from the prisons of one bishop during one episcopate (John Buckingham of Lincoln) see *CPR, 1383–5*, p. 120; *CPR, 1385–5*, p. 87. Escapes form the subject of two chapters (10 and 11) in Ralph B. Pugh, *Imprisonment in Medieval England*, corr. repr. (Cambridge, 1970).

⁴⁸ *Rot. Parl.*, iii, p. 466.

⁴⁹ Emden, *BRUO*, ii, p. 854; Wilkins, *Concilia*, iii, pp. 255, 260.

⁵⁰ R.G. Davies, 'The Attendance of the Episcopate in English Parliaments, 1376–1461', *Proceedings of the American Philosophical Society*, 129 (1985), pp. 59, 70.

⁵¹ *Chronicon Adae de Usk*, ed. and trans. Sir Edward Maunde Thompson (London, 1904), p. 58; *The Chronicles of London*, ed. Charles Lethbridge Kingsford (London, 1905), p. 63; *Thomae Walsingham Historia Anglicana*, ed. Henry Thomas Riley (RS, London, 1864), ii, p. 247, 'multis aspectantibus'; *Johannis de Trokelowe et Henrici de Blaneforde necnon . . . Annales*, ed. H.T. Riley (RS, London, 1866), p. 336 makes the same point. This chronicle places the execution in the year beginning March 25.

⁵² *Rot. Parl.*, iii, p. 479.

⁵³ McFarlane, *JW*, pp. 119–20, 152.

⁵⁴ The suggestion was made by Peter McNiven, *Heresy and Politics in the Reign of Henry IV* (Woodbridge, 1987), pp. 89–90.

⁵⁵ Wilkins, *Concilia*, iii, p. 260.

⁵⁶ *Provinciale*, p. 293 n.d., 'debent comburi seu ignes cremari, ut patet in quadam constitutione Frederici, quae incipit, "ut commissi"'.

⁵⁷ Wilkins, *Concilia*, iii, p. 254; see J.H. Wylie, *History of England under Henry the Fourth* (London, 1884–8), vol. iv (index) for references to the constable and the marshal.

⁵⁸ '"Ego," inquit Archiepiscopus, "committo te judicio saeculari", et militi marescallo dixit, "Accipite eum vos, ut secundum legem vestram puniatur"', *Johannis de Trokelowe*, ed. Riley, p. 336.

⁵⁹ Lambeth Palace Library, Reg. Arundel (Canterbury) ii, f. 179ᵛ.

⁶⁰ *The Church in London 1375–1392*, ed. A.K. McHardy (London Record Society, 13, 1977), p. 7; John Stow, *A Survey of London*, ed. C.L. Kingsford (Oxford, 1908), i, p. 260; Richard Newcourt, *Repertorium Ecclesiasticum Parochiale Londinense: An Ecclesiastical Parochial History of the Diocese of London*, 2 vols (London, 1708–10), i, p. 303.

⁶¹ *Chronicon Adae de Usk*, 2nd edn (London, 1904), p. 222, n. 1. Thompson invented the parish of 'St Osyth Walbrook' and many have followed him down this path of error.

⁶² Newcourt, *Repertorium*, I.304.

⁶³ Hudson, *PR*, pp. 80–1, and references.

⁶⁴ PRO, C237 (Bills on Special Pardons), 24/2/144.

⁶⁵ Dr Crook in conversation; see also his 'Derbyshire and the English Rising of 1381', *Historical Research*, 60 (1987), pp. 9–23, for use of this PRO class.

⁶⁶ PRO, KB 27 (King's Bench Plea Roll)/548, m. Rex 8d. The pardon is also to be found on the pardon roll C67/30 m.23. It is interesting to speculate on whether, during his imprisonment in the Marshalsea, he encountered Richard Benet, *alias* Benedict Wolman, 'a Southwark inn-keeper who had once been an under-marshal of the Marshalsea of the royal household, presumably during the reign of Richard II'. He was imprisoned in 1404, probably for involvement in the countess of Oxford's conspiracy, and was later one of the leaders of Oldcastle's rebellion: Charles Kightly, 'The Early Lollards: a survey of Lollardy activity in England, 1382–1428' (D. Phil. thesis, York University, 1975), pp. 468–9.

⁶⁷ PRO, KB 27/555 m. 19d.

⁶⁸ Goodman, *John of Gaunt*, p. 73; Hudson, *PR*, p. 64.

⁶⁹ Newcourt, *Repertorium*, ii, pp. 81, 203, 258, 319–20, 331–2, 347, 402.

⁷⁰ *CPR, 1396–9*, p. 146; *CPR, 1399–1401*, pp. 181, 402, 403.

71 *CCR, 1392-6*, pp. 84, 241, 496; *CCR, 1396-9*, pp. 131, 279; PRO, C237/24/2/141, 157, 173. Prof. David Smith tells me that Morker is in the parish of Markington, which lies between Ripon and Ripley.

72 PRO, C237/24/2/173.

73 PRO, C237/24/2/144; he was described as being of the county of Oxfordshire in *ibid.*, no. 147; see also *ibid.*, nos. 146, 173, 233. Roskell *et al.* (eds), *The History of Parliament*, iii, pp. 307–10, charts his career from *c.* 1404.

74 John Aston, in 1382; for example Margaret Aston, 'Wycliffe and the vernacular', in *FF*, pp. 41–4; and Kightly, 'Early Lollards', p. 435.

75 I am grateful to Miss Melanie Barber of Lambeth Palace Library for discussing the composition and physical appearance of the manuscript with me, and for her suggestions on this unusual record.

76 Other decorated examples at the start of convocation proceedings can be found at I, ff. 54, 57, and II, ff. 22, 28. In other places a blank square was left for the insertion of a decorated capital 'C' which was never filled in; I, ff. 62ᵛ, 65, 71, 76.

77 There is apparently no palaeographical term to describe this enlarged and impressive writing; 'Heading Hand' would describe it exactly.

78 Wilkins, *Concilia*, III, pp. 254–5. The heading *Articuli objecti Willelmo Sawtre*, p. 255, does not occur in the manuscript.

79 Only in 1406–7, following more Lollard agitation, see Hudson, *PR*, p. 15, and Kightly, 'Early Lollards', pp. 470–1.

80 Margaret Aston, '*Corpus Christi* and *Corpus Regni*: Heresy and the Peasants' Revolt', *P&P*, 143 (1994).

81 For example, the London crowd seems to have taken the accused's side during John Aston's trial in 1382, and there had been Lollard-inspired unrest in 1386.

82 *Chronicon Adae de Usk*, ed. Thompson, p. 45.

83 J.H. Wylie, *History of England under Henry the Fourth* (London, 1884–98), i, pp. 161–4.

84 *Ibid.*, p. 57.

85 Kightly, 'Early Lollards', pp. 451–2.

86 See J.A. Sharpe, *Judicial Punishment in England* (London, 1990), chap. 1, for an interesting discussion on the uses of punishment.

87 Emden, *BRUO*, ii, pp. 854–5.

88 *DNB*; the article is by R.L. Poole. Thanks are due to Mrs J.M. Horne for the reference and for drawing my attention to this episode. More detail is given in Matthew Spinka, *John Hus: A Biography* (Princeton, 1968), p. 247.

7

RICHARD WYCHE, A CERTAIN KNIGHT, AND THE BEGINNING OF THE END*

Christina von Nolcken

Thanks especially to Anne Hudson, we have been becoming conversant with the written texts through which the Lollards partly made their bid for influence.[1] Various shorter studies have also been telling us about features of these texts' style.[2] And Peggy Knapp, in her *Chaucer and the Social Contest*, has briefly brought these interests together into a discussion of that larger phenomenon we might term Lollard discourse.[3] She has suggestively related this discourse to the Lollards' history and ideology.[4] As the title of her book indicates, however, she worked with an eye mainly to Chaucer, and her interest in Lollard discourse is finally in how it intersects with other discourses in Chaucer's fiction. We still await such a discussion conducted with an eye to the Lollards themselves.[5] In what follows I will make a tentative start at providing this. I will concentrate on a single moment in the story of the discourse, though one that must have repeated itself with variations many times before the story was over, and on a single text exemplifying this moment. I shall call the moment the beginning of the end; the text will be the letter that Richard Wyche wrote to a friend in about March 1403, while he was being held under suspicion of heresy by Walter Skirlaw, bishop of Durham 1388–1406.[6] I offer my discussion of this in the present forum because it was largely thanks to a certain knight that Wyche's letter came to exemplify so relatively late a moment in the story I am concerned with. But before I can turn to this letter I need to make a few observations about Lollard discourse in general.[7]

* * *

As must be obvious to any reader of what seem to be the Lollards' most characteristic texts, their authors very often prefer an essentialising to a particularising rhetoric. They do this perhaps most markedly in relation to themselves. They represent the struggle they are engaged in not so much as between particular persons at a particular time as between Christ and Antichrist or, in slightly less essentialised terms, as between a group of *trewe prechours, trewe preestis, pore cristen*

* I thank Margaret Aston, Janel Mueller and Jay Schleusener for commenting on drafts of this paper. Its shortcomings are my own.

men, pore prestis, and the like, headed by Christ, and a group of *false prechouris, false prestis, veyn religious, anticristis clerkis,* and the like, headed by Antichrist. They represent themselves less as particular persons than as a group of *pauperes sacerdotes, pauperculi sacerdotes, pore men,* and the like. And when they do use the singular of themselves they provide no individualising details: *a symple creature* claims responsibility for the Wycliffe Bible translation, for example; *quidam ruralis simplex discipulus* for a tract on images now in Prague University Library MS. X. E. 9, fols. 210ᵛ–214.

What these authors made of themselves rhetorically, they also seem to have aspired to in their lives. At the very least, they seem to have done this as they produced their written texts. As F.D. Matthew observed in 1880, there is a 'certain sameness' about these texts; it is a sameness Matthew probably associated with the texts' content but which, we are now learning, is enhanced by their diction and possibly by other features of their style.[8] And the Lollards do not seem to have cultivated this certain sameness only when they wrote. References like Geoffrey Chaucer's Host's 'I smelle a Lollere in the wynd', or his Shipman's concern that the Parson will gloss and teach the Gospel, suggest the Lollards also cultivated it when they spoke.[9] References to them as clad in 'vestibus de russeto' suggest that despite their dislike of symbolic religious habits they cultivated a certain sameness too in their own overall appearance.[10] And their contemporaries seem regularly to have found this certain sameness in the Lollards' demeanour.[11] As Henry Knighton remarks in his *Chronicon* (under 1382, though in a section probably written rather later):

> Et hoc acsi essent de uno gignasio educati et doctrinati, ac etiam de unius magistri schola simul referti et nutriti. (And this as if they had been educated and taught in a single school and even nurtured together in the classroom of a single master.)[12]

Self-representations of those in marginal cultures often begin in a mainly collective consciousness.[13] But the kind of thinking the Lollards inherited – at however great a remove – from John Wycliffe also encouraged them to privilege the essential.[14] His realism meant that they admitted no disjunction, in theory, between temporal being as we perceive it in particular appearances here, and the more essentialised forms of being that for Wycliffe were located ultimately in God.[15] And in conjunction with his biblicism it helped them look from one to the other in practice as well. For like Wycliffe, they held that the Bible, while having its accidental being in words written by particular persons about particular times, had its more essential being in the revealed Word of God. Its account of Christ's struggle against his temporal opponents accordingly became a version of his more essential struggle against the forces of evil at any time; it enabled the Lollards to pronounce on their own struggle in what they could safely assume was the language of Truth.[16] When the Lollards emphasise their collective fidelity, simplicity and poverty they are only doing rhetorically what they hoped they were also doing in fact. They are resolving themselves towards Christ.[17]

Like Wycliffe, the Lollards were well aware that our fallen reason cannot interpret appearances here with any assurance.[18] They regularly acknowledge that we cannot know for sure whether we belong in the eternal Church of Christ:

[A]l ȝif eche man schulde hope þat he be lyme of holy chirche, neþeles he schulde suppose þis byneþe byleue and wiþ a drede, but ȝif God tolde hym specially what ende þat he schulde haue.[19]

And they accept that we cannot really identify those surrounding us:

[S]omme men ben now hooly men, as ankerus, hermytes and freris, and eft þei ben apostotaas and dyon enemyes of Crist. Al þis is hud þing, for ȝif suche men semon to doon yuele, and somme syche semon to do good, as ben manye ipocrytis, neþeles þe ende is hyd of whyche þei schulden take þer name.[20]

But because the Lollards treated the relation between essential and accidental or, in the case of the individual here, between inner and outer, as if along a continuum, they could also treat it as if it were relatively transparent. They make confident guesses about who belongs where in the ultimate scheme of things:

[W]e may not ȝit wite for certeyn which persone is of cristis spouse of alle þe men þat wandren heere, but we may gesse & þat is ynow. As we gessen þat þis man þat holdiþ wel cristis lawe is a leme of hooly chirche, þe which chirche is oure modir. So we gessen of an-oþer man þat reuersiþ cristis lawe, þat he is a leme of þe fend & no part of hooly chirche.[21]

They relate a person's inward *will* directly with his outward *words* and *works*:

For, as her wordes sownen and her werkis schewen to mannes doom, dredynge and louynge feiþfulli God, her wille, her desir, her loue, her bisinesse ben moost sett for to dreden to offenden God and to loue for to plesen him in trewe knowynge and in feiþful kepynge of hise heestis. And aȝenward þei þat ben seid to ben in þe feiþ of holy chirche in Schrouesbirie and elliswhere, bi open evedence of her prowde, enuyous, malicious, coueitous, leccherous and oþere ful vicious wordis and werkis, neiþer knowen, neiþer haue wille to knowe, neiþer to occupien her wittis to knowe truli and effectuelli þe feiþ of holi chirche.[22]

They fully anticipate that even in this temporal life *will* will somehow out. According to an indignant Lollard, after Nicholas Hereford stopped preaching the Word he couldn't even get his pronunciation right:

And I am very sorry for you, that you, who, in times past have excellently well
and fruitfully preached the gospel in the pulpit, do now as well fail in the
congruity of the Latin tongue, as in the other science natural. For, as it was
heard, thrice in one lecture you said 'appetītis;' that is to say, pronouncing the
middle syllable long, which thing not only the masters, but also the young
scholars understood. And many other faults there were in grammar, which for
shame I dare not recite.[23]

As the above passages indicate, Lollard authors did not always locate their discussion
at the more essentialising end of their continuum – far from it. 'A Lollard Chronicle
of the Papacy' concerns itself with the particulars of human history, for example,
discussing how secular rulers have very often been righteous – like Charlemagne,
who had the right to choose his own bishops (pp. 178–9, ll. 111–21), or King Alfred,
who founded Oxford to ensure that no unlearned man have office in the church
(pp. 179–80, ll. 136–49) – and how popes have almost always been corrupt – like
Pope Joan who had a child by her lover (p. 179, ll. 127–35), or Pope Boniface who
obtained the papacy by deceit and 'made þe vj book of decretallis' (p. 192,
ll. 530–2).[24] And more pertinent in the present discussion, William Thorpe's
Testimony, a work that may well have been influenced by Wyche's letter, concerns itself
with its author's questioning by Archbishop Thomas Arundel at Saltwood Castle on
7 August 1407.[25] But even when Lollard authors work with such particulars, they
retain an essentialising perspective. Granted, we sometimes have to accept this
mainly on trust. But the cues are often there. 'A Lollard Chronicle of the Papacy'
marks the significance of the particular events it treats by quoting the Fathers and
St Paul on how things will be in the last times (pp. 186–7, ll. 343–55), for example,
or on the duties of secular rulers at all times (p. 188, ll. 393–414). And Thorpe
regularly reminds his reader of the significance of his experience. He explicitly aligns
it with that of a somewhat detemporalised figure of Christ:

And where, ser, ȝe seie þat I haue troublid þe comounte of Schrouesbirie, and
manye oþer men and wymmen, wiþ my techynge, þis doynge if it þus be is not to
be wondrid of wiise men, siþen alle þe comountee of þe citee of Ierusalem was
troublid wiþ þe techynge of Cristis owne persone, þat was veri God and man and
þe moost prudente prechour þat euere was or schal be (pp. 44–5, ll. 691–6).

And already in his Prologue we find him associating evil in the world with
Antichrist:

And hereþoruȝ þe Lord is wraþþid greetli and moued to take hard veniaunce, not
oonli on hem þat doon þis yuel, but also vpon alle hem þat consenten to þese
antecristis lymes, whiche knowen eiþir miȝte knowen her malice and her
tirauntrie, and ouȝten to wiþstonde her viciousnesse and wol not (p. 24, ll. 12–17).

Had the Lollards been left to themselves, their discourse might have simply continued in its certain sameness until it reached the end of its story. But the Lollards had defined this discourse while challenging a still powerful institutional church, and the more successful their challenge threatened to be, the less the church could afford to neglect its perpetrators.[26] Rhetorically, the Lollards' opponents often attacked them in essentialising terms resembling the Lollards' own. The clerk introducing William Swinderby's case confidently writes of the 'preachers, or more truly execrable offenders of the new sect, vulgarly called Lollards', for example, and Archbishop Arundel refers to Wycliffe as 'the son of the old serpent, or rather the herald and pupil of Antichrist himself' ('serpentis antiqui filius, immo et ipsius Anticristi previus et alumnus').[27] But at a more practical level the Lollards' opponents also worked hard to destroy any group identity the Lollards might have felt. Even when these opponents were dealing with fairly large numbers, as in the diocese of Norwich in 1428–31, they treated their suspects as many individuals.[28] They put pressure on them to denounce other individuals by name.[29] They examined witnesses separately and singly.[30] They played them off one against another.[31] One way or another they forced them to come to terms with their own particularity. Lollard discourse did sometimes persist into the sixteenth century, to merge with new reformist discourses;[32] it even managed to retain something of its sameness while doing this.[33] But it was also often completely silenced well before this later date. And where it did survive that tended to be only after it had been partly reabsorbed into some of the very discourses it had originally defined itself against.

Most of our information about how the Lollards responded to prosecution comes from records kept by their opponents. These records reveal a Lollardy rather different from the one I have been describing – a fragmented version, the possession of many idiosyncratic individuals rather than of any single group.[34] Where the authors of the Lollard works I have been considering tended to uniformity in even the most accidental features of their language, the Lollards whose views these records report seem to have delighted in varying such features. As Aston has shown, for example, where William White provided for the possibility of a doctrine of consubstantiation by maintaining that 'no priest . . . has the power of making Christ's body; but after the sacramental words have been uttered by such a priest, material bread remains on the altar' ('nullus sacerdos . . . habet potestatem conficiendi corpus Christi; sed post verba sacramentalia a tali presbytero prolata, panis materialis remanet in altari'), his pupils managed completely to destroy this possibility. They turn the host into 'pure material bread' or 'only a cake of material bread' until one of them can maintain that 'the sacrament that priests call the true body of Christ has no eyes to see, ears to hear, tongue to speak, hands to touch, or feet to walk, but it is a cake made of wheat flour'; and another can suggest that if the consecrated Host was the true body of Christ 'a thousand priests would make a thousand gods, and afterwards all such gods, eaten and digested, [would be] evacuated in base, stinking privies'.[35] These records can tell us something about Lollard discourse at its more central moments, if sometimes also at some of its more bizarre ones. They can also tell us about the all-but-complete silencing of this discourse. But they tell us little about what might happen to this discourse between those moments. Wyche's letter helps fill the gap.

* * *

Wyche's letter is one of only two surviving documents in which a Lollard describes his experience while on trial; the other is Thorpe's much better known *Testimony*.[36] In many ways the two works resemble each other closely. Wyche is, however, concerned with rather more than just the details of his questioning: enjoining a friend's daughter to live the life of a virgin only if she is doing this for Christ, for example (p. 542, ll. 1–27), or warning another friend against the pride that can accompany poverty (p. 543, ll. 20–3). And where the *Testimony* is highly crafted, and enjoyed an extensive circulation both at home and abroad, Wyche's letter is rushed and informal. Also, its circulation always seems to have been relatively restricted. Like the *Testimony* it is preserved in Latin, though only in a single copy. Unlike the *Testimony* it is not also preserved in English.[37] Wyche may well have originally worked in this language, for the friend he primarily addresses is a layman – he has a wife and mother-in-law (p. 543, ll. 23–4) – and at least one other layman, a certain 'Bynkfeld' (p. 541, l. 29), figures among Wyche's hoped-for readers.[38] But his letter seems to have remained unknown among the later Lollards, and it never reached the English Reformers.[39] It was discovered late in the last century by J. Loserth, in a Bohemian manuscript containing mainly works by Wycliffe and John Hus.[40]

The letter undoubtedly belongs in the company it found in its manuscript for, as we shall see, Wyche was a reader of Wycliffe's works and he was to correspond with Hus. Hudson has also recently pointed out that the manuscript contains a Latin copy of another work by an English Wycliffite, the sermon preached by William Taylor at St Paul's Cross on 21 November 1406, which certainly originally circulated in both Latin and English.[41] Wyche's immediate crime seems to have involved preaching against fraternal begging, and after his arrest he is first asked about this (p. 531, ll. 15–16).[42] As soon as he asserts that such begging is against the Law of God (p. 531, l. 17), however, he is also questioned on other hallmarks of Lollard belief – oral confession, unlicensed preaching and, above all, the Eucharist.[43] He is evidently writing for persons fully attuned to how he thinks, and he does not pretend to reproduce everything he said. He sums up much of what he said about whether preachers should be licensed by the bishop with a breezy 'et multa alia verba habuimus in ista materia' (p. 531, l. 36), for example, and he sums up a section on the Eucharist with a similarly breezy 'et tunc plura verba alia huiusmodi' (p. 532, l. 22). But he reproduces quite enough to confirm that the authorities were right to suspect him of being, as the bishop puts it, 'unu(s) de secta Lolardorum' (pp. 531, l. 40–532, l. 1). Admittedly, he twice makes the un-Lollard-sounding concession that oral confession is necessary for salvation (pp. 533, l. 1–5, 536, ll. 11–21).[44] But as we shall see, he also says he doesn't thereby mean to deny Wycliffe's stand on this issue, and on the other issues he is clearly Lollard. He justifies having preached without licence by citing the gospel, Gregory, and other doctors on the need for priests to preach God's Law under any circumstances (p. 531, ll. 38–9).[45] And he steadfastly affirms that the accidents of the bread and wine remain after the words of consecration at the Eucharist.

For the Lollards' opponents, it was enough for suspects to hold such conclusions to convict them of heresy.[46] But Wyche also makes it clear that he has fully espoused the kind of thinking that led to these conclusions.[47] He does this perhaps most clearly in relation to the Eucharist. He regularly looks to the Host in its most material manifestation, refusing to allow that there can be no bread after the words of consecration (pp. 532, ll. 20–2, 538, l. 30–539, l. 9). But he also looks to its more essential being, insisting that it is indeed the true body of Christ (p. 532, ll. 14–15). Like Wycliffe at times, he remains vague about what actually happens to it in this higher order of being – the substance – after the words of the consecration.[48] But he steadfastly resists his opponents' claim that what remains on the altar is the true body only in the appearance (*specie*) of bread (p. 532, ll. 16–19). For him it is the true body in the form (*forma*) of bread (pp. 532, ll. 14–15, 539, ll. 1–4).[49] Like Wycliffe, therefore, he cannot finally allow that the substance of the Host can change or be annihilated without taking its accidents with it.[50] When a Franciscan Master of Theology adduces the analogy between the change of Moses' rod into a serpent (Exod. 4. 3–4) and that of the Host from bread to body of Christ (p. 538, ll. 37–41), Wyche retorts that neither Scripture nor the doctors say that the substance of the rod was annihilated or destroyed. What they say is that it was turned into a serpent ('nec scriptura nec doctores dicunt quod substancia virge fuit annichilata vel destructa sed conversa in colubrum' p. 538, ll. 42–3).[51]

Wyche also reveals this kind of thinking in what he has to say about the Bible. Again, he regularly refers to this in its most material manifestation, the words on the page, although as he has no copy with him he cannot always do this accurately: he accepts as biblical the words 'misterium fidei' in the consecration of the wine at the Eucharist, for example (p. 540, ll. 23–30).[52] But when asked whether there is material bread he points out that the word 'materialis' never occurs in Scripture (pp. 532, ll. 20–2, 536, l. 3), and when he is assured that the whole church believes that the Eucharist is not bread after consecration he challenges his opponents to show him that same negative in the Law of God (p. 538, ll. 32–3).[53] Like Wycliffe he is very much against glossing or adding to the actual words of the Bible (pp. 536, ll. 7–8, 537, ll. 44–5).[54] But he is also well aware that many copies of the Bible contain errors, and like Wycliffe he finally cautions that God's Law does not lie primarily in the written words of the Bible's ink and parchment (p. 540, ll. 30–2).[55] Like Wycliffe too, he evidently holds that one should read the words of the Bible in relation to their authors' and, ultimately, God's intention.[56] When his opponents mockingly suggest that because St Paul said every man may have a wife he must have been in favour of clerical marriage, he points out that what St Paul meant was that marriage was preferable to fornication (p. 533, l. 38). And when his opponents point to what they apparently take as St Paul's addition of 'enim' to Christ's 'hoc est corpus meum' (Matt. 26.26, Mark 14.22, Luke 22.19), he objects that this 'enim' is merely confirmatory (p. 536, ll. 10–11).[57]

Like the Lollard authors mentioned above, Wyche also has not let this kind of thinking affect only what he has to say about particular Lollard tenets. He has also let it affect his shaping of his own career.[58] He is an ordained priest of the diocese of Hereford,[59] but he probably acquired his distinctive views while at Oxford; there is even a slight chance that he acquired some of them directly from Wycliffe.[60] And like most if not all of those who aspired to be Lollard Poor Priests, he has been roaming the country preaching what he would consider the Word – he refers to the bishop's accusation that he and one Jacobus had subverted the people in Northumberland (p. 535, ll. 47–8), and the community he has most recently been sustaining was situated in or near Newcastle.[61] He is determinedly unworldly – it was due to a fall, he assures his readers, that he hired a horse on his way to the bishop (p. 531, ll. 11–13).[62] While not courting martyrdom – he says he would gladly be freed (p. 534, l. 37) – he has not rejected the temporal imprisonment and death any full *imitatio Christi* might demand. And his self-representation has obviously been influenced by other Poor Priests: in giving the details of his trial he resembles St Paul (in Acts 24, for example), and like Paul in his various imprisonments he writes to his friends – even to the extent that like Paul (2 Tim. 4.13) he asks these friends for books (pp. 543, ll. 29–36, 544, ll. 1–4).[63]

Given Wyche's evident Lollardy, and given his career to date, there seems every reason to expect that in his letter Wyche would be concerned explicitly to align his present struggle against the authorities with Christ's struggle against Antichrist. Of all the Lollard works I know, however, his letter is the most consistently particularising.[64] Wyche refers to what may be a blood brother (p. 544, l. 1) as well as his sufferings from stomach ache (p. 541, l. 22), and haemorrhoids (p. 541, l. 25). He addresses a particular person (p. 531, l. 1), and through him other particular persons, even giving some of their names – John May and his wife (p. 541, l. 30), 'Bhytebi' (p. 541, l. 29), 'magistro meo de Balknolle' (*ibid.*), 'Bynkfeld' (*ibid.*), 'Roberto Herl' (p. 542, l. 27), 'Laudens' and 'Gre[n]e' (p. 543, l. 20). He requests specific *quaterni*, and describes in detail how these should be smuggled to him via Henry of Topcliff, brother of the Topcliff who married William Corpp's sister (p. 543, ll. 37–41).[65] He specifies when his interrogations occurred – he was first brought before the bishop on 7 December, for example (p. 531, l. 13) – who was standing or sitting where (pp. 535, ll. 14–15, 18; 539, ll. 16–22), what was asked and by whom. He writes in what readers of Lollard texts would probably agree is a highly idiosyncratic style, cautious, evasive, sometimes even grimly humorous. And although he describes a struggle, it is between the Father of the Lie and the Father of Lights, and it remains within himself (pp. 536, l. 24–537, l. 12).[66] He doesn't give Antichrist a look-in.

Admittedly, what Wyche doesn't do explicitly, he is to some extent doing implicitly. When, after hours of argument, the bishop comments 'either he is outside the faith for sure or we are' and Wyche adds for the benefit of his readers 'and he spoke the truth' ('Vel ipse pro certo est extra fidem, vel nos; et verum dixit' p. 537, ll. 46–7), his words seem loaded with implication about who belongs where in the larger scheme of things.[67] And he doesn't altogether withhold the cues that he is regarding his experience from some essentialising perspective. When he refers to a sermon he had preached about the rewards awaiting those who are persecuted here, for example, he is clearly locating both himself and his readers on the right side (pp. 541, l. 38–542, l. 1).[68] He complains that the bishop and his associates would find even Christ a heretic – though it is perhaps telling that his is not a slightly detemporalised Christ like Thorpe's (p. 541, ll. 15–17). And as we shall see, the conflict within himself is one that the Father of Lights will finally win.

It might seem at first that Wyche, like Thorpe, has simply chosen to locate his discussion towards the particularising end of the Lollard continuum, therefore, though if so he has located it somewhat nearer this end than Thorpe has. He is, after all, writing a personal letter, and he is addressing a far more specific audience than Thorpe's 'diuerse frendis' and 'oþere special frendis' (p. 25, ll. 30, 32–33).[69] He may also have had a personal preference for working in a relatively particularising mode. Even so, there remains good reason for suspecting that the difference between his letter's discourse and that of Thorpe's *Testimony* is rather more fundamental than this. For unlike Thorpe, who represents himself as writing after only one day of inconclusive questioning, Wyche has been under considerable pressure, including intellectual pressure, from the authorities for some time. He has been in prison for some three months, in considerable pain and without hope of release. He has been alternately cajoled with promises of temporal preferment and threatened with a terrible death (pp. 533, ll. 7–14, 540, ll. 11–21). The fact that he was more than once placed near the fire during questioning was perhaps meant to remind him of what that death would be (pp. 539, l. 21, 540, ll. 18–19).[70] He has been confronted with the recantation Purvey made on 5 March 1401 (p. 537, ll. 19–20), and although he doesn't rise to the bait it is hard to imagine that he was not worried by it.[71] He has withstood these pressures with admirable success – to the extent that at the time of writing he has been pronounced a heretic and is awaiting degradation from the priesthood, confiscation of his goods (pp. 540, ll. 49–541, l. 3) and quite possibly death by burning – as he puts it, the 'diem sollempnem' (p. 544, l. 8).[72] But during the time he describes he has also partly given in. He has allowed the knight of my title to persuade him to swear an oath of obedience to the laws and constitutions of the institutional church. When assessing the nature of his discourse we have to take account of his dealings with this knight.

* * *

That Wyche has been intensely worried by these dealings is indicated by the disproportionately large space he assigns them in his narrative. What he describes as having led up to them is roughly this. When he first presents himself for questioning, the bishop demands that he swear an oath of obedience to the laws and constitutions of the church as specifically contained in the Decretum, Decretals, Sext and Clementines (p. 531, ll. 19–22).[73] Wyche refuses. At first he gives no reason for doing this ('et non respondi ei verbum', p. 531, ll. 25–6). Later he resorts to legalistic quibbling, pointing to insufficiencies in the laws and constitutions (pp. 533, l. 16–534, l. 2).[74] The deadlock lasts for some weeks: it is only broken when the bishop sends the knight, together with a *notarius presbyter* and the *cancellarius* (p. 534, ll. 3–5), to negotiate with Wyche in the prison.

Wyche almost certainly looked to the knightly class to spearhead the reform of the church.[75] He has also already received verbal support from two members of this class early in the present proceedings (p. 532, ll. 26–7).[76] Although the present knight comes from the bishop, therefore, Wyche's initial response to him is positive; as he puts it at the time of writing: 'It seemed to me that he was a reliable man' ('(A)pparuit michi quod ille esset solidus homo', p. 534, l. 4). The knight tells Wyche he wants them to work out a satisfactory wording for the oath (p. 534, ll. 6–7). Wyche launches yet again into why he cannot swear the oath as it stands (p. 534, ll. 8–25). But this time he also looks towards compromise. He juxtaposes his very Lollard-sounding objection that one is not held to obey any law or precept except insofar as it conforms to the will of God, with the observation that laymen are not bound to obey laws pertaining to the office of the pope, bishops or priests (p. 534, ll. 21–4). The knight seizes on Wyche's implication: 'Richard, could you find it in your conscience to obey the law of the catholic church insofar as is relevant to you?' ('Ricarde, potesne invenire in consciencia tua ad obediendum legi ecclesie catholice in quantum ad te pertinet?', p. 534, ll. 25–7). Although he probably mainly wanted to provide Wyche with the saving 'in quantum ad te pertinet' he has also provided some other wording Wyche can use. Wyche immediately picks this up, to formulate a version of the oath he would be willing to swear: 'I know the law of God is the law of the catholic church and far be it but that I should obey the law of our God insofar as it applies to me' ('scio quod lex Dei est lex ecclesie catholice et absit quin obedirem legi Dei nostri in quantum ad me pertinet', p. 534, ll. 27–8).

Wyche seems to have been well aware that an essentialising wording can embrace a range of specific applications, including some that the Lollards would have said lacked any grounding in Truth.[77] Like other Lollards, he also seems to have been prepared to exploit this range.[78] Some weeks before the incident involving the knight he was asked whether auricular confession was necessary for salvation (p. 533, ll. 1–2). He conceded that it was: 'Necessarium est, dixi' (p. 533, l. 2). On that occasion the authorities didn't press matters, although the chancellor, who throughout the proceedings proves very much Wyche's match, realised that they would have to pin Wyche down further before accepting his answer: 'God knows you will tell us to whom and when before you depart from here' ('Deus scit tu dices nobis cui et quando antequam abhinc recesseris', p. 533, ll. 2–3). Wyche doesn't explain what was in his mind as he made this concession. But he provides some commentary for the benefit of his readers the second time he makes it. He then acknowledges that the good Wycliffe ('bonus Wicleff') had denied the need for such confession (p. 536, l. 14).[79] But he also notes that Wycliffe was speaking in the manner of the sophists ('ad modum loquendi sophistarum', p. 536, l. 15), whereas he himself is speaking in terms of Scripture. Virtue of some kind, he then observes, is necessary for the salvation of the soul ('Quelibet virtus est de necessitate salutis anime cuilibet', p. 536, ll. 15–17).[80] He is infuriatingly cryptic; evidently, he could expect his readers to supply a good deal of his meaning.[81] But his sense is presumably similar to that expressed in the tract Matthew called 'Of Confession': 'To make hoolynesse in men is confession nedful; and þerfor shuld hooly churche witt sumwhat of confession'.[82] Where Wycliffe was referring to confession as members of the institutional church on earth would have understood this, Wyche was referring to the need for members of the Church of Christ to acknowledge their own sinfulness.

Wyche also does not explain what was in his mind when he proposed his new version of the oath. Given his equivocations over confession, however, we can assume that here too he was seeking a wording that could be variously interpreted. If for him the term 'Catholic church' could mean the essentialised *Congregatio Praedestinorum* of the Lollards, for his opponents it could still mean the institutional church on earth, peopled both by those who would be saved and by those who would not.[83] And if for him the law of this church could mean the essentialised Law of God as revealed in the Bible, for his opponents it could still mean the canon laws of this institutional church. So the knight must have seemed to Wyche to have been playing into his hands when he approved of his proposal: 'Tu bene dicis' (p. 534, l. 29). That Wyche will not finally be able to control even part of the oath's public meaning is implied by what the knight says next, however: 'You may keep that [oath] of yours in your heart and let it be your oath, and you may swear it as delimited in your heart' ('Custodias istud in corde tuo et sit istud iuramentum tuum, et iures tu istud in corde tuo limitatum', p. 534, ll. 29–30).

When Wyche formulated his version of the oath, he was evidently hoping this would be the version he would actually swear in public. When the knight tells Wyche to keep his version in his heart, however, he is probably assuming that the version Wyche will then swear will continue to be the bishop's. Wyche realises there is a problem and cautiously points out that in such circumstances he should accept the oath according to the judge's intention and not his own ('Sed vos scitis bene, dixi, si reciperem iuramentum a iudice, oportet me recipere secundum intentum iudicis et non secundum meum', p. 534, ll. 30–32). The knight, perhaps unaware of what exactly is at stake, assures him that the bishop will accept Wyche's version of the oath ('Pro certo scias, quod dominus meus reciperet a te iuramentum istud, quia sum missus a Domino meo ad te ad tractandum tecum super isto iuramento', p. 534, ll. 32–4). Wyche should probably have refused to continue negotiating, on the grounds that his opponents were almost certainly unable to understand the oath as he would wish. But when the knight also indicates that the bishop will release Wyche from the original oath ('Et si volueris sic facere, dominus meus absolvet te ab alio iuramento et sic facies bonum finem', p. 534, ll. 35–6), he gives way. He still insists that he will swear only provided the bishop will receive the oath as Wyche himself defines it, and he again spells out what this will mean ('si dominus meus voluerit facere sicut vos dicitis et recipere a me istud iuramentum limitatum in corde meo, hoc est, quod teneor obedire legi Dei, in quantum ad me pertinet', p. 534, ll. 43–6). But even when the chancellor objects: 'By God, you will swear as we want before you leave' ('Per Deum, tu iuras sicut nos volumus antequam recesseris', p. 534, ll. 47–8), Wyche lets the knight reassure him: 'Ne dubites' (p. 534, l. 46).

On the next day Wyche is brought before the bishop and given a fresh text of the oath to read through. All the authorities have done is insert a version of Wyche's 'in quantam ad me pertinet' into what must have been the oath's original text. It now reads:

> I Richard Wyche of the diocese of [Worcester] swear that each catholic is firmly and precisely held by the laws and constitutions contained in the Decretum, Decretals, Sext and Clementines and that, insofar as concerns me, I am willing to obey them, and that if I should happen to preach anything against the same in future I will confess myself fallen into heresy, also, if I have any books against them I will send them to the bishop around Easter. (Ego Richardus Vicz Virgoniensis diocesis iuro quod quilibet catholicus tenetur firmiter et precise legibus et constitucionibus in Decretis, Decretalibus, Sexto et Clementinis contentis et, quantum ad me attinet, volo obedire eisdem et si contingat me in posterum aliquid contra easdem predicare me in heresim lapsum confiteor, eciam, si quos contra eos libros habeo, circa diem Pasce ad episcopum destinare.) (p. 535, ll. 7–12)[84]

Wyche complains to the knight that the oath was not the one of their agreement, and says he will never swear it (p. 535, ll. 15–16). The knight continues to push him in the direction he may well have thought Wyche had agreed to go: 'Will you not swear the oath as delimited for yourself in your heart?' ('Non, dixit, iures tu iuramentum tibi in corde tuo limitatum?', p. 535, ll. 16–17). Again Wyche should probably have refused to continue negotiating, this time on the ground that he could not thus separate what was in his heart from what he said. But he gives way once more, although not without again spelling out his intention to the bishop: 'Lord,' he says, 'if you are willing, I will swear the oath of the agreement but only as delimited for me for swearing in the heart by my master [this] knight' ('Domine, iuramentum pacti mihi modo limitatum in corde a magistro meo hic milite ad iurandum volo iurare, si volueritis', p. 535, ll. 19–20). Hoping that the bishop would accept the oath of their agreement, he kisses the Bible as the oath is read out ('At ille: Iures tunc. Pone manum super librum. Et posui, et ipsi legerunt illud iuramentum pacti; et cum legissent, osculatus sum librum; speravi episcopum non recepturum a me nisi iuramentum pacti; sicut et pactum voluit, si veritas staret', p. 535, ll. 20–4).

Hudson has suggested that what the authorities wanted in all this was a recantation, even if only in words, that they could then use as propaganda:

> As presented by Wyche, this device was suggested by his opponents, presumably on the grounds that the recantation, albeit illusory, of so notable a Lollard would be of more propaganda use than his execution.[85]

They could certainly have used such propaganda, for during Wyche's imprisonment at least three other priests, including very probably the 'Bhyteby' Wyche refers to (p. 541, l. 29), were denounced to Skirlaw for heretical activity.[86] But if this was all the authorities wanted, they pushed their luck too far. For as soon as Wyche had sworn this first oath, they confronted him with further oaths on the Eucharist and confession (p. 535, ll. 24–5), pointing out that the first oath implied his willingness to swear these (p. 535, ll. 29–30). Wyche later quotes one of these oaths from memory; it seems far too specifically worded for him to have been able to interpret it except in the terms intended by his opponents:

> It is to be held and believed by all that the bread and wine placed on the altar in the consecrating service of the priest are transubstantiated after the words of consecration into the true body and blood of Christ. And after the words of consecration the bread and wine that were previously in that place do not remain there, but in that place is the body of Christ. [Catholice est tenendum et credendum quod panis et vinum que ponuntur in altari ministerio sacerdotis consecrando post verba consecracionis sunt transsubstanciata in verum corpus et sanguinem Christi. Et post verba consecracionis non remanet ibi panis et vinum que prius ponentur sed ibi est corpus Christi.] (pp. 537, l. 48–538, l. 5)

This time there can be no provision for any saving 'in quantum ad me pertinet'. Hardly surprisingly, Wyche refuses to swear. He is returned to prison, and although he describes further confrontations with the authorities they get no further concessions from him, at least until after he has written the present letter.

* * *

When Wyche refuses to swear the further oaths he obviously thwarts the authorities: to this extent his was the victory. Yet the authorities have also had a victory of sorts, and one which may suggest that what they wanted was not so much any recantation in word as to convince Wyche – to really convince him – that his ideas were unsoundly based. Had Wyche sworn the initial oath in the relatively unspecific terms he had suggested, he would have been able to maintain a transparent relationship between his will and his words both in his own eyes and in those of his Lollard readers. But he obscured this relationship when he accepted his opponents' more specific terms. Admittedly, his opponents had at first seemed willing to let him define the meaning of what he swore, but as soon as they confronted him with the further oaths they made it clear that they fully intended to hold him to the conventional meaning of his words. Where Wyche had hoped – or half-hoped – that they would let him speak in his own language, they have forced him to speak in theirs. Wyche now has either to accept that he has spoken thus in will as well as in word (and as a committed Lollard he can hardly do this), or he has to accept that there can be a real and exploitable disjunction between a person's will and what he actually says. He is having to confront the possibility that his Lollard assumptions need not hold.

As Smalley has pointed out, Wycliffe came to his realism after something akin to a religious conversion.[87] It is appropriate, therefore, that when Wyche moves away from this realism it is also partly in response to a religious experience. He tells his readers that after refusing to swear the further oaths he agonised for three days over 'that confounded oath' ('illo iuramento intoxicato', p. 536, l. 25). God, he believed, had deserted him (although he recognises at the time of writing that this was in order later to recall him) and the Father of the Lie was tempting him (presumably simply to go ahead and give in). Finally he called for help to the 'Father of Lights' ('ad patrem luminum', p. 536, l. 29), and his prayer was heard: '(A)ccording to his grace he (the Father of Lights) brought the agreement back to memory and the manner of the agreement with the knight just as is written above, and how I never thought and how it did not enter my mind and how I never had the will to swear that oath but the oath as delimited by the knight' ('Et ex sua gracia reduxit ad memoriam pactum et modum pacti cum milite sicut prescribitur, et quomodo numquam cogitavi nec in mentem ascendit, et nunquam habui voluntatem ad iurandum illud iuramentum, sed iuramentum limitatum a milite') (p. 536, ll. 40–4). The scene ends appropriately, with Wyche praising and thanking God in words paraphrasing Psalm 34.7–9 (pp. 536, ll. 44–537, l. 12).[88] What the knight had begun, the Father of Lights has continued: Wyche has by now moved a good way towards accepting that the disjunction between what we intend and what we actually say may be absolute. He is beginning to pay far more than lip service to the view that this is a world in which sensible appearances betray interpretation.

When Wycliffe formulated his realist position it was explicitly to counter those he termed 'Ockham et multos alios doctores signorum'.[89] He was reacting, thus, against the empiricist theory of knowledge we (perhaps wrongly) usually term nominalist.[90] It was against these doctors' theory that the universal terms by which our reason essentialises particulars are mere words, devised by ourselves, that Wycliffe evolved his own arguments about the real being of universals or archetypes. And it was against their insistence on a possible disjunction between sensible and intellectual being that he evolved his arguments concerning the continuity between the two. To be sure, Wycliffe was hardly dealing with the same opponents as Wyche was. But Wyche's opponents did represent an institutional church whose members, for Wycliffe as well as his followers, suffered from the same kind of temporally obsessed thinking as Wycliffe's doctors. If these doctors were wedded to their signs, so too were the members of this church:

> For al þo holynesse þat þei do to þe Chirche her moder myght þei do wiþoute suche weddynge to hor sygnes; ffor so did Crist and his apostels, lyvynge wiþ þo puple. And þerfore fle ypocrisye, and be scolere of treuthe; and ouþer seme þat þou art, or be þat þou semes.[91]

If the doctors could not raise their minds above the temporal, nor could these members:

> [þ]e fende wiþ hise membris what wiþ ypocrisie, þat is feyned hoolines, what wiþ blynd pite, þat regneþ in þe seculeris, he haþ encombrid Cristis chirche wiþ miche worldli muk & ouerladde oure modir wiþ temporal possessioun þat sche mai not rise to heuenli contemplacioun.[92]

Wyche's discourse is being reabsorbed into a descendant of the very discourse Wycliffe had originally worked against.

Wyche would probably have resisted the idea that his assumptions had begun to approach those of his opponents. He would probably have claimed that where these opponents looked only to appearances, he sought essentials: what God meant in the Bible rather than its words on the page, what he himself meant by his oath rather than how its words might sound. But no less than his opponents he now lacks rational access to these essentials. And without this access he is even less able than his opponents to pronounce on the significance of appearances here, for as a Lollard he no longer has the accumulated authority of the institutional church to fall back on.[93] Early in the proceedings Wyche was asked who will judge whether a human law accords with the Law of God. He answered with ostensible confidence that the Law of God will (p. 533, ll. 21–2). On a later occasion the chancellor asks him who will judge whether obeying canon law sometimes means infringing the Law of God. Wyche's reply seems less confident;

it is certainly less civil: 'God knows' ('Deus scit'), he says (p. 534, l. 13), in the expletive that became his cognomen, 'Godwote'.[94] His words here may still have borne the same implication as his earlier answer. They may also suggest an awareness that he is losing his hold on his Lollardy. Had they come after his dealings with the knight they would almost certainly have suggested this.

Wyche's opponents seem almost to have contrived their later action in order to bring home to him how little able we are to interpret temporal appearances. In a confrontation that took place some weeks after he swore 'illud iniquum iuramentum' (p. 529, l. 27), Wyche again tries to explain to the bishop what he meant by it. He reiterates how he had agreed to swear the oath in his heart as delimited by the knight and how this oath specified that he was held to obey the law of God insofar as it concerned him: 'Pro certo, dixi, nunquam intendebam nec unquam cogitavi illud iuramentum sed iuramentum pacti limitatum in corde meo ab isto reverendo milite; quod fuit istud quod teneor obedire legi Dei in quantum ad me pertinet' (p. 539, ll. 28–31). He then looks to the knight for confirmation: 'Non dixistis: Iures tu iuramentum in corde tuo limitatum?' But far from supporting Wyche, the knight denies ever having said this, 'Istud miles negavit' (p. 539, ll. 34–5). He even gets angry when Wyche observes that it is a great sin for a man to deal treacherously with his brother: 'Are you saying that I have dealt treacherously with you? ('Dicis tu, dixit, quod ego tractavi tecum in dolo?', p. 539, l. 45). If ever there was a specialist in potentially misleading appearances, this knight must have seemed that specialist to Wyche. Hardly surprisingly, Wyche's response sounds more like that of someone from the uncertain world of a *Piers Plowman*, say, than of the writer of a Lollard text: 'I don't say so, as I don't know your heart' ('Non sic dico, dixi, quia nescio cor vestrum', p. 539, l. 46).[95] Like the knights who approved of Wyche's views on the Eucharist, this one may have been well-disposed towards him. He may equally well have always been against him. He may have been initially well-disposed and then altered his position. He may even have been part of a cunning plot – possibly a diabolically cunning one – calculated to deprive Wyche of his Lollard premises. Wyche leaves us guessing: the main effect of this part of his narrative is to underscore how bewildering appearances can be.

When assessing the nature of Wyche's discourse, we should not simply locate his letter at the particularising end of the Lollard continuum, therefore. We should also recognise that its author has been losing his ability to view essential being along this continuum. Pressures exerted by the opposition and especially those exerted by the knight have meant that his Lollard discourse has begun to lose its distinctive identity. Granted, on particular tenets Wyche remains determinedly Lollard and, as we shall see, he will finally die for his beliefs. Despite his probable disillusionment with the present knight, he will also maintain contacts with the knightly class. In a future letter he will even deploy a rhetoric of the kind I have been associating with Lollard discourse at its more central moments. But in the story of this discourse, his present letter can only spell the beginning of the end.

* * *

Some Lollards, when they found themselves making the kind of compromises Wyche was making, would probably have admitted their changed way of thinking and capitulated.[96] Not so Wyche. Instead, he became one of the most long-lived and probably one of the most influential of the fifteenth-century Lollards.[97] He remained in prison for a time after he wrote his letter, but between October 1404 and March 1406 he was brought by writ of *corpus cum causa* into the chancery court at Westminster, where he submitted and was released.[98] The terms on which he submitted leave little room for ambiguity: they concern the Eucharist, obedience to the Decretum, Decretals, Sext and Clementines, unlicensed preaching and the legitimacy of fraternal begging (despite the chancellor's mutterings, Wyche's original answers on confession seem to have been accepted as satisfactory).[99] Nevertheless, on 8 September 1410, the very day on which Sir John Oldcastle, that most notorious member of the gentry ever to be associated with the Lollards, wrote to King Wenceslas' favourite courtier, Voksa of Valdštejn (or in his absence to Zdislav of Zviřetice), Wyche wrote to Hus.[100] His letter deploys an essentialising rhetoric of the kind I have been associating with Lollard discourse at its more central moments.[101] In October 1417 Wyche and a certain William Broune were being questioned at Westminster about money belonging to Oldcastle.[102] We do not know what the result of this questioning was. Two years later, however, Wyche was brought before the convocation of Canterbury as having long been under vehement suspicion of errors and heresies.[103] Pending further investigation he was remanded to the Fleet prison, from which he was nevertheless released in July 1420.[104] He then served for many years as a vicar in Kent and Essex.[105] In 1440 he was convicted as a relapsed heretic before the bishop of London, and on 17 June he and his servant Roger Norman were burned on Tower Hill.[106]

Wyche seems to have been able to conduct his lengthy career as a Lollard partly thanks to the very compromises we have seen him learning to make. With his burning, however, we reach another moment in the story of Lollard discourse, one very close to the end. As Wyche's various recantations show, he had subscribed during his career to the characteristically Lollard views that images and the Cross should not be worshipped and that pilgrimages to Rome or Jerusalem were no more useful than staying at home.[107] He had also preached against offerings to images.[108] But after his death 'þe peple in greet multitude' held him a saint, erecting a cross and offering silver and waxen images at the place where he was burned.[109] It was only the intervention of the authorities that prevented them from turning the place into a site of pilgrimage.[110] Lollard discourse has here become almost entirely indistinguishable from some of the discourses it had once opposed.

Yet Wyche's letter does not only point towards this end. It also points to new beginnings. Wyche never specifies exactly why he originally wrote the letter; he seems to have thought he was using it primarily to provide the community he has just left with information about his questioning.[111] But he has also evidently used it to help influence the way in which members of this community would interpret his own conduct. As we have seen, he could to some extent rely on their understanding what he meant when he seemed to speak against Lollard principles concerning confession. But his relief when the Father of Lights confirmed that he had not willed the oath of allegiance, suggests that even Wyche himself had trouble interpreting what he intended when he actually swore this oath. Not only has the pressure brought to bear on him by his opponents caused him to lose any confident access he might once have had to the wills of persons around him; it has also caused him to lose any confident access he might have had to his own will. It is surely for such reasons that he has done in his letter something Lollard authors usually saw little need for. He has attempted to reach and expose to scrutiny what the Middle Ages would have termed his 'inner man'.[112]

Because Wyche's letter never reached the English Reformers it never directly influenced later Protestant writing (although as already noted it may have had some indirect influence via Thorpe's *Testimony*).[113] But in its anxious exposure of Wyche's inner man it looks towards certain much later forms of English Protestant discourse. Stephen Greenblatt has characterised these forms while also commenting on why they are rare among the early Protestants:

> [W]e associate Protestantism with . . . the alternately anguished and joyful self-reflection of Bunyan's *Grace Abounding* [1666] or Fox's *Journal* [1694]. But significantly, among the early Protestants we find almost no formal autobiography and remarkably little private, personal testimony. The kind of self-consciousness voiced in these forms, the sense of being set apart from the world and of taking a stance toward it, the endless, daily discursiveness of later generations, is only in the process of being shaped, while the traditional methodology for the examination of conscience and the ritual forgiveness of sin by virtue of the Church's power of the keys have been bitterly renounced.[114]

Greenblatt does acknowledge that, exceptionally, some early Protestants produced such forms, although he points only to Martin Luther and the Marian martyr John Bradford as having done so.[115] Even these examples belong to the Renaissance rather than the Middle Ages, however, and only one is from England. Had Greenblatt known Wyche's letter it would have provided him with an earlier – very likely the earliest – example of such writing in England. Here, as so often in their 'premature reformation', the Lollards have fully anticipated later developments.[116]

Notes

[1] See the articles collected in Hudson, *LB*, and the comprehensive discussion in Hudson, *PR*.

[2] In, for example, H. Hargreaves, 'Wyclif's Prose', *Essays and Studies*, new ser. 19 (1966), pp. 1–17; P.A. Knapp, *The Style of John Wyclif's English Sermons* (The Hague and Paris, 1977); J.M. Mueller, *The Native Tongue and the Word: Developments in English Prose Style, 1380–1580* (Chicago, 1984), pp. 40–55; C. von Nolcken, 'A "Certain Sameness" and Our Response to It in English Wycliffite Texts', in

R.G. Newhauser and J.A. Alford (eds), *Literature and Religion in the Later Middle Ages. Philological Studies in Honor of Siegfried Wenzel*, Medieval & Renaissance Texts & Studies (Binghamton, NY, 1995), pp. 191–208. For discussions of Wycliffe's written style see, for example, W. Mallard, 'Clarity and Dilemma – the *Forty Sermons* of John Wyclif', in G.H. Shriver (ed.), *Contemporary Reflections on the Medieval Christian Tradition: Essays in Honor of Ray C. Petry* (Durham, NC, 1974), pp. 19–38; P. Auksi, 'Wyclif's Sermons and the Plain Style', *Archiv für Reformationsgeschichte*, 66 (1975), pp. 5–23.

³ P.A. Knapp, *Chaucer and the Social Contest* (New York and London, 1990).

⁴ *Ibid.* See esp. pp. 63–76, 'Coming to Terms with Wyclif'.

⁵ A new generation of scholars is also beginning to write about this discourse; I am indebted to Janet Harris and Fiona Somerset for showing me their unpublished work (see below, n. 78 and 81). See also H. Barr, *Signes and Sothe: Language in the Piers Plowman Tradition* (Cambridge, 1994), which I read only after completing this paper.

⁶ All references to this letter will be by page and line to F.D. Matthew (ed.), 'The Trial of Richard Wyche', *EHR*, 5 (1890), pp. 530–44; translations from the Latin are my own. On the letter's date and the circumstances surrounding its composition see M.G. Snape, 'Some Evidence of Lollard Activity in the Diocese of Durham in the Early Fifteenth Century', *Archaeologia Æliana*, 4th ser. 39 (1961), pp. 355–61; C. Kightly, 'The Early Lollards: A Survey of Popular Lollard Activity in England, 1382–1428', D. Phil. thesis (University of York, 1975), pp. 12–21.

⁷ For a fuller working-out of the argument in the following four paragraphs as well as references for the forms quoted in them see von Nolcken, 'A "Certain Sameness"'.

⁸ Matthew, *EWW*, p. xlviii (the 1880 and 1902 editions are here the same); for discussion of similarities of diction in the Lollards' texts see Hudson, *LB*, pp. 165–80; G. Cigman, '*Luceat Lux Vestra*: The Lollard Preacher as Truth and Light', *RES*, new ser. 40 (1989), pp. 485–9.

⁹ *Canterbury Tales* II (Bl), ll. 1173, 1179–83 in *The Riverside Chaucer*, ed. L.D. Benson *et al.*, 3rd edn (Boston, MA., 1987); for further such references see Hudson, *LB*, pp. 166–8.

¹⁰ As by Henry Knighton and Thomas Walsingham, cited by Hudson, *PR*, p. 145 and n. 170; on the Lollards' appearance see further Hudson, *PR*, pp. 144–7. On their opposition to the symbolic religious habits which they associated mainly with the mendicants see, for example, R.D. Kendall, *The Drama of Dissent: The Radical Poetics of Nonconformity, 1380–1590* (Chapel Hill, NC, 1986), p. 40.

¹¹ See, for example, the comments in the sermons in Oxford Bodleian Library MS Bodley 649 quoted by Hudson, *PR*, p. 146: 'Magnam sanctitatem ista secta ostendit exterius, abstinent multis in aperto, incedunt in simplici apparatu, loquntur pauperime et pallide respiciunt'; and Worcester Cathedral Library Ms. F. 10 quoted by G.R. Owst, *Literature and Pulpit in Medieval England: A Neglected Chapter in the History of English Letters and of the English People*, 2nd edn (Oxford, 1961), p. 374: 'For we se now so miche folk, and specialiche thes lollardes, thay go barfot, thei go openhed, ȝe, thei wassche sothylike hir clothes withowtyn with teres of hir eȝen', and further, Aston, *LR*, p. 6 and n. 15.

¹² *HK*, p. 302; translation my own.

¹³ On the importance of a collective consciousness in the history of women's autobiography, for example, see S.S. Friedman, 'Women's Autobiographical Selves: Theory and Practice', in S. Benstock (ed.), *The Private Self: Theory and Practice of Women's Autobiographical Writings* (Chapel Hill, NC, and London, 1988), esp. pp. 38–44.

¹⁴ On this point see, for example, G. Leff, *Heresy in the Later Middle Ages*, 2 vols (Manchester and New York, 1967), ii, pp. 500–3; Mallard, 'Clarity and dilemma', pp. 22–4.

¹⁵ On Wycliffe's realism see further Leff, *Heresy*, ii, pp. 500–10 and, for example, J.A. Robson, *Wyclif and the Oxford Schools: The Relation of the 'Summa de Ente' to Scholastic Debates at Oxford in the Later Fourteenth Century* (Cambridge, 1961), pp. 141–95; A. Kenny, *Wyclif* (Oxford and New York, 1985), pp. 1–30; 'The Realism of the *De Universalibus*', in A. Kenny (ed.), *Wyclif in his Times* (Oxford, 1986), pp. 17–29; J.I. Catto, 'Wyclif and Wycliffism at Oxford 1356–1430', in J.I. Catto and R. Evans (eds), *The History of the University of Oxford*, ii (Oxford, 1992), pp. 190–3.

¹⁶ Wycliffe argues the Bible as the ground of Truth throughout his *De Veritate Sacrae Scripturae* (c. 1377–78), ed. R. Buddensieg, 3 vols (WS, London, 1905–7). He explicitly notes that Scripture

ought to provide the model for all human speech at, for example, I, p. 205. On how the Wycliffites viewed scriptural language see, for example, M. Hurley, '"Scriptura Sola": Wyclif and his Critics', *Traditio*, 16 (1960), p. 295; A.J. Minnis, '"Authorial Intention" and "Literal Sense" in the Exegetical Theories of Richard Fitzralph and John Wyclif: An Essay in the Medieval History of Biblical Hermeneutics', *Proceedings of the Royal Irish Academy*, 75, section C, no. 1 (1975), pp. 27–30; D.L. Jeffrey, 'Chaucer and Wyclif: Biblical Hermeneutic and Literary Theory in the XIVth Century', in D.L. Jeffrey (ed.) *Chaucer and scriptural tradition*, Ottawa (1984), pp. 115–23, esp. p. 122; G.R. Evans, *The Language and Logic of the Bible: The Road to Reformation* (Cambridge, 1985), pp. 119–20; R. Copeland, 'Rhetoric and the Politics of the Literal Sense in Medieval Literary Theory: Aquinas, Wyclif, and the Lollards', in P. Boitani and A. Torti (eds), *Interpretation: Medieval and Modern. The J.A.W. Bennett Memorial Lectures, Eighth Ser., Perugia, 1992* (Cambridge, 1993), pp. 14–23. On Wycliffe's biblicism see, for example, Robson, *Wyclif and the Oxford Schools*, pp. 163–4; B. Smalley, 'The Bible and Eternity: John Wyclif's Dilemma', *Journal of the Warburg and Courtauld Institutes*, 27 (1964), pp. 73–89; Leff, *Heresy*, ii, pp. 511–16; Kenny, *Wyclif*, pp. 56–67; Catto, 'Wyclif and Wycliffism', pp. 195–8, 209.

[17] On the model see M. Wilks, '*Reformatio Regni*: Wyclif and Hus as Leaders of Religious Protest Movements', *SCH*, 9 (1972), p. 119; C. von Nolcken, 'Another Kind of Saint: A Lollard Perception of John Wyclif', in A. Hudson and M. Wilks (eds), *From Ockham to Wyclif*, *SCH*, subsidia 5 (Oxford, 1987), p. 436 and n. 48. For the qualities the Lollards associated with Christ – poverty, meekness, simplicity and patience – see William Thorpe's *Testimony* in *Two Wycliffite Texts: The Sermon of William Taylor, 1406; The Testimony of William Thorpe, 1407*, ed. A. Hudson (EETS 301, 1993), p. 71, l. 1534. All references to the *Testimony* will be to this edition by page and line.

[18] See, for example, John Wyclif, *De Ecclesia*, ed. J. Loserth (WS, London, 1886), pp. 5, ll. 24–7, 77, ll. 9–13; *Opus Evangelicum*, ed. J. Loserth, 2 vols (WS, London, 1895–6), II, p. 216, ll. 5–10.

[19] Hudson & Gradon, *EWS*, II, p. 2, ll. 39–42.

[20] *Ibid.*, p. 4, ll. 79–84.

[21] *De Officio Pastorali* (Matthew, *EWW*, p. 422).

[22] Thorpe, *Testimony*, p. 44, ll. 669–78. On the words-work-will continuum see J.A. Burrow, 'Words, Works and Will: Theme and Structure in *Piers Plowman*', in S.S. Hussey (ed.), *Piers Plowman: Critical Approaches* (London, 1969), pp. 111–24.

[23] As translated by Foxe, *A&M*, III, p. 189.

[24] As Talbert points out, 'A Lollard Chronicle of the Papacy' is 'obviously meant to support by historical examples the doctrine that all jurisdiction depends upon righteousness' (E.W. Talbert (ed.), 'A Lollard Chronicle of the Papacy', *Journal of English and Germanic Philology*, 41 (1942), p. 163). All references to this work are to Talbert's printing by page and line.

[25] Wyche and Thorpe were both active in the north of England at much the same time (for Thorpe's activity there see Thorpe, *Testimony*, p. 29, ll. 180–5), and they may have known each other. Kightly has suggested that Wyche's 'domini Wilhelmi Corpp' (p. 543, l. 41) may be a scribally corrupt form of Thorpe ('Early Lollards', pp. 4, 17). See further Hudson, *Two Wycliffite Texts*, pp. lvii–lix.

[26] As Aston has remarked, '[I]t becomes clear that the heretics continued to survive and to make recruits because they reflected developments which were widespread and which were taking place in the whole of society, not merely in unorthodox circles' (*LR*, p. 213).

[27] As translated by Foxe, *A&M*, iii, p. 109; *Snappe's Formulary and Other Records*, ed. H.E. Salter (Oxford, 1924), p. 134.

[28] For these proceedings see Tanner, *HT*, *passim*. For accounts of the procedure in trials, *Reg. Chichele*, I, pp. cxxix–cxxxvii; Thomson, *LL*, pp. 220–36.

[29] See the wording of the standard recantation as described by Tanner in *HT*, p. 6, and as exemplified by Matilda Fletcher (*ibid.*, p. 132); see also the terms of the oath Thorpe refuses to swear (*Testimony*, pp. 34–5, ll. 353–60). For accounts of the fear this could lead to see J. Fines, 'Studies in the Lollard Heresy. Being an Examination of the Evidence from the Dioceses of Norwich, Lincoln, Coventry and Lichfield, and Ely, during the period 1430–1530', D. Phil. thesis (University of Sheffield, 1964), pp. 175–7; Hudson, *PR*, pp. 161–3.

[30] As pointed out by C.E. Welch, 'Three Sussex Heresy Trials', *Sussex Archaeological Collections*, 95 (1957), p. 61.

[31] As illustrated by Thorpe's *Testimony*. Thorpe seems to have been arrested together with another 'ȝonge man' from whom Arundel has confiscated a roll; the young man is not present when Arundel questions Thorpe about the contents of this roll (*Testimony*, p. 76, ll. 1697–1704). Arundel later plays on Thorpe's ignorance by telling him the young man has submitted (pp. 90–1, ll. 2152–72).

[32] On the later history of Lollardy see Hudson, *PR*, pp. 446–507. On its links with the Reformation see A.G. Dickens, *The English Reformation*, 2nd edn (London, 1989), pp. 49–60; *idem*, *Lollards and Protestants in the Diocese of York 1509–1558*, 2nd edn (London, 1982), pp. 1–15. See further J.F. Davis, *Heresy and Reformation in the South East of England 1520–1559* (London, 1983) on how by the mid-sixteenth century 'Lollardy had proved a reservoir that flowed into many channels' (p. 149).

[33] On similarities between texts and communities widely separated in time and space see Hudson, *PR*, pp. 10–11.

[34] On this point see Thomson, *LL*, esp. pp. 239–50. Kendall has also described Lollardy's 'subsidence towards the idiosyncratic and the ill-defined', though he also comments on the 'unity behind its diversity' (*Drama of Dissent*, p. 15).

[35] Aston, *LR*, pp. 91–2. Hudson has suggested that these variations represent the result of discussion and conversations among the Lollards (*PR*, p. 193).

[36] On this link between the two works see J. Fines, 'William Thorpe: An Early Lollard', *History Today*, 18 (1968), p. 496.

[37] On the transmission of the *Testimony* see Hudson, *Two Wycliffite Texts*, pp. xxvi–xxxvii, and pp. xli–xlv on the probability that it was originally in English.

[38] Kightly suggests that 'Bynkfeld' is Henry Bynkefelde (or Bingfield), a prominent citizen of Newcastle at this time, or some member of his family ('Early Lollards', p. 17 and n. 2). Wyche seems to distinguish between those who will be able to read the letter – 'Bhytebi', 'magistro meo de Balknolle', and 'Bynkfeld' (p. 541, l. 29) – and those its main recipient should merely greet – 'Johanni Maya cum uxore sua' (p. 541, l. 30), 'Laudens' and 'Gre[n]e' and his wife (p. 543, l. 20), his addressee's wife and mother-in-law (p. 543, ll. 23–4). It is perhaps more likely that Wyche is distinguishing between those who can and cannot read the vernacular than between those who can and cannot read Latin.

[39] Where Foxe rehearses the whole of Thorpe's *Testimony*, for example (*A&M*, iii, pp. 249–85), all he knows about Wyche are events accompanying his death (*ibid.*, pp. 702–3). He does also include a translation of the letter Wyche wrote to John Hus in 1410 (*ibid.*, pp. 506–7), but he represents this as coming from one 'Ricus Wichewitze, priest unworthy' (p. 507) whom he does not seem to associate with Wyche. On this letter see below, n. 100.

[40] Prague University Library Ms. III. G. 11, ff. 89ᵛ–99ᵛ. On the manuscript, see J. Truhlář, *Catalogus Codicum manu scriptorum latinorum qui in C.R. Bibliotheca Publica atque Universitatis Pragensis asservantur*, 2 vols (Prague, 1905-6), I, pp. 213–15; A. Hudson, 'William Taylor's 1406 Sermon: A Postscript', *Medium Ævum*, 64 (1995), pp. 100–6.

[41] *Ibid.*; for discussion of Taylor and the text of his sermon in English see Hudson, *Two Wycliffite Texts*, pp. xi–xxvi, ll. 1–23.

[42] Among the errors listed against Wycliffe in 1382 was the statement that the friars were obliged to earn their living by the work of their hands and not to beg (*Fasc. Ziz.*, p. 282); when William Rymington argued sometime after the summer of 1381 that it is lawful for friars to beg and meritorious to give liberally to them, Wycliffe replied that the approval of the Roman court does not make friars' begging lawful, *Opera Minora*, ed. J. Loserth (WS, London, 1913), pp. 222–3.

[43] William Sawtrey was burned especially for his views on the Eucharist (*Fasc. Ziz.*, pp. 408–11); on Sawtrey see P. McNiven, *Heresy and Politics in the Reign of Henry IV: The Burning of John Badby* (Woodbridge, 1987), pp. 79–92. In the same year Purvey revoked, among others, views on the Eucharist, confession, and the duty to preach even without licence (*Fasc. Ziz.*, pp. 400–7).

[44] For Wycliffite views concerning oral confession and absolution see Hudson, *PR*, pp. 294–301, and below, n. 79.

[45] Wyche does not reproduce his quotations from these authorities, so we cannot associate his choice of passages with any particular source. He could have got more than enough such material from the Wycliffite *Floretum/Rosarium* under *Predicare/Predicacio*. For this entry in the Middle English translation of the latter see *The Middle English Translation of the 'Rosarium Theologie'*, ed. C. von Nolcken, Middle English Texts 10 (Heidelberg, 1979), pp. 85–92.

[46] For their criteria see, for example, the lists of tenets the authorities drew up against Wycliffe himself (*Fasc. Ziz.*, pp. 245–57, 110, 277–82), or the lists of questions they put to suspects (for two such lists see Hudson, *LB*, pp. 133–5). Such lists are sometimes refuted in Lollard tracts: see especially 'On the Twenty-Five Articles' (Arnold, *SEW*, iii, pp. 454–96); 'Sixteen Points on which the Bishops accuse Lollards' (Hudson, *Selections*, pp. 19–24, 145–50).

[47] For another attempt to isolate criteria that might help define a work as Lollard, see Cigman, '*Luceat Lux Vestra*', who focuses on such features as the nuances of such polarities as that between *few* and *many*, or *true* and *false* (p. 483).

[48] See, for example, *De Apostasia*, ed. M.H. Dziewicki (WS, London, 1889), pp. 119–31, where Wycliffe tries to define the essence of the sacrament; on Wycliffe's difficulties on this point see M. Keen, 'Wyclif, the Bible, and Transubstantiation', in A. Kenny (ed.), *Wyclif in his Times* (Oxford, 1986), pp. 1–16, at 10. For Wycliffe's views in general see, for example, Leff, *Heresy*, ii, pp. 549–57; Kenny, *Wyclif*, pp. 80–90; H. Phillips, 'John Wyclif and the Optics of the Eucharist', in Hudson and Wilks (eds), *From Ockham to Wyclif*, pp. 245–58; Hudson, *PR*, pp. 281–4; M. Rubin, *Corpus Christi: The Eucharist in Late Medieval Culture* (Cambridge, 1991), pp. 324–7.

[49] Wyche's wording is of a kind frequently used by Lollards working in the vernacular: see, for example, the two texts Knighton records as Wycliffe's confessions on the Eucharist (Hudson, *Selections*, p. 17, ll. 2–3, 20–2); 'The Song of Moses' (Arnold, *SEW*, iii, p. 36, l. 28); 'þe Pater Noster' (*SEW*, iii, p. 106, l. 17); Hudson & Gradon, *EWS*, i, pp. 675–7, II, p. 375, l. 261; Thorpe, *Testimony*, p. 31, l. 236. As Wycliffe notes (*De Apostasia*, p. 84, i. 19–35), *forma* can be taken for the substantial or the accidental form. That the Lollards' use of *forma* without further specification could confuse, especially given how imprecise such terminology was in English by contrast with Latin, is indicated by its use also by those determined to separate themselves from the Lollards. Margery Kempe, for example, who when accused of being a Lollard unambiguously clears herself of not believing in transubstantiation (*The Book of Margery Kempe*, ed. S.B. Meech and H.E. Allen (EETS 212, 1940), p. 115, ll. 10–18), elsewhere longs to receive communion 'wher owyr mercyful Lord Crist Ihesu fyrst sacryd hys precyows body in þe forme of bred & ȝaf it to hys discipulys' (*Book*, p. 72, ll. 16–18) and weeps because of the love she feels for the sacrament 'whech sche stedfastly beleuyd was very God and Man in þe forme of breed' (*Book*, p. 138, ll. 34–5). Thomas Hoccleve also seems to have missed the point in his comment about John Badby (as quoted by Rubin, *Corpus Christi*, pp. 328–9). On the differences between the vernacular and Latin in respect to such terms see Margaret Aston, 'Wycliffe and the Vernacular', in Aston, *FF*, pp. 27–72, esp. pp. 43–9. For an anti-Lollard preacher who was not confused in this way see H.L. Spencer, *English Preaching in the Late Middle Ages* (Oxford, 1993), p. 188. It is for such reasons that the chancellor tries to pin Wyche down further after he has made this formulation, 'An est ibi panis materialis vel non?' (p. 532, l. 20).

[50] When Rymington claimed that by God's omnipotence the accidents remain in the sacrament without substance, for example, Wycliffe replied that Augustine said an accident cannot exist without a subject, and that we can say the bread is supernaturally changed into Christ's body but naturally remains bread (*Opera Minora*, pp. 212–14).

[51] Thomas Netter of Walden also associates the Eucharist with Moses' rod (*Doctrinale Antiquitatum Fidei Catholicae Ecclesiae*, ed. B. Blanciotti, 3 vols (Venice, 1757–9; repr. Farnborough, 1967), ii, cols. 308–9); that this analogy was standard is indicated by its use in a version of the lections for the octave of Corpus Christi that became incorporated in Jacobus de Voragine's *Golden Legend*: see further Margaret Aston, 'Corpus Christi and Corpus Regni: Heresy and the Peasants' Revolt', *P&P*, 143 (1994), p. 46.

[52] That he has no Bible with him is made clear by his request for biblical material at the end of his letter (p. 543, ll. 28–40) and by his asking his opponents for a Bible when they want him to write

down what he believes on the Eucharist (p. 538, ll. 16–17). Archbishop Arundel will later refuse to let Thorpe have a Psalter he had confiscated from him in Canterbury on the ground that Thorpe will select verses from it to use against the authorities (*Testimony*, p. 51, ll. 891–5).

[53] Wyche will maintain such an attitude towards the Bible: when he submits one of his revocations later in his career (see further below, p. 143), he will ask that the church reject anything he says that is not grounded in scripture (*Fasc. Ziz.*, p. 370).

[54] See for example Wyclif, *De Civili Dominio*, ed. R.L. Poole and J. Loserth, 4 vols (WS, London, 1885–1904), i, pp. 118–24; *De Veritate Sacrae Scripturae*, i, p. 405, ll. 16–18. There are also many statements to this effect in the Lollards' texts: see, for example, Hudson & Gradon, *EWS*, i, pp. 357–8, ll. 65–9; 'þe Pater Noster' (Arnold, *SEW*, III, p. 112, ll. 25–7); 'How Men Ought to Obey Prelates' (Matthew, *EWW*, pp. 37, l. 22–38, l. 2), 'Of Confession' (*ibid.*, p. 329, ll. 17–21). On Wycliffe's attitude towards the interpretative traditions of the church see Hurley, '"Scriptura Sola"'; H.A. Oberman, *The Harvest of Medieval Theology: Gabriel Biel and Late Medieval Nominalism*, 3rd edn (Durham, NC, 1983), pp. 371–8.

[55] See, for example, Wyclif, *De Benedicta Incarnatione*, ed. E. Harris (WS, London, 1886), p. 73, ll. 8–10, referred to by Smalley, 'Bible and Eternity', p. 83; Wyclif, *Opus Evangelicum*, ii, p. 36, ll. 15–27.

[56] On Wycliffe's reading the Bible in this way see Minnis, '"Authorial Intention"', pp. 11–27; A. Hudson, 'Biblical Exegesis in Wycliffite Writings', in *John Wyclif e la tradizione degli studi biblici in Inghilterra* (Genoa, 1987), pp. 71–5; Copeland, 'Rhetoric', pp. 14–17. Wycliffe had reached this position after arguing in about 1372–4 with the Carmelite, John Kenningham, over what it meant to say that each word of the Bible was absolutely and eternally true. For his exchanges with Kenningham see *Fasc. Ziz.*, pp. 453–76, and further Robson, *Wyclif and the Oxford Schools*, pp. 161–70; Smalley, 'Bible and Eternity', pp. 86–7.

[57] There is no *enim* in modern copies of the Vulgate at 1 Cor. 11.24, and its equivalent does not appear in either version of the Wycliffite Bible (Forshall & Madden, *HB*, IV, p. 359). It does appear in the words of consecration in early copies of the Sarum missal (*The Sarum Missal edited from three early manuscripts*, ed. J.W. Legg (Oxford, 1916), p. 222), however, and in such quotations of these words as that from Hugh Ripelin of Strassburg's *Compendium Theologicae Veritatis* in the Lollard *Rosarium Theologie* (*Middle English Rosarium*, p. 71, ll. 23–4).

[58] On the 'living non-literate textuality' discernible among various heretical groups, including the Lollards, see R.N. Swanton, 'Literacy, heresy, history and orthodoxy', in Biller and Hudson (eds), *Heresy and Literacy*, pp. 285–6.

[59] For Wyche's diocese, see *Fasc. Ziz.*, p. 501.

[60] The manuscript containing Wyche's letter also contains a brief piece on the Eucharist by someone writing while Wycliffe was still active in Oxford. W.R. Thomson has suggested that this is a production by an amanuensis of Wycliffe's, 'carefully recording yet another of his master's peremptory challenges to his mendicant opponents, probably still in 1381 – though a case for late 1380 would not be out of court' (*The Latin Writings of John Wyclyf: An Annotated Catalog*, Pontifical Institute of Mediaeval Studies, subsidia mediaevalia 14 (Toronto, 1983), p. 74). This work is included by J. Loserth in his edition of Wycliffe's *De Eucharistia* (WS, London, 1892), pp. 347–8. In its other two manuscripts this piece is attributed (obviously wrongly) to Wycliffe, though in the *contenta* of the present manuscript the ascription 'Rychardo Vicz' is written over an erasure of 'Joh. Wycleph' (Thomson (ed.), *Latin Writings*, pp. 73–4). Given that Wycliffe left Oxford in 1382, and Wyche will still be alive in 1440, we should almost certainly reject this ascription. Yet it remains just possible that Wyche heard Wycliffe lecture in the early 1380s, for students regularly started attending Oxford at fifteen (H.B. Workman, *John Wyclif: A Study of the English Medieval Church*, 2 vols (Oxford, 1926), i, p. 52) and in his present letter Wyche remarks that he has held his views on the Eucharist since his youth (p. 539, ll. 1–4). Whether or not Wyche encountered Wycliffe, however, as M. Lambert has put it, 'he argued so skilfully with the assessors of the bishop of Durham, and was so familiar with Wycliffe's views that he must have had an academic background' (*Medieval Heresy: Popular Movements from the Gregorian Reform to the Reformation*, 2nd edn (Oxford, 1992), p. 246); on Wyche's possible academic connections, see further no. 61.

61 Snape considers this Jacobus was probably a priest called James Nottingham who was cited to appear before Bishop Skirlaw on 23 February 1403; when he failed to appear he was excommunicated and cited to appear on 14 March; when he again failed to appear he was cited to appear on 6 April ('Some Evidence', pp. 356–7). But Hudson suggests that Jacobus was William James, a Fellow of Merton College (*PR*, p. 90); work being done by Maureen Jurkowski on the visits of Merton Fellows to the College manors strengthens this possibility. On what was meant by preaching the Word see Spencer, *English Preaching*, pp. 134–49; on the Poor Priests and how they seem to have conducted themselves see G. Lechler, tr. P. Lorimer, *John Wycliffe and his English Precursors* (London, 1884), pp. 189–201; H.L. Cannon, 'The Poor Priests: A Study in the Rise of English Lollardry', *Annual Report of the American Historical Association*, 1, (1899), pp. 451–82; Workman, *John Wyclif*, ii, pp. 201–5; Thomson, *Latin Writings*, p. 281.

62 For a Lollard call to men of the church to sell their fat horses see 'On the Twenty-Five Articles' (Arnold, *SEW*, iii, pp. 494–5); for one directing them not to have possessions and ride but to go on their feet as Christ and the apostles did see Aston, *LR*, p. 23 and n. 88. As Hudson points out, the Lollards were satirised for their expensive clothes in two sets of answers to the same questions; she suggests that there must have been some tale about this circulating in academic or fraternal circles (*PR*, pp. 146–7). G.R. Owst refers to a sermon in BL, MS. Harley 2276 which accuses the Lollards of becoming proud as soon as any worldly wealth comes to them (*Preaching in Medieval England: An Introduction to Sermon Manuscripts of the Period c. 1350–1450* (Cambridge, 1926; reissued New York, 1965), pp. 139–40).

63 Hudson also notes that Wyche is here placing himself in the apostolic tradition of persecution (*PR*, p. 222). On the importance of St Paul to later religious autobiographers like Bunyan see P. Delany, *British Autobiography in the Seventeenth Century* (London and New York, 1969), pp. 29–31.

64 E.W. Talbert and S.H. Thomson, 'Wyclyf and his Followers', in J.B. Severs (ed.), *A Manual of the Writings in Middle English 1050–1500*, vol. ii (Hamden, Conn., 1970), pp. 517–33, provides a useful guide to Wycliffe's and the Lollards' writings, supplemented by Hudson, *LB*, pp. 1–12, 249–52.

65 See further above, notes 25 and 38.

66 The appellation 'Father of the Lie' ('pater mendacii') is from John 8.44, 'mendax est, et pater eius', translated in the Wycliffite Bible (Forshall & Madden, *HB*, IV, p. 261) as 'he is a lyiere, and fadir of it' (Early Version); 'he is a liere, and fadir of it' (Later Version); it is an appellation favoured by Wycliffe in, for example, *De Apostasia*, pp. 27, l. 10, 67, l. 3, 121, l. 12; see also *Opus Evangelicum*, ii, p. 21, ll. 19–20. The appellation 'Father of Lights' is from James 1.17, 'a Patre luminum' translated (*HB*, IV, p. 596) 'the fadir of liȝtis' (Early Version); 'the fadir of liȝtis' (Later Version); see further *Middle English Dictionary*, eds H. Kurath, S.M. Kuhn *et al.* (Ann Arbor, MI., 1952–), *s.v.* 'light' n., 9 (d).

67 Thorpe will also comment on how completely unable he is to communicate with his opponents (*Testimony*, p. 93, ll. 2245–7); see further von Nolcken, 'Another Kind of Saint', p. 439.

68 The sermon was on the text 'Non est igitur servus maior domino suo; si me persecuti sunt et vos persequentur' (John 15.20). It seems to have been unconnected with the sermon on John 15.17–25 (Common of an Apostle) in the main Lollard sermon cycle (Hudson & Gradon, *EWS*, ii, pp. 11–15).

69 There are few Wycliffite letters to compare it with. Loserth prints nine by Wycliffe (*Opera Minora*, pp. 1–18), but these are formal rather than personal, as is the letter printed by W.R. Thomson, 'An Unknown Letter by John Wyclif in Manchester, John Rylands University Library MS. Eng. 86,' *Mediaeval Studies*, 43 (1981), pp. 535–6, as well as the vernacular version of his letter to Pope Urban (Arnold, *SEW*, III, pp. 504–6). Also formal are the letters by Lollards listed below, n. 100.

70 How terrifying the experience of being questioned for heresy was is conveyed by Margery Kempe in her account of her trial before the Archbishop of York: '& hir flesch tremelyd & whakyd wondirly þat sche was fayn to puttyn hir handys vndyr hir cloþis þat it schulde not ben aspyed' (*Book*, p. 124, ll. 24–6).

71 How anxious such cases make Thorpe is indicated in that it is he, not Arundel, who first brings them up (*Testimony*, pp. 39, l. 499–42, l. 610). He refers to Nicholas Hereford, John Purvey, Robert Bowland and Philip Repingdon; his opponents later return to these cases when trying to make

Thorpe give way (pp. 88, l. 2084–89, l. 2119). On the date of Purvey's recantation see Hudson, *LB*, p. 87.

[72] When Wyche writes his letter Sawtrey is the only Lollard actually to have been burned, in the first week of March 1401. Wyche is explicitly threatened with burning when one 'Magister Augustinus' comes to plead with him (p. 533, ll. 13–14).

[73] Wyche seems to be objecting only to having to swear obedience to the canon laws of the established church, not to swearing an oath. Lollards frequently objected to doing the latter, often on the grounds of being asked to swear by a creature, that is, by a relic, a saint, or the Bible in its material being, and sometimes on the grounds that it was against God's Law to swear any oaths at all. See further H.G. Russell, 'Lollard Opposition to Oaths by Creatures', *American Historical Review*, 51 (1945–6), pp. 668–84; Hudson, *PR*, pp. 371–4. Thorpe will object to swearing by the Bible on the grounds that it is wrong to swear by a creature (*Testimony*, p. 34, ll. 332–48). As Russell points out, the issue provided both sides with a convenient rallying point (p. 677).

[74] Canon law was regarded by Wycliffe and his followers as man's unjustifiable addition to God's Law. The extreme Lollard view was that it had been created by a corrupt church to further its own ends, and that it conflicted with the Law of God as revealed in the Bible and as belonging to the archetypal apostolic church. For Wycliffe's views see, for example, *De Civili Dominio*, ii, p. 178, ll. 20–34; the Lollards' tracts and sermons also abound with disparaging references to canon law: see Hudson & Gradon, *EWS*, ii, p. 89, ll. 22–5; *An Apology for Lollard Doctrines*, ed. J.H. Todd, Camden Society, 14 (1842), pp. 73–80; as well as to decrees and decretals: see *EWS*, ii, p. 58, ll. 114–18, iii, p. 2, ll. 13–18; 'How religious men should keep certain Articles' (Matthew, *EWW*, p. 225, ll. 2–5), and to the 'pope's law': see *EWS*, iii, pp. 103, l. 72, 223, l. 53; 'Of Dominion' (*EWW*, p. 291, l. 29). The pope's law is frequently associated with Antichrist: see *EWS*, i, pp. 489, l. 76, 659, ll. 80–3. Examples of decrees conflicting with God's Law are given in the twenty-sixth of the *Thirty-Seven Conclusions (Remonstrance against Romish Corruptions in the Church*, ed. J. Forshall (London, 1851), pp. 78–82). On Lollard attitudes to canon law see further Hudson, *PR*, pp. 378–82.

[75] On how Wyclif saw the chief hope of reform as lying with the king and secular nobility, see Leff, *Heresy*, ii, pp. 542–5, Lambert, *Medieval Heresy*, pp. 236–7; for a brief allusion to how the Lollards saw this as lying with the gentry see McFarlane, *JW*, p. 147; on the relationship of the movement with the gentry see McNiven, *Heresy and Politics*, pp. 46–62. Characteristic in its appeal to the secular power is the concluding prayer of 'On the Twenty-Five Articles': 'God for his grate mercy distroye errouris and heresies of Anticristis chyrche, and make knowen þo treuþis of holy Chirche, and encrese riȝtwysenys, pes, and charite, and lyȝte þo hertes of lordus, to know and distroye þo heresies of þo Chirche, þat pride of prestis lese not þis worlde' (Arnold, *SEW*, iii, p. 496, ll. 1–5); for Lollard approval of the knights of the realm see Hudson and Gradon, *EWS*, ii, p. 64, ll. 107–9; 'But o counfort is of knyȝtus, þat þei saueron myche þe gospel, and han wylle to redon in Englisch þe gospel of Cristus lyȝf'.

[76] As pointed out by Workman, *John Wyclif*, ii, p. 380: 'Even in the north of England, where lollards were few, at the trial of Richard Wyche for heresy in December 1400 [sic] two knights in the audience could not suppress their verdict: "He seems to us to believe well"'. Workman was countering those like W.T. Waugh, 'The Lollard Knights', *Scottish Historical Review*, 11 (1913–14), pp. 55–92, who had concluded that Lollardy held little appeal for the upper classes; especially thanks to McFarlane's investigations (*LK*, pp. 135–261) we now mostly agree with Workman. For an extreme claim as to the importance to Lollardy of the so-called Lollard Knights see M. Wilks, 'Royal priesthood: the origins of Lollardy', in *The Church in a Changing Society: Conflict – Reconciliation or Adjustment?* (Proceedings of 1977 CIHEC Conference, Uppsala, 1978), pp. 63–70; for discussion of what these knights represented in that larger culture of the times see J.A. Tuck, 'Carthusian Monks and Lollard Knights: Religious Attitude at the Court of Richard II', *Studies in the Age of Chaucer, Proceedings of the New Chaucer Society*, 1, 1984: P. Strohm and T.J. Heffernan (eds), *Reconstructing Chaucer* (Knoxville, TN, 1985), pp. 149–61. For the suggestion that such members of the gentry remained important in the reign of Henry IV see McNiven, *Heresy and Politics*, pp. 72–8; Hudson, *PR*, pp. 110–17.

[77] For discussion by Wycliffe of how a term might be used without proper grounding in Scripture

see for example *Opus Evangelicum*, i, p. 97, ll. 25–37 (with reference to 'potestas'); ii, pp. 21–2 (with reference to 'pater' and 'magister'); for references to these examples and further discussion see Evans, *Language and Logic*, pp. 114–16. As Evans points out (p. 116) the author of the General Prologue to the Wycliffe Bible is explicitly concerned with the problems presented by words 'that hath manie significacions vndur oo lettre'.

⁷⁸ See Wycliffe's discussion of such a device (*De Veritate Sacrae Scripturae*, i, pp. 50, l. 20–51, l. 10). The first statement John Aston made on the Eucharist in 1382 was intended to be ambiguous, as was probably the confession of Hereford and Repingdon: see McNiven, *Heresy and Politics*, p. 39; Hudson, *PR*, pp. 283–4. Such a device may partly explain why the Lollards often submitted and then returned to their views with seeming ease, though they seem also to have been helped by their belief that oaths sworn by creatures, or even oaths in general, were illegitimate (see above, n. 73), as well as by their belief that they need not recognise the validity of any oaths to an institution that lacked real authority. See further Fines 'Studies in the Lollard Heresy', p. 40 (on the Lollards as 'habitual word-twisters'); Hudson, *PR*, pp. 158–60 (on how returning ambiguous answers seems to have been taught in the Lollard schools). I am indebted to M. Janet Harris for showing me her unpublished 'Lollardy and the Function of Language in Fifteenth-Century English Heresy Trials' (1994) and to F.E. Somerset for showing me her 'Vernacular Argumentation in *The Testimony of William Thorpe*', in *Mediaeval Studies*, 58 (1996), in which she discusses how the Lollards protected themselves through the careful deployment of general and conditional statements.

⁷⁹ In, for example, *Sermones*, ed. J. Loserth, 4 vols (WS, London, 1887–90), i, pp. 304–10; ii, pp. 62, l. 26ff, 138, l. 24ff; among the points declared heretical from his writings in 1382 was one claiming that if a man were to be truly contrite all eternal confession is either redundant or useless for him (*Fasc. Ziz.*, p. 278). Wycliffe's stand is more like Wyche's in his response to Rymington (*Opera Minora*, pp. 252–3), and he admits the potential usefulness of confessing to a priest in his *De Eucharistia et Poenitencia* (*De Eucharistia*, pp. 329–43; esp. p. 333).

⁸⁰ I have not yet tracked down this passage; it does not feature either as authoritative quotation or as analytic heading under *Virtus* in the Wycliffite collections of preachers' *distinctiones*, the *Floretum* and its shorter version, the *Rosarium* (perhaps the most likely place to look for it) or in the *Floretum* under *Salus* (an entry not contained in the *Rosarium*). I do not necessarily accept, with Matthew, that the passage is introduced by the term 'scripture' despite the lack of break in the manuscript (Prague University Library Ms. III. G. 11, fol. 93ᵛ). Wyche may be indicating that his interpretation of the term 'confession' is grounded in Scripture.

⁸¹ Somerset discusses how Thorpe, helped by God's grace, uses the methods of a disputation *De sophismatibus* to neutralise Chrisostom's 'it is synne to swere wele' ('Vernacular Argumentation', forthcoming). Wyche seems to be relying on similar methods, as he claims that despite appearances he in fact agrees with Wycliffe. Somerset also discusses how Thorpe then structures an argument around the equivocal senses of *vertue*; Wyche seems to be relying on such methods here too.

⁸² Matthew, *EWW*, p. 327, ll. 20–2. Like Wycliffe, Lollard authors sometimes acknowledge that confessing to a priest can have its benefits, but they also stipulate that the priest needs to be good and the person confessing truly contrite. See, for example, the fourth of the *Twenty-five Articles* (Arnold, *SEW*, pp. 461–2), and the ninth of the *Thirty-Seven Conclusions* (*Remonstrance*, pp. 21–2).

⁸³ On Lollard conceptions of the church see, for example, Leff, *Heresy*, ii, pp. 516–21; Hudson, *PR*, pp. 314–27.

⁸⁴ As noted above (p. 134), Wyche is of the diocese of Hereford, not Worcester; he will later want to invalidate the oath because it gets his diocese wrong (p. 541, ll. 7–10).

⁸⁵ Hudson, *PR*, p. 160.

⁸⁶ Snape, 'Some Evidence', p. 356. Snape here suggests that 'Bhetebi' was John Whitby, who was excommunicated for non-appearance on 17 February 1403 and cited to appear on 14 March.

⁸⁷ Smalley 'Bible and Eternity', pp. 74, 77–81.

⁸⁸ That Wyche uses the psalm in this way may counter Hudson's observation that the Lollards strikingly differ from the later English Puritans in not using the psalms either privately or in Lollard

gatherings 'as a scripturally-justified form of poetry' (*PR*, p. 195); the Psalmist, with his alternate despair and exaltation and his intense conversations with the Lord would be a model for seventeenth-century Protestant autobiographers like Bunyan; see further Delany, *British Autobiography*, p. 28.

[89] See W.J. Courtenay, *Schools and Scholars in Fourteenth-Century England* (Princeton, NJ, 1987), pp. 348–55, esp. pp. 350–1 and n. 60. See also, for example, Wycliffe's reference to how he differs from the 'sectis signorum' (*Fasc. Ziz.*, p. 125) and John Tissington's indication that Wycliffe referred to his opponents as 'doctores signorum' (*ibid.*, p. 166).

[90] On the term see Kenny, *Wyclif*, pp. 5–8.

[91] *Lincolniensis* (Arnold, *SEW*, iii, p. 231, ll. 14–18); for a similar comment by Wyclif see *Opus Evangelicum*, ii, p. 59, ll. 30–40.

[92] *The Lanterne of Liȝt*, ed. L.M. Swinburn (EETS 151, 1917), p. 95, ll. 10–14 (punctuation my own).

[93] As Hudson observes (*PR*, p. 316), this was a point that Netter was well aware of (*Doctrinale*, ii, cols. 739–40, 742); she discusses the point further in relation to Thorpe in 'William Thorpe and the Question of Authority', in G.R. Evans (ed.), *Christian Authority: Essays in Honour of Henry Chadwick* (Oxford, 1988), pp. 127–37, esp. p. 137.

[94] We learn of his cognomen from an order to set him free from prison on 15 July 1420, where he is referred to as 'Richard Wyche clerk, otherwise called Richard Godwote' (*CCR, 1419–22*, p. 82). Wyche also confidently uses the tag in an exchange with the knight: 'Deus scit quod *ita* fuit', p. 539, l. 35.

[95] For discussion of the world of *Piers Plowman* in relation to that of the Lollards see C. von Nolcken, '*Piers Plowman*, the Wycliffites, and *Pierce the Plowman's Creed*', *Yearbook of Langland Studies* 2 (1988), pp. 71–102.

[96] Like Hereford, arrested for preaching in support of Lollardy in 1387, who had abandoned his Lollardy by 1391 (Hudson, *Two Wycliffite Texts*, pp. 109–10, note to ll. 499–501); or Repingdon, who submitted in 1382 (*ibid.*, pp. 111–12).

[97] For Wyche's career see Emden, *BRUO*, iii, p. 2101 and references. For another Lollard whose career seems similarly vacillating see Hudson's account of William Taylor in *Two Wycliffite Texts*, pp. xvii–xxv. Aston also seems to have returned to his Lollardy after recanting in 1382 (Hudson, *Two Wycliffite Texts*, p. 112, note to l. 570), as does Purvey after recanting in 1401 (*ibid.*, pp. 110–11, note to ll. 499–501).

[98] *Reg. Chichele*, i, p. cxxxiv; iii, p. 57.

[99] *Fasc. Ziz.*, pp. 501–5.

[100] As McFarlane puts it, 'it is fairly obvious that they were accomplices' (*John Wycliffe*, p. 162); see further M. Spinka, *John Hus, a Biography* (Princeton, NJ, 1968), p. 117. For Wyche's letter, see *M. Jana Husi Korespondence a Dokumenty*, ed. Václav Novotný (Prague, 1920), pp. 75–9; it has been translated into modern English in *The Letters of John Hus*, with introductions and explanatory notes by H.B. Workman and R.M. Pope (London, 1904), pp. 32–4 (the translation is based on that of Foxe), and in *The Letters of John Hus*, translated from the Latin and the Czech by M. Spinka (Manchester, 1972), pp. 213–15. For Oldcastle's letter see J. Loserth, 'Ueber die Beziehungen zwischen englischen und böhmischen Wiclifiten', *Mittheilungen des Instituts für oesterreichische Geschichtsforschung* 12 (1891), pp. 266–7; in about 1413 Oldcastle will similarly write to the king (*ibid.*, pp. 268–9). What seems to have been an intimacy between Wyche and Oldcastle may have gone back a long way: Oldcastle grew up in Herefordshire (W.T. Waugh, 'Sir John Oldcastle', *EHR*, 20 [1905], pp. 435–6), which was also Wyche's diocese (above, p. 134).

[101] The letter abounds with references to Antichrist, for example, and its fight is ultimately between those who get their help from the Lord ('a domino') against his adversary Antichrist ('eius adversarium Antichristum') (*M. Jana Husi Korespondence*, p. 78). It also leaves no doubt as to where Hus and his associates stand in this fight.

[102] F. Devon (ed.), *Issues of the Exchequer . . . from Henry III to Henry VI* (London, 1837), pp. 352–3; Thomson lists William Brown as a Woodstock glover involved in Oldcastle's rebellion (*LL*, p. 55).

[103] *Reg. Chichele*, iii, pp. 56–7.

[104] *CCR, 1419–22*, p. 82.

[105] Emden, *BRUO*, iii, p. 2101 and references.

[106] Thomson, *LL*, p. 149 and references.

[107] *Fasc. Ziz.*, pp. 501–5. The document containing this revocation dates from some time between October 1404 and March 1406. It mentions Innocent VII, elected 17 October 1404 as pope (p. 505) and Walter (Skirlaw), who died on 24 March 1406, as bishop of Durham (p. 501); see further Snape, 'Some Evidence', p. 359.

[108] *Fasc. Ziz.*, pp. 370–2; Netter tries to answer Wyche's use here of Sap. 13. 10ff. (*Doctrinale*, iii, cols. 967–9).

[109] *Six Town Chronicles of England,* ed. R. Flenley (Oxford, 1911), p. 114; see also *ibid.*, p. 101.

[110] Foxe, *A&M*, iii, p. 703; Thomson, *LL*, pp. 149–50.

[111] He must also have wanted to reassert his links with this community; as he says he will not be writing to it again (p. 541, l. 28), he must have believed this was his farewell. As indicated above (p. 132), he is also still striving to fulfil certain pastoral commitments. He also needed money and books (pp. 543, l. 37–544, l. 5).

[112] For the term see Thorpe, *Testimony*, p. 36, l. 421, and *Middle English Dictionary, s.v.* 'inner' adj. 2 (a). This 'inner man' will play an important part in later Protestant writing; Delany for example comments on Luther's dominant concern with this and on how his internalisation of religion led to the anguish and neurotic conflicts which entered into the standard emotional repertoire of seventeenth-century spiritual autobiographers (Delany, *British Autobiography*, p. 34).

[113] On the *Testimony*'s anticipating later Protestant hagiography see Hudson, *Two Wycliffite Texts*, pp. lvi–lix.

[114] S. Greenblatt, *Renaissance Self-Fashioning from More to Shakespeare* (Chicago, 1980), p. 85. For discussion of such later English Protestant writing see, for example, B.J. Mandel, 'Bunyan and the Autobiographer's Artistic Purpose', *Criticism*, 10 (1968), pp. 225–43; J. Webber, *The Eloquent 'I': Style and Self in Seventeenth-Century Prose* (Madison, WI., 1968), esp. pp. 15–52; Delany, *British Autobiography*, esp. pp. 27–39, 55–104; D. Ebner, *Autobiography in Seventeenth-Century England: Theology and the Self* (The Hague and Paris, 1971), esp. pp. 22–71.

[115] Greenblatt, *Renaissance Self-Fashioning*, p. 271, n. 28. There are of course other examples; Janel Mueller has drawn my attention to Queen Katherine Parr's *Lamentation of a Sinner* (1547), for example. Notable too is *The Autobiography of Thomas Whythorne*, ed. James M. Osborn (Oxford, 1961), and esp. pp. 145–67, where Whythorne describes his introspective responses to the plague of 1563 (I am grateful to Margaret Aston for this reference).

[116] The term 'premature reformation' derives from the title of Hudson, *PR*.

8

LAWYERS AND LOLLARDY IN THE EARLY FIFTEENTH CENTURY*

Maureen Jurkowski

Common lawyers suffered generally from a bad press in late medieval England,[1] and they fared no better at the hands of Wycliffite writers. According to the author of one tract, 'False men of lawe . . . norischen pledynge and debate among men', in order to 'have a veyn name and wynnen hem a litil worldly stynkynge muk with goddis curs'. Their catalogue of sins included the perversion of law and truth, the disinheritance of rightful heirs, the corruption of lords, and religious hypocrisy.[2] All the more surprising is it then, to find that many of the gentry supporters of the Lollard heresy in the early fifteenth century were in fact common lawyers – that is, practising members of the legal profession in its various manifestations. This paper will discuss both the careers and the involvement in the Lollard heresy of several of these lawyers, before exploring possible connections between their professional lives and their heretical views.

It is necessary first, however, to provide a definition of the late medieval common lawyer and some account of his professional activities. Because lawyers are often disguised in record sources as 'gentlemen', they can be difficult to recognise, and the identification is further obscured by the wide range of activities of what contemporaries often called a 'man of law'. This problem of identification is particularly acute in regard to the lower reaches of the profession in the later fourteenth and fifteenth centuries – those primarily under consideration here; these lawyers remain under-studied and ill-defined.[3] At the pinnacle of the profession stood the 'serjeants-at-law', an élite group of the most talented lawyers who commanded large fees for pleading cases before the king's courts at Westminster, especially in the court of Common Pleas where they enjoyed a monopoly of pleading. It was from their ranks that the judiciary was appointed.[4] Entitled to wear a special livery, serjeants were skilled in the intellectually demanding arts of 'counting' and pleading, the process by which opposing parties in litigation attempted to frame an issue for the jury's determination which could settle a case in their favour.[5]

The next rungs down in the legal hierarchy were occupied by an amorphous

* I am grateful to Dr Paul Brand and Dr Nigel Ramsay for reading and commenting on this paper. All remaining errors are my own.

group known as 'apprentices-at-law', the most gifted of whom were eventually called to the rank of serjeant. The term 'apprentice' was applied to practising lawyers who had received legal training in the central law courts, or to students who were currently receiving such training. These lawyers might practise as advocates, attorneys, advisers, clerks or officials,[6] and in 1379 were deemed to fall into three income brackets.[7] Taxed in 1379 at the same level as serjeants, senior apprentices pleaded cases in the king's courts other than the Common Pleas. Attorneys represented clients in court, handling all procedural, pre-trial matters, and liaising with the serjeants or senior apprentices engaged by their clients to plead.

By the mid-fourteenth century, apprentices and clerks in the civil service had organised themselves into hostels called inns in the area of the Temple, for the purposes of education and shared accommodation.[8] Consultation with clients took place after the morning court session in the vicinity of the inns – in nearby churches and in the porch of St Paul's Cathedral.[9] Because they were frequently in and around the law courts, many attorneys, particularly those in the early stages of their careers, secured casual employment in matters connected with the courts, for instance, by hiring themselves out as mainpernors – that is, as bail bondsmen, and guarantors of the good behaviour of pardoned persons and the court appearances of defendants in civil and criminal suits.[10]

Practising in the county and other local courts and advising clients in the localities, there was another layer of lawyers, about whom we know a good deal less. Some of these may also have been engaged on occasion as attorneys in the law courts at Westminster,[11] and may have belonged to London inns, but most of them probably confined themselves to local matters, advising the lesser gentry and yeomanry, and wielding influence among the mercantile oligarchies of the largest county towns.[12]

In addition to advocacy in court, an important and lucrative part of a lawyer's practice was the provision of counsel to individuals and institutions, and he was usually paid an annual retaining fee for both services. His employers were great magnates and wealthy knights, bishops and abbots, cities and towns, and religious corporations of every description, many of whom retained legal experts in each court and government department, as well as a team of legal advisers to oversee their affairs as a council.[13] Arbitration of his client's disputes was also an important aspect of the services expected from a fee'd lawyer,[14] but many of the duties he performed were of an administrative nature. These were often related to the acquisition and management of the client's landed estate: lawyers acted as feoffees, superintended the sale or purchase of land, provided safe custody for deeds, arranged marriage jointures, drafted wills, served as executors and oversaw inquisitions post mortem.[15]

There was great demand for such services, as well as a sharp rise in litigation business in the second half of the fourteenth century, owing to a variety of factors, and the number of legal practitioners must have grown accordingly.[16] Increased competition over land and the growing complexity of the law governing its descent were the chief reasons,[17] but the field of contract law also saw an increase in business. Free men and women of all social classes had become more and more preoccupied with legal protection in their ordinary daily activities, a preoccupation which expressed itself in the regular use of penal bonds with conditional defeasance to guarantee the performance of the most routine of covenants and obligations.[18] It is little wonder then, that the legal profession became a 'growth industry' where there were tremendous opportunities for men of talent and ambition.

A development related to the rise in the numbers of common lawyers was the laicisation of the civil service, a revolutionary change which began in the early fifteenth century. The new tendency to appoint to royal administrative posts laymen instead of ordained clerks, whose numbers were falling, can first be perceived in the Exchequer.[19] Clerks were traditionally rewarded for their services through preferment to ecclesiastical benefices, but laymen required another form of payment, and it was the Exchequer which offered the most in the way of financial incentives. Here, officers were well placed to obtain custody of escheats, wardships and other available sources of crown patronage. Equally, there was considerable scope for profitable financial wheeling and dealing with crown debtors and creditors.[20] Other departments of royal administration, however, soon followed suit, and by 1430 most financial officers were laymen.[21]

There was considerable overlap between these lay administrators in royal service and the personnel staffing the estates and households of the great magnates.[22] The distinction was further blurred by the Lancastrian usurpation of 1399, for the crown was thereafter served by two bureaucracies – that of the royal government and that of the duchy of Lancaster, which continued to be administered separately.[23] As in other magnate establishments, many of the duchy's top administrative posts, such as chief steward, receiver-general, bailiff, feodary and auditor, were filled by lawyers. Equally, it was the lawyers who chiefly staffed the offices of county administration. They made up the bulk of the increasingly powerful commissions of the peace: a single lawyer, together with another member, could constitute a quorum to hold sessions and hear indictments. They often served as undersheriffs and escheators, and were frequently appointed by the crown to investigative and other administrative commissions.[24] Thus, despite an obvious long-term trend of bureaucratic specialisation, in the short term there was 'an increased occupational mobility and adaptability across the widened range of lay careerism'.[25] By the early fifteenth century new opportunities existed for lawyers at all levels of the profession in both law and administration in the service of both private and public employers.

The career of Thomas Tykhill of Aston-on-Trent, Derbyshire provides a fine example of a lawyer who took full advantage of these opportunities.[26] Born into an obscure, lesser gentry family in southern Derbyshire,[27] he probably received legal training at a London inn of court during the reign of Richard II. By 1399, he was employed as an attorney for John Burghill, bishop of Coventry and Lichfield, whom he probably served until 1405, when the bishop sued him for the return of documents in his keeping.[28] He may also have found early employment as a legal adviser to a local peer, Richard, lord Grey of Codnor.[29]

Although he was undoubtedly talented and clever, it was the political circumstances of the Lancastrian ascendancy which brought him the rapid success that then followed. In 1398 he was appointed a justice of the peace in Derbyshire under John of Gaunt, duke of Lancaster and the greatest landowner in the county, and from 1401 until his arrest in January 1414 he continued to sit on the commission.[30] As an 'apprentice-at-law', he was also paid a retaining fee by the duchy to serve on its team of legal advisers from 1409 to 1416.[31] It was in the administration of Henry, Prince of Wales, however, that his career was made. From 1405 to 1414 he was chief steward of the northern part of all the prince's lands in the Principality of Wales, the Earldom of Chester and the Duchy of Cornwall, as well as a paid member of the prince's council.[32] As such he was given wide powers and duties, and played an important role in both the prince's legal and administrative affairs and in the conduct of his war against the Welsh rebels.[33] In February 1410, when the prince was in control of the king's council,[34] Thomas Tykhill was appointed the king's attorney in the court of Common Pleas, the Exchequer of Pleas and the Chancery; he was to represent the king's interests in all suits brought before these courts.[35] By now a knowledgeable lawyer and administrator, he was frequently appointed to judicial and other royal commissions concerned with the king's revenue.[36]

His standing in the county had understandably risen, but although he must have collected fees from a number of employers[37] and had amassed a compact estate in Derbyshire centred on his residence at Aston-on-Trent, his financial success was on a modest scale.[38] Promotion to the serjeantcy would have brought him to a new level of prosperity and was the next logical step in his career path. By April 1413, however, there were signs that all was not well between him and the newly-crowned king.[39] This discord may have had its roots in rumours of curious goings-on on the Tykhill estates.

In 1410, the same year in which he had become king's attorney, Thomas Tykhill and his wife Agnes[40] began sheltering in their home a Lollard preacher called William Ederyk. Known also as William 'Tykelpriest', Ederyk was said to have preached his heretical views in Derby, Chaddesden, and in towns where the Tykhills owned property – Aston, Tutbury and Castle Donington.[41] His preaching tours in Leicestershire led Bishop Repingdon to make enquiries in the locality and to examine one of his converts in 1413, but the backing of the prominent Tykhills evidently dissuaded him from summoning Ederyk himself.[42]

The prosecution of Sir John Oldcastle signalled danger for all Lollard supporters, and the Tykhills must also have felt under threat: on 30 December William Ederyk set off for the revolt in London with a small contingent of men from the adjoining village of Thulston.[43] After the rebels' defeat, Ederyk still enjoyed Tykhill's protection. He escaped back to Aston from St Giles's Fields and remained at large until captured at the end of 1414 near Kenilworth Castle; by January 1415 he had procured the king's pardon.[44] Tykhill meanwhile had had his post of king's attorney taken from him and by 25 January 1414 he was imprisoned in the Tower, together with other gentry supporters taken into custody on the king's special orders.[45] Among these were two other members of the Derbyshire gentry – Sir Thomas Chaworth, a prominent knight whose part in the revolt remains unknown,[46] and Henry Bothe, usually referred to as an esquire of Littleover, who was also a practising lawyer.

A younger son of Thomas Bothe of Barton in Eccles, Lancashire,[47] Henry Bothe (or del Bothe) had settled in Littleover, Derbyshire by the 1390s, around which time he also married Isabel, daughter of an established member of the local gentry, John Fynderne of Findern.[48] Bothe's legal practice was purely local in its scope, and it would appear that his expertise lay primarily in the field of conveyancing and the law of real property. From about 1400 onwards, 'he was continuously in demand as a trustee and witness to local property transactions'.[49] A lawsuit of 1410 reveals that he represented clients at the Derby bailiffs' court (the borough court), a service which he had probably long provided, for in 1400 he had sat as one of three arbitrators in a dispute between the bailiffs and a townsman.[50] He is also known to have acted as an advocate at assizes held in the county.[51] When Margery Clitheroe was planning to divorce her husband Richard in 1413, she sought Bothe's advice at a meeting at Calwich Priory in Staffordshire on how to safeguard her portion of the estate, and he agreed to ride to London on her behalf and treat with Clitheroe for a settlement.[52]

Bothe's long association with the house of Lancaster had begun by January 1395 when he obtained letters of protection of six months' duration for travel to Ireland in the company of Thomas, duke of Gloucester.[53] He welcomed with open arms the return from exile of Henry earl of Derby in 1399, and was among the small group of gentry later rewarded with a life annuity for accompanying the new king to his first parliament,[54] a move which probably stood him in good stead again, later. In February 1403 he climbed the first rung of the ladder of county administration when he was named escheator of the counties of Nottingham and Derby, a post he held again from 1409 to 1410,[55] but his progress on this front was temporarily halted.

At some time in 1413 Bothe began maintaining at his home in Littleover the Lollard chaplain Walter Gilbert of Kibworth Harcourt, Leicestershire, and in June of that year, and on other occasions, Bothe himself was said to have publicly preached heresy.[56] What exactly it was that he preached is unknown. Like

Ederyk, Walter Gilbert led a small contingent of men to the Oldcastle revolt, though apparently not one composed of Derbyshire men, as his forces were drawn from the villages around Kibworth Harcourt.[57] Bothe must have been implicated in the rising after Gilbert's capture, however, for by 25 January he had joined Tykhill in the Tower. Unlike Tykhill, his goods were confiscated like those of a convicted felon by the Derbyshire escheator.[58]

Both, nevertheless, escaped lightly from this dangerous episode. They were forced to remain a few months in the Tower, during which time they were treated liberally, after large bonds had been posted by friends and relations guaranteeing their behaviour.[59] In May both were released on payment of another bond pending their treason trials in Michaelmas term 1414, at which they were acquitted.[60]

The third Derbyshire lawyer to play a part in these affairs was Henry Bothe's brother-in-law, John Fynderne of nearby Findern – perhaps the most interesting of these men. His rise to prominence is again associated with that of the Lancastrians, as well as with his close friendship with John Cokayne, a pillar of Henry IV's regime as Chief Baron of the Exchequer from 1400 to 1412 and a justice of the court of Common Pleas from 1405 to 1429.[61] Scion of a well-established armigerous family,[62] Fynderne's career before 1399 is obscure, but he was probably the same man who served as a bailiff of the town of Derby in 1389–90.[63] In this capacity he would have presided over the town's court, and as steward of Burton Abbey, his landlord, he would have performed the same service at the abbot's manorial court.[64]

There is no evidence that he ever acted as an advocate for anyone else, but he usually represented himself on the many occasions in which he brought suits before the king's courts, and was very skilled in the manipulation of legal procedure.[65] In November 1399 he was appointed to the Exchequer post of apposer of foreign estreats,[66] and although the appointment was undoubtedly political, he must have possessed the requisite skills. His task was to approve the accounts rendered by sheriffs at the Exchequer for the fines and amercements levied in the king's courts which they had collected – a job which required a thorough knowledge of legal process and records.[67]

The benefits of this post were many. The potential for bribery and extortion of the sheriffs was considerable, and it ensured that Fynderne's influence would be felt both at Westminster and in the provinces.[68] This influence manifested itself in various ways: he was appointed to several administrative commissions,[69] he found many private employers wishing to use his services, and he was able to secure a share of the crown's patronage in the form of wardships, leases and forfeitures.[70] Together with John Cokayne, he speculated in real estate in London and elsewhere, purchasing tenements and rents and passing them on to others.[71] He lent money to a variety of individuals, often recording the transactions on the Exchequer rolls.[72] Among his clients were a peer, Reginald, lord Grey of

Ruthin,[73] a prominent king's knight, Sir Richard Arundell,[74] and Dru Barentyne, a wealthy London goldsmith.[75] He was also paid for counsel to the duchy of Lancaster.[76]

One form of crown patronage which he pursued with a particular vigour was the leasing of the possessions of the alien priories, which were taken into the king's hands in 1403 for the duration of the war with France. He procured the 'farm' of the priories of Lapley in Staffordshire and Hinckley in Leicestershire and, for a short time, of Tutbury in Staffordshire.[77] In August 1404 he gave security, with Sir John Oldcastle, for custody of the priory of Craswall in Wales, which was strategically located for the campaign then being waged against the Welsh insurgents.[78]

In 1413 Fynderne and his brother-in-law Henry Bothe were embroiled in a bitter dispute, when both were summoned before the king.[79] Nevertheless, John Fynderne was among the mainpernors who posted a bond of 1,000 marks to guarantee Bothe's behaviour in the Tower after his arrest for Lollardy the following year.[80] He was also a friend and neighbour of Thomas Tykhill. The two together witnessed deeds of their mutual friends and neighbours,[81] and Tykhill had served as a trustee in Fynderne's acquisition of the manor of Potlock from his kinsman John Took, releasing his interest to him in a deed of 1409.[82] Moreover, Tykhill and Bothe were not the only members of the Derbyshire gentry to become involved in the Lollard heresy. John Prynce, an esquire of Windley and close friend of Thomas Tykhill's, was also indicted in the aftermath of the Oldcastle revolt, for preaching heretical views at Windley in June 1413 and at other times and places.[83] Both Fynderne and Bothe had witnessed land conveyances along with John Prynce and his brother Richard for their mutual friends the Iretons in early 1414.[84] William Marshall, 'gentleman' of Stretton-en-le-Field, where John Fynderne was lord of the manor, was also presented by jurors as having expressed Lollard views at Stretton in October 1413.[85] Marshall and Fynderne later fell out, but from 1412 to 1415, Marshall had witnessed several documents relating to Fynderne's purchase of the manor of Stretton-en-le-Field.[86] Neither Marshall nor Prynce ever answered to these charges before the King's Bench although, together with Thomas and Agnes Tykhill and Henry Bothe, they were ordered to purge themselves before their ordinary, which all except Marshall did in 1418.[87]

Tykhill would never become a serjeant-at-law, but both he and Bothe retained a local prominence; neither was ever found to be involved with the heresy again.[88] John Fynderne, however, for a time remained an active bail bondsman for imprisoned Lollards. While Oldcastle was in hiding and the threat of another rising persisted, several suspected Lollards were imprisoned without charge in the Marshalsea. After the threat had dissipated with Oldcastle's capture and execution in December 1417, these men were released to mainpernors who guaranteed their future behaviour and undertook to produce them for examination upon request. Three times in 1418 John Fynderne and his kinsman

John Took, who were not otherwise active as mainpernors, posted bonds with others to free men who had been in custody on suspicion of Lollardy.

The first of these suspected Lollards was Henry Jeke, a gentleman of Tamworth, Staffordshire, and Wigston, Leicestershire, who in January undertook to cease holding heretical opinions.[89] In March, William Glasier of Barton under Needwood, Staffordshire, and Thomas Praty of Solihull were released to Fynderne and Took after pledging not to speak publicly or privately against church doctrine.[90] Finally, in July Fynderne and Took were among a group of six mainpernors to whom six detained men were delivered[91] – one was John Grene, a weaver of Chaddesden, Derbyshire, who had taken part in the revolt,[92] and another was Nicholas Taillour of Leicester, by then a seasoned veteran of heresy.[93] Among the bail bondsmen was also a former fellow of Merton College, Oxford, with a long history of involvement in Lollardy, to whom we shall later return – Thomas Lucas. In sum, it seems more than a coincidence that John Fynderne (who died in 1420)[94] should have both taken the part of and found himself surrounded by so many adherents to the heresy, however fleeting their commitment to it may have been.

In Wigston, Leicestershire, another well-established, if less prominent, family was at the centre of heresy – the Fridays.[95] Richard and John Friday first appear as witnesses to a land conveyance in Wigston in 1393; they and their younger brother Ralph all owned land in the town.[96] Richard Friday, who by 1414 made his residence at South Croxton, was variously referred to as 'gentleman' and 'prentys of lawe',[97] and by 1397 had built a thriving practice as an attorney in the court of Common Pleas.[98] Among his employers was Philip Repingdon, bishop of Lincoln, for whom he held court at Leicester as his steward in 1414.[99] It is Ralph Friday, however, who is the chief interest here. He, too, was undoubtedly a common lawyer.

Between the years 1401 and 1409 at least, Ralph appears to have owned property and perhaps to have resided partly in Oxfordshire, possibly after attendance at one of the Oxford business schools.[100] By 1409, however, he was back in Leicestershire permanently,[101] and within the next two years married Alice, the widow of John London, a property-owner in Leicester and former mayor of the town.[102] The first sign that Ralph was active as an attorney comes from 1405, when he began to operate in London as a professional mainpernor, reaching a peak of activity in this occupation in 1409.[103] By 1413 Ralph was representing clients in the court of Common Pleas, and by 1418 also in the King's Bench; in 1424 he was appointed as an attorney at an assize in Leicester.[104] All of his clients were drawn from Leicestershire and it is likely that his practice was chiefly local. In Wigston, where he lived until at least 1455, he witnessed several land conveyances from 1418 to 1432.[105]

Wigston, where Ralph engaged in sheep-farming,[106] was the subject of an investigation by Archbishop Arundel in 1402 following reports that heresy was rife in the village among both lay folk and clerics. In 1413 Bishop Repingdon again made enquiries there, and found that three men of prominent families were involved in the heresy. They possessed English books and had asserted their right to preach. A fourth man, John Friday, 'was said to have consorted with Lollards'; all had to post bonds for their good behaviour and swear not to hold such opinions.[107]

Another visitation of that same year revealed that a yeoman called John Belgrave, who also had property interests in Leicester and Wigston, held some remarkable views of which he was forced to purge himself.[108] Among his seven compurgators, all of whom were from prominent families, was Ralph Friday, and it should thus come as no surprise that both Belgrave and Friday were indicted for holding Lollard beliefs in the aftermath of the Oldcastle revolt.[109] Neither was charged with complicity in the revolt, but, as is well known, Friday is credited with having been an eloquent speaker against the papacy and with having declared that Archbishop Arundel was a 'disciple of the Antichrist and a murderer of men'.[110] Less well-known is that Friday, together with Thomas Lucas and others, also stood surety for the purchase of pardons by three Buckinghamshire Lollards in June 1414.[111] Despite his indictment, he himself appears never to have been taken into custody nor to have suffered any ill consequences for his beliefs.[112]

Possibly also to be counted among the supporters of the heresy in Leicestershire was another attorney operating in the court of Common Pleas, John Howes of Howes. From at least 1397 he was a filacer of the court – that is, he was responsible for enrolling entries of the mesne process of actions brought before the court in certain counties.[113] It would have been very convenient for him to further the suits of his clients in the course of his duties; the post could thus provide a stepping stone for a career as an attorney.[114] On occasion, Howes appeared for clients in court[115] and was evidently thought expert enough to be appointed to the quorum of the peace commission in Leicestershire in 1418.[116]

Aside from the fact that he was sought by the crown in 1414 for unspecified trespasses in Nottinghamshire,[117] where he also owned property,[118] there is only one fleeting indication that he held Lollard sympathies. In 1421 he was delivered by the king's justices from Nottingham Castle gaol where he had been imprisoned on a charge that he had supplied food, drink and money to the fugitive John Oldcastle at Hickling Rise, Nottinghamshire, in December 1416.[119] The allegation may have been entirely malicious, but it is worth noting that a few weeks later, Oldcastle was spotted in the vicinity, at Swarkestone Bridge, Derbyshire, close by the estates of Tykhill, Fynderne and Bothe.[120]

So far, only lawyers who apparently embraced the Lollard heresy in the full flight of their legal careers have been discussed. In the case of Thomas Compworth, an esquire of Thrupp, Oxfordshire, however, the order of events was reversed. The story of Compworth's refusal to pay tithes to the abbot of

Oseney, his condemnation as a heretic by Bishop Buckingham in 1385, and his trial before the university chancellor at Oxford, survives in a chronicle account and has been discussed by Anne Hudson, Alison McHardy and others.[121] K.B. McFarlane also noted that Compworth was among a group of heretics in Northampton who in 1392 allegedly enjoyed the protection of the mayor of that town.[122] Compworth's later prosperity has also been remarked upon, but his career as a lawyer has gone virtually unnoticed.[123]

By 1396 he had begun to act as a bail bondsman, and by the first decade of the fifteenth century had established a legal practice in the capital. In addition to finding bail for defendants (at law) and mainprising for pardons, he served often as a financial guarantor for men seeking crown patronage.[124] He is first found representing clients in the court of Common Pleas in 1410.[125] His main residence was at Helmedon, Northamptonshire, but his marriage around 1406 to Elizabeth, daughter and heiress of William Hondsacre, also brought him property in Warwickshire.[126] Two important clients were Maud, lady Lovell of Titchmarsh, Northamptonshire, and John Holand, earl of Huntingdon; he probably was of counsel to both.[127] As defendants in a lawsuit of 1415, he and his frequent associate William Ardern described their occupation as 'apprenticii ad legem, in eadem lege eruditi'.[128] In 1413 Compworth was named to the quorum of the peace commission in Northamptonshire, but, perhaps significantly, he was left off the commission appointed in February 1414.[129] There is no evidence, however, of any further involvement with the heresy. Between 1421 and 1426, he served three terms as county escheator, and in 1427 was elected to represent Northampton in Parliament.[130]

The last man to be discussed here also appears to have taken up practising law in later life. Thomas Lucas is known to most of us in another guise – that of a Merton College fellow with a record of heretical activity. A fellow by 1391 and a Master of Arts by 1403, he was one of four Merton scholars arrested for their unorthodox views and imprisoned in Beaumaris Castle, Anglesey, from 1395 to 1399.[131] Lucas was never charged with complicity in the revolt itself, but it has been suggested that he and John Mybbe, principal of Cuthbert Hall, were the Oxford scholars referred to by Bishop Repingdon who were busy stirring up trouble in Oxford at the time of the 1414 uprising.[132]

By late 1416 Lucas had joined forces with the supporters of the pseudo-Richard II and was openly plotting against the king, writing and distributing handbills in the streets of London and elsewhere.[133] In these bills and in a letter to the Emperor Sigismund, he urged the confiscation of clerical temporalities. Sigismund passed this letter on to the king, and Lucas, styled 'master of arts of Andover, Hampshire, gentleman', was duly arrested and charged with treason. He pleaded not guilty, whereupon a jury was summoned rather promptly, and in Trinity term 1417 acquitted him.[134] Perhaps we should not be too surprised by this leniency, for there is reason to believe that Lucas enjoyed influence in Westminster, where the case was both pleaded and tried.

Until 1406 Lucas was involved in the administration of Merton College, where the part played by the fellows in estate management was unusually large.[135] He and three other Merton fellows with whom he was imprisoned in 1395 all appear to have acted as receivers of the college, both before and after their arrest, riding to various manors and collecting rent monies from their bailiffs and tenants.[136] Lucas was later sued to account for monies received from college properties in the counties of Buckingham and Leicester,[137] and made at least three journeys to oversee the administration of the Northumberland and Durham manors.[138] After his release from prison in 1399, Lucas had returned to the college and was appointed a junior proctor of the university for 1403–4. He was still in good standing at the college in 1408, when he borrowed twelve volumes from Merton College library by agreement with the subwarden.[139]

By 1410, however, he was embroiled in a bitter struggle with the warden, Edmund Bekynham, and other fellows, which manifested itself in several lawsuits brought before the king's courts, and it is evident that by then Lucas had been expelled from the college.[140] In 1409 he sued Bekynham and three fellows in two separate actions in the Common Pleas, for the return of bills and muniments. After various delays, Lucas managed to win his case against Bekynham at Westminster in June 1413, and was awarded £200 in damages (or £40 and the return of the chest of muniments).[141] Bekynham immediately appealed the case to the King's Bench on a writ of error, and began a series of ostensibly spurious suits against Lucas in retaliation, including one that the latter had forcibly taken three books from the college in 1401.[142] The appeal was aborted when Bekynham died in February 1416, and whether Lucas ever received his chest or money is unknown.[143] In all of these cases he always represented himself in court, whether plaintiff or defendant, and whether filing the simplest of writs to further the proceedings or submitting the pleadings at trial.[144]

That Lucas had now begun to practise as a common lawyer and was often in London is suggested further by his frequent appearance from 1410 as a bail bondsman and common mainpernor. It was not only imprisoned Lollards whom he bailed, although he did help such men on a number of occasions;[145] he also gave surety for the court appearances of defendants in a variety of suits.[146] From 1416 onwards he was often described as being 'of Andover', where he owned property,[147] and on other occasions he was said to be 'of London',[148] but he clearly retained Oxford ties, for in Michaelmas 1419 he appeared as an attorney in the King's Bench court in a trespass suit between two fellows of Balliol College. His client, Thomas Chace, a future chancellor of the university, alleged that he had been assaulted by one Richard Collyng.[149] No more is known of that case, for it was transferred from that court to the jurisdiction of the university chancellor,[150] but it may serve as an example of just one of the many instances in which Lucas continued to associate with Oxford clerks and scholars.[151]

In 1413 Lucas began to represent clients in the King's Bench court,[152] and by the 1420s he was doing the same in the court of Common Pleas,[153] although it was as a King's Bench attorney, and perhaps pleader, that he was most active in the years 1417 to 1423.[154] The geographical scope of his client-base expanded over these years from Oxford and Berkshire to include other parts of England.[155] On at least three occasions he acted as an attorney in civil actions for men who were previously associated with the Lollard heresy: in 1418 for Robert Cringleford, a goldsmith of London,[156] in 1421 for John Wille, a clerk of Oxford,[157] and in 1422 for Thomas Crompe, a pardoner of Hereford.[158] Lucas, it seems, was a Lollard lawyer in more than one sense. A truly fascinating character, he has been largely overlooked as a link between the academic and gentry Lollards, and the adherents of the sect in many different places.

Tykhill, Bothe, Fynderne, Friday, Compworth, Lucas and perhaps also Howes – we have by now seen enough lawyers, either circumstantially or firmly linked with Lollardy, to suggest that there might have been something which particularly attracted men in this profession to the heresy. One factor that must be noted straight away is that, apart from Henry Bothe, all of these men spent significant amounts of time in London – so much so, that any notion that they were provincial gentlemen whose worlds were bounded by the narrow concerns of local society must be wholly discarded. They were urbane and worldly, in touch with the latest trends in the capital. On the other hand, the fact that all were from areas where several other supporters of the heresy could be readily found, suggests that locality was also a factor.

Secondly, and it is this point that I would like to stress, they were highly literate individuals who had prospered largely because of the power which their literacy gave them. They must have possessed enormous confidence in their own abilities to argue and to reason, and to form and hold opinions. Such a measure of confidence, I would maintain, would naturally have predisposed them to look favourably upon the central component of the Wycliffite credo – that laymen were legitimately entitled to read Scripture for themselves and to draw conclusions about its meaning. Moreover, the related idea that the Word of God was open to distortion through the glossing of unworthy or corrupt priests would have seemed highly plausible to them. Distortion of texts was something that lawyers knew about. Indeed, I would like to suggest that lawyers shared a characteristic here with academic Wycliffites and Lollard writers: all were highly skilled in textual analysis – written texts were at the centres of their worlds. Lawyers owed their skill with texts to the experience of practising law and, perhaps above all, to the legal training acquired at the courts and the inns, a training comparable in some ways to that offered at the universities, and one which is worth looking at in some detail to develop the point further.

It is probably safe to assume that the education of lawyers (and other members of the gentry) began with attendance at a town grammar school, for it is now evident that by the late Middle Ages, most average-sized towns had a school at which elementary reading and grammar were taught.[159] Indeed, John Fynderne's village of Findern appears to have had a school in 1420 when a William Kelme, 'scolemayster', figures among his tenants there.[160] Thereafter, knowledge of legal and business practices could be gained by service as an apprentice to an attorney or clerk in a lord's household, and/or by appointment (often hereditary) to posts such as bailiff or steward.[161]

Formal training in business and common law practices, however, had become increasingly common for aspiring lawyers, as two fourteenth-century indentures attest. The first, dating from 1323, was a marriage agreement which provided for the education of the husband at an Oxford school for one year, and then for four further years among the apprentices at the court of Common Pleas.[162] That this programme of study was standard is confirmed by a second indenture, dating from 1380 and making similar provision.[163] The Oxford schools in question were of course the business schools, which had long given instruction in letter-writing, casting accounts, conveying property and elementary legal procedure.[164]

The education at the king's courts in Westminster referred to in the indentures clearly consisted of more than the mere observation of pleading and court procedure. Such informal self-help methods were combined with formal instruction at the inns of court and chancery where students and practising attorneys alike lived. To be sure, regular attendance at the courts was the main feature of the training, and students sat or stood in a special section designated the 'crib', where they took notes and were sometimes addressed specifically by the justices.[165] Concerned solely with the salient points of law debated by the serjeants and justices, these notes circulated among students and became known as 'yearbooks'.[166] Other reading material was available to them, such as treatises on the forms of original writ, conveyancing and pleading, and formularies and collections of statutes.[167]

As for formal teaching, it is evident that lectures for students of the common law were being given from 1278, probably at Westminster.[168] In the early fourteenth century disputations as learning exercises were taking place in a form similar to the disputations which formed a part of the university course in civil law. Hypothetical cases were put to students who were to show their ability to choose and apply the appropriate writs and pleadings, arguing opposing views with each other.[169] By the middle of the fourteenth century and the emergence of the inns, these disputations had evolved into extremely complex moot cases – cases which became known by mnemonic names and continued to be debated there for centuries. The moots were again concerned with the choice of writs and the forms of pleading, constituting a re-enactment of the tentative oral pleading of a real court, in which serjeants were allowed to test their arguments before committing themselves to their plea of record.[170]

Meanwhile, another form of learning exercise developed out of the early lectures – readings on the statutes.[171] These readings were not to reach their

fully-fledged form until the late fifteenth century, when an apprentice was called to
the bar at his inn to expound on the early statutes before the senior apprentices of
his inn (or 'benchers') during the vacations, but prototype readings were taking
place at a much earlier date. A few extant texts show their evolution from short
questions and answers to collections of notes – all on statute law. In a reading on
the Statute of Westminster II dating from the 1420s, each statute is analysed clause
by clause; the reader describes the common law prior to the statute, explains the
effect of the legislation, and demonstrates its application to specific cases.[172]

These early readers, to quote J.H. Baker, 'were not expected to give a wholly
original performance, but to expound and develop the traditional learning
surrounding their texts'. By the later fifteenth century, this exegesis of the statutes
is known to have been delivered in a prescribed, chronological order, and this
was probably the case from early on.[173] In a certain sense, therefore, this series of
the major statutes came to comprise a fixed corpus of text. As described by
Professor Baker, the exercises in which this corpus was analysed were both
conceptually and in practical terms similar to the analyses traditionally carried
out by academics (and Wycliffite writers) on another set text – the Bible.[174]

Similar principles of textual analysis applied in the dissection of the legal
arguments pleaded in court, as recorded by the apprentices in their notes, and in
the practice moots. The discussions reported in the yearbooks invariably turned on
whether or not the original writ 'was good', that is, whether the action being sued
could be maintained in the fixed form of the writ in which it had been presented to
the court; an action was tried not simply as a set of facts but on how well these facts
had been manipulated within the form of the writ and the options open to the
attorneys at the pleading stage.[175] Standardised writs, as such, embodied another
form of set text to which medieval lawyers had to address themselves.

Successful performance in the learning exercises of the inns before their seniors
was the means by which aspiring lawyers advanced. Participation in these, as well
as the actual experience and observation of pleading in court, ensured that lawyers
would become skilled in argument and analysis. They learned not only how to
penetrate to the heart of an argument, but also how to pervert an argument
through the subtle art of sophistry, and how to use information selectively for their
own ends. This experience directly parallels the textual analysis required in the
formulation of theological argument at the universities, against the sophistication of
which the Lollards complained bitterly.[176] Nevertheless, despite being deplored in
others, the manipulation of text was equally employed by Wycliffite writers: they
used the work of orthodox writers in a very selective fashion to find authority for
their own heretical views.[177] Knowing full well the dangers inherent in 'glossing' a
text, which he might have likened to the exercise of 'giving colour',[178] a common
lawyer may have been particularly receptive to the Wycliffite insistence on the
primacy of holy writ alone in matters of theology.

The degree of participation by the lawyers discussed here in the learning exercises of the inns cannot be measured, but all of those who can be shown to have frequented the Westminster courts probably had at least some contact with the inns and the education offered there, and all would have developed a critical habit of mind shaped by the rigours of legal advocacy. Thomas Tykhill, who was granted the right to wear a serjeant's livery in 1412, must have fared well in moots and readings. For a Master of Arts like Thomas Lucas, and indeed anyone versed in the tradition of the university disputation, the analysis of texts and the debates of inn and court alike would have been familiar exercises.[179]

Certainly, intellectual curiosity and an appetite for learning was characteristic of medieval common lawyers, for wide tastes in reading can often be perceived from the books that they owned. The libraries of Thomas Kebell, Roger Townshend and John Cokayne[180] spring to mind, to name but a few.[181] None of the heretical lawyers discussed here left any evidence of book ownership (nor indeed any wills), and understandably so, but one whom I have omitted, William Stourton of Stourton in Wiltshire, a lawyer placed on K.B. McFarlane's list of possible 'Lollard knights', did.[182] It is worth noting that Stourton, who died in 1413, had simultaneously held a post identical to that of Thomas Tykhill in the administration of Henry Prince of Wales as chief steward of the southern part of his estates, and had likewise sat on the prince's council.[183] Another lawyer, John Bount of Bristol, bequeathed in his will of 1404 a 'book of gospels in English', which he said was then in William Stourton's possession.[184]

Undoubtedly there were other reasons which attracted their support for the heresy, reasons which may have had more to do with their status as members of the gentry. The most obvious element of appeal, of course, was the Lollard plan for the disendowment of the clergy, a plan which would have benefited the gentry directly.[185] This scheme must have seemed agreeable to John Fynderne, with his interest in the possessions of the alien priories,[186] and it was clerical disendowment which Thomas Lucas advocated in his ill-advised letter to the Emperor Sigismund in 1416. Other conscious appeals to gentry support have been detected in many features of Lollard book production, which have been discussed by Margaret Aston and Anne Hudson.[187]

For those lawyers who were also active administrators in royal service, there may well have been a more specific focus to their anti-clericalism. As mentioned earlier, the rapid expansion of the legal profession in the late medieval period coincided with the development of a new careerism among laymen as employees in the king's and in private bureaucracies. This was a development which would have been welcomed by John Wycliffe and his followers. The denunciation of the 'Caesarean clergy' for its participation in royal administration was a central element of Wycliffe's criticism of men in holy orders, derived from his theory of dominion. It was a theme expressed in many of his works which found a resonance in the anti-clerical mood of late fourteenth-century society,[188] and which furnished a convenient ideology for the new breed of professional men.

Writers of Wycliffite tracts continued to harp on this theme. It received its lengthiest treatment in a long anti-clerical tract now contained in Lambeth Palace MS 551. This text, entitled 'The Clergy May Not Hold Property', includes a final section specifically dealing with the subject, under the subtitle: 'On the Wrongfulness of the Clergy holding Secular Office'.[189] Rather than present a coherent argument, the author of this section offers a host of carefully chosen citations from biblical and patristic sources to support the view that secular lords withhold priests 'in seculer bissynes' at the peril of the souls in their care and, lest the weight of these authorities be taken too lightly, a series of quotations in the original Latin follows to drive the point home.[190]

The Wycliffite text known as the 'Thirty-Seven Conclusions', which has been dated on the basis of internal evidence to *c.* 1395,[191] also dealt with this subject. It went further, in specifically naming the offices from which clerics should be barred – those in the Chancery, Treasury, Privy Seal and the Exchequer, as well as the stewardship of lands and halls in the service of both of the king and private lords.[192] At several points, the text addresses secular lords directly, and may have been written for the same audience as that of the 'Twelve Conclusions' posted on the doors of Westminster Hall during the Parliament of 1395.[193]

Other tracts subtly express views which would have held a similar appeal for the new class of lay administrators. One such tract is included in a collection of three Wycliffite texts, all written in a single hand and in the dialect of Derbyshire – now Bodleian MS Douce 273.[194] Entitled 'Tractatus de Regibus', the text is a skilful distillation of Wycliffe's theory of dominion, culled from various of his works.[195] The king's right and duty to reform a church gone wrong is its chief subject: the endowment of the clergy, its role in government and the abuse of its power of excommunication are all decried. The text patiently approaches its climax and apparent purpose – the persuasion of the king and nobility to reverse its policy of sanctioning the imprisonment of Lollard preachers, which was also a concern of the author(s) of the 'Thirty-Seven Conclusions'.[196] The other two tracts in the manuscript – 'On the Twenty-Five Articles'[197] and 'On the Seven Deadly Sins'[198] – are similar in style and tone. An unorthodox version of the *Lay Folks Catechism* was also originally bound in with these three tracts;[199] the whole manuscript was probably copied for a layman in the late fourteenth or early fifteenth century, possibly for one of the men discussed here.[200]

Although such tracts have not yet received the treatment they deserve, it is evident that many were intended for an audience of laymen, for the role of the king and the secular nobility as reformers of the corrupt Church is a theme running through these and other Wycliffite writings. It would appear that at least some of the lawyers and administrators who served lay rulers were willing if not eager to embrace this role. Intellectual curiosity and a confidence in their own ability to discover the meaning of sacred texts may have played an equal part. It is tempting to attribute to these lawyers sentiments similar to those which prompted Robert Plumpton, a student at the Inner Temple, to write to his mother enclosing a copy of the New Testament in about 1536. She was not to doubt her ability to understand it, he said, 'for God will give knowledge to whom he will give knowledge of the Scriptures, as soon to a shepperd as to a priest, yf he ask knowledg of God faithfully'.[201] If not to a shepherd, certainly to a lawyer.

Notes

[1] E.W. Ives, 'The Reputation of the Common Lawyer in English Society, 1450–1550', *University of Birmingham Historical Journal*, (1960), pp. 130–61.

[2] Two copies of this tract entitled 'Three things destroyen this world', survive: one in Corpus Christi College, Cambridge, MS 296, and one in Trinity College, Dublin, MS 244. The text has been printed in Matthew, *EWW*, pp. 182–4. Similar sentiments are expressed in another tract also published in this volume and also contained in the same two manuscripts, entitled 'Of servants and lords' (esp. pp. 234, 237–8). See also 'The Grete Sentence of Curs Expounded', printed in Arnold, *SEW*, iii, p. 332.

[3] A valuable, but brief, work on this subject is N.L. Ramsay, 'What was the Legal Profession?' in M.A. Hicks (ed.), *Profit, Piety and the Professions* (Gloucester, 1990), pp. 62–71. See also E.W. Ives, 'The common lawyers in pre-Reformation England', *TRHS*, 5th ser., 18 (1968), pp. 145–73, and for the paucity of work done on the subject of fifteenth-century attorneys J.H. Baker, 'The Attorneys and Officers of the Common Law', *Journal of Legal History*, 1 (1980), pp. 182–3.

[4] In addition to the Common Pleas, there was the court of King's Bench, and the common law courts of the Exchequer and Chancery. Judges were created by royal appointment, while serjeants were admitted to the order by the Common Pleas justices and called to their 'estate and degree' by a royal writ of subpoena. On the serjeants generally, see J.H. Baker, *The Order of Serjeants-at-Law* (London, 1984).

[5] The clearest account of medieval pleading is in J.H. Baker, *An Introduction to English Legal History*, 3rd edn (London, 1990), pp. 90–4. For counting, *Novae Narrationes*, ed. E. Shanks and S.F.C. Milsom (Selden Society, 80, 1963).

[6] Baker, *Introduction to English Legal History*, p. 182.

[7] The graduated income tax of that year was levied at 40s for 'great' (senior) apprentices, 20s for 'other' apprentices and 6s 8d for both apprentices 'of lesser estate' and attorneys: *Rot. Parl.*, iii, pp. 57–8.

[8] On education at the early inns, see J.H. Baker, *The Third University of England: the inns of court and the common-law tradition*, Selden Society Lecture (London, 1990), pp. 5–16, and on the early inns themselves, see Baker, *Introduction to English Legal History*, pp. 182–4; S.E. Thorne, 'The Early History of the Inns of Court', *Graya*, 50 (1959), pp. 79–96, reprinted in his *Essays in English Legal History* (London, 1985), pp. 137–54; R.F. Foxburgh, 'Lincoln's Inn of the 14th century', *Law Quarterly Review*, 94 (1978), pp. 363–82.

[9] M. Hastings, *The Court of Common Pleas in Fifteenth Century England* (Ithaca, 1947), pp. 38–42.

[10] That groups of lawyers banded together for this purpose, perhaps while students, is the impression gained by an examination of the class of documents in the PRO known as Chancery Special Bail Pardons (C237) for the reigns of Henry IV and V. The employment of common law attorneys as mainpernors is a subject which has not received the attention it deserves.

[11] Evidence that the same professional attorneys acted in both the county and the king's courts exists from the early fourteenth century: R.C. Palmer, 'County Year Book Reports: the professional lawyer in the medieval county court', *EHR*, 91 (1976), pp. 776–801. How long and to what extent this continued to be the case is a matter of speculation.

[12] The drafting of the increasing number of petitions to the king and parliament was largely the work of lawyers operating at this level. Their role in local society had become greater, as had the importance of the county courts in the late Middle Ages: J.R. Maddicott, 'The County Community and the Making of Public Opinion in Fourteenth Century England', *TRHS*, 5th ser., 28 (1978), pp. 28–41.

[13] The retention of common lawyers by ecclesiastical bodies had become common practice by the mid-fourteenth century, when they replaced the canon lawyers who had previously advised such bodies: N.L. Ramsay, 'Retained Legal Counsel, *c.* 1275–*c.* 1475', *TRHS*, 5th ser., 35 (1985), pp. 95–112.

[14] It is now widely accepted that many, if not most, legal disputes were settled by arbitration; see C. Rawcliffe, 'The Great Lord as Peacekeeper: Arbitration by English Noblemen and Their Councils in the Later Middle Ages' in J.A. Guy and H.G. Beale (eds), *Law and Social Change in British History* (London, 1984), pp. 34–53; E. Powell, 'Arbitration and Law in England in the Late Middle Ages', *TRHS*, 5th ser., 33 (1983), pp. 49–67. A fee'd lawyer would have played a large part in such proceedings, whether serving on a panel of arbitrators chosen to settle a dispute, or appearing as his client's representative before such a body.

[15] Ives, 'The Reputation of the Common Lawyer', pp. 159–60.

[16] This is admittedly an impressionistic view (judging in part from the size of the rolls), but it stands to reason, even if it could be shown that the number of attorneys operating in the central courts remained constant. See, however, the complaint made in the parliament of 1455 about the surfeit of such attorneys in Norfolk and Suffolk: *Rot. Parl.*, v, pp. 326–7.

[17] The increasing popularity of entails and enfeoffments in the fourteenth century, moreover, contributed greatly to the development of an entirely new court in the Chancery, where remedy for their abuses could be provided by virtue of the Chancellor's equitable jurisdiction. See M.E. Avery, 'The History of the Equitable Jurisdiction of Chancery before 1460', *BIHR*, 42 (1969), pp. 131–44.

[18] The widespread use of such bonds is patently evident in the Common Plea rolls where complaints of broken contracts, for which one brought an action of debt, exist in great profusion (PRO, Court of Common Pleas, Plea Rolls, CP40). See A.W.B. Simpson, 'The Penal Bond with Conditional Defeasance', *Law Quarterly Review*, 82 (1966), pp. 392–422; R.C. Palmer, *English Law in the Age of the Black Death, 1348–1381* (Chapel Hill, 1993), pp. 62–91.

[19] Dr Storey has suggested, moreover, that the clergy were reluctant to take up these posts, because of popular criticism that they neglected their spiritual duties in doing so: R.L. Storey, 'Gentlemen-Bureaucrats', in C.H. Clough (ed.), *Profession, Vocation and Culture in Later Medieval England*, (Liverpool, 1982), pp. 100–4. See above, pp. 46–7.

[20] *Ibid.*, pp. 104–5. On the laicisation of the Exchequer, see further: J.L. Kirby, 'The Rise of the Under-Treasurer of the Exchequer', *EHR*, 72 (1957), pp. 666–77; J.C. Sainty, 'The Tenure of Offices in the Exchequer', *EHR*, 96 (1965), pp. 449–57.

[21] Namely, the king's household, chamber and great wardrobe, and the office of clerk of the works: Storey, 'Gentlemen-Bureaucrats', p. 100. The so-called 'writing offices' of Chancery and Privy Seal, where more specialist skills were needed, held out much longer: J. Catto, 'The King's Servants', in G.L. Harriss (ed.), *Henry V: The Practice of Kingship* (Oxford, 1985), pp. 77–9.

[22] R.A. Griffiths, 'Public and Private Bureaucracies in England and Wales in the Fifteenth Century', *TRHS*, 5th ser., 30 (1980), pp. 109–30.

[23] R. Somerville, *The Duchy of Lancaster*, 2 vols (London, 1953–70). The estates and household of the Prince of Wales, which includes the Principality of Wales, the Earldom of Chester and the Duchy of Cornwall, was also a private, but royal, administrative unit: W.R.M. Griffiths, 'The Military Career and Affinity of Henry Prince of Wales, 1399–1413' (M.Litt. thesis, Oxford University, 1980); A.E. Curry, 'The Demesne of the County Palatine of Chester in the Early Fifteenth Century' (M.A. thesis, Manchester University, 1977), pp. 1–45.

[24] Ramsay, 'What was the Legal Profession?' (n. 3 above), pp. 68–9.

[25] D.A.L. Morgan, 'The Individual Style of the English Gentleman', in Michael Jones (ed.), *Gentry and Lesser Nobility in Late Medieval Europe* (Gloucester, 1986), pp. 25–6.

[26] For a fuller investigation of Thomas Tykhill's life and involvement with Lollardy, see M. Jurkowski, 'Lancastrian Royal Service, Lollardy and Forgery: The Career of Thomas Tykhill', in R.E. Archer (ed.), *Crown, Government and People in the Fifteenth Century* (Stroud, 1995), pp. 33–52.

[27] The Derbyshire Tykhills, who had settled in Chellaston by the early fourteenth century, were a

branch of the Tickhills of Tickhill of southern Yorkshire, from whom three clerks in royal service in the early fourteenth century were drawn: J.L. Grassi, 'Clerical Dynasties from Howdenshire, Nottinghamshire and Lindsey in the Royal Administration, 1280–1340' (D.Phil. thesis, Oxford University, 1960), pp. 486–9. For deeds of the early Tykhills in Derbyshire, see: Derbyshire Record Office (DRO), D2375M/101/3; D779B/T71; Sheffield City Archives, Bagshawe Collection 2469.

[28] *CPR, 1396–99*, p. 531; PRO, CP40/577, rot. 7d. In Easter term 1399, moreover, Thomas Tykhill was a mainpernor for the court appearance of the bishop's vicar-general, to answer two debt charges: PRO, CP40/553, rot. 329d. On Walter Bullock, the vicar-general, see Emden, *BRUO*, p. 303.

[29] It was certainly the patronage of Lord Grey after his fall from grace which kept him prominent in the affairs of Derbyshire: *CPR, 1413–16*, pp. 393–4, 418. Grey also headed all the peace commissions to which Tykhill was appointed during the reign of Henry IV; see below. As early as 1398 Tykhill owned land in Astwith in Ault Hucknall, far from his other properties, but perhaps leased from Grey, who also had an estate there: PRO, CP40/548, rot. 75; CP40/616, rot. 7.

[30] *CPR, 1396–99*, p. 531; *1399–1401*, p. 558; *1401–5*, p. 516; *1405–08*, p. 490; *1413–16*, p. 418.

[31] He represented the duchy interests at assizes in Derbyshire, Leicestershire and Staffordshire from 1409, and from 1411 he sat on the duchy council: Jurkowski, 'Thomas Tykhill', p. 34.

[32] His annual fee of office was £20, plus expenses at 6s 8d per day in dangerous Cheshire and 4s elsewhere. In 1408 the latter were more than £48 in arrears. He was also paid 5 marks per annum to serve on the council: PRO, Special Collections, Ministers' Accounts, SC6/813/23, fols. 5–5v.

[33] Jurkowski, 'Thomas Tykhill', pp. 34–5; Bodleian Library, MS Tanner 196, fols. 3v–5v; G. Roberts, 'The Anglesey Submissions of 1406', *Bulletin of the Board of Celtic Studies*, 15 (1952), pp. 39–61.

[34] P. McNiven, 'Prince Henry and the English Political Crisis of 1412', *History*, 65 (1980), pp. 1–16.

[35] The formal appointment was only to the Common Pleas, but he appeared on the king's behalf in all three courts: *CPR, 1408–13*, p. 163; *Select Cases in the Court of King's Bench*, ed. G.O. Sayles (Selden Society, 6, 1965), pp. xc–xci; Jurkowski, 'Thomas Tykhill', p. 36.

[36] *CFR, 1399–1405*, pp. 251–4; *CPR, 1408–13*, pp. 172, 182, 227, 431, 475; *1413–16*, p. 148; PRO, Exchequer, Lord Treasurer's Remembrancer, Originalia Rolls, E371/177, rots. 14–15; E371/179, rot. 21.

[37] One employer was the cathedral priory of Ely, who retained him as legal counsel in London from 1420 to 1424, and perhaps much earlier: Jurkowski, 'Thomas Tykhill', p. 48.

[38] He owned lands in Aston-on-Trent, Chellaston, Wilne, Marston, Shardlow, Scropton and Astwith, all in Derbyshire, and in Castle Donington, Leicestershire and Tutbury, Staffordshire: *ibid.*, p. 37; PRO, CP40/903, rot. 338.

[39] His tenure of the posts of king's attorney and chief steward was confirmed in 1413, but fishing rights in Melbourne, granted to him as a mark of favour by Henry IV, were taken away and in April 1413 bestowed upon another duchy servant, Peter Melbourne. In October the king was compelled to write to the resentful Tykhill, insisting that he surrender the rights to Melbourne: PRO, Duchy of Lancaster, Miscellaneous Books, DL42/17, fols. 1, 72.

[40] They were married by 1396. Agnes's family name is unknown, but she brought to Tykhill a life interest in lands in Tutbury and Scropton, previously held by John Duffield of Tutbury: DRO, D779B/T76; PRO, DL42/4/99, fol. 119.

[41] PRO, Court of King's Bench, Ancient Indictments, KB9/204/1, mm. 59–61.

[42] After hearing a sermon by Ederyk in Castle Donington church on Easter Sunday 1413, a 'sutor' named John Anneys was said to have preached in taverns and other public places, that one need not confess all one's sins to a priest and that all bishops and doctors serving the church were fools, and everyone knew it: C. Kightly, 'The Early Lollards': A Survey of Popular Lollard Activity in England, 1382–1428 (D.Phil. thesis, University of York, 1975), pp. 32–4, cf. Lincolnshire Archives Office, Visitation Book Vj/o, fols. 10, 14, 14v, 16, 16v.

[43] Ederyk had been fitted out with armour and his men promised wages of 1 mark each: PRO, KB9/204/1, mm. 59–61.

⁴⁴ PRO, Court of King's Bench, Recorda, KB145/5/2/1. The tradesmen who had formed Ederyk's group were also pardoned: Jurkowski, 'Thomas Tykhill', p. 39.

⁴⁵ *CPR, 1413–16*, p. 150; PRO, Court of King's Bench, Coram Rege Rolls, KB27/611, rot. 13 rex.

⁴⁶ He was released without charge: PRO, KB27/611, rot. 13 rex; PRO, Chancery, Recognisances, C259/7, m. 5.

⁴⁷ C. Rawcliffe, 'Henry Booth', in J.S. Roskell, Linda Clark and Carol Rawcliffe (eds), *The History of Parliament. The House of Commons 1386–1421*, 4 vols (Stroud, 1993), i, p. 288; Bodleian Library, MS Dodsworth 149, fols. 157ᵛ, 163.

⁴⁸ They were married by Trinity term 1394, when they were sued in the Common Pleas for detinue of goods: PRO, CP40/535, rot. 28d. It is difficult to conclude other than that the 'Elisabeth', wife of Henry Bothe, who appears only in a final concord of 1408 for a messuage and dovecot in Derby, was a scribal error for 'Isabel': *Derbyshire Feet of Fines, 1323–1546*, ed. H.G.H. Garratt and C. Rawcliffe (Derbyshire Record Society, 11, 1985), p. 74; PRO, Court of Common Pleas, Feet of Fines, CP25(1)/39/42, m. 18. This solution would solve the chronological problems acknowledged by Dr Rawcliffe, see Rawcliffe, 'Henry Booth', p. 290, n. 2. Henry and Isabel's son and heir, John, was of age by June 1416: DRO, D2375M/13/3(4). Isabel died in 1441 and was buried in the church of Findern, where the incised slab of her tomb remains today: L. Jewitt, 'Findern and the Fyndernes', *The Reliquary*, 3 (1863), pp. 189–90; N. Pevsner, *Derbyshire*, 2nd edn, revised by E. Williamson (London, 1978), p. 215.

⁴⁹ Rawcliffe, 'Henry Booth', p. 289.

⁵⁰ PRO, CP40/598, rot. 423 (where he sued his client for his fee of 40s); PRO, Exchequer, Exchequer of Pleas, E13/117, rot. 6.

⁵¹ PRO, Justices Itinerant, Assize Rolls, JUST1/1514, rot. 69d; JUST1/1524, rot. 17; JUST1/1537, rot. 19d.

⁵² Bothe's own deposition on the matter survives among the early Chancery proceedings: PRO, Chancery, Early Chancery Proceedings, C1/6/318.

⁵³ Rawcliffe, 'Henry Booth', p. 289.

⁵⁴ PRO, DL42/16, fol. 67.

⁵⁵ Rawcliffe, 'Henry Booth', pp. 288, 290.

⁵⁶ PRO, KB9/204/1, mm. 57–67.

⁵⁷ PRO, KB9/204/1, mm. 57–67; KB27/614, rot. 45 rex.

⁵⁸ The order to the escheator for the valuation and confiscation of all his lands, goods and chattels was given on 26 January, and stated that Bothe was in exigent for outlawry for treasons and felonies. The goods, valued at £13 11s 4d consisted of livestock, seed stocks, sown fields, and some household goods: PRO, Exchequer, King's Remembrancer, Escheators' Files, E153/2450B, mm. 2, 4–5; PRO, Exchequer, Pipe Office, Pipe Rolls, E372/261, Not-Derb dorse. In 1416, Bothe was allowed to buy back the goods: PRO, Exchequer, Tellers' Rolls, E405/31, rot. 1.

⁵⁹ *CCR, 1413–19*, pp. 116, 121.

⁶⁰ *CCR, 1413–19*, p. 124; PRO, C259/7, m. 5; KB27/614, rots. 15, 24 rex.

⁶¹ *The Judges of England 1272–1990*, ed. J.C. Sainty (Selden Society, Suppl. Series, 10, 1993), pp. 68, 93. Cokayne had been a successful lawyer under Richard II in London, where he was the city's recorder from 1394 to 1398. He was very clearly connected with the Lancastrians, however, serving as chief steward of the northern part of the duchy of Lancaster from 1399 to 1400: E. Foss, *The Judges of England, with Sketches of their Lives*, 9 vols (London, 1848–64), iv, p. 303; Somerville, *Duchy of Lancaster*, i, p. 418.

⁶² For the family's early history and its legendary foundation by a crusading knight, see M. Craven, 'Sir Geoffrey de Finderne and His Flower', *Derbyshire Archaeological Journal*, 103 (1983), pp. 91–7.

⁶³ DRO, D185/R3.

⁶⁴ Fynderne's father, also John, had been the abbey's steward in the 1360s: *A Calendar of Charters*

and Other Documents belonging to the Hospital of William Wyggeston at Leicester, ed. A.H. Thompson (Leicester, 1933), pp. 203–5. The stewardship was hotly contested, but John Fynderne appears to have held the post from 1404 to 1416 at least, and in 1406 was said also to be a member of the abbot's council: Staffordshire Record Office [SRO], D603/A/ADD/1939; D603/A/ADD/632; BL, MS Loan 30, fols. 150ᵛ–151ᵛ.

65 See, for example: PRO, CP40/614, rot. 367d; CP40/615, rot. 554d; CP40/625, rot. 131d.

66 He held the post from 1399 to 1406 and again from 1410 to 1412: *Officers of the Exchequer*, ed. J.C. Saintly (List & Index Society, Special Series, 18, 1983), pp. 78–9.

67 W.H. Bryson, 'A Book of All the Several Officers of the Court of Exchequer . . . According to the State of the Exchequer at this Day, January 1641 by Lawrence Squibb', *Camden Miscellany XXVI* (Camden 4th ser., 14, 1975), pp. 108–15.

68 On corruption in the apposer's office, see C.H. Haskins and M.D. George, 'Verses Written on the Exchequer in the Fifteenth Century', *EHR*, 36 (1921), pp. 58–67.

69 *CPR, 1402–05*, p. 502; *CCR, 1401–05*, p. 319; *1405–08*, p. 229; PRO, Exchequer, King's Remembrancer, Memoranda Rolls, E159/186, rot. 1. He sat also as an assize justice in Nottinghamshire in 1403: PRO, Chancery, Patent Rolls, C66/369, m. 11d; CP40/585, rot. 145.

70 *CPR, 1399–1401*, p. 380; *1402–05*, p. 82; PRO, E372/247 (Derb-Not); *CFR, 1399–1405*, p. 230; PRO, Duchy of Lancaster, Accounts Various, DL28/4/4, fols. 5, 18ᵛ; *CFR, 1405–13*, p. 68.

71 Corporation of London Record Office [CLRO], Hustings Roll (137) 12, 19; (139) 34, 35; (140) 18, 19; *Calendar of Plea and Memoranda Rolls . . . at the Guildhall 1413–1437*, ed. A.H. Thomas (Cambridge, 1963), pp. 9, 12, 56–8; PRO, KB27/626, rots. 17d, 24; CP40/635, enrolled bills 1d; CP40/636, rots. 171, 418; CP40/642, rot. 426; E13/134, rots. 5–5d; E13/135, rot. 6d; *Feet of Fines for Essex, 1327–1422*, ed. R.C. Fowler (Essex Archaeological Society, 3, 1949), p. 254; *CCR, 1413–19*, pp. 384, 387; *CCR, 1429–36*, pp. 596–8.

72 See the recognisances section of the King's Remembrancer's Memoranda Rolls (PRO, E159) from 1402 to 1409.

73 Fynderne acted as a conveyancing agent for Grey after the latter's release from captivity by Owyn Glyndŵr, who had held him to ransom for 10,000 marks: G.H. Fowler, 'Records of Harrold Priory', *Publications of the Bedfordshire Historical Record Society*, 17 (1935), pp. 172–4; L.H. Butler, 'Robert Braybrooke, Bishop of London (1381–1404) and his kinsmen' (D.Phil. thesis, Oxford University, 1951), pp. viii, 438–9. Fynderne may have been involved in the negotiations for Grey's release; he certainly bought lands sold by Grey to raise the ransom money and in 1404 was appointed to a commission to investigate the concealment of lands in Shropshire forfeited by Glyndŵr's accomplice Edmund Mortimer: F.G. Hipkins, 'The State of Repton Manor from the Reign of Henry I to that of Henry V', *Journal of the Derbyshire Archaeological and Natural History Society*, 24 (1902), p. 77; *CPR, 1402–05*, p. 502.

74 PRO, KB27/615, rot. 29, where Fynderne was said to be of Arundell's counsel.

75 PRO, KB27/599, rot. 78d; KB27/600, rot. 44; KB27/603, rots. 5, 14, 15d rex; KB27/609, rot. 9d rex; *CCR, 1408–13*, pp. 338–9. Barentyne's connection with Fynderne probably came through Cokayne, who had been involved with the goldsmith since at least 1403; the same is undoubtedly true of Lord Grey who was Cokayne's father-in-law by 1394; CLRO, Hustings Roll 131 (46); 144 (33); *Derbs. Feet of Fines*, pp. 63–5.

76 PRO, DL28/4/2, fol. 13ᵛ; DL28/4/7, fol. 10ᵛ.

77 *CFR, 1399–1405*, pp. 196–9, 241–2. He and John Cokayne were later accused of having obtained custody of Tutbury by producing false documents which misrepresented the priory's status: A. Saltman, 'The Priory of Tutbury', *Victoria County History, Stafford*, iii (London, 1970), pp. 335–8.

78 *CFR, 1399–1405*, p. 249; R. Graham, 'The Order of Grandmont and its Houses in England', in her *English Ecclesiastical Studies* (London, 1929), pp. 210–11, 226–7; Griffiths, 'Military Career', pp. 32–6 (see above, n. 23).

79 PRO, Exchequer, Exchequer of Receipt, Issue Rolls, E403/614, m. 1. Two men summoned with them – Hugh Erdeswick and Edmund lord Ferrers of Chartley – were involved in large-scale

disorder in Staffordshire, see E. Powell, *Kingship, Law and Society. Criminal Justice in the Reign of Henry V* (Oxford, 1989), pp. 208–16. For the dispute between Fynderne and Bothe, PRO, KB27/610, rot. 80, rot. 16d rex; DRO, D2375M/24/55.

[80] The other mainpernors were Bothe's Lancashire relations: *CCR, 1413–19*, p. 116.

[81] Derby, Local Studies Library, Every Deed 3494; *Derbs. Feet of Fines*, p. 74.

[82] DRO, D2375/24/55. Tykhill personally acknowledged the authenticity of his release to Fynderne at the Exchequer in May 1411: PRO, E159/187, rot. 1 Easter term recognisances.

[83] PRO, KB9/204/1, m. 59; KB27/627, rot. 9. On his evidently close relationship with Tykhill, with whom he may have had family ties, PRO, KB9/1056, mm. 33–5; BL, Wolley Charter, I, 85.

[84] BL, Add. MS 6671, fols. 28–9.

[85] PRO, KB9/204/1, m. 66.

[86] *CCR, 1409–13*, pp. 353–4; *Wyggeston Charters*, pp. 207–8; *CCR, 1413–19*, p. 273. Among many references to his quarrel with John Fynderne beginning in 1417, see PRO, KB27/624, rot. 60d; CP40/629, rot. 403; KB9/1055, m. 22.

[87] PRO, KB27/627, rots. 9d, 12d, 14 rex; KB27/628, rot. 19 rex. Marshall was still being sought for this reason in 1426: KB27/669, rot. 12d rex.

[88] Bothe was elected four times to parliament – in 1420, 1423, 1425 and 1427. On the later careers of Tykhill and Bothe, see Jurkowski, 'Thomas Tykhill', pp. 40–52; Rawcliffe, 'Henry Booth', pp. 288–91.

[89] PRO, KB27/627, rot. 12. Fynderne may have been motivated here by a favour owed to Thomas Farnham, another of the mainpernors and Jeke's brother-in-law: PRO, CP40/625, rot. 131d.

[90] Both men were also accused of supporting Oldcastle: PRO, KB145/5/7.

[91] PRO, KB145/5/6; KB27/629, rot. 17d rex.

[92] He was part of a group which left for the revolt from Derby. Although pardoned in Easter term 1415, he was still in Newgate prison in September of that year: PRO, KB9/204/1, m. 58; KB27/616, rots. 23–23d rex; PRO, Exchequer, King's Remembrancer, Sheriffs' Accounts, E199/26/30.

[93] Kightly, 'Early Lollards', pp. 11, 134–5; PRO, KB9/204/1, m. 141. He had allegedly been released earlier: KB27/613, rot. 6 rex.

[94] PRO, CP40/641, m. 12; PRO, Chancery, Inquisitions Miscellaneous, C145/300, m. 18.

[95] The Fridays had lived at Wigston since the later twelfth century, when a Ralph Friday witnessed the earliest Wigston charter: W.G. Hoskins, *The Midland Peasant* (London, 1957), pp. 31–2, 53, 71, 74, 78. Yet another Ralph Friday witnessed many charters in the following century: *Wyggeston Charters*, nos. 867–8, 873–5, 881, 883, 886, 888, 890, 892, 895–6, 899, 902–3, 905–7.

[96] PRO, CP40/551, m. 439; *Wyggeston Charters*, nos. 653, 1023, 1032; Hoskins, *Midland Peasant*, p. 31.

[97] PRO, KB27/617, rot. 1 attorneys; CP40/613, rot. 34. In 1398 he represented his brother John in a suit over land in Wigston: PRO, CP40/551, rot. 439.

[98] PRO, CP40/544, rots. 27, 438; CP40/551, rot. 439; CP40/564, rot. 287d; CP40/587, rot. 90d; CP40/589, rot. 326d; CP40/616, rot. 138.

[99] PRO, KB27/612, rot. 11 rex.

[100] In two instances, he sued debts in the Common Pleas which originated in the county. On two other occasions, he mainprised for a pardon, listing his residence as in the county of Oxford, which indicates that he had property there meant to serve as collateral for the mainprise: PRO, CP40/561, rot. 321; CP40/562, rot. 461; PRO, Chancery, Special Bail Pardons, C237/38, mm. 30, 31.

[101] He was also referred to as 'of county Leicester' in 1407 and in the same year acted as a guarantor in the county with his brother Richard: PRO, C237/30, mm. 17, 22; C237/31, m. 109d; C237/32, mm. 50, 190, 233, 270.

[102] PRO, KB27/602, rot. 19; KB27/603, rot. 18d; KB27/605, rot. 43d. John London was also elected MP for the borough in 1401: C. Kightly, 'John London', in Roskell *et al.* (eds), *History of*

Parliament, ii, p. 616. Elizabeth, named as his wife by Dr Kightly, was probably married to John, his son.

103 He mainprised for at least thirteen pardons in that year. See the several bonds posted in the years 1405 to 1416, usually with the same group of attorneys – perhaps members of his inn – in PRO, C237/28, m. 10; C237/29, m. 74; C237/30, mm. 17, 22; C237/32, mm. 30, 31, 50, 138, 139, 149, 163, 178, 190, 233, 270, 280, 308; C237/37, m. 29, 120; C237/38; mm. 187, 204, 205; C237/39, mm. 22, 31. He was also an active guarantor of court appearances with Leicestershire attorneys, including his brother Richard, in 1414 and 1415, following the sessions held before the king in Leicester in April–May 1414: PRO, KB27/614, rot. 2 fines, rots. 30d, 36–36d; KB27/615, rot. 1d fines.

104 PRO, CP40/611, rot. 409; CP40/628, rot. 282d; CP40/635, rot. 1 attorneys; CP40/644, rot. 2 attorneys; KB27/629, rot. 1 attorneys; KB27/642, rot. 1d attorneys; KB27/648, rot. 1 attorneys; JUST1/1537, rot. 29.

105 *Wyggeston Charters*, nos. 1001, 1006–7, 1012, 1023, 1032.

106 In a trespass suit brought against three men in 1413, he claimed that sixty-eight sheep had been abducted from him there: PRO, CP40/611, rot. 409.

107 J. Crompton, 'Leicestershire Lollards', *Transactions of the Leicestershire Archaeological and Historical Society*, 44 (1968–9), pp. 26, 28–9.

108 For Belgrave's opinions, see: *ibid.*, pp. 29–30, and for his earlier clashes with ecclesiastical authorities, see: Hudson, *PR*, p. 77; Kightly, 'Early Lollards', p. 112.

109 Both Friday and Belgrave were called Lollards: PRO, KB9/204/1, m. 141.

110 McFarlane, *JW*, p. 174.

111 These were John Angret, parson of the church of Islehampstead Latimer, Richard Norton of Wycombe and Richard Freman of Rickmansworth: PRO, C237/37, m. 120.

112 Belgrave and eight others from Leicester, however, were imprisoned in the Marshalsea until June 1414, when they were delivered to Bishop Repingdon for correction: PRO, KB27/613, rot. 6 rex; BL, Add. MS 38525, ff. 28–28ᵛ; PRO, KB145/5/2/1. Friday did suffer at the hands of enemies, however, see *Select Cases in Chancery, 1364–1471*, ed. W.P. Baildon (Selden Society, 10, 1896), pp. 123–4.

113 The membranes on which he entered mesne process have his name written in the bottom right-hand corner. See, for example: PRO, CP40/544, rot. 338; CP40/617, rot. 477. On the Common Pleas filacers, Hastings, *Court of Common Pleas*, pp. 145–7.

114 William Armeston and Thomas Cowley both rose to prominence as attorneys in the early fifteenth century by this means. Armeston became the duchy of Lancaster's attorney in the Common Pleas, and Cowley succeeded to the post of king's attorney in the King's Bench court: PRO, CP40/551, rot. 493; Somerville, *Duchy of Lancaster*, i, p. 457 (Armeston); J.B. Post, 'King's Bench Clerks in the Reign of Richard II', *BIHR*, 47 (1974), p. 161 (Cowley).

115 PRO, CP40/544, rots. 75, 338d; CP40/616, rot. 138. As a defendant in a lawsuit for debt in 1422, he was described as a 'gentleman attorney in the Common Bench': CP40/644, rot. 1d attorneys.

116 PRO, E371/183, rot. 23. In 1419 he sat in sessions on three occasions: PRO, Exchequer, Lord Treasurer's Remembrancer, Miscellaneous Rolls, E370/160/3, m. 18.

117 PRO, KB27/613, rot. 6d fines, rot. 29 rex.

118 Namely in Radclif and Kinalton: PRO, CP40/551, rot. 473; CP40/583, rot. 1 enrolled bills.

119 PRO, JUST3/195, rot. 37. He was also accused of having committed a theft in 1404.

120 The story told by the approver Robert Rose is discussed in Kightly, 'Early Lollards' (n. 42 above), p. 41.

121 Hudson, *PR*, pp. 80–1; A.K. McHardy, 'Bishop Buckingham and the Lollards of Lincoln Diocese', *SCH*, 9 (1972), pp. 133–4; and see McHardy above, p. 119–20.

122 McFarlane, *JW*, pp. 141–5; PRO, Special Collections, Ancient Petitions, SC8/142/7099.

123 Apart from a brief mention in Kightly, 'Early Lollards', pp. 107–8. It is possible (but unlikely,

I think) that the Thomas Compworth now embarking upon a legal career was the son of the heretical Thomas Compworth. In 1395 a Thomas Compworth 'the younger' was pardoned for a murder and robbery committed at Thrupp in 1387: *CPR, 1391–96*, p. 600. Significantly, one of his mainpernors for a later pardon of the same crime was William Sawtrey, the chaplain burned for heresy in 1401: A.K. McHardy, above, Chapter 6, pp. 119–21. It was perhaps also the younger Compworth who was involved with the Lollards of Northampton.

[124] *CCR, 1396–9*, pp. 68, 405; *CFR, 1399–1405*, p. 58; PRO, C237/26, m. 27; KB27/570, rot. 1d fines, rot. 2 rex; C237/27, m. 408; *CFR, 1405–13*, pp. 84, 132; PRO, CP40/595, rot. 262; KB27/608, rots. 27–29d; *CFR, 1413–22*, pp. 46, 64, 260; *1422–29*, pp. 186–7.

[125] PRO, CP40/598, rot. 158d. He also appeared as an attorney in Chancery: PRO, Chancery, Recorda, C260/130, m. 32.

[126] Namely, the manors of Withybrook and Wishaw: PRO, CP40/583, rot. 1d enrolled bills; CP25/1/248/67, m. 43; CP40/589, rot. 260d; CP40/590, rot. 53. Moreover, Elizabeth was also co-heiress to the Northamptonshire manor of Newbold, as a descendant of William Swynford through her mother; the manor was recovered at assize in 1424: JUST1/1537, rots. 41–41d.

[127] PRO, E371/180, rot. 14; C260/130, m. 32; KB27/621, rot. 13 rex, rot. 1d attorneys; PRO, Chancery, Warrants, C81/1423, m. 18. In a charter of instruction to her feoffees, Lady Lovell directed that Compworth was to receive an annuity of 5 marks from her estate: *CCR, 1419–22*, p. 125.

[128] PRO, KB27/618, rot. 47.

[129] PRO, E371/178, rot. 50. He also had been appointed to the quorum of an enquiry commission of 1412: E371/177, rot. 8.

[130] *List of Escheators for England and Wales* (List & Index Society, 72, 1971), p. 95; *CFR, 1413–22*, p. 13; Kightly, 'Early Lollards', pp. 107–8. His date of death is unknown. According to the inquisition post mortem of John Neville, an esquire of Gayhurst, Buckinghamshire, whom he had served as a feoffee, Compworth was still alive in October 1438: PRO, Exchequer, Inquisitions Post Mortem, E149/164, m. 3.

[131] Emden, *BRUO*, p. 1170; M. Aston, 'Lollardy and Sedition, 1381–1431', in Aston, *LR*, p. 22, first published in *P&P*, 17 (1960).

[132] Mybbe was arrested for his part: J.I. Catto, 'Wyclif and Wycliffism at Oxford 1356–1430', in J.I. Catto and R. Evans (eds), *The History of the University of Oxford*, ii, *Late Medieval Oxford* (Oxford, 1992), pp. 252–3. For Mybbe's later involvement with the obdurate heretical priest Thomas Drayton, see below (n. 157) and Kightly, 'Early Lollards', pp. 250–7.

[133] Such bills reportedly appeared in London, St Albans, Northampton, Reading and Canterbury: Thomson, *LL*, pp. 16–17; KB27/624, rot. 9 rex.

[134] The jurors appeared after only one distraint: PRO, KB27/624, rot. 9 rex; KB145/5/5/1.

[135] T.H. Aston, 'The External Administration and Resources of Merton College to circa 1348', in J.I. Catto (ed.), *The History of the University of Oxford*, i, *The Early Oxford Schools* (Oxford, 1984), pp. 331–6, 344.

[136] These were William James, John Gamylgay and Richard Whelpington. They visited the manors of Barkby and Kibworth Harcourt (Leics.), Cheddington (Bucks.), Embleton and Ponteland (Northumb.) and Stillington and Seaton Carew (Co. Durham): Merton College, Oxford, Merton College Archives [MCA] 5611, 5613, 5614, 6278–81, 6285, 6586; PRO, CP40/544, rot. 33; CP40/551, rot. 387d. For the northern manors, see below.

[137] PRO, CP40/614, rots. 113, 485d. It was alleged that he had received £4 from the bailiff of Cheddington, Bucks., between Christmas 1394 and Easter 1395, for which he never accounted. Unfortunately, the relevant bailiff's account does not survive. No further details are available about his receipts in Leicestershire, but no liveries to him appear in any of the bailiffs' accounts for that period: MCA 6278–81 (Kibworth Harcourt); MCA 6586 (Barkby).

[138] In the autumns of 1400, 1405 and 1406: MCA 3727, 6143, 6144. William James also travelled to the northern manors in 1400, and John Gamylgay was there in 1390, 1391 and 1393. Before his

death in 1406, Richard Whelpington made the same journey at least seven times (1389–93, 1402–3): MCA 3718–20, 3723, 4186b, 6089–91, 6093–94, 6119, 6123, 6126–8, 6135, 6143, 6154.

139 F.M. Powicke, *The Medieval Books of Merton College* (Oxford, 1931), pp. 73, 188. He was paid as a fellow until 1406: MCA, 3732; Emden, *BRUO*, p. 1170.

140 A fifteenth-century hand noted alongside their names on the college's official list of fellows that both Lucas and Gamylgay had been expelled: MCA 413 (*Catalogus Vetus*), fol. 13v.

141 PRO, CP40/599, rot. 220d; CP40/611, rot. 7.

142 PRO, KB27/610, rot. 39; CP40/611, rots. 158, 173, 199, 443, 551d, 601; CP40/614, rots. 113, 396, 485d.

143 Lucas continued to seek the damages awarded to him by the Court from Bekynham's executors: PRO, KB27/622, rot. 62. For Bekynham's date of death: rot. 74.

144 In Michaelmas term 1413, Lucas did designate three attorneys who might appear on his behalf to defend against Bekynham's writ of error in the King's Bench, but does not appear to have used them: PRO, KB27/610, rot. 1d attorneys.

145 As stated above, Lucas was a mainpernor, together with Ralph Friday and four others, for a group of three Buckinghamshire Lollards in June 1414, and with John Fynderne and others, for six men incarcerated for suspicion of heresy, who were released from prison in July 1418: PRO, C237/37, m. 120; KB27/629, rot. 17d rex; KB145/5/6. In Easter term 1415 three Northamptonshire men indicted for complicity in the Oldcastle revolt appeared in court with pardons. They were released on condition that they purged themselves, and four lawyers gave surety for their behaviour – one of these was Lucas: KB27/616, rot. 1 rex.

146 *CCR, 1409–13*, p. 321; PRO, CP40/598, rot. 42; CP40/612, rot. 130; *CCR, 1413–19*, p. 376; PRO, KB27/619, rot. 1 fines; KB27/621, rot. 21; KB27/631, rot. 16d rex; KB27/637, rots. 44d, 55d, rot. 2 fines, rot. 11d rex; KB27/641, rots. 1d, 2 fines; KB27/642, rot. 1 fines.

147 In an action for debt which he brought against a smith of Andover, he claimed to have leased lands and tenements there to a Robert Stacy for an annual rent of 5 marks in 1406: PRO, CP40/636, rot. 419. See also his prosecution of Stacy's widow for debt in 1419: CP40/632, rot. 330. A trespass suit begun in 1419 indicates that he also owned property in Cholsey, Berkshire, together with Gilbert Kymer, principal of Hart Hall in Oxford, who was later to achieve prominence as university chancellor and physician to Humphrey, duke of Gloucester: PRO, KB27/634, rot. 38; KB27/635, rot. 15; KB27/636, rot. 15; Emden, *BRUO*, pp. 1068–9. Another suit for trespass at Cholsey reveals that Lucas (with four others) also held a messuage and land there as a feoffee of John Frere and Matilda Hay: PRO, KB27/635, rots. 24–24d. In 1413 and 1420 he represented John Hay, described the following year as the 'vicar of the church of Cholsey', in a trespass suit: KB27/609, rot. 1d attorneys; KB27/637, rot. 44d; KB27/639, rot. 66d.

148 PRO, KB27/621, rot. 21; KB27/637, rot. 44d; KB27/638, rot. 87. These were all cases in which Lucas was acting as a mainpernor and the significance of the domicile he gave for himself was to indicate where his collateral for the bond was located. He must therefore have also owned property, or at least rents, in London.

149 For Chace and Collyng, see Emden, *BRUO*, pp. 379–80, 466.

150 Richard II had given the chancellor the privilege of hearing all pleas between university scholars in actions arising in Oxford: PRO, KB27/634, rots. 73–73d.

151 PRO, KB27/621, rot. 21; KB27/634, rot. 38; KB27/635, rots. 15, 24–24d; KB27/636, rots. 8d, 15; KB27/637, rot. 44; KB27/642, rot. 57, rot. 1 fines; KB27/647, rot. 1 fines.

152 PRO, KB27/609, rot. 1d attorneys; KB27/610, rots. 1–1d.

153 PRO, CP40/646, rots. 1d, 3d attorneys.

154 There was a lull in his advocacy from 1414 to 1416, and in 1423 his activities in the courts appear to have ceased.

155 Particularly London, Middlesex and the home counties, but also East Anglia and, on one occasion, Northumberland: PRO, KB27/626, rots. 1–2 attorneys; KB27/627, rot. 1d attorneys; KB27/629, rot. 44, rot. 1 attorneys; KB27/638, rots. 1–1d attorneys; KB27/639, rot. 1 attorneys;

KB27/640, rot. 1 attorneys; KB27/641, rots. 1–1d; KB27/642, rot. 1 attorneys; KB27/643, rot. 5, rot. 1 attorneys; KB27/644, rot. 1 attorneys; KB27/645, rots. 1–1d attorneys; KB27/646, rot. 5 rex, rot. 1 attorneys.

[156] The suit against Cringleford alleged trespass: PRO, KB27/629, rot. 1d attorneys. Cringleford was among the Londoners arrested in 1414 for participation in the Oldcastle revolt. At the time of the revolt, Cringleford was living in St Bartholomew's Hospital; his goods (which included £66 13s 4d in money) and property were confiscated by the London escheator, but he was pardoned in October 1414: Kightly, 'Early Lollards', p. 507; PRO, Exchequer, Pipe Office, Escheators' Accounts, E357/24, m. 49; E153/2340.

[157] Together with one William Felton, he paid a fine in the King's Bench for Wille, who had been convicted of a trespass in Oxfordshire against Alice Stone: PRO, KB27/642, rot. 1 fines. Wille is to be identified with John Wille, rector of St Lawrence's church, Bristol, and an associate of the Lollard priest, Thomas Drayton. Together with John Mybbe (see above), he was a compurgator for Drayton, who was accused of heresy in Bristol with William Taillour in 1420. Wille, Mybbe, Drayton and William Felton then held adjoining benefices in Bristol: Kightly, 'Early Lollards', pp. 250–7; Hudson, *PR*, pp. 125–6; W. Barrett, *The History and Antiquities of the City of Bristol* (Bristol, 1789), p. 481.

[158] The executors of John Banbury of Warwickshire accused Crompe of having stolen money from the latter four years earlier: PRO, KB27/643, rot. 5, rot. 1 attorneys. Archbishop Arundel had at some point condemned Crompe both for supporting Oldcastle and for heresy, as stated in a pardon for these crimes secured from Archbishop Chichele in May 1416: *Reg. Chichele*, iv, p. 151.

[159] N. Orme, *Education in the West of England 1066–1548* (Exeter, 1976), pp. 4–12.

[160] PRO, KB27/638, rot. 45.

[161] For example, John Fynderne's tenure of the stewardship of Burton Abbey, see above. On these routes to a career as an attorney, see Ramsay, 'What was the Legal Profession?', pp. 68–9.

[162] The fact that this agreement was made between two minor Lancashire gentry families suggests that this practice was widespread; it was not merely commonplace among the wealthier and more urbane members of this class: M.J. Bennett, 'Provincial Gentlefolk and Legal Education in the Reign of Edward II', *BIHR*, 62 (1984), pp. 203–6.

[163] The length of the period of study was evidently not specified in this indenture, however, which is recited in a lawsuit: E. Rickert, *Chaucer's World* (London, 1948), p. 55. Further evidence that this practice was common can be found in some fourteenth-century verses in BL Add. MS 12270, fol. 215 (ll. 19–20) which speak of young men who have come by an agreement to learn in the Bench (Common Pleas) after schooling in Oxford: *Readings and Moots at the Inns of Court*, ed. S.E. Thorne and J.H. Baker (Selden Society, 105, 1989), ii, p. xxixn.

[164] H.G. Richardson, 'Business Training in Medieval Oxford', *American Historical Review*, 46 (1941), pp. 259–80.

[165] P.A. Brand, 'Courtroom and Schoolroom: the Education of Lawyers in England prior to 1400', *BIHR*, 60 (1987), pp. 150–1; *Readings and Moots*, ii, pp. xxv–xxvi.

[166] A.W.B. Simpson, 'The Circulation of Yearbooks in the Fifteenth Century', *Law Quarterly Review*, 73 (1957), pp. 494–505; E.W. Ives, *The Common Lawyers of Pre-Reformation England* (Cambridge, 1983), pp. 147–66.

[167] Brand, 'Courtroom and Schoolroom', pp. 151–65; P.A. Brand, *The Origins of the English Legal Profession* (Oxford, 1992), p. 113; Richardson, 'Business Training', pp. 269, 275, 278.

[168] Brand, 'Courtroom and Schoolroom', pp. 151–62; Brand, *Origins*, pp. 117–18.

[169] For the origins of the university disputations and for the similarities between civil and common law disputations: *Readings and Moots*, ii, pp. xvi–xxii.

[170] *Ibid.*, pp. xxxiii–xlix. For tentative pleading, Baker, *Introduction to English Legal History*, pp. 93–4.

[171] For what follows here, see J.H. Baker, 'Learning Exercises in the Medieval Inns of Court and Chancery', in his *The Legal Profession and the Common Law* (London, 1986), pp. 9–15; *Readings and Moots at the Inns of Court*, ed. S.E. Thorne (Selden Society, 71, 1952), i, pp. xvii, lxi, lxvii–iii.

[172] The earliest of these texts dates from the 1340s and was set out in chronological order by

statute from Magna Carta to the legislation of Edward I. Another 'reading' of *c.* 1374 deals only with Magna Carta: Baker, 'Learning Exercises', pp. 14–15.

[173] So much is suggested by the text from the 1340s, see n. 172 above.

[174] Moreover, the early readings, together with subsequent commentary added to them, were preserved by law students for centuries and bound in with later readings. As such, the readings and commentary formed an exegetical supplement to the body of received text, in a relationship perhaps analogous to that between the writings of the Church Fathers and the Bible: *Readings and Moots*, i, pp. lx–lxi.

[175] See, for example, *Year Books of Henry VI, 1 Hen VI, AD 1422*, ed. C.H. Williams (Selden Society, 50, 1933), which has a parallel text translation into English.

[176] Hudson, *PR*, pp. 224–7.

[177] *Ibid.*, pp. 209–16, 250–4, 274–5.

[178] On the meaning and origins of this phrase, see D.W. Sutherland, 'Legal Reasoning in the Fourteenth Century: The Invention of "Color" in Pleading', in M.S. Arnold, T.A. Green, S.A. Scully and S.D. White (eds), *On the Laws and Customs of England, Essays in Honor of Samuel E. Thorne* (Chapel Hill, 1981), pp. 182–94.

[179] Lucas was not the first scholar from Merton College known to have taken up a career as a common lawyer. He was preceded in this by the remarkable Ralph Strode, a logician of international renown and a friend of both Wycliffe and Chaucer, who became a common pleader for the city of London in 1373. See Emden, *BRUO*, pp. 1807–8. For Strode's correspondence with John Wycliffe, see W.R. Thomson, *The Latin Writings of John Wyclif* (Toronto, 1983), pp. 234–8; *Johannis Wyclif Opera Minora*, ed. J. Loserth (WS, 1913), pp. 10–11, 175–200, 258–312, 398–404. I am obliged to Dr J.I. Catto for telling me of Strode in conversation.

[180] Kebell: Ives, *The Common Lawyers* (n. 166, above), pp. 362–7; Townshend: C.E. Moreton, 'The "Library" of a Late Fifteenth-Century Lawyer', *The Library*, 6th ser., 13 (1991), pp. 338–46; Cokayne: M. McGregor, 'Bedfordshire Wills proved in the Prerogative Court of Canterbury 1383–1548', *BHRS*, 58 (1979), pp. 8–11; F. Wormald, 'The Fitzwarin Psalter and its Allies', *Journal of the Warburg and Courtauld Institutes*, 6 (1943), pp. 10–11.

[181] See also the comments of Dr Christine Carpenter on the book ownership of Warwickshire lawyers: C. Carpenter, *Locality and Polity, A Study of Warwickshire Landed Society, 1401–1499* (Cambridge, 1992), p. 205.

[182] McFarlane, *LK*, p. 215. See also p. 100 above.

[183] PRO, Exchequer, King's Remembrancer, Miscellanea, E163/6/41, mm. 01, 017, 022, 032; SC6/813/23, fols. 2–2ᵛ, 5ᵛ; Duchy of Cornwall Records, Accession Rolls, E306/2/7; Bodleian Library MS Tanner 196, fols. 3ᵛ–5ᵛ. On Stourton's career, see J.S. Roskell and C. Kightly, 'William Stourton', in Roskell *et al.* (eds), *History of Parliament*, iii, pp. 496–9.

[184] Other legacies in Bount's will include 2 marks to Robert, manciple of the Middle Temple, and his new book of statutes to his beloved fellow, John Beoff, an apprentice of the court (i.e., an apprentice-at-law): T.P. Wadley, *Notes or Abstracts of the Wills in the Great Orphan Book and Book of Wills in the Council House at Bristol* (Bristol, 1886), p. 73.

[185] For the text and a full discussion of the Disendowment Bill presented in Parliament in 1410 and perhaps earlier, see: Hudson, *Selections*, pp. 135–7, 203–7; M. Aston, '"Caim's Castles": Poverty, Politics and Disendowment', in Aston, *FF*, pp. 95–131.

[186] He also leased the temporalities of Burton Abbey from the crown during the voidance of the abbot in 1400, together with another Derbyshire lawyer: *CPR, 1399–1401*, p. 380; PRO, E159/179, rot. 1 (Hilary recognisances).

[187] M. Aston, 'Lollardy and Literacy', in Aston, *LR*, pp. 208–12; M. Aston, 'Lollardy and the Reformation' in *LR*, pp. 228–9; A. Hudson, 'A Lollard Quaternion', in Hudson, *LB*, pp. 193–200.

[188] Wycliffe dealt with this subject in *De Ecclesia*, p. 292, ll. 3–7; *De Civilio Dominio*, iii, pp. 173, l. 14–176, l. 7; *Opera Minora*, pp. 48, l. 10–49, l. 26; *De Officio Regis*, pp. 27, l. 3–29, l. 10, p. 52, ll. 4–24, cf. P. Gradon, 'Langland and the Ideology of Dissent', *Proceedings of the British Academy*, 66 (1981), pp. 189–90.

[189] Printed in Matthew, *EWW*, pp. 359–404. Similar views are also expressed in at least two other tracts printed by Matthew (pp. 168, 246–7), in a sermon printed in Arnold, *SEW*, i, p. 270, and in the *Twelve Conclusions of the Lollards* which were posted on the doors of Parliament and St Paul's Cathedral in 1395. For the latter, see: Hudson, *Selections*, p. 26.

[190] Another version of this tract exists as a sermon in BL, Egerton MS 2820: Hudson, *PR*, p. 28.

[191] *Remonstrance against Romish Corruptions in the Church*, ed. J. Forshall (London, 1851), pp. vii–xiii, and *passim.*, where the text is printed.

[192] From conclusion II, quoted in Hudson, *PR*, p. 346. For a Latin version of the 'Thirty-Seven Conclusions', see H.F.B. Compston, 'The Thirty-seven Conclusions of the Lollards', *EHR*, 26 (1911), pp. 738–49. See Anne Hudson's chapter above.

[193] Hudson, *PR*, p. 316. For the suggestion that the 'Thirty-Seven Conclusions' was the other book referred to in the *Twelve Conclusions*, in which 'the same matters and many others had been set forth in the vernacular language', see *Remonstrance*, pp. ix–x.

[194] A. McIntosh, M.L. Samuels and M. Benskin (eds), *A Linguistic Atlas of Late Medieval English*, 4 vols (Aberdeen, 1986), i, p. 185.

[195] Printed in *Four English Political Tracts of the Later Middle Ages*, ed. J.P. Genet, Camden Society, 4th ser., 18, (1977), pp. 1–20.

[196] Hudson, *PR*, p. 217.

[197] Written in 1388 at the earliest, it is a point-by-point refutation of a list of errors of the Lollards submitted to the king by the clergy in the parliament of that year. Professor Hudson has suggested that the date of composition was later: Hudson, *PR*, p. 210n. Point XIV advocated clerical disendowment and condemned the secular employment of the clergy. Found only in Douce MS 273, it is printed in Arnold, *SEW*, iii, pp. 454–96.

[198] This tract appears in another manuscript of Wycliffite material as well, written also in Derbyshire dialect: Bodleian Library MS 674, and in Trinity College, Dublin, MS 245; J.E. Wells, *A Manual of the Writings in Middle English 1050–1400* (New Haven, 1916), p. 471; T.K. Abbott (ed.), *Catalogue of the Manuscripts in the Library of Trinity College, Dublin* (Dublin, 1900), p. 36. The text is printed in Arnold, *SEW*, iii, pp. 119–67.

[199] This copy of the *Lay Folks Catechism* now comprises two other Bodleian MSS: MS Douce 274 and MS Eng.th.e.181. This version contains an unsettling mix of orthodox commonplaces and Wycliffite invective: A. Hudson, 'A New Look at the Lay Folks Catechism', *Viator*, 16 (1985), pp. 251–8, and 'The Lay Folks' Catechism: A Postscript', *Viator*, 19 (1988), pp. 307–9.

[200] The small volume is neatly and uniformly written; the first initial of every chapter in each tract is decorated with gold leaf.

[201] *The Plumpton Correspondence*, ed. T. Stapleton, reprinted with a new introduction by K. Dockray (Gloucester, 1990), pp. 231–4.

9

HUSSITISM AND THE POLISH NOBILITY

Paweł Kras

The role of the nobility in promoting heresy in medieval Europe has already been widely recognised, but there is still a need for comparative research into various aspects of this problem. The participation of Languedoc knights in the Cathar movement; the support of English gentry for Lollards; the role of Czech nobility in the Hussite movement; all these examples highlight the important part the nobility played in supporting religious dissent and promoting anti-clerical ideology in the Middle Ages.

This paper on the dissemination of Hussite ideas among the nobility in late medieval Poland is intended to broaden this historical perspective. First of all a few words should be said about the sources which provide a historian with information on the spread of Hussitism in Poland. The most important source for any research in the late medieval history of Poland is the chronicle *Annales seu Chronicae incliti regni Polaniae Libri XII*, written by Jan Długosz (1415–80), a close associate of the Cracow bishop, Zbigniew Oleśnicki (1423–55), who was a bitter enemy of Hussitism. According to Długosz's account, Hussite ideas did not affect the Polish nobility, except for two noblemen, Spytko of Melsztyn (d. 1439) and Abraham Zbąski (d. 1442). The Polish chronicler, an advocate of church privileges, charged both aforementioned nobles with adhering to Hussitism in order to gain political and economic advantage.[1]

Długosz's information about the Hussite noblemen can be verified by means of ecclesiastical records (*acta episcoporum, acta causarum seu iudiciorum, acta capitulorum*)[2] which provide data about accusations of heresy in fifteenth-century Poland. Unfortunately, any attempt to estimate the total number of suspect noblemen is hindered by the considerable destruction of these documents. Another deficiency of the ecclesiastical registers is the lack of complete records of the proceedings against noblemen who were interrogated under a charge of heresy.[3]

The ecclesiastical registers of four Polish dioceses (Gniezno, Poznań, Płock and Włocławek) yield the names of thirty-eight Polish nobles suspected of heresy during the fifteenth century. Within this group sixteen persons were charged with receiving Communion in both kinds, but owing to the incomplete and patchy records, the charges against only ten nobles can be verified by means of their interrogations before ecclesiastical courts.[4]

Recent research has shown that Hussite ideas affected Polish society on a very

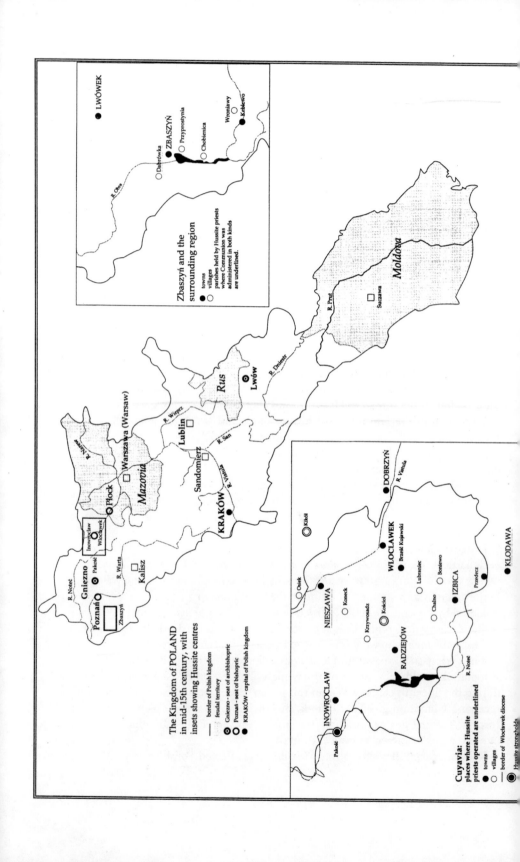

The Kingdom of POLAND
in mid-15th century, with
insets showing Hussite centres

— border of Polish kingdom
.... feudal territory

◎ Gniezno - seat of archbishopric
◉ Poznań - seat of bishopric
● KRAKÓW - capital of Polish kingdom

Zbaszyń and the
surrounding region

● towns
○ villages
parishes held by Hussite priests
where Communion was
administered in both kinds
are underlined.

Cuyavia:
places where Hussite
priests operated are underlined

● towns
○ villages
◉ border of Włocławek diocese
◎ Hussite strongholds

limited scale, but at least nine Polish Hussites were burnt at the stake.[5] None of them was a nobleman, although some of those burned had been closely linked with their noble protectors.

A number of reasons help to explain why the Hussite movement did not gain much popularity among the Polish nobility.[6] One of the most important is the absence of social and religious circumstances comparable to those in Bohemia, where the nobility supported the Hussite programme as a means of their political and social advancement. The Hussite movement was a complex religious and socio-national phenomenon specific to fifteenth-century Bohemia, a country far more developed than Poland in its economy, society and education. Therefore, what seemed to the Bohemian nobility a reason for identifying with Hussite ideas, did not similarly motivate the Polish nobility.[7]

For most Polish nobles, Hussitism did not offer any alternative to the traditional church, but appeared rather as a disaster, a misfortune which had happened to the Czech nation. Negative opinions of the Hussites were commonplace in Poland and based upon a widespread fear of the 'Czech heresy', which was considered a serious danger to Polish society. Hussites were widely regarded not only as enemies of the church, but also as dangerous rebels whose activity threatened totally to overthrow the prevalent socio-political order in the region.[8] Most of the Polish nobility acknowledged the destructive character of the Hussite movement and, despite individual sympathisers, a hostile attitude towards Hussite ideas prevailed among them. Observing the decline of Bohemia under the Hussite leadership, they looked with disdain at the overthrow of traditional feudal institutions, and at the growing political activity of townspeople and peasants.[9]

On the other hand, soon after the council of Constance (1414–18), the Polish clergy launched a campaign to protect Polish society against the spread of Hussitism. In 1420 the provincial synod of the Polish clergy issued the anti-Hussite regulations, *Remedia contra haereticos*, which forbade Poles to go to Bohemia and claimed that any Pole who visited that country was 'infected by the impure Hussite heresy'. Special ecclesiastical commissions were to be established in each diocese, to interrogate Poles returning from Bohemia. Such persons were obliged to recant heresy before the ecclesiastical courts and to take an oath never to go to Bohemia without the permission of their bishop. According to these regulations, any individual who upheld the idea of, or received, Communion in both kinds was suspected of Hussite ideas and should recant their heresy before the ecclesiastical court.[10] In addition, the suspicion of Hussitism was attached to anyone who had either stayed in Bohemia or possessed heretical books.

In the 1420s cooperation between the state and the church in suppressing heresy grew closer and stronger and severe measures against heretics were introduced by the king to support ecclesiastical censures. In the anti-Hussite edict of Wieluń, enacted on 9 April 1424, King Władysław Jagiełło called on all Poles staying in Bohemia to return immediately to Poland or they would be declared heretics and their estates confiscated. Furthermore, the adherents and propagators of Hussite ideas were threatened with the loss of their titles, offices and dignities.[11] In one of the later promulgations of these anti-heretical laws, capital punishment was also prescribed against those who broke the royal bans and went to Bohemia.[12]

The royal anti-heretical regulations, with their consequences for common law, may have been regarded as a serious infringement of the liberties and privileges of the Polish nobility,[13] but there is no trace of nobles' opposition to them. Furthermore, in June 1424 the Polish and Lithuanian nobility signed the act of anti-Hussite confederation which was intended to stop the departure of Polish knights to Bohemia, and to back the royal anti-heretical laws. The participants of the confederation declared their defence of the Catholic church and swore to struggle against heretics both within the country and outside. They also promised to assist the ecclesiastical authorities in searching for suspect persons and capturing heretics.[14] The determination of the Polish nobility to prevent the dissemination of Hussite ideas was also expressed during the provincial land diet in Jedlna, in 1430, at which heresy was considered a serious threat to the public order and integrity of the Polish kingdom, and heretics were ordered to be prosecuted with all means at the state's disposal.[15]

Despite the royal and ecclesiastical bans, a number of Polish knights went to Bohemia and fought on the Czech side against the anti-Hussite crusades organised by Sigismund of Luxembourg and Martin V. Most of them were in the retinue of Prince Sigismund Korybut, who was first dispatched to Bohemia in 1421 as the representative of Vitold, the Great Duke of Lithuania, and then returned there in 1424, trying on his own initiative to become a Czech king.[16] Noble participants of Korybut's expeditions had a good opportunity to become familiar with Hussite ideas and services.[17] Some of them took the opportunity to acquire Hussite books and bring them back to Poland. Several denunciations are recorded in fifteenth-century ecclesiastical registers concerning the possession of heretical books by noblemen. Unfortunately, apart from the information about their heretical character and Czech origin, their titles and contents remain unknown.[18]

Distribution of heretical books became a popular way of propagating Hussite or Wycliffite ideas among the Polish nobility. In 1449 Andrew Gałka of Dobczyn (c. 1400–51), a Wycliffite scholar at the university of Cracow, was charged with popularising Wycliffe's teaching among high-ranking nobles. On the margins of Wycliffe's treatises, which he had copied and commented on, Gałka put the names of three powerful noblemen (Peter Szafraniec, Cracow subchamberlain, Andrew Tęczyński, and Lukas Górka, voivode of the Poznań region) to whom he intended to give Wycliffe's works.[19] Having found these codices in his apartment, the Cracow clergy charged Gałka with attempting to incite the Polish nobility against the clergy. He himself denied any such intention. There is no doubt that Gałka enjoyed the protection of an unknown nobleman whom he asked to defend him at the royal court against ecclesiastical slanders of heresy while he was in exile in Silesia.[20]

The rise of Hussite influences in Poland took place in the 1430s and was made possible by two factors: the emergence of noble opposition headed by Spytko of Melsztyn and Abraham Zbąski,[21] and the friendly relations between Poland and Hussite Bohemia, first in the years 1431–3 and then in 1438–9. There is much evidence to argue that a sudden advance of Hussitism coincided with the political upheaval which followed the death of Władysław Jagiełło. After the succession of his young son, Władysław II, to the Polish throne in 1434, royal authority was considerably weakened, as two opposing groups of nobles engaged in a struggle to seize control of the country. After the death of Jagiełło the bishop of Cracow, Zbigniew Oleśnicki, became the most influential figure in power, and secured his position by promoting his supporters to the crucial offices in the state administration.[22] In the political struggle, the direct attack of the opposition group was aimed at the Cracow bishop, well-known as an uncompromising enemy of the Hussites and an advocate of the strong position of the church.

His political adversaries were led by Spytko of Melsztyn, who belonged to one of the most powerful clans in Poland. The origins of his family's fortune go back to the reign of Casimir the Great (1333–70), but considerable political and economic advances were achieved by his father Spytko, who was a key official at the royal court in the first decade of Jagiełło's reign in Poland (1385–1434). After the death of Jagiełło, the position of Melsztyński's clan underwent a rapid political and economic decline. The royal endowments (the Sambor region in Ruthenia) which Jagiełło had granted to Spytko's father were taken back from his clan and given to Oleśnicki's supporters, the clan of Odrowąż.[23] This loss made Spytko of Melsztyn a bitter enemy of the Bishop Oleśnicki and a leader of a group of young nobles (*iuniores*), members of prestigious clans, who suffered a similar decline. In 1434 Spytko, together with the nobles from Great Poland, opposed the coronation of the young prince Władysław which was promoted by the bishop of Cracow. Soon after, he was one of the initiators of a campaign against tithes and played a leading part in the land diet of Sieradz of 1435, at which a compromise payment was arranged between the ecclesiastical authorities and the nobles.[24]

Spytko's political activity achieved its climax in 1438, when most of the Polish nobility supported the unsuccessful attempt to place Prince Casimir, the younger brother of Władysław III (1434–44), on the Czech throne. In the spring of 1438 the Czech land diet of Mielnik, attended mostly by the Utraquist and Taborite gentry, elected Casimir king of Bohemia, in opposition to the earlier election of Albrecht of Habsbourg supported by the Catholic nobles.[25] Notwithstanding the protest of Zbigniew Oleśnicki, Władysław III supported the intervention in favour of his brother, promoted by a group led by Spytko of Melsztyn and Abraham Zbąski,[26] and launched a military campaign to Silesia. The Cracow bishop was forced to accept the royal decision on condition that the country should be protected against the influx of Hussite ideas. The confederation which he convened in Nowy Korczyn in April 1438 condemned Hussitism as a danger for the public order, and threatened its protectors with severe secular punishment.[27] But the defeat of the Polish intervention in Bohemia sealed the fate of Spytko of Melsztyn and his party. Zbigniew Oleśnicki made use of the failure of pro-Czech policy to suppress the noble opposition in Poland.

At the beginning of May 1439 Spytko rose in rebellion against the Cracow bishop and endeavoured to seize power in the country. His sudden attack on the supporters of Bishop Oleśnicki, who convened in Nowy Korczyn, did not bring him success. On the contrary, his military action frightened most of his previous allies and was condemned by the king, Władysław III, who declared him an enemy of the country. In consequence, his tiny army was easily defeated at the battlefield of Grotniki and Spytko himself was killed.

Recent research has shown that Spytko's rising was primarily a political action aimed at overthrowing Oleśnicki's group. Despite Spytko himself adopting Hussite ideas and becoming an advocate of Utraquist Communion, there is no evidence that Hussitism played any significant role in the political activity of his group.[28] Spytko may have tried to promote Hussitism as part of the struggle against the Cracow bishop, but his efforts were unsuccessful. Most Polish nobles were reluctant to pursue their political and economic goals through the adoption of Hussite ideas.

The activity of noble opposition in the years 1434–9 facilitated the dissemination of Hussite ideas in Polish society. Strangely enough, the spread of Hussitism in Poland coincided with the Prague compacts of 1436 and the subsequent return of Sigismund of Luxembourg to Bohemia, which put an end to the revolutionary phase of the Hussite movement. In the years 1435–45 the most active Hussite centres emerged in Great Poland (around Zbąszyń) and Cuyavia (around Pakość and Nieszawa).

Well-organised Hussite centres were found mainly on the noble estates whose owners either adhered to Hussite ideas or protected their dissemination. The emergence and existence of groups of Polish Hussites was made possible only through the protection of the nobles whose social and political position guaranteed their safety and immunity.

Two relatives of the powerful clan of Nałęcz, Abraham Zbąski and his brother-in-law Abraham of Kębłow are the best-known Hussite nobles in Poland. It is difficult to date precisely the beginnings of Hussite practices in the area around Zbąszyń, but there is no doubt they were introduced by the two above-mentioned nobles who, in the struggle against the local clergy, went so far as to replace the Catholic clergy by heretical priests. For at least five years (1436–40) Abraham Zbąski and Abraham Kębłowski protected Hussite priests, attended heretical services, and rejected any attempt by the Poznań bishop to reintroduce Catholic practices in their lands.[29] Claiming the sovereignty of their estates, they both denied episcopal jurisdiction and refused the bishop's right to conduct visitations. Their anti-clerical attitude gained some popularity among the inhabitants of

Zbąszyń, who in the absence of Abraham Zbąski, in 1440, denied the jurisdiction of the Poznań bishop and declared their obedience to their landlord.

Against this background it is worthwhile to take a closer look at Abraham Zbąski, whose name was closely linked with the history of Hussitism in Poland. Zbąski was one of the richest and most influential noblemen in Great Poland in the first half of the fifteenth century. He was born into the old and prestigious noble clan of Nałęcz, whose members had played an important role at the royal court and had appointed to important royal offices.[30] In 1430 he became an active politician and a leader of the nobility in Great Poland.[31] He gained much favour at the royal court of Władysław Jagiełło, who granted him new royal endowments as a reward for his services.[32] After 1432 Zbąski acted as royal judge for Great Poland, one of the key functions in the state administration.[33]

In 1431 he was dispatched by Jagiełło to Prague, to take part in the Czech land diet. The principal aim of his diplomatic mission to Bohemia was to negotiate the participation of the Czech delegation in the council of Basel.[34] At that time Zbąski was already a member of the pro-Hussite party which pursued the policy of reinforcing the diplomatic ties with Hussite Bohemia against Oleśnicki's party, which promoted the alliance with Sigismund of Luxembourg. When, in 1431, the pro-Hussite group came to power at the royal court, the hostile attitude towards the Czech Hussites was replaced by more friendly policy. In this new political situation Zbąski may have been useful in promoting a new relationship with the Czechs.[35]

Zbąski's mission to Bohemia in 1431 probably provided an occasion for him to learn about Hussite thought.[36] After the death of Władysław Jagiełło, he lost his firm position at the court and joined the malcontent group of the nobility whose influence on state policy was ended by the rule of Oleśnicki. In the climate of growing hostility between the two parties, Zbąski engaged in a struggle for the reform of tithes, demanding both a reduction and reorganisation of their payment. Together with Spytko of Melsztyn, he played a leading part in putting forward these demands during the provincial land diet for Great Poland in Piotrków, in August 1434. Probably the failure of this action encouraged him to take further individual steps.[37] In 1435 Zbąski denied tithes to the local clergy and encouraged neighbouring nobles to do the same.[38]

His disobedience to the clergy provoked the intervention of the Poznań bishop, Stanisław Ciołek, who summoned him before his court under a charge of spreading errors.[39] When Zbąski refused to appear, Ciołek excommunicated him and imposed an interdict on his estates. The ecclesiastical censures did not change Zbąski's attitude, and the conflict between the Poznań bishop and the nobility, followed by the subsequent escape of the latter to Cracow, enabled Zbąski to avoid punishment.[40]

It is worth noting that during his conflict with Bishop Ciołek Zbąski continued to perform his duties as royal judge of Poznań, and carry out his public activities.

He presided over the provincial land court, judged the cases subject to his office, and issued formal documents, even for the monasteries and the Poznań consistory. Despite the fact that Zbąski was excommunicated, the validity of his legal acts was not questioned. His heretical reputation did not disturb his political career at the royal court, and he accompanied the king at the land diets in 1436 and 1439.[41] Until 1440 his position was strong enough to ignore ecclesiastical censures and protect Hussites on his estate.

It was as late as the beginning of 1439 that a new bishop of Poznań, Andrzej Bniński, from the powerful clan of Łodzia, undertook a new initiative against the Hussites of Zbąszyń.[42] The Poznań bishop carried out the visitation of the Zbąszyń region and interrogated persons suspected of heresy. In October 1439, during the absence of Zbąski, Bniński, accompanied by the starost (royal governor) of Great Poland,[43] came to Zbąszyń, but he was not allowed to enter the castle where the heretical priests and town officials had fled to avoid interrogation.[44]

The clan of Bniński was directly engaged in the conflict between the Poznań bishop and Abraham Zbąski. In 1439, in the Poznań town hall, Zbąski was assaulted with a sword by the bishop's cousins, Peter and Albert, and only avoided a fatal stroke by quickly hiding under the table.[45] On the mediation of Zbąski's relatives, Bniński agreed to stop his action and seek a peaceful solution. Once again Zbąski was summoned before the episcopal court, but when he did not appear the bishop repeated the excommunication and called upon the royal officials to enforce his verdict. Finally, under pressure from the ecclesiastical and secular authorities, in November 1440 Zbąski gave up his support for Hussite ideas and recanted his heresy in Poznań cathedral.[46]

According to the testimony of Zbąszyń inhabitants, Abraham Zbąski was personally responsible for introducing and sponsoring Hussite services in both the town and the surrounding region. His decision to replace Catholic services by Hussite ones encountered no opposition, and his relatives, parish priests and the inhabitants of Zbąszyń and the adjacent villages all attended heretical masses in the parish churches. The members of his family (his wife Katherine, mother Świętosława and daughter Anna), when interrogated before the Poznań bishop in 1442, acknowledged that Zbąski had forced them to follow his devotion to Hussite services, particularly to Utraquist Communion, which he had considered necessary for salvation.[47] Similarly, Nicolaus, the parish priest of Zbąszyń, explained his attendance at the Hussite services by his obedience to the will of his benefactor and admitted that he had distributed Communion in both kinds in order to retain his parish living.[48]

On the initiative of Abraham Zbąski, the Hussite priests celebrated a simplified mass modelled upon the Taborite (*missa sicca*) without lighting the candles and ringing the bells. The priest who sang the mass was dressed in a plain russet garment with a stole round his neck. During the interrogation of Zbąszyń Hussites, it turned out that new heretical services had been introduced by the Hussite priests, including evening songs which had gained much popularity. The most obvious evidence of the spread of Hussitism in Zbąszyń was Utraquist Communion, frequently distributed among the laity. The episcopal notary noted that Communion in both kinds had provoked a great scandal among the faithful, and led to the profanation of Christ's blood, which was often spilt from the chalice.[49]

Apart from securing Hussitism in his estates, Zbąski intended to promote Hussite ideas in the neighbouring area by means of personal contacts with neighbouring noblemen, and by sending out Hussite missionaries. In February 1439 two Hussite agitators from Zbąszyń were captured in Lwówek by the parish priest while they were preaching to the peasants in the inn.[50] The ecclesiastical registers also recorded the names of five nobles who were associated with the Hussite centre in Zbąszyń: Abraham of Kębłów, Peter Oganka of Chobienica,[51] Jan Tłuczymost of Wolikowo,[52] Stanisław Wilgosz[53] and Elżbieta of Gostyń.[54] Each of them was cited to appear before the episcopal court and to recant heresy.

The episcopal registers recorded thirteen Hussite priests who lived in Zbąszyń and the surrounding area, under the protection of Abraham Zbąski. Some of them, like Nicolaus, parish priest of Zbąszyń, had their parish livings on his estates, and adhered to heresy lest they should be deprived of their endowments. The others came to Zbąszyń from outside Zbąski's territory; some of them may have fled from very distant areas and found refuge under Zbąski's protection: for instance John of Cuyavia or John Longinus from Ruthenia. In 1440 Abraham promised to hand over all the heretical priests to the bishop. Their fate after being put on trial was varied – five of them were burnt at the stake, two managed to escape from the episcopal jurisdiction and continued their heretical activity in Great Poland,[55] whereas two others recanted heresy and were forced to change their parish living.[56] Some Hussites of Zbąszyń managed to flee to Bohemia and avoided episcopal interrogation.[57]

As has already been stressed, the emergence of the Hussite centre in Zbąszyń depended on the wishes of Abraham Zbąski, and Hussite ideas were openly held by those who lived there as long as their protector supported them. Therefore, his recantation of heresy and return to the Catholic church doomed the Zbąszyń Hussites. Yet, notwithstanding the loss of their protector, the Hussites persisted in Zbąszyń for some years.[58] In 1443 the bishop of Poznań ordered some inhabitants of Zbąszyń to wear yellow crosses on their outer garments as a sign of their penance for heresy.[59] Zbąszyń and the surrounding area gained a bad reputation in the eyes of the clergy, and some individuals suspected of heresy swore neither to go to Bohemia nor to visit the Zbąszyń region (described as *loca suspecta*).[60]

Another Polish area which became notorious for Hussite ideas lay in Cuyavia, in the northern part of the Polish Kingdom. The first information about Hussites in this region dates from 1424, when Szymon, the parish priest of Koneck, appeared before the ecclesiastical court to abjure Wycliffite and Hussite opinions. Szymon was charged with denying the church's right to temporal possessions and propagating Utraquist Communion.[61] Six years later he was summoned once again and interrogated about seven priests who had fled from Cuyavia to Bohemia.[62]

Unfortunately, owing to the gap in *acta officialatus* of the Włocławek diocese for the years 1430–80, it is hard to reconstruct the development of heresy in the area where, in the opinion of the Polish clergy, Hussite ideas flourished widely under the protection of noble families. The Płock chapter, which supervised a search for heretics in the diocese of Płock,[63] regularly discussed the spread of heresy in the Dobrzyń region, an eastern part of Cuyavia.[64] The persistence of heresy in Cuyavia also became a matter of concern to church officials outside this region. The vicar general of the Cracow diocese, John Elgot (d. 1452) complained to the bishop of Płock, Paul Giżycki (1439–63), about the negligence of his officials, who let the heresy flourish in the area under his jurisdiction. Elgot pointed to the Dobrzyń region as a centre of heresy, where Hussite ideas spread without any constraint and a number of noble families received Communion in both kinds from heretical priests.[65]

Most information about Hussite nobles in Cuyavia can be derived from the records of the trial of the Hussites of Nieszawa, which took place in 1480. The trial revealed that several noble and merchant families in Cuyavia had been widely known (*ex fama publica, in communi opinio*) for heresy, and that Hussite services including the distribution of Utraquist Communion were held in the area between Pakość and Nieszawa. According to the testimony produced during the trial, persons suspected of heresy lived in Pakość, Nieszawa, Inowrocław, Brześć Kujawski, Kościół, Bodzanówek, Sinki, Lupsin and Osięciny.[66] The parish priest Nicolaus of Kościół claimed that a vast territory of Cuyavia, spreading from Korzecznik in the north to Krzywosądza in the south, should be burnt because it was settled by heretics.[67]

The most active advocates of heresy in this region belonged to noble families. In Kościół heretical ideas were adopted and protected by two noble families, the owners of the village: Peter of Moszczana, castellan of Dobrzyń, and his wife, called the Moszczeńscy, and Krystyn of Kościół and his wife Helena Krzywosądzka.[68] The crucial role in promoting and supporting Hussite ideas was played by noblewomen: lady Moszczeńska, Helena Krzywosądzka and Grzimka of Bodzanówek. Moszczeńska, Helena and Grzimka organised meetings with suspect priests and secured the maintenance of heretical ideas in their families. In Kościół Helena Krzywosądzka supported two of her sons, Szymon and Krystyn, who joined a heretical group, but turned against her third son Albert, castellan of Kowal, who despite her efforts rejected Hussite ideas.[69] Likewise, Grzimka tried to encourage her daughter-in-law Anna Redecka to receive Communion in both kinds.[70]

The records of the 1480 trial make it difficult to define the ideology of Hussite groups in Cuyavia. In the testimony delivered before the court the charges of heresy were usually based on such hazy suspicions as belonging to a sect, attending suspect meetings or having contacts with unknown persons. The only clear charge refers to Utraquist Communion being considered necessary for salvation. The ecclesiastical court found this a sufficient evidence of heresy and thoroughly examined the circumstances of receiving Communion in both kinds.[71]

Although the trial in 1480 revealed about forty persons suspected of heresy, only five of them were brought before the ecclesiastical court. This can be explained by the fact that most of the suspects died before the trial. Among five Hussites interrogated in 1480 there was only one petty nobleman – Frydan of Lupsino. His adherence to Hussitism seems to be characteristic of other Polish noblemen: his heresy lay in his devotion to Utraquist Communion, which he claimed was necessary for salvation. In his testimony Frydan declared that he had received Communion in both kinds for the first time while fighting together with the Czech army in Silesia (probably in 1474). He had then served for a certain time in Skrzynno as a chamberlain of Anna Mszczujowa, who was an advocate of Hussitism. After his return to Cuyavia he continued to receive Utraquist Communion from various priests.[72] Moreover, Frydan tried to propagate Hussite ideas by means of heretical books. He gave one of them to his neighbour Nicolaus Jurkowski who committed it to his parish priest and gave evidence in court.[73]

In Pakość the adherents of Hussite ideas were protected by the noble owners of the town, who organised meetings in their house, took care of heretical priests, and promoted the distribution of Utraquist Communion. It may be argued that the Pakość Hussites set up an élite heretical group, which consisted of the owner's family, their servants and some high-ranking members of local society, such as the mayor.[74]

On 7 April 1441 the wife of the owner of Pakość, Anne Maternina, and three other women, appeared before Archbishop Wincenty Kot of Gniezno (1436–48) to abjure a charge of heresy. All of them admitted having received Communion in both kinds from a parish priest, who at that time was imprisoned.[75] Between then and 1455 seven other inhabitants of Pakość were summoned by the ecclesiastical officials under suspicion of holding Hussite ideas.

Hussite nobles in Cuyavia did their best to secure the secrecy of their religious activity, and opposed any attempts at disclosure. In 1431 a nobleman, Bartłomiej of Kościół, organised an assault on an unknown inquisitor who inspected the area of Boniewo while searching for heretics. The inquisitor was seriously injured, his eyes were gauged out and nose cut off. The culprit was prosecuted by the royal officials and his estates were confiscated, but thanks to the support of his friends he escaped from Poland and found refuge in Silesia.[76] Some time later, Grzimka, one of the eager advocates of Utraquist Communion, prevented a meeting between her daughter-in-law and a deputy judge (*officialis*) of the Włocławek bishop, which might have revealed her heresy.[77] The noble protectors of Hussitism in Kościół did not hesitate to expel the parish priest Abraham after he had preached against heresy.[78] Likewise, in 1450 the Hussites in Pakość reacted angrily against the parish vicar Andrew after he had preached against Materna's family, and publicly criticised their support of heresy. There is no doubt that Andrew's sermons aroused the concern of the local Hussites, who threatened to drown him in a river if he did not stop his hostile preaching.[79]

Thanks to the links which bound together the heretical groups in Cuyavia, the circulation of books and brochures as well as the movement of heretical priests were made possible. Contacts between heretical families were well-developed, and the Hussite priests easily moved from one village to another in order to hold heretical services and distribute Communion in both kinds. A number of inhabitants of Cuyavia visited Bohemia and took part in Hussite services there.[80] There is some evidence that some families had strong links with the Czech Hussites, received heretical books from Bohemia, and sent their children to study in Prague.[81]

Assessing the attitude of the Polish nobles towards the Hussite movement, two points deserve to be emphasised. On the one hand, most of them regarded Hussitism as a serious threat to the stability of feudal structures and a danger for their privileged position in the society. On the other, the Hussite programme may have provided some nobles with arguments to restrict the political influence of the clergy and to criticise tithes.[82] Only a few of them adhered to Hussitism for religious reasons and considered this a spiritual adventure in their search for new forms of piety outside the Catholic church. Nevertheless, for all of them, interest in Hussite ideas proved a matter of temporary fascination and discontent with the traditional church, which expired as soon as they found it dangerous for their social position. They supported Hussite ideas and ignored traditional services to the extent that opposition to the Catholic church did not produce serious political or personal consequences. The episcopal registers make it clear that all Hussite noblemen who appeared before the ecclesiastical courts failed to persist in their sympathy for Hussite ideas and finally returned to the bosom of the church.

Notes

[1] *Iohanni Dlugosii Historiae Polonicae Libri XII*, ed. A. Przeździecki, i–v, in *Opera omnia*, x–xiv (Cracow, 1873–9) – hereafter cited as Długosz – particularly Długosz, iv, pp. 606–10.

[2] Most materials of heresy interrogations in fifteenth-century Poland were edited in *Acta capitulorum necnon iudiciorum ecclesiasticorum selecta*, ed. B. Ulanowski, i–iii (Cracow, 1874–1918, *Monumenta Medii Aevi Historica*, xiii, xvi, xviii; hereafter cited as *AC*); other records in *Monumenta historiae dioecesis Wladislaviensis*, ed. W. Neuman, iv (Włocławek, 1884); hereafter cited as *MHDW*; *Acta capitulorum Cracoviensis et Plocensis selecta*, ed. B. Ulanowski, in *Archiwum Komisji Historycznej*, vi (Kraków, 1891); hereafter cited as *AC Ploc.*; *Gnesner Hussitenverhöre 1450–1452*, ed. A. Kunkel in *Mitteilungen des Instituts für österreichische Geschichtsforschung*, 38 (1920), pp. 314–25. The records of the ecclesiastical trials of the Hussites of Zbaszyń were published by J. Nowacki, *Biskup poznański Andrzej Bniński w walce z husytami Zbąszynia. Nieznane karty z procesów husyckich roku 1439* [The Poznań bishop Andrew Bniński fighting against the Hussites in Zbąszyń. Unknown Records of Hussite trials in 1439], *Roczniki Historyczne*, 10 (1934), pp. 249–78; hereafter cited as *AC Pozn*.

[3] On the state of ecclesiastical records see H.E. Wyczawski, *Przygotowanie do studiów w archiwach kościelnych* [Introduction to Research in Church Archives] (Kalwaria Zebrzydowska, 1989).

⁴ My own data are based upon the published records of ecclesiastical courts of the four above-mentioned dioceses, see n. 2 above. There is still much discussion on the approximate number of Polish Hussites. A Czech scholar, Josef Macek, listed the names of 159 Polish Hussites among whom he numbered only sixteen nobles. Macek wrongly listed a few nobles who were not directly accused of heresy and omitted a number of other Hussite nobles. J. Macek, *Husyci na Pomorzu i w Wielkopolsce* [Hussites in Pomerania and Great Poland] (Warsaw, 1955), pp. 188–90. Macek later argued that for the years 1430–50 the total number of Polish Hussites consisted of 37 per cent of priests, 30 per cent of townspeople, 20 per cent of peasants and 11 per cent of nobles, but he failed to produce any precise numbers: J. Macek, *Jean Huss et les traditions hussites* (Paris, 1973), p. 224.

⁵ Marxist historiography claimed that the Hussite movement gained much popularity in Poland – see E. Maleczyńska, *Ruch husycki w Czechach i w Polsce* [The Hussite Movement in Bohemia and Poland] (Warsaw, 1959) – but recent research has proved that Hussite ideas were adopted only by a few Poles; S. Bylina, 'Problém ohlasu husitství v Polském království' [The Problem of Hussite Influences in the Polish Kingdom], in *Jihlava a basilejská kompaktata* (Jihlava, 1992), pp. 135–49.

⁶ For more information on the historical evolution of Polish nobility and their position in medieval society see A. Gąsiorowski (ed.), *The Polish Nobility in the Middle Ages* (Wrocław, 1984).

⁷ On the participation of the Czech nobility in the Hussite movement see F. Šmahel, *Husitská revoluce* [The Hussite Revolution], i, (Prague, 1993), pp. 259–88.

⁸ S. Bylina, 'Wizerunek heretyka w Polsce późnośredniowiecznej' [The Image of the Heretic in Late Medieval Poland], *Odrodzenie i Reformacja w Polsce*, 30 (1985), pp. 5–21; U. Borkowska, *Treści ideowe w dziełach Jana Długosza. Kościół i świat poza Kościołem* [The Ideological Contents in the Writings of Jan Długosz. Church and the World outside the Church] (Lublin, 1984), pp. 61–70; P. Kras, '*Furor Hussitarum* – the Hussite Movement in the Selected Accounts of Fifteenth-Century Chronicles from East Central Europe', in U. Borkowska (ed.), *Universal and Regional Ideas in the Chronicles from East Central Europe* (Lublin, 1996), pp. 84–108.

⁹ The widespread feelings about Hussitism were rightly expressed in the speech of the Polish king Władysław Jagiełło to the Czech delegation which came to Cracow in 1431: '*illico florentissimum Regnum vestrum adeo depressum et conculcatum est, ut nec Regem habeatis nec pontificem, nec victimam Universitas Pragensis, fons nationum irriguus aruit. Principes et barones a serviis et rusticis gladio submoti sunt, templa incensa, corpora sanctorum disiecta et vidata, virgines stupratae, religiones sacrae pessundatae et exclusae, omnia videntia et impetus non consilium, non ratio gubernat, et etsi aliqui baronum et nobilium supersint, hi tamen a rusticorum genere, qui in ingenucrium successerunt fortunas, adeo, obriti sunt, ut resurgendi et rem publicam defendendi et capessendi nullam habeant facultatem*', Długosz, iv, p. 539.

¹⁰ *Statuty synodalne wieluńsko-kaliskie Mikołaja Trąby z 1420 roku*, (The Provincial Statutes of Mikołaj Trąba from 1420), ed. J. Fijałek and A. Vetulani (Cracow, 1950), pp. 48–55.

¹¹ On the cooperation between royal and ecclesiastical officials in the struggle against heretics in medieval Poland see W. Wójcik, 'Pomoc świecka dla sądownictwa kościelnego w Polsce średniowiecznej' [Secular Support for Ecclesiastical Jurisdiction in Medieval Poland], *Prawo Kanoniczne*, 3 (1960), fasc. 3–4, pp. 35–86.

¹² *Volumina legum Polonicarum*, ed. J. Ohryzko, i (Petersburg, 1859), p. 38.

¹³ On the social and political advancement of the Polish nobility in the late Middle Ages, S. Gawęda, *Możnowładztwo małopolskie w XIV i pierwszej połowie XV wieku* [The Nobility of Little Poland in the Fourteenth and the first half of the Fifteenth Century] (Cracow, 1966).

¹⁴ 'The confederation was a result of the lawless expedition of Sigismund Korybut to Bohemia which caused protests and indignation throughout Europe'; *Codex epistolaris Vitoldi, Magni Ducis Lithuaniae 1376–1430*, ed. A. Prochaska (Cracow, 1882), pp. 633–4. Antoni Prochaska compared the Polish–Lithuanian resolution with the Act of anti-Hussite Confederation of Bingen in 1424, which defined the means of fighting against Czech Hussites; idem, 'Dwa związki antyhusyckie' [Two Anti-Hussite Associations], *Kwartalnik Historyczny*, 11 (1987), pp. 689–744.

¹⁵ *Codex epistolaris saeculi decimi quinti*, ed. A. Sokołowski and J. Szujski, ii (Cracow, 1898), p. 235 (henceforward quoted as *CE*).

¹⁶ Długosz, iv, pp. 328–30; H. Kaminsky, *A History of the Hussite Revolution* (Berkeley and Los Angeles, 1967), pp. 60–2, 77. A detailed study of the activity of Sigismund Korybut in Bohemia was produced by J. Grygiel, *Życie i działalność Zygmunta Korybutowicza* [Life and Activity of Sigismund Korybut] (Wrocław, 1988), particularly pp. 77–105.

¹⁷ For a few such cases see *AC*, ii, p. 870.

¹⁸ *AC Ploc.*, p. 105, No. 420; a nobleman John Kryski of Baboszewo in the Płock diocese possessed '*libellum in quo continetur heresis*' (1481); during the meeting of the Płock canonry in 1472 the general vicar showed '*libellum heresim in se continentem primo quod communicare simplices sub utraque specie non esset peccatum, item quod eciam pueri communicarentur sicut adulti etiam sub utraque specie, item (quod) bona temporalis dnis spiritualibus reciperentur . . .*'; *ibid.*, p. 106, no. 426.

¹⁹ *CE*, ii, pp. 63–4, 68–71; on Andrew Gałka, M. Schlauch, 'A Polish Vernacular Eulogy of Wycliff', *JEH*, 8 (1959), pp. 53–73.

²⁰ In a letter to the unknown Polish nobleman (probably Łukasz Górka) he wrote: '*Magnifice domine! Ad episcopum Cracoviensem modernum sum delatus, quod legissem et scripsissem libri Magistri Iohannis Wicleph ac incitassem Baroniam Regni contra sacerdotes . . .*'; *Codex diplomaticus Universitatis studii generalis Cracoviensis*, ed. A. Stenzel, ii, (Cracow, 1888), pp. 115–16.

²¹ E. Maleczyńska, *Ruch husycki*, pp. 172–4; A. Sochacka, 'Konfederacja Spytka z Melsztyna z 1439 r., Rozgrywka polityczna czy ruch ideologiczny?' [Confederation of Spytko of Melsztyn from 1439. A Political Game or Ideological Movement?], *Rocznik Lubelski*, 16 (1973), pp. 46–7.

²² Sochacka, 'Konfederacja Spytka', pp. 47–53.

²³ *Akta grodzkie i ziemskie* [Records of Town and Land Courts], ed. O. Pietruski and K. Liske, iv (Lwow, 1873), p. 25.

²⁴ Sochacka, 'Konfederacja Spytka', pp. 46–8.

²⁵ A detailed study of the Polish candidate for the Czech throne was written by R. Heck, *Tabor a kandydatura jagiellońska w Czechach (1428–1444)* [Tabor and the Jagiellonian Candidature in Bohemia, 1438–1444] (Wrocław, 1964); on the impact of the election of Casimir on the internal situation in Poland see also R. Heck, 'Walka ideologiczno-propagandowa o kandydaturę Jagiellońska w Czechach w roku 1438' [The Ideological and Propagandist Struggle for the Jagiellonian Candidature in Bohemia in 1438], *Śląski Kwartalnik Historyczny Sobótka*, 18 (1963), pp. 96–119.

²⁶ The act of confederation is published in Z. Ohryzko (ed.) *Volumina legum Polonicarum*, i, p. 64.

²⁷ *Ibid.*, pp. 63–4.

²⁸ The chronicler John Długosz was not convinced of Spytko's inclination towards Hussite ideas. At the beginning of his account of Spytko's rebellion he wrote: '*Spitho de Melsthin propter Bohemicam haeresim seditionem faciens, collecto exercitu vincitur et in proelio interficitur*'. On another occasion he put in doubt the accusations of Spytko's involvement in Hussitism: '*Creditus est Spitho praefatus non malevolentia aut pertinacia sed cerebri debilitate facinus huiusmodi peregisse, et Communionem utriusque speciei necessariam ad salutem credisse . . .*'; Długosz, iv, pp. 606–7; Sochacka, 'Konfederacja Spytka', pp. 54–62.

²⁹ J. Macek, *Jean Huss*, pp. 224–5.

³⁰ He was son of Jan Głowacz of Leżenice and Nowy Dwór (d. 1399), voivode of Mazovia, and Jadwiga of Graboszewo. Zbąski inherited the town of Zbąszyń with the surrounding region which had been given to his father by King Władysław Jagiełło; A. Gąsiorowski, 'Husyty Abrahama Zbąskiego działalność publiczna' [Public Activity of the Hussite Abraham Zbąski], *Śląski Kwartalnik Historyczny Sobótka*, 36 (1981), p. 139.

³¹ In Długosz's account of Zbąski's struggle against the Cracow bishop, the chronicler stressed his various abilities and drew attention to his prominent services in the state administration. He seems to have been surprised by Zbąski's adherence to heresy: '*In aliis quidam rebus vir singularis ingenii erat, et in consulendi pro republicae, praeter coronationem Wladislai* [Długosz mentions the coronation of the ten-year-old son of Jagiełło, Władysław, which was forced by the Cracow bishop], *quamvis est dissuasisse, partes meliores sequebatur, ut dolerent omnes boni ingenium tam industrium et callidum ad illa haeresis studia convertisse*'; Długosz, iv, p. 610.

32 In 1423 he appeared in the noble jury of Kościany for the first time. In 1425 he was awarded 140 marks from the neighbouring royal possessions in Rogoziniec as a token of the king's favour. In 1430 he accompanied the king at a provincial diet in Kościana; A. Gąsiorowski, 'Husyty Abrahama Zbąskiego', p. 140.

33 The office of royal judge was very prestigious and profitable. After 1432 Zbąski started to appear more often in various documents and his signature is to be found on such documents as the privilege of Cracow (in 1433) and compromises between the king and Sigismund Korybut (1432, 1434); A. Gąsiorowski, 'Husyty Abrahama Zbąskiego', p. 140.

34 *Urkundliche Beiträge zur Geschichte des Hussitenkrieges*, ed. F. Palacký, Bd 2, (Prague, 1873), pp. 205–6, No. 734; R. Heck, 'Walka', pp. 53–8.

35 In July 1432 King Władysław Jagiełło signed a military alliance with the Orebites against the Teutonic Knights and in the following year the Czech–Polish expedition to Prussia took place. O. Odložilik, 'Husyci na brzegu Bałtyku w 1433' [The Hussites at the Baltic Seaside in 1433], *Rocznik Gdański*, 7–8 (1933–4), pp. 81–125; J. Macek, *Husyci na Pomorzu*, pp. 32–8.

36 Długosz, iv, p. 544; *AC Płoc.*, p. 445. Josef Macek argued that Zbąski's visit to Bohemia made him familiar with the Hussite programme and incited him to claim secularisation of ecclesiastical possessions; J. Macek, *Jean Huss*, p. 225.

37 Długosz, iv, p. 561.

38 On 6 November 1435 a nobleman, Przecław of Lubiechowo, informed the church authorities in Poznań about the agitation against tithes which was stirred up by Zbąski among Poznań nobility. His account shows that Zbąski's action gained considerable support; *AC*, ii, p. 506, no. 1065.

39 *AC*, ii, p. 44, no. 208.

40 In the spring of 1436, Bishop Ciołek left Poznań after the death of his brother Andrew, who was starost (royal governor) of Great Poland; J. Nowacki, *Dzieje archidiecezji poznańskiej* [The History of the Poznan Archdiocese], vol. 2 (Poznań, 1964), p. 84; A. Gąsiorowski, 'Husyty Abrahama Zbąskiego', p. 141.

41 *Ibid.*, pp. 143–4.

42 J. Nowacki, *Biskup poznański*, pp. 249–58; M. Mastyńska, 'Biskup Andrzej Bniński, cz. 1' [Bishop Andrew of Bniński, part 1], *Roczniki Historyczne*, 9 (1933), pp. 184–98.

43 The fact that after 1436 Krzesław of Kurozwęki, relative of bishop Bniński, was starost of Great Poland played an important part in suppressing the Hussites of Zbąsyń. Krzesław commanded nine hundred troops who accompanied the Poznań bishop during his visitation of Zbąszyń in October 1440. He also took part in a few trials against the heretics and burned six of the Zbąszyń Hussites after their condemnation by the episcopal court; *AC*, ii, p. 517, no. 1097.

44 *Ibid.*

45 *Johanni Dlugosii Catalogus episcoporum* (vita Andrei de Bnin) in *Opera omnia*, i, p. 510; Długosz, iv, p. 608.

46 '*sufficienter ut spero purgaverim, ita ut non esset opus videre meo ac humanitati satisfacere volens, non compulsus, nec metu alicuius concussus, sed ultranea mea voluntate nescio, quod meo scire, aliter fidem tenuissem aut credissem sicut sancta Ecclesia credit . . .*'; *AC*, ii, pp. 519–20, no. 1002.

47 *AC*, ii, p. 532, no. 1141.

48 *AC Pozn*, p. 273.

49 *AC Pozn*, pp. 265–75; J. Nowacki, *Biskup poznański*, pp. 254–6.

50 A nobleman, Maciej Gądkowski, declared during the trial that one of the captured – the Hussite priest Miklasz of Gniezno – had preached heretical ideas in the Polish army which had been dispatched to Silesia in 1438; *AC Pozn*, pp. 266–8.

51 At the time of the bishop's visitation of Zbąszyń, in the neighbouring village of Chobienica, Peter Oganka overtly declared his adherence to Hussite tenets and participation in the services at which Communion in both kinds was distributed; *AC*, ii, p. 518, no. 1098.

52 He appeared before the bishop on 7 September 1440 and recanted heresy, in particular swearing never again to receive Communion in both kinds; *AC*, ii, p. 513, no. 1087.

53 *AC*, ii, p. 522, no. 1111.

54 Acta officialatus Poznaniensis from 1439, f. 21; M. Mastyńska, 'Biskup Andrzej Bniński', p. 193.

55 The information about the burning of Hussite priests from Zbąszyń is recorded by John Długosz in his biography of Andrew Bniński (*Catalogus episcoporum Poloniae*) in *Opera omnia*, i, pp. 511–12) and in *Liber mortuorum monasterii Lubinensis ordinis s. Benedicti*, ed. W. Kętrzyński in *Monumenta Poloniae Historica*, v (Lvov, 1888), p. 606. Several years later the councillor of Zbąszyń Nicholaus Grunberg was also burned as a heretic, but the first mention of his death occurred as late as 1470; *AC*, ii, p. 596, no. 1330.

56 Mikołaj of Zbąszyń; Jakub of Wroniany *AC Pozn*, p. 277.

57 Długosz, iv, p. 610.

58 The last entry concerning the Zbąszyń Hussites is recorded in the *acta officialatus* of the Poznań diocese in 1453; *AC*, ii, p. 569, no. 1353.

59 *AC*, i, p. 53, no. 263.

60 *AC*, ii, p. 554, no. 1207.

61 *AC*, iii, pp. 223–4, no. 479.

62 *AC*, iii, p. 230, no. 504. As the *acta officialatus* of the Włocławek diocese for the years 1430–80 were destroyed there is no means of studying the development of Hussite ideas in this area for fifty years. The first page of *acta officialatus* from 1480 started with the trial of the Hussites in Nieszawa.

63 *AC Płoc.*, pp. 85–109; J. Serczyk, 'Husytyzm na Mazowszu w drugiej połowie XV wieku' [Hussitism in Mazovia in the second half of the Fifteenth Century], *Studia z dziejów Kościoła w Polsce*, 1 (1960), pp. 161–80.

64 *AC Płoc.*, pp. 92, 99–100, (nos. 354, 383, 386).

65 The letter was written between 1450 and 1452; *CE*, i, pp. 347–8.

66 *AC*, iii, pp. 234–45, nos. 515–532; *MHDW*, iv, pp. 15–19.

67 *AC*, iii, p. 243, no. 527.

68 Moszczeński was castellan of Dorzýn and Krysten of Kościot was steward (*dapifer*) of Brześć Kujawski; *AC*, iii, pp. 241, 242, nos. 524, 527.

69 *AC*, iii, p. 242, no. 572.

70 *AC*, iii, p. 242, no. 527.

71 This charge was included in all verdicts against five Hussites who were interrogated in 1480; *AC*, iii, pp. 242, 244–5, 246, nos. 526, 530, 532; *MHDW*, iv, pp. 15–18.

72 *AC*, iii, p. 245, no. 531.

73 *AC*, iii, p. 239, no. 520.

74 *AC*, ii, pp. 197–200, no. 524; the testimony of Katherine of Nieszawa, interrogated in 1480, put the mayor of Pakość on the list of persons suspected of heresy; *AC*, iii, p. 515, no. 234.

75 *AC*, ii, p. 132, no. 383.

76 On 20 May 1480 Albert of Miąsko in his denunciations described an assault on the inquisitor which took place around 1430; *AC*, iii, p. 244, no. 529.

77 *AC*, iii, p. 243, no. 527.

78 *AC*, iii, p. 243, no. 529.

79 '. . . *si iurabitis quod contra dnam Materninam et suos pueros de heresi proclamare non debebitis, aut eciam, ipsam quomodo prodere, extunc mittemus te, si vero non submergevisi, extunc inducens iuramentum praestit, ut eidem mandaverant*'; *AC*, ii, p. 200, no. 524.

80 A few such cases of the inhabitants of Pakość are recorded in *Gnesner Hussitenverhöre 1450–1452*, pp. 321–5; see also the interrogation of Stanisław, parish priest in Pakość, who lived for a certain time in Prague, where he listened to Jan Rokicana's sermons and acquired Hussite books; *AC*, ii, pp. 192–3, no. 521; ii, p. 197, no. 524.

81 In Cracow Jan Elgot, vicar general of the Cracow bishop, talked to a student from the Dobrzyń region, who had been forced by his parents to study in Prague; *CE*, i, p. 347.

82 General remarks on this phenomenon in: J. Kłoczowski, *Europa Słowiańska w xiv–xv wieku* [Slavic Europe in the Fourteenth and Fifteenth Centuries] (Warsaw, 1984), pp. 147–52.

10

CONNECTIONS BETWEEN LOLLARDS, TOWNSFOLK AND GENTRY IN TENTERDEN IN THE LATE FIFTEENTH AND EARLY SIXTEENTH CENTURIES*

Rob Lutton

Tenterden and the surrounding Weald of Kent sustained traditions of heterodoxy from the early fifteenth century through to the Reformation and beyond. A number of possible explanations have been given for the continuity of Lollardy and what seems to have been a general susceptibility to religious dissent on the Weald. One of these explanations seizes upon the existence of a cloth industry which created the networks along which textile middlemen spread Lollard ideas to economically insecure wage-earning artisans, who were the obvious audience for anti-clericalism and 'chiliastic prophecies'.[1] An alternative view, proposed by Alan Everitt, sees this tradition as having more to do with a 'restless individualism' or 'freedom of the wold', linked to its relative isolation and, in particular, its remoteness from ecclesiastical control.[2] Taking yet a different approach, Anne Hudson has looked to the continuity of Lollard ideas within families over a number of generations as perhaps the best way to account for the survival of dissent in certain areas.[3] These explanations are not mutually exclusive, partly because they do not all seek to explain the same thing. The first two are more concerned with identifying the conditions, whether socio-economic, geographical or political, within which heterodox ideas gained appeal. The third, on the other hand, is more of an explanation of the survival of those ideas, and as such offers a method by which to test and explore the wider question of susceptibility to heterodoxy.

The approach adopted here therefore puts the family centre-stage and seeks to comment on the relationship of Lollardy to more orthodox forms of piety in Tenterden, and in particular its appeal to Wealden families in the late fifteenth and early sixteenth centuries. In addition, some questions will be raised regarding the relationship of Lollardy to later developments in the form of both orthodox and unorthodox radicalism. In the process it is hoped that something

*I would like to express my thanks to Dr R.G. Davies for his comments on an earlier draft of this paper, and to Mr A.F. Butcher not only for his many helpful suggestions, but for his sustained interest and support.

will emerge about the social, economic and political contexts of Lollardy in
Tenterden and its region. In this sense, to make the family the unit of analysis is a
deliberate attempt to adopt the most adequate method for beginning to describe
and analyse a particular local and regional culture.[4] Family therefore provides a
starting point, as well as a method for reconstructing certain social and economic
formations and political situations which may have given rise to particular
mentalities, more open than others to heterodox ideas.

This reconstruction begins in the middle of a story, with Stephen Castelyn, a cutler
of Tenterden, who abjured certain heretical opinions before Archbishop William
Warham in May 1511.[5] Castelyn was one among over fifty suspects embroiled in the
Kentish heresy trials which ran from 29 April 1511 to June 1512. Tenterden was
recorded as the home parish of twelve of these, with the rest coming predominantly
from parishes nearby, or from the Maidstone area.[6] Stephen Castelyn's particular
errors concerned the sacrament of the altar, pilgrimage, images, confession and
absolution. These opinions were in accord with those of the other Kentish suspects as
a whole. This is probably because they were all questioned along the same lines: on
the sacrament of the altar, baptism, confirmation, confession and absolution,
priesthood, matrimony, extreme unction, pilgrimage, images, and the consecration of
bread and water. Not all the suspects abjured on all points, but almost all denied
transubstantiation, were hostile to pilgrimage and to the veneration of images, and
around one third opposed confession.[7] Stephen Castelyn's involvement in the trials,
as a witness as well as a suspect, allows us to retrace at least some of his religiously
divergent steps leading up to 1511. Together with a number of other suspects,
Castelyn gave evidence against Edward Walker of Maidstone. Walker was
subsequently burned for his activities, it seems largely because of his role as ringleader
of the Lollard group with which Castelyn was involved from, at latest, May 1509.

According to the depositions, Castelyn first met the group on May Day 1509, in
Edward Walker's house at Maidstone. In addition to Castelyn and Walker, Robert
Raynold of Cranbrook (and possibly at one time of Tenterden) and William Baker,
also of Cranbrook, were present. Both Baker and Raynold concur on the main
subject of discussion, the former telling how 'evryche of them commyned, held,
concluded and beleved that the sacrament of the aulter, that the preest dude holde
above his hede at the sacrying tyme, was not crists body, flesshe and bloode, but
oonly brede', and the latter stressing how it was 'a thing made in mynde and for
the remembraunce of criste for the people, for crists owne body was in heven and
his worde was in erthe'. According to Baker, on the same occasion 'every of theym
had communicacion ayenst pilgremage and worshipping of seynts and of offeryngs.
And then and there they and every of theym concluded that it shuld not be
profitable for mannyes soule. In so moche that aftir the said communicacion this
deponent, whiche was mynded to goo and offer to the roode of grace, outdrewe his
mynde and went not thider but gave his offeryng to a poore man'.[8]

The next recorded meeting involving Castelyn was some seven months later in

The church of St Mildred, Tenterden, with its dominating west tower (the finest in Kent), built in the second half of the fifteenth century. The biggest group of defendants in 1511–12 came from the town and many penances were ordered to be performed in the parish church. (By permission of Kent Messenger Group Newspapers)

John Bampton's house at Otham, Bampton, at Christmas time, 1509. Also present were John Bampton, his brother Richard Bampton of Boxley, Robert Bright of Maidstone, Thomas Feld, William Baker of Cranbrook, William Riche of Benenden and a young man of around seventeen who came with Riche. Together they 'commyned, held, beleved and affermed that the sacrament of the aulter was not the body of Criste but oonly brede'. That night, Castelyn excepted, the men went on to Edward Walker's house in Maidstone, where they drank together and continued to hold forth against the miracle of the mass until they were forced to stop by the arrival of the gaoler's wife.[9] The depositions tell us that seven weeks later Castelyn joined in another heretical meeting, which took place at Shrovetide (on, or shortly before, 12 February) 1510. This is the only episode recounted by Castelyn himself, revealing how:

in the house of the said Edward Walker at Maidston, in the kechyn by the fyre on the evenyng, the said Edward Walker, Robert Hylles and this deponent [Castelyn] commyned togider ayenst the sacrament of thaulter. And then and ther they three and every of theym concluded and said that the sacrament of the aulter was but oonly brede, doon in a mynde to call people togider, and god was oonly in heven. And also, as he remembreth, they commyned agaynst pilgremages.[10]

The last gathering that we know about at which Castelyn was present was around St Bartholomewtide (24 August) 1510, in Walker's house along with Robert Raynold and John Bampton, where they once again discussed and spoke against the sacrament of the altar.

Although there were meetings at which Castelyn was not present over this period of time, it is apparent that he was more than just a peripheral member of the group. Some details about reading in these conventicles are suggestive as to his role. On one occasion when Castelyn seems to have been absent William Baker confessed to have read to the group from

a booke of Methewe where yn was conteyned the gospell in Englisshe at the whiche redyng the said John Bampton, William Riche, Edward Walker and the said yongman were wele contentid and pleasid saying that it was pitie that it might not be knowen openly the whiche redyng in the saide booke as they understod it was agenst the sacrament of thaulter baptisme matrymony and preesthode.

Baker claimed to have given the book to John Bampton, and that he did not know where Bampton had put it. There is no mention of the book in Bampton's deposition. Significantly though, he claimed that he could not remember whether it was Baker or Castelyn who had read on this occasion.[11] Although we should probably trust Baker's own confession to having read from the book, Bampton's confusion suggests at least that Castelyn was known to be capable of reading to the group, and maybe even that he had read at other times.

Moving further away from the trials of 1511, it seems that Stephen Castelyn did not learn his heresy directly from Edward Walker and his circle. His own abjuration states that he had held heretical opinions from around 1507, when he would have been about nineteen.[12] Insight into the earlier stages of his heresy is gained from evidence he gave against William Carder. Carder also lived in Tenterden, and was one of the ringleaders in the area. Some years before, he had come to Kent from Lincolnshire, the home of his Lollard parents. His mother was originally from Tenterden, but had fled some forty years before for fear of persecution. Carder had supposedly been responsible for teaching and sharing his opinions with a number of people in the parish.[13] The only information we have on Castelyn's relationship with Carder is his own testimony, in 1511, that about three years previously, once again in Maidstone, 'William Carder of Tenterden taught hym first to belive ayenst the sacrament of thaulter that it was not goodes body, flesshe and bloode, but oonly brede . . .'. It seems that Castelyn's relationship with Carder was the bridge to his involvement in the Maidstone group. This is made all the more likely by the fact that Robert Hilles of Tenterden, and William Riche of the nearby parish of Benenden, who were also involved in the Maidstone conventicles, both gave evidence against Carder.[14] Castelyn's more than occasional presence in the Maidstone area suggests that he may have been apprenticed or have regularly worked or traded there, away from his home parish and family in Tenterden. There is the tantalising possibility that he was apprenticed to Walker, who like Castelyn, was a cutler. There is, however, nothing to prove this, and for the time being the most that can be said is that, as was often the case, trade or professional connections seem to have been important in drawing a new convert into a Lollard circle.[15]

So far we have concentrated only on Stephen Castelyn himself and his involvement in heresy from 1507 to 1511. It is now time to turn to his family in Tenterden in order to try and place his divergence from orthodoxy under Carder, Walker and others in some sort of context. The surviving evidence which relates to the Castelyn family of Tenterden in this period is relatively plentiful, in particular comprising seven last wills and testaments dated from 1473 to 1532. These represent four generations of the family, and it is partly because of the survival of their wills, that the Castelyns appear as one of the more enduring families in the parish.[16]

Stephen had a brother named William who died towards the end of 1510, but for whom unfortunately we have no surviving will (See p. 204 for the Castelyn family tree). We get closest to Stephen in the will of his sister-in-law, William's wife Katherine, which contains what may be the only direct reference to him outside the records of the heresy trials. Katherine died shortly after William, at the beginning of 1511, and Stephen was an executor and witness to her will. Katherine left Stephen 'half of my husband's remaining steel and a hundred weight of iron', indicating that the brothers may have practised the same or at least similar trades.[17] As well as a brother, Stephen also had three sisters named Alice, Julian and Joan.[18] Stephen appears to have been named after his father, who, to distinguish him from his son, will be referred to as Stephen Castelyn senior.[19] Stephen Castelyn senior was most probably one of the two sons of Robert Castelyn junior who died in 1487.[20] Robert in turn was one of the three sons of Robert Castelyn senior who died in 1473.[21] Having traced Stephen Castelyn's family back over three generations, it is possible to assess the character of Castelyn family piety over a period of almost forty years.

It makes sense to begin with the last will and testament of Robert Castelyn senior, dated 21 September 1473, the first surviving representation of Castelyn piety.[22] As is the case for all the Tenterden wills in this period, Robert senior's has an

The Castelyn Family of Tenterden

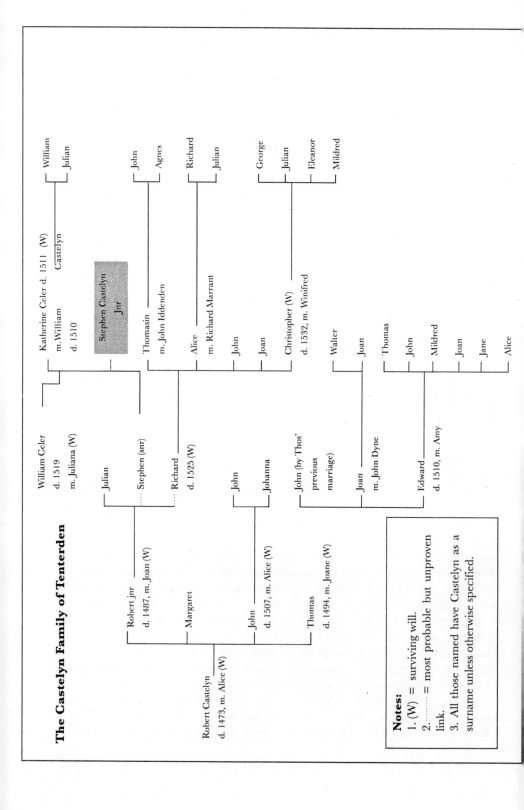

Notes:
1. (W) = surviving will.
2. .... = most probable but unproven link.
3. All those named have Castelyn as a surname unless otherwise specified.

orthodox testamentary preamble, and he left a relatively small sum of 4*d* for tithes forgotten to the high altar of Tenterden parish church.[23] In writing his will, Robert concentrated on providing for his family, making bequests of household goods to his wife Alice, his sons Robert, John and Thomas and his daughter Margaret. To what extent the exclusion of any bequests for such things as masses, obits or other traditional religious arrangements was due to pressure on limited resources is impossible to gauge from his will alone. The low payment for tithes forgotten might suggest that money was in short supply for Robert, but meagre payments to high altars do not necessarily reflect a lack of wealth or low social status.[24]

Fortunately, it is not impossible to place Robert Castelyn senior socially in Tenterden. He is recorded in 1463 as a witness, along with four other men, to a grant of two acres of land in Tenterden by Thomas Pytlesdon esquire, Thomas Carpynter and Thomas Jan junior to Robert Donny, all of the parish.[25] The Pytlesdon family had their seat on the manor of Pitlesdon in Tenterden, just west of the town, and Thomas Pytlesdon served as the borough's first bailiff in 1449–50 when the town was annexed as a limb to the Cinque Port of Rye in Sussex. He went on to serve as bailiff again in 1450–1, and 1458–9.[26] Thomas Carpynter was another leading figure in the town who served as bailiff in 1478–9, 1488–9 and 1495–6.[27] The Jans do not appear to have been prominent in town government but held what appear to have been not insubstantial lands in Tenterden and Halden.[28] Robert Donny, to whom the grant of land was made, served as bailiff in 1455–6.[29]

Robert Castelyn's name appears last in the list of witnesses to this grant, which leads with Thomas Haymes, followed by William Harenden, William Wygge and Thomas Baynden. Thomas Haymes was possibly the same individual or of the same family as Thomas Heynes, a chaplain, who in 1498 held and granted lands in Tenterden together with, among others, Sir Richard Guildford, knight.[30] We have no other record of the activities in the parish of the fourth witness, Thomas Baynden. However, something can be said about Harenden and Wygge. Harenden was bailiff in 1457–8, and he and Wygge acted in tandem as rentiers, leasing the whole or half of a parcel of property comprising a messuage, gardens, arable and woodland totalling fifteen acres, between 1449 and 1450. Wygge held lands in his own right as early as 1451, and as late as 1474.[31] These glimpses of political and economic activity suggest that Harenden and Wygge belonged to leading families of middling status in Tenterden; the sort of men of good reputation and of enough weight and standing to have witnessed such a land transaction. That Robert Castelyn senior acted alongside and on behalf of such leading figures in the town, including Thomas Pytlesdon esquire, a member of a local gentry family, sheds at least some light on his social status.[32] It therefore does not seem to be stretching things too far to say that the Castelyn family, at least from the 1460s, was one of the more established families in Tenterden.

To return to the question of Robert Castelyn senior's last will and testament, these indications of his social status tend to undermine the notion that the rather sparse and completely family-centred character of his deathbed piety was entirely due to a lack of available resources. It suggests that there was at least some element of choice in the way he made his will, and that his actions and words, and the form in which they were recorded, were self-consciously austere. It is of course possible that Robert was limited to certain types of resources; in other words, that he was largely restricted to making bequests of household goods, having already devised his lands and bequeathed the bulk of any cash. This might explain why his payment for tithes forgotten was only 4d and why there are no other cash bequests in his will. This said, there are numerous examples of Tenterden wills which make sometimes extensive cash bequests either wholly or in part on the strength of goods or lands to be sold by executors. That Robert did not make this sort of arrangement in order to fund bequests to church fabric or for masses and prayers, suggests that such concerns were not as important to him as they were to some of his fellow parishioners.[33]

Fourteen years later, at the end of August 1487, Robert Castelyn junior made a will which closely adhered to the tenor of testamentary piety set by his father.[34] An orthodox preamble and payment for tithes forgotten, once again of 4d, was accompanied by bequests to family. Robert junior left his messuage and gardens to his wife Joan, and ensured that Alice, his mother, could complete her days in the house and gardens in which she already lived. On their deaths all this was to go to his sons, who, as already explained, are most satisfactorily identified as Richard and Stephen. All, that is, except for 20s left to his daughter Julian. He also mentioned his sister Margaret in his last will. Departing somewhat from the pattern of his father's will, Robert junior's contains a request for the residue of his estate to be distributed by his wife for his soul, his parents' souls and all the Christian faithful. As is often the case with these formulae, however, this probably had more to do with scribal convention than personal aspiration. Even if it reflects Robert's wishes we have no way of knowing how any residue was to be employed, and so this clause in no way disrupts the continuity of testamentary expression between father and son. This continuity involved the absence of traditionally orthodox pious elements such as bequests for masses, obits, lights and chantries, and – what was most probably a cause as much as a consequence of this omission – concentration upon immediate family.

When it came to making their wills, tradition – or at least transmitted values – seems to have provided some important guiding principles for the Castelyns, whilst the range of choices available dictated the ways in which these values were applied. John Castelyn, son of Robert senior and brother to Robert junior, is a good example of how Castelyn family piety was passed on and moulded in new ways by changing fortunes and circumstances. He made a will in January 1507, with an orthodox preamble, in which he left 2s 2d to the high altar of St Mildred's, the parish church, for his forgotten tithes.[35] This relatively large sum is confirmation of Castelyn family wealth and status and suggests that at least in one branch of the family, by the early sixteenth century Castelyn fortunes were on the up and up.[36] This is not to say though, that such a large discrepancy between John's payment and those of his father and brother was entirely due to differences of wealth. It may have had more to do with the form which available wealth took, and the degree of diversity of resources available at death. John certainly appears to have had greater access to liquid capital than his father and brother, the major part of which, 66s 8d, he devoted to his daughter Joan's dowry. He also bequeathed goods to his wife Alice and son John. In his last will he made provision – but only in the event of his daughter not marrying – for 20s to go towards repairs of Tenterden parish church, 20s to be left to Thomas Weldysh, and the residue to go to poor maidens, and other charitable purposes. Like his father and brother before him, John made no arrangements for masses, obits or prayers, or bequests for images or lights, and in terms of definite arrangements no explicitly religious bequests. If John departed in any way from the tenor of testamentary piety laid down and followed by his forebears, it was only in terms of the strategy he employed for dispensing different types of resources. He still concentrated almost wholly upon providing for immediate family, and only then, in the form of secondary measures, did he attend to the issues of the maintenance of the parish church, charity and the welfare of real or fictive kin. John neither procured liturgical intercessions, nor left us with any signs of adherence to saints' cults.

Just as transmitted values could be mediated by the nature of available resources, so they could also be moulded in their expression through the variety of pressures brought to bear by social relationships. This is true of Joan Castelyn, the widow of Thomas Castelyn, the third of Robert senior's sons. Her will, written in December 1494, is of the same character as the other Castelyn wills, but her bequests reflect her own particular social network and sense of obligation and responsibility.[37] She left 4d in tithes forgotten and gave 4d to repairs of the parish church – the first definite gift to church fabric in the surviving Castelyn wills. The rest of her testament is devoted to bequeathing household goods to a total of eighteen individuals. Eleven of these gifts were to close relatives: her daughter and her daughter's family, grandchildren, a nephew's children (Stephen Castelyn senior's daughters) and '*filio mariti mei*'. She also made bequests to the daughters of Robert Eastlyng, and six gifts to women whose precise relationships to her are not immediately apparent. Whilst not noticeably departing from family tradition, Joan included a wider circle of people within the compass of her bequests than her father-in-law or brothers-in-law. This is best seen as mediation of family piety through a particular set of social relationships, in part to do with her being a woman and a widow.[38]

This brings us back to Katherine Castelyn, Stephen Castelyn's sister-in-law, who died in 1511, the year of the heresy trials. It appears that both she and her husband William Castelyn, who died late the previous year, lived only to their late twenties. Two children are mentioned in Katherine's testament, and yet her parents, William and Julian Celer, were beneficiaries, her father an executor, and her mother a witness. Parental influence provides the best explanation for the divergence of Katherine's testamentary piety from the pattern of earlier Castelyn wills. Katherine made a series of four small bequests to lights. Three of these were also patronised in her mother's will eight years later. Because of this familial continuity Katherine's testamentary piety is best seen as being closer to that of the Celer family than the Castelyns, this being a good illustration of the importance of life span and the pressures of the deathbed in the will-making process.[39]

Our reconstruction has now brought us back to where we began – the mid-point of our story – the years in which Stephen Castelyn became involved in Lollardy. This has not only been a reconstitution of family, but also of family piety, seen in the transmission of values between two generations over some thirty-four years from 1473 to 1507. The tenor of this family piety was surprisingly coherent, and arguably formed an important element in Stephen Castelyn's interest in heterodoxy. There is certainly nothing which emerges from a collective reading of these wills which was contrary to Lollard ideas, and seen in a positive way there is much in accordance with them. Indeed the Castelyn wills may represent an extremity of orthodox piety which rendered its adherents particularly susceptible to Lollardy.

The significance of the continuity of testamentary expression in the Castelyn wills can be better appreciated when all those which have shared features are compared to the Tenterden wills as a whole.[40] (See figure 1.) A total of fifty-four out of 246, or 22 per cent of those made from 1470 to 1535, share the Castelyns' lack of traditionally religious elements.[41] These fifty-four wills are distributed between forty-five different testator-surnames, and a total of eight surnames appear more than once as makers of these wills, the Castelyns leading with three. Including the Castelyns, in three out of the eight cases the wills have been established as belonging to the same family. In the remaining five cases there is nothing to rule out family connections, but as yet no evidence has been found which proves that they existed. For the sake of convenience I shall refer to these groups of individuals as families, whilst bearing in mind the provisional nature of this description.[42] Although these families represent only 18 per cent of the surnames, together they share seventeen out of the fifty-four, or 32 per cent of the Castelyn-like wills. This shows that there was a marked tendency for these wills to be continuous within *certain* families.[43] This suggests, firstly, that like the Castelyns, for some individuals, in some families, the making of a will without attention to traditional religious concerns involved elements of real choice and the prioritisation of some concerns over and above others, rather than the restrictions of limited resources alone. Secondly, it appears that the Castelyns' approach to will-making, borne out of familial tradition, was not as idiosyncratic as it was reflective of a more widely shared sense of values, which were passed on from one generation to the next, among a certain group of families. This group perhaps represented a particular direction in the pattern of local or regional piety, and offers a broader scope within which to explore the appeal of Lollardy in Tenterden. Whether or not these families formed a relatively coherent interest group remains to be seen. Their social positions, political roles and kinship networks within the parish have yet to be fully investigated.

For the time being, the Castelyns offer a very good case study of one of these families. This is especially due to the survival of two more wills which allow for the continued reconstruction of the family and the completion of the story of their piety up to the 1530s. The first belongs to Richard Castelyn and is dated April 1525. From evidence both in and outside his will it seems that Richard was around fifty years old at least at his death. He was most probably one of the sons of Robert

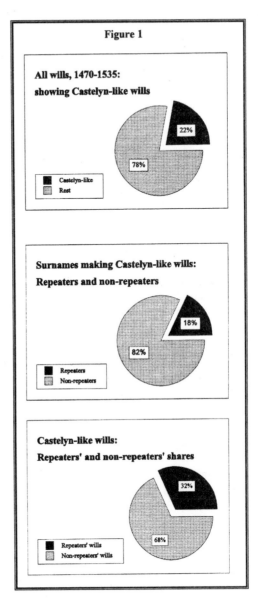

Figure 1

All wills, 1470-1535:
showing Castelyn-like wills

- Castelyn-like
- Rest

22%
78%

Surnames making Castelyn-like wills:
Repeaters and non-repeaters

- Repeaters
- Non-repeaters

18%
82%

Castelyn-like wills:
Repeaters' and non-repeaters' shares

- Repeaters' wills
- Non-repeaters' wills

32%
68%

Castelyn junior, and so Stephen Castelyn the heretic's uncle. Richard left 3s 4d in tithes forgotten, followed by a gift of 8d every quarter for three years after his death to the Jesus mass. He apportioned 20s to his funeral, 20s to his month's mind, and arranged for a yearly obit in Tenterden parish church for seven years at 6s 8d a year. He went on to leave 4d to each of his godchildren, and 6s 8d to each of four of his grandchildren. This is clearly a very different will from those examined so far for the family, with a conspicuous presence of cash bequests, and more outwardly and traditionally orthodox religious arrangements expressed in relative detail.[44]

Richard's son Christopher Castelyn acted as his father's executor, and died only seven years later, in 1532. In terms of religious bequests, his will closely resembles his father's. He left 2s in tithes forgotten, 6s 8d in wax to the light before the sacrament in St Mildred's, 4d every quarter for six years to the Jesus mass, 26s 8d divided equally between his funeral and month's mind, and 10s to his year's mind. His wealth is attested to not only by these bequests but, in addition, by a dowry of £10 for his daughter Julian. In his last will he made an arrangement for 6s 8d a year to be paid for masses and diriges in St Mildred's for seven years.[45] As was the case with the other members of the Castelyn family, the continuity of pious attitudes between father and son is revealed in these bequests. This can be seen particularly in the occurrence of gifts to the Jesus mass in both texts, of the same overall amount of 8s. They also left similar amounts for obsequies. The exactly duplicated arrangement for a yearly obit over seven years represents a common phenomenon of late medieval wills. This may have been the same arrangement delayed by Christopher as executor of his father's will, and so included in his own, or alternatively it represented the continuation of a familial tradition as, after all, it was seven years since his father's death and so an opportune time to renew the endowment.[46]

To all intents and purposes these two wills are entirely orthodox. How then can such a seeming rupture from earlier family traditions be explained, whilst retaining family as a useful motif in the dynamics of piety? At a first glance the answer seems to lie in Richard's and Stephen's status and wealth. Richard's standing is illustrated by his involvement in other families' wills as witness or executor on five recorded occasions from 1498 to 1519.[47] He served the parish community in a more formal capacity as one of the two or four named *parochiani* in Tenterden in 1505, 1506, and 1515, presumably the parishioners sworn in to make presentments to the visitations of those years.[48] His wealth, at least in part, lay in lands and tenements in both Tenterden and the neighbouring parish of Rolvenden. He was among the wealthier townsfolk: in 1512/13 as a baron of the confederation of the Cinque Ports, a fifteenth of his goods and chattels in the hundred of Tenterden were assessed at 10s, which can be compared to an average of 15s for all those combarons who owned property in the hundred, assessed at the same time.[49] Christopher may have surpassed his father in prestige and status, serving as churchwarden for two consecutive years in 1521 and 1522.[50] He was feoffee to a will in 1513, and then again in 1518 and 1524, and he was witness to a will in 1532, just two months before he wrote his own.[51]

Although Richard and Christopher appear to have boosted the Castelyn family fortunes since the last decades of the fifteenth century it is easy to over-emphasise their rise in influence, wealth and status. To begin with, in the late fifteenth and early sixteenth centuries, only a minority of richer families were likely to succeed in one parish for over four generations as they did.[52] It is unlikely that Richard and Christopher's wealth was all 'new money' and it probably owed much to the economic achievements of their forebears. Moreover, this apparent social and economic lift might be more of an illusion than a reality, since Tenterden as a whole was benefiting from industrial and agricultural developments which took place across the Kentish Weald from the end of the fifteenth century.[53] In relative terms, when compared to their contemporaries Richard and Christopher may have been no wealthier than Robert Castelyn senior.

Richard and Christopher's wills undoubtedly represent a shift in Castelyn testamentary piety towards greater sophistication and variety. This perhaps owed something both to the growing diversification of Castelyn economic interests, and their developing role within the institutions of parish, town and region. This is not to deny Richard and Christopher any genuine piety, but rather to see the expression of their beliefs as part and parcel of their social relations and range of available resources. This change in the way the Castelyns went about expressing their piety forms part of a more general trend in the Tenterden wills. The incidence of Castelyn-like wills over time (that is, those like the early Castelyn wills, which lack traditionally orthodox religious bequests) can be used as a basic indicator of the changing level of elaboration of testamentary expression. They fell steadily from 33 per cent of all those made in the 1470s, to 14 per cent from 1530 to 1535. This may have been due to a growth in the importance of the will as a vehicle in the expression and arrangement of post-obit piety, as well as perhaps also pointing to a real shift in piety, towards more ostentatious and traditionally orthodox arrangements. Such developments more than likely though had something to do with the changing nature of the community over the period, that is, as already suggested, a rise in prosperity for many of those families for whom we have wills, and the diversification of those economic interests which could be legitimately transformed into symbolic gifts.

At this stage some suggestions can be made concerning the identification of a coherent but nonetheless dynamic familial mentality, sympathetic to both the continuities and discontinuities of Castelyn testamentary expression, as well as Stephen's divergence into heresy. A helpful starting point is provided by Poos's work on Essex, which suggests that among '. . . the broad middling range of rural people . . .' in this period, there was a scepticism of secular and ecclesiastical authority, which caused a reaction leading to '. . . a desire for greater involvement in communal life . . .', a growing parochial activism and an essentially conservative concern with the morality of local clergy. What we know about the dynamics of Castelyn piety accords not only with such attitudes but with the suggestion that, as in Essex, they were '. . . reinforced by both theologically orthodox and Lollard-influenced lay piety'.[54] The increasing presence of the Castelyns in communal life from the early sixteenth century heralded a new involvement for the family in structures of authority whose traditional claims had certainly been questioned for some time by adherents to Lollard ideas in and around Tenterden, and which may well have been more openly and widely criticised within the orthodox community. The pattern of the early family wills up to 1507 is explicable if seen in terms of a certain degree of scepticism towards the structures of traditional orthodox religion, a scepticism which may have encouraged Stephen Castelyn to engage in more active dissent. The later wills bespeak a different sort of activism – certainly more orthodox, and probably more integrated into the mainstream of religious life.

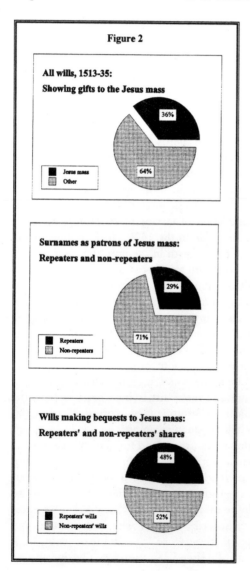

Figure 2

All wills, 1513-35:
Showing gifts to the Jesus mass

- Jesus mass   36%
- Other   64%

Surnames as patrons of Jesus mass:
Repeaters and non-repeaters

- Repeaters   29%
- Non-repeaters 71%

Wills making bequests to Jesus mass:
Repeaters' and non-repeaters' shares

- Repeaters' wills   48%
- Non-repeaters' wills 52%

Richard's and Christopher's involvement in parochial religion, and their attitudes to orthodox devotion, are perhaps best illustrated by their patronage of the Jesus mass. Although it is never referred to as such in the Tenterden wills, this was probably the mass of the Holy Name of Jesus. From the middle of the fifteenth century this was one of the most popular of all votive masses in England, and was part of the wider development of devotional forms surrounding the person and sufferings of Christ, which grew in popularity at this time.[55] In Kent, the Jesus mass was established in Sandwich and Lydd in the 1460s, and was being celebrated in at least one of the parish churches of Canterbury within a decade. It appears to have taken a further thirty years to reach the Weald.[56] Bequests begin in the Tenterden wills in 1513, run to the end of the sample in 1535, and usually consist of sums of money ranging from 4*d* to 3*s* 4*d*. These occur in forty-two of the 117 wills, or 36 per cent made between the two dates.[57] (See figure 2.) Analysis of these bequests by surname reveals that nine out of thirty-one or 29 per cent of the surnames which are represented by bequests to the cult, accounted for a total of twenty out of forty-two, or 48 per cent of gifts made. In seven out of the nine cases of repeating surnames, all those wills bearing the same surname were made by people of the same family. In the other two cases this cannot yet be proved but is not unlikely. It is therefore, on the whole, legitimate to think of these nine groups of wills as belonging to nine different families. Thought of in this way, the spread of bequests reveals a general tendency for patronage of the Jesus mass in Tenterden to be specific to particular families, such as the Castelyns. In other words, to an unquantifiable, but nevertheless significant degree the cult was formed and sustained by bonds of family and household rather than being purely to do with individual choice or independent expression of religious sentiment.[58] In addition, the Castelyns were not the only family in Tenterden who left wills devoid of specifically religious bequests and then went on to support the Jesus mass. (See figure 3.) In fact, nine out of seventeen, or 53 per cent of those families who made Castelyn-like wills, and for whom we have at least one will made from 1513 to 1535, also made bequests to the Jesus mass. Put the other way round, a total of nine out of fifteen or 60 per cent of those families who supported the new cult and for whom we have other wills, also left Castelyn-like wills.[59] This points to a marked correlation concentrated within certain families between the making of wills which lack specifically religious gestures, and adherence to the Jesus mass in Tenterden. What is more, the overwhelming trend, as was the case with the Castelyns, was one of movement over time from sparse testamentary piety to support of the new cult. For families like the Castelyns the Jesus mass may have been an attractive option in post-obit piety simply because it was new, and represented a fresh aspect of orthodox devotion which provided just the right niche for those who may have been dissatisfied with the many saints' cults which were established in the parish.[60] In addition to the appeal of novelty it may also have been attractive to these families because it encapsulated a peculiarly Christocentric strand of orthodox devotion, which whilst being within the bounds of orthodoxy, was in a certain sense radical.[61]

I have now moved from discussing one individual to reconstructing his family and something of its piety, and to saying some broader things about religious attitudes in Tenterden as a whole. On the one hand this has been in the form of a story about the Castelyn family, pieced together from fragments of available information in order to try and put Stephen Castelyn's heterodoxy into some sort of context. On the other hand, the Castleyns have also been used as a case-study, in order to shed light on religious culture at Tenterden. Although other families have been cited to support the inferences which have been drawn from the Castelyn family, this has so far only been done in a statistical fashion, which

Figure 3: Spread of wills for those surnames which repeat one or more times, showing Castelyn-like wills, those containing bequests to the Jesus mass, and those which have neither of these features. (Only those surnames for which there is at least one surviving will dated 1513 or later are included, this being the date from which bequests to the Jesus mass began.)

Key:
* = Castelyn-like wills
† = Jesus mass wills
§ = wills which have neither of the above features

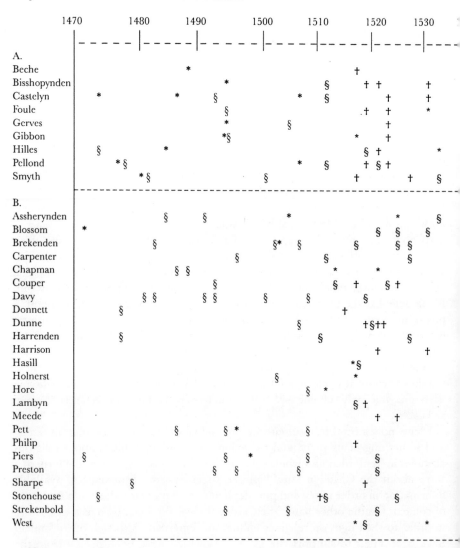

Note:

A: = surnames for which there are both Castelyn-like and Jesus mass wills.

B: = surnames for which there are either Castelyn-like or Jesus mass wills, and/or those with neither of these features.

means that the pattern of piety to which the Castelyns adhered is in danger of being presented in the image of their testamentary story alone, and that is not the intention here. As I have already suggested, it appears that other families shared similar values to those of the Castelyns and worked them out in a like-minded, but often subtly different, manner.

One such family were the Pellonds. Like the Castelyns, the Pellonds were directly affected by the heresy trials of 1511, William Pellond of Tenterden abjuring heretical opinions and receiving his sentence of penance on 17 December 1511.[62] The family was involved in the tailoring or drapery business by the sixteenth century, and appears to have held land in and around Tenterden from as early as the late fourteenth century.[63] The Pellonds were perhaps of higher status and older pedigree in Tenterden than the Castelyns. As early as 1464, in the assessment on the men of the Cinque Ports, William Pellond's grandfather, Thomas Pellond senior, paid 5s 4d as a fifteenth on his goods and chattels in the hundred.[64] Although none of the family is recorded as serving in parish offices, at some time between 1530 and 1532 a William Pellond was admitted as a freeman of Tenterden.[65]

The earliest will which survives for this family is dated July 1477, and belonged to Thomas Pellond senior. He had a large family of at least five sons and four daughters who, along with his grandchildren, dominate his testament and last will. His grandson William Pellond, convicted in the heresy trials thirty-four years later, is possibly included in these bequests.[66] Thomas left a total of 20s and various household goods to family and kin, as well as 5 marks for his daughter Margaret's dowry, 3s 4d to each of his executors who were his sons John and Adam, and 4d to each of his godchildren. He paid 12d in tithes forgotten and made no bequests for masses or prayers. In his last will, however, he made a detailed bequest for the paving of a footway in the parish. Concentration upon providing for family and kin and a conspicuously isolated endowment for public works therefore typify Thomas's testamentary priorities.[67]

Like the Castelyns, a total of seven wills survive for the Pellonds in Tenterden, and Thomas's is one of two among them which lack any explicitly religious bequests. The significance of the continuity of testamentary expression within families has already been noted, and this is reinforced here, as Thomas's son, William Pellond senior, made the second Pellond will in 1508, which was devoid of any explicitly religious elements. This is all the more significant because he was the father of William Pellond, the known heretic. William senior also left 12d in tithes forgotten, but did not even attend to public works. The sparseness of his testamentary piety is perhaps best understood as part of a tradition passed from father to son, similar to that adhered to by the Castelyns.[68]

William junior's two cousins, Moyse and Richard Pellond, both left wills which have much in common, and in terms of their place in the tenor of Pellond family piety, are best compared with those of Richard and Christopher Castelyn. In

1519, Moyse Pellond left 6s 8d to the chapel of St John the Baptist in the hamlet of Small Hythe, Tenterden. Among his bequests was a gift of a portion of russet cloth to a poor maiden of the parish. He also stipulated that 13s 4d be distributed to priests, clerks and poor people, and for a drinking for the health of his soul on his burial day, and 6s 8d at his month's mind. Beneath the witness list is one last bequest of 12d to the maintenance of the Jesus mass within Tenterden parish church.[69] This may be compared with his brother Richard Pellond's testament of six years later: beginning where his brother left off, he gave 20d a year for sixteen years to the Jesus mass. After this he devoted 40d to be given to poor people in the parish every Good Friday for sixteen years, and then stipulated that a yearly obit be conducted for his soul in St Mildred's for sixteen years, within 'the twelve days', at 3s 4d a year. At both his burial and month's mind 20s were to go to priests, clerks, and in meat and drink, and 10s to poor people. At his year's mind, 20s was to be given to priests, clerks and poor people. After a number of cash bequests to family and godchildren, he left 20s to the mending of each of a footway and a 'streetway' between Tenterden and Small Hythe. These arrangements were to be funded by lands in Wittersham and Heronden being put out to farm for sixteen years. Lastly, a house and garden at Eastgate were to be sold; ten marks of the proceeds were to pay for a year's temporary chantry in St Mildred's, and the residue was to be distributed to poor people.[70] Richard's bequests in particular are a good indication of the wealth of the Pellond family by the 1520s, and suggest that they, like the Castelyns, and no doubt other leading families in Tenterden, were growing in prosperity at this time.[71] The endowments from lands at farm indicate the increasing complexity of the moral and religious economy, within which a wider range of available resources were set aside for pious purposes. Elsewhere in England at this time, the transmission of such endowments between family members seems to have involved an awareness of the symbolic value of specific parcels of property.[72]

Like the later Castelyn wills these also indicate adherence to the Jesus mass. Unlike the Castelyns however, Moyse and Richard Pellond placed a shared and unusual emphasis upon charity to the poor and public works, indicating an entirely orthodox, but possible radical, mentality which viewed charitable or civic gifts as being equal in value to procured masses and prayers. Whilst not all wanting to equate this attitude with Lollardy, it is relevant, all the same, that a strand of good works such as this has been found in wills of known Lollards in the Chilterns.[73] Indeed, this reminds us of William Baker's statement in the heresy trials of 1511, that after talking against pilgrimage, images and offerings with Stephen Castelyn and others, he decided not to make an oblation to the Rood of Grace but gave it instead to a poor man.[74] Both Pellond and Castelyn family piety appears to have been thoroughly orthodox, but theirs was a particular style of orthodoxy, grown from seeds which, under the right conditions, had also given rise to an appreciation of Lollard criticisms of the traditional religious order.

These ideas about the common origins and likenesses of Lollardy and radical orthodoxy are reminiscent of J.A.F. Thomson's thoughts on Tenterden. He concluded that '. . . there is nothing to show that convinced Lollards made up anything more than a minority in Tenterden, but . . .' that '. . . the majority was not vindictive towards them'.[75] Although we shall never know just how many convinced Lollards there were in Tenterden, on this first point I am inclined to think that Thomson is right. It is hoped that the evidence presented here helps to some degree to explain why he also seems to be accurate on the second.

To begin with, it is apparent that Lollards were not socially marginalised in Tenterden, but drew interested followers from well-established and leading families, and were certainly not predominantly members of an artisan underclass as proposed by J.F. Davis. This was of course not just a Wealden phenomenon but has been shown to have been the case in other Lollard areas, to the extent that sympathy and protection, from elements of local élites, helped to sustain the continuity of heterodox ideas.[76] At Tenterden, the testamentary evidence from these families suggests that there existed a mentality among at least some influential quarters of town society which was favourably disposed towards Lollard ideas. In addition, there seems to have been a connection, through these families, between Lollardy and later orthodox radicalism. A more obvious continuity, not explored here, is that between Lollardy and Protestantism. I raise this not because the Castelyns and Pellonds have left any signs that they were Protestants by the 1530s, but because Stephen Castelyn's and William Pellond's social status goes some way to bridging the social gulf set by Peter Clark, between his Lollard 'artisans' and 'small peasant farmers' on the Weald, and the Lutheran converts there who, in his opinion, tended to be 'substantial men or clergy'. If the Castelyns and the Pellonds are anything to go by, then any notion of social distinction between Lutherans and Lollards needs to be revised. Lastly, it is suggested here that alongside the flow and apprehension of certain ideas, whether Lollard, Lutheran or humanist, the particular mentality of those families from whom converts were drawn also dictated the geographical and social spread of dissent. The Castelyns and the Pellonds seem to have been especially susceptible, and ideally placed to lean in both Lollard and radically orthodox directions at different times. Once the pace of reform had quickened in the 1530s, they may also have found much to seize upon in Protestantism.[77]

Before anything more definite can be said, much more needs to be done to identify other families in Tenterden, and elsewhere on the Weald, who were involved in Lollardy. In this way it may be possible to judge whether or not Stephen and William were typical of the sorts of people who diverged into heresy. Whilst they cannot be described as 'poorer folk', we know very little as yet about the social background of the majority of other Lollards in the region.[78] In terms of the general complexion of local piety, families of relatively high social status such as the Castelyns and the Pellonds were most likely to have been among the trendsetters, and to have exerted a disproportionate influence upon patterns of religious devotion. To what extent they themselves were influenced by more powerful interest groups is a question to which I will now attend.

In Kent, county and local power was largely in the hands of the gentry. Those large landowners who did exist were predominantly rentiers with estates concentrated in the east of the county. West Kent, the Weald included, was characterised by relatively small gentry estates of less than a thousand acres. By the mid-sixteenth century, Tenterden was typical of those large Wealden parishes which could '. . . contain the estates – and the pretensions – of two or three gentry of the status of knight or esquire, as well as several smaller fry known only as "gent"'. These gentry landowners leased the vast proportion of their lands to a whole range of tenants, most of whom were relatively small men with no more than a hundred to a hundred and fifty acres and most twenty, thirty or fifty acres.[79] There was therefore much potential for the creation of complex relationships between townsfolk and local and county gentry.

By at least the beginning of the sixteenth century the Castelyns had seemingly strong connections with the Foule family.[80] This link was shared to a lesser extent by the Pellonds.[81] The Foules provided Tenterden with bailiffs on five separate occasions from 1480 to 1540 and by 1541, probably due to a combination of both office-holding and aspiration, John Foule was describing himself, or was being described, as *generosus*.[82] Significantly, they were also among those families who patronised the Jesus mass.[83] The Foules probably represent the next notch up from the Castelyns in Tenterden's social hierarchy. They were one of those families who occupied the ambiguous grey area between yeomen-townsfolk and lesser gentry.

Another family, with which the Castelyns, Pellonds and the Foules all had connections, was that of the Hales.[84] The Hales's original seat, Hales Place, was in the neighbouring parish of High Halden, but they had moved to Tenterden in the latter half of the fifteenth century, and through marriage and purchase built up their estate there over the following two generations. In the early sixteenth century Sir John Hales, of the Dungeon, Canterbury, held the seat and it was subsequently inherited by his third son, Edward Hales esquire.[85] John Hales served as bailiff in Tenterden in 1504–5, but his professional and political careers were to take him further afield.[86] After becoming a member of Gray's Inn he built up his reputation as a lawyer both in London and beyond, and was elected MP for Canterbury in 1514. In 1522 he was appointed third baron of the exchequer and was promoted to second baron in 1528, a position he held until his death in 1539. Although his religious convictions cannot easily be separated from his political commitments, it would seem that by the late 1530s he tended towards the conservative in terms of attitudes to reform of the church. Not only his son-in-law Walter Hendley, but also his nephew, Christopher Hales, were among the conservative group of magistrates who reacted against Protestant reform in the late 1530s and early 1540s.[87]

Christopher Hales's career was however, far from unambiguous, and suggests that he and his kinsmen sought some degree of reform of the old religious order. Also a member of Gray's Inn, he became MP for Canterbury in 1523, Solicitor General in 1525 and was appointed Attorney General in 1529. His career was capped by his becoming Master of the Rolls in 1536. In 1533 he was actively involved in the investigation of Elizabeth Barton, the Nun of Kent, who had quickly become a focus of popular Catholic sentiment. In the 1530s he formed an important part of Thomas Cromwell's patronage network in the county, probably worked with him on drafting and enacting the early Reformation legislation, and benefited greatly in the process from grants of lands which had formerly belonged to the monasteries of Kent. It does seem though, that once he was established politically – and perhaps once he had emerged from the shadow of Cromwell – his lack of sympathy for more sweeping reform, particularly at the level of parochial religion, meant that he took an essentially conservative line. His sense of antagonism towards popular Protestant radicalism is best illustrated by the quarter sessions of 1538, at which his group of magistrates took the opportunity to persecute Protestants in the parishes of Kent.[88]

A third member of the family, Sir James Hales, the eldest son of John Hales, was, however, more committed to reform. He earned a reputation as a leading Protestant lawyer and, among other things, drafted the Chantries Act of 1547. It was probably not just obstinacy or a zeal for the letter of the law which led to his clash with the Marian regime in 1553. His insistence that Catholics be prosecuted for nonconformity at the Kent assizes of that year landed him in prison. He may already have been unbalanced before this, but the experience of imprisonment and the arguments of a colleague and other men who visited him in the Fleet appear to have driven him to try to take his own life. Shortly after his release, in 1554, he was more successful, drowning himself in a stream outside Canterbury.[89]

The Hales family therefore represent something of a mixed reaction to the changes of the Reformation period. John and Christopher were, it seems, willing to move with the times, especially when there were such great gains to be made in office and seigneurial lordship. Basically orthodox in their religious sentiments, they were, it seems, motivated by an anti-clericalism which was directed most forcibly against the monasteries. James moved much faster than his father and cousin, perhaps too readily for his own good. Whilst John and Christopher would have been hostile to Lollardy, their desire for limited Erastian reform was not incompatible with the sort of piety expressed by families like the Castelyns and Pellonds from the teens and twenties of the sixteenth century. That the family still had a strong influence in Tenterden politics by the early 1540s, is shown by the fact that Edward Hales esquire, the successor to the family seat, served as bailiff on three occasions.[90] As well as the benefits of political networks, the clannish nature of Kentish gentry families which meant that '. . . within the same parish there could reside gentlemen, yeomen, and husbandmen, all bearing the same name and all in one way or another related', probably allowed them considerable power in and around Tenterden.[91]

An even more important gentry family with influence in Tenterden were the Guildfords. There is evidence of connections between members of the Guildford family, the Foules, the Castelyns and the Haleses, which underlines how the nature of landholding and the land market on the Weald brought townsfolk and gentry into close contact.[92] The Guildfords were one of the two leading county gentry families in central and west Kent. They held perhaps three to four thousand acres centred on the manor of Halden in Rolvenden, and by the early sixteenth century they had acquired two manors in neighbouring Tenterden.[93] The Weald was very much within the Guildford sphere of influence, and Tenterden perhaps their greatest power-base in their struggles with the Nevilles in the early sixteenth century, to the extent that in 1505 Sir Edward Guildford was able to close Tenterden market as an act of retaliation against Neville aggression. Control of the Cinque Ports was a cherished prize in this conflict, and by the early 1520s, the Lord Wardenship was in Guildford hands, further adding to their influence in Tenterden. The long-running conflict between these two families was expressed in religious terms, the Nevilles becoming identified with Catholic opposition to Henrician reform, whilst the Guildfords built up a reputation for unorthodoxy.[94]

When Sir John Guildford made his intensely orthodox will in 1493 and wished his '. . . out beryng to be made not pomposely' and that at his year's mind a plain stone with epitaphs rather than a tomb be laid on him, he unwittingly left a portent of his family's radical but decidedly unorthodox stance in the future.[95] In the late 1520s when anti-clericalism had gathered pace in Kent, the Guildfords led the attack on church court fees. They were also intellectually important, as Sir Henry Guildford was a friend and correspondent of Erasmus, and the family were instrumental in circulating humanist ideas amongst the government circle of the county, ideas which may have provided one of the main sources of inspiration for the radical Protestant group centred on Canterbury which emerged over the next decade. At the same time, Lutheranism began to take root on the Weald and in the Medway valley, the areas where the Guildford clan held greatest sway.[96]

Especially because of their struggles with the religiously conservative Nevilles, the Guildfords may have found it convenient to provide a safe environment for some of their less-than-orthodox neighbours in and around Tenterden in the late fifteenth and early sixteenth century. There was, after all, at this time common ground between Tenterden as a rising urban centre, and the gentry families who sought to take advantage of new industrial developments on the Weald. Good relations with leading parish and town families like the Castelyns, Pellonds and Foules would have been the very building-blocks of sound policy and economic advancement. It was perhaps through these connections that families who had previously strayed into heresy, learned new and radical ideas which appealed to their own moralising piety. It is possible that the ease with which new converts were made to Lollardy in the early sixteenth century, and the subsequent precocious development of Protestantism in the region, owed something to the Guildfords' political ambitions and patronage networks. The Guildfords took advantage of the vacuum created by the Weald's isolation from those structures of government which worked to shore up traditional religion elsewhere in the county, and had a vested interest in keeping things that way. As a result they may have helped to maintain the cohesion of a regional culture which fostered dissenting mentalities.

Notes

1 J.F. Davis, 'Lollard survival and the Textile Industry in the South-east of England', *SCH*, 3 (1966), pp. 191–201.

2 A. Everitt, *Continuity and Colonization; The Evolution of Kentish Settlement* (Leicester, 1986), pp. 221–2. See also Everitt, 'Nonconformity in Country Parishes', in J. Thirsk (ed.), *Land, Church and People. Essays presented to Professor H.P.R. Finberg* (The Agricultural History Review, 18, 1970, Supplement), pp. 178–99. See also Andrew D. Brown, *Popular Piety in Late Medieval England: The Diocese of Salisbury 1250–1550* (Oxford, 1995), pp. 219–22, where dislocation from ecclesiastical control and certain social, economic and demographic features shared by the cloth towns of the claylands of Berkshire, Wiltshire and Dorset are presented as important factors in creating susceptibility to heresy and dissent. For some recent thoughts on economic determination of the distribution of heterodoxy, see Margaret Spufford, 'The importance of religion in the sixteenth and seventeenth centuries', in Spufford (ed.), *The World of Rural Dissenters, 1520–1725* (Cambridge, 1995), pp. 40–64.

3 Hudson, *PR*, pp. 121, 134–7, 456–64. 'Dissent as a phenomenon transmitted within the family', has recently been given more attention in, Spufford (ed.), *The World of Rural Dissenters*, esp. pp. 23–9.

4 For some stimulating thoughts on the regional dimension of late medieval piety, see Norman P. Tanner, 'The Reformation and Regionalism: Further Reflections on the Church in Late Medieval Norwich', in J.A.F. Thomson (ed.), *Towns and Townspeople in the Fifteenth Century* (Gloucester, 1988), pp. 129–47.

5 London, Lambeth Palace Library, Register of Archbishop William Warham, vol. I (hereafter Reg. Warham), ff. 161ᵛ–162ʳ. Stephen Castelyn was sentenced on 11 September 1511; *ibid.*, f. 168ʳ.

6 The proceedings extend from ff. 159ʳ–175ᵛ in Warham's register; Norman Tanner's edition (see Chapter 11 below) is appearing shortly.

7 This rough description of the general pattern of the recorded beliefs is drawn from J.A.F. Thomson's work on the trial records rather than any thorough survey of my own: Thomson, *LL*, p. 189.

8 Reg. Warham, ff. 174ʳ–174ᵛ.

9 *Ibid.*, f. 174ᵛ: depositions of Robert Bright and William Baker against Edward Walker.

10 *Ibid.*, f. 174ʳ.

11 *Ibid.*, f. 174ᵛ.

12 Stephen Castelyn's age at the time of the trials is twice given as 23, and he confessed to holding heretical opinions for four years: *ibid.*, ff. 169ᵛ, 174ʳ, 161ᵛ.

13 Hudson, *PR*, pp. 136, 156.

14 Reg. Warham, f. 169ᵛ.

15 See, for example, Hudson, *PR*, pp. 130–1.

16 Only three other families left as many surviving wills as this between 1470 and 1535, namely

the Bregendens, the Davys and the Pellonds. After these come the Assherynden, Bisshoppynden, Couper, Dunne, Piers and Smyth families, who were each responsible for five or six wills. There are 246 surviving wills for Tenterden from 1470 to 1535; of these 224 are enrolled in the Archdeaconry Register of Canterbury, 13 are to be found in the Canterbury Consistory Court Register and one is an Office Copy related to the Archdeaconry Register, all of which are housed at the Kent Archive Office, Maidstone. A remaining eight are Prerogative Court of Canterbury wills, to be found at the PRO.

[17] Maidstone, Kent Archives Office [KAO], PRC 3, Canterbury Archdeaconry Act Book (hereafter Cant. Arch. Act. Book), III, f. 77; PRC 17, Canterbury Archdeaconry Register of Wills (hereafter, Cant. Arch. Reg.), XI, f. 183.

[18] We know about Stephen's sisters because they were remembered in Joan Castelyn's testament of 1495: Cant. Arch. Reg., VI, f. 96.

[19] There is no extant will for Stephen Castelyn senior. We know that he was Stephen and William's father from William Claidich's testamentary endowments set down in 1505. Claidich left 6s 8d and part of the residue of his estate to each of the sons and daughters of Stephen Castelyn senior, and singled out William to receive lands, tenements and a messuage: Cant. Arch. Reg., X, f. 20.

[20] Robert Castelyn junior did not name his sons in his last will, but stipulated that after the deaths of his wife and mother, his messuage and gardens were to pass to them: Cant. Arch. Reg., V, f. 5. By establishing all those relationships which one can be sure about for the Castelyn family as a whole, it is possible to judge who was the most likely father of Stephen Castelyn senior. Whilst weighing all the available evidence in order to come to the most reasonable conclusion, this method still leaves room for error.

[21] Cant. Arch. Reg., II, f. 347.

[22] *Ibid.*

[23] Thirty-two out of 246, or 13 per cent of testators, left 4d or less in tithes forgotten between 1470 and 1535. Twelve of these omitted to make any such payment altogether, and one left 2d.

[24] Such bequests have been used by Gottfried as a rough index of wealth, although he provides no basis for his assertion that the amount given was fixed by legal statute as a certain proportion of the testator's liquid wealth: see R.S. Gottfried, *Bury St. Edmunds and the Urban Crisis: 1290–1539* (Princeton, 1982), pp. 125–9, 260; *idem.*, *Epidemic Disease in Fifteenth Century England* (Leicester, 1978), p. 31; see also M.L.A. Higgs, 'Lay Piety in the Borough of Colchester, 1485–1558', (Ph.D. thesis, University of Michigan, 1983), pp. 200–2, where Gottfried's method is followed. For criticism of this, see R.H. Hilton's review of Gottfried's *Bury St. Edmunds*, in *Urban History Yearbook*, 1983, p. 185. R.B. Dinn, who has also worked on Bury St Edmunds, compared the high altar payments of thirty-two testators to their 1523/4 lay subsidy assessments and found a broad but consistent correspondence, payments rising with the assessed wealth of testators. As a result, he suggests that payments 'may have been linked to the wealth or income of the testator' in a similar way to tithes, although he does provide examples of cases where this correspondence would appear to have broken down: R.B. Dinn, 'Popular Religion in Late Medieval Bury St Edmunds', (Ph.D. thesis, University of Manchester, 1990), pp. 64–8. Whether this was a formalised system, regulated or at least prompted by parish clergy, or an informal practice motivated more by the piety of testators, either way the size of payments, in the majority of cases and in a broad way, could have been dictated by the amount of disposable wealth available at the time of writing the will. The prevalence and size of bequests for tithes forgotten varied from place to place and from time to time in late medieval England. In Norwich, the inclusion of 'for tithes forgotten' in the wording of bequests to high altars only regularly appears from the 1490s, and Tanner cautions that this may have had as much to do with a change in scribal fashion as with the growing scruples of parishioners: N.P. Tanner, *The Church in Late Medieval Norwich* (Toronto, 1984), pp. 5–6. It seems best to view these payments as arising from the difficulties of assessing personal tithes during life, and therefore when it came to death it was a matter of individual conscience and/or clerical coercion as to how much should be bequeathed. It is more than

likely that local customs developed whereby a certain proportion of one's available resources at death came to be considered as adequate recompense for any negligence, deliberate or unknowing, during life. At the same time, it would be wrong to exclude the possibility of a voluntary element within these bequests. In other words, some gave more than would normally have been expected and some gave less: J.A.F. Thomson, 'Tithe Disputes in Later Medieval London', *EHR*, 78 (1963), p. 2; S.L. Thrupp, *The Merchant Class of Medieval London* (Ann Arbor, University of Michigan Press, 1962), p. 185; E. Duffy, *The Stripping of the Altars* (New Haven and London, 1992), pp. 356–7. See below, n. 71.

25 Maidstone, KAO, U410, Roberts Mss., T21.

26 E. Hasted, *The History and Topographical Survey of the County of Kent* (Canterbury, 1797–1801), this edn 1972), vii, p. 206; Maidstone, KAO, Te/C1, ff. 13ʳ–16ᵛ, 140ʳ.

27 KAO, Te/C1, ff. 140ᵛ–ʳ.

28 Stephen Jan, 1471, Cant. Arch. Reg., II, f. 131; Richard Jan, 1495, Cant. Arch. Reg., VI, f. 133.

29 KAO, Te/C1, f. 140ʳ.

30 KAO, U410, Roberts Mss., T12.

31 KAO, Te/C1, f. 140ʳ; BL, Add. Chs., 16319, 56976, 56977, 16322, 16326.

32 As he comes last in the order of precedence in the list, it may be that he did not share such high social status as Harenden and Wygge but, nevertheless, that he is named at all suggests that he was not far beneath them. For an example of how witness lists in deeds have been used in this way elsewhere, see C. Dyer, 'The Rising of 1381 in Suffolk: its Origins and Participants', *Proceedings of the Suffolk Institute of Archaeology and History*, 36 (1985), Appendix xi, p. 285.

33 For example, William Stonehouse, in his will written in 1513, stipulated that his ploughs, wains and harrows be sold to fulfil the terms of his testament, which included cash bequests for his funeral, month's mind and year's mind, to church fabric, and to family, kin and friends: Cant. Arch. Reg., XII, f. 227. Thomas Hicks, in 1522, arranged for lands in the neighbouring parish of Rolvenden to be sold for £23 in order to fulfil his extensive testamentary bequests: *ibid.*, XV, f. 228. Other testators who followed this practice of converting household goods or lands into cash bequests include: Richard Baker, 1504, *ibid.*, X, f. 92; Thomas Blusshe, 1473, *ibid.*, II, f. 291; Stephen Blossom, 1522, *ibid.*, XV, f. 128; Thomas Chapman, 1487, *ibid.*, V, f. 9; John Haredyng, 1506, *ibid.*, IX, f. 245; Philip Harenden, 1513, *ibid.*, XII, f. 312; Stephen Smith, 1482, *ibid.*, III, f. 450.

34 *Ibid.*, V, f. 5.

35 Canterbury Consistory Register of Wills, IX, f. 65.

36 Only about a quarter of the Tenterden wills contain payments of 2s or more to high altars.

37 Cant. Arch. Reg., VI, f. 96.

38 Joan's testament is rather typical of women's wills in this period, which tend to include bequests to a wider and more extensive range of friends and associates than those of their male counterparts. See, for example, P.H. Cullum, '"And Hir Name was Charite": Charitable Giving by and for Women in Late Medieval Yorkshire', in P.J.P. Goldberg (ed.), *Woman is a Worthy Wight: Women in English Society, c. 1200–1500* (Stroud, 1992), p. 185.

39 Cant. Arch. Act. Book, III, f. 77; Cant. Arch. Reg., XI, f. 183; PRC 16/1, Cant. Arch. Office Copy, f. 100. For some thoughts on deathbed pressures, see C. Marsh, 'In the Name of God? Will-Making and Faith in Early Modern England', in G.H. Martin and P. Spufford (eds), *The Records of the Nation* (Woodbridge, 1990), pp. 230–3, and Duffy, *Stripping of the Altars*, pp. 315–23.

40 A precise definition is required for this category of wills. Any will which has bequests for masses, chantries, obits, prayers, or to images, lights, religious houses, or parish churches, in whatever form, is excluded (so for example, Joan Castelyn's will is excluded due to her gift of 4d to the fabric of the parish church). Included among those which are left are those which have only formulaic and vague requests for the disposal of the residue of the estate, usually for the health of the testator's soul and sometimes also for others such as parents and all the faithful deceased (this is the case in Robert Castelyn junior's will, which is included). In many cases the residue is simply entrusted to the

executors with no mention of what it might be used for. Also included are a small number which fulfil the first criteria and contain bequests for such things as temporary chantries, charitable gifts, church fabric and for general distribution for the testator's soul only to be carried out in the event of a specified heir not inheriting, usually because of death before a stipulated age, or failure to marry. These bequests were second order arrangements, perhaps having the character of afterthoughts in the will-making process. There are in fact only nine wills which fulfil the first criteria and which also contain reversionary bequests of this sort. Four of these were for chantries, the rest being for such things as church fabric, charitable gifts or for general and unspecified distribution for the soul (John Castelyn's will is an example of this last kind, which contains a reversionary arrangement including a gift to church fabric and a charitable bequest in the event of his daughter not inheriting).

[41] Although it is difficult to compare this figure with findings in other places it does seem high. For example, from a survey of over 2,500 wills, mainly from the Midlands and made in the first decades of the sixteenth century, it has been estimated that only 3–4 per cent contain no religious bequests: J.J. Scarisbrick, *The Reformation and the English People* (Oxford, 1984), pp. 3, n. 2, 6.

[42] The problems of establishing family connections between individuals can be considerable, and the successful reconstruction of a family over two or more generations often depends on whether sons are named in wills, or on explicit references to relationships by blood or marriage in these or other sources. It is often the case that wills bearing the same surname made in adjacent or nearby parishes hold the keys which will unlock these problems of reconstruction, and until these are consulted it is neither possible to rule out nor to confirm any of the five cases which remain in doubt. It is important to note however, that in all five cases at least two of the wills out of all those bearing the same surname have been successfully linked by a relationship of parenthood or marriage. It is much harder to establish relationships between brothers, and so the greatest difficulties are to do with orientating different branches of one family. This, of course, is not to mention the problems involved in establishing affinal connections. It is not surprising that the three successfully reconstructed families have, on the whole, left larger numbers of wills than the five which remain open to question: the Assheryndens, 5 wills; the Castelyns, 7; and the Pellonds, 7. The others are the Chapmans who have left 4; the Gibbons, 4; the Hilles, 5; the Jans, 3; and the Wests, 3.

[43] It is significant that the total number of wills made by the eight families amount to only 15 per cent of all those which survive for the period, compared to 32 per cent of Castelyn-like wills. Looked at in a different way, in relation to more enduring families only, the total number of wills left by the eight families amount to 26 per cent of all those wills which survive for those surnames for which we have two or more wills; and yet the same eight families account for 49 per cent of the Castelyn-like wills left by more enduring surnames. This shows a clear bias towards familial continuity in the making of this type of will.

[44] Cant. Arch. Reg., XVI, f. 293.

[45] Cant. Arch. Reg., XXI, f. 58.

[46] For examples and discussion of the continuity of anniversary and chantry endowments within families, see Clive Burgess, "'By Quick and by Dead": wills and pious provision in late medieval Bristol', *EHR*, 102 (1987), pp. 837–58.

[47] John Symme, 1498, Cant. Arch. Reg., VIII, f. 41; Agnes Bocher, 1500, *ibid.*, VII, f. 250; Joanne Gerves, widow, 1504, *ibid.*, X, f. 19; Philip Harenden, 1513, *ibid.*, XII, f. 312; Katherine Foule, widow, 1519, *ibid.*, XV, f. 64.

[48] Canterbury, Cathedral Archive, Z.3.2, Archdeacon's Court Libri. Cleri. and Visn. Acta., 1501–8 (hereafter, Arch. Visn. Acta.), 2nd section, ff. 4^v, 25^v; Z.3.3., *ibid.*, 1514–16, f. 51^v. Brown, *Popular Piety in Late Medieval England*, p. 78.

[49] Cant. Arch. Reg., XVI, f. 293; PRO, E179, 231/228.

[50] Z.3.4, Arch. Visn. Acta., 1520–23, ff. 20^r, 68^r.

[51] Philip Harenden, 1513, Cant. Arch. Reg., XII, f. 312; William Cowper, 1518, Cant. Cons. Reg., XII, f. 174; George Strekenbold, 1524, Cant. Arch. Reg., XVI, f. 269; William Foule, 1532, *ibid.*, XIX, f. 273.

52 The erosion of the land–family bond, amongst other factors, had by the fifteenth century created some local populations which were highly mobile and, by the sixteenth century, parishes predominantly made up of nuclear households which were isolated in terms of blood and marriage: R.J. Faith, 'Peasant Families and Inheritance Customs in Medieval England', *Agricultural History Review*, 14 (1966), pp. 77–95; Z. Razi, 'The Myth of the Immutable English Family', *P&P*, 140 (1993), pp. 4–5, 33–42; C. Dyer, 'Changes in the size of peasant holdings in some West Midland villages 1400–1540', in R.M. Smith (ed.), *Land, Kinship and Life Cycle* (Cambridge, 1984), p. 281; M.E. Mate, 'The East Sussex Land Market and Agrarian Class Structure in the Late Middle Ages', *P&P*, 139 (1993), p. 48; K. Wrightson, 'Kinship in an English Village: Terling, Essex 1500–1700', in Smith (ed.), *Land, Kinship and Life Cycle*, pp. 315–16. However, throughout the fifteenth century, arguably in all types of community, there were those families who retained their continuity for a number of generations. By the beginning of the sixteenth century, owing to a combination of factors, there was a tendency in some areas towards a greater stability and continuity for some families – predominantly the wealthiest: for example, see C. Dyer, 'Changes in the size of peasant holdings', pp. 287–94. In his recent excellent survey of the literature on geographical mobility in early modern England, Peter Spufford suggests that as little as 15–25 per cent of family name groups survived in one parish for as many as three generations, and that this may have been as true of the fifteenth as of the sixteenth and seventeenth centuries. He attributes family stability to a combination of wealth and landholding, ample economic opportunities and the natural ability of certain families to produce male sons: 'The comparative mobility and immobility of Lollard descendants in early modern England', in Spufford (ed.), *The World of Rural Dissenters*, pp. 314, 320–1, 323, 330.

53 P. Clark, *English Provincial Society from the Reformation to the Revolution: Religion, Politics and Society in Kent 1500–1640* (Sussex, 1977), pp. 7–8, 14; M.L. Zell, 'A Wood-Pasture Agrarian Regime: The Kentish Weald in the Sixteenth Century', *Southern History*, 7 (1985), pp. 69–93.

54 L.R. Poos, *A Rural Society after the Black Death: Essex 1340–1525* (Cambridge, 1991), p. 273.

55 Duffy, *Stripping of the Altars*, pp. 45, 109, 113–16, 236; R.W. Pfaff, *New Liturgical Feasts in Later Medieval England* (Oxford, 1970), pp. 62–83; E.G.C.F. Atchley, 'Jesus Mass and Anthem', *Transactions of the St Pauls Ecclesiological Society*, 5 (1905), pp. 163–9.

56 *Testamenta Cantiana: East Kent*, ed. A. Hussey (London, 1907), pp. 285, 202, 48. The pattern of dissemination of the cult was remarkably similar in the diocese of Salisbury: Brown, *Popular Piety in Late Medieval England*, pp. 86–7.

57 Although relatively late in its introduction into the parish, once established the Jesus mass appears to have been very popular in Tenterden, compared to other places for which we have information. For example, in Bury St Edmunds the cult began in 1456 and 9 per cent of lay and clerical testators mentioned the mass or gild of Jesus from 1449–1530. At its most popular, in the years 1459–68 and 1479–82 it appeared only in 19 per cent of wills: R.B. Dinn, 'Popular Religion in Late Medieval Bury St Edmunds', pp. 195–200. In Norwich the Jesus mass was the most popular of votive and indulgenced masses mentioned in wills 1440–1532. Even so, only 11 per cent of lay and clerical testators left bequests to the Jesus mass over the same period: Tanner, *Church in Late Medieval Norwich*, pp. 94, 102–3, 220–1 (percentage figure is adapted from Appendix 11). See also, L.M.A. Higgs, 'Lay Piety in the Borough of Colchester', pp. 236–40, and Brown, *Popular Piety*, pp. 138–42.

58 It might be argued that this is due to the relatively abundant survival of wills made by members of these nine families, compared with those of the families which are represented by the remaining twenty-two bequests. Such an argument does not, however, adequately explain the distribution of gifts. All the wills – whether they contain bequests to the Jesus mass or not – made by the nine families between 1513 and 1535 constitute only 22 per cent (26 out of 117) of all wills made between these two dates, and this may be compared with their share of 48 per cent of bequests to the Jesus mass. By taking only those surnames for which there are at least two surviving wills made from 1513 to 1535, the transmission of affiliation to the Jesus mass within certain families becomes even more apparent: a total of twenty-one surnames repeat at least once in terms of will-making during the period in question, and these account for fifty-five wills. Out of these, the nine families were

responsible for twenty-six, or 47 per cent, and yet the same nine families made twenty out of twenty-four, or 83 per cent of the bequests to the Jesus mass by these twenty-one 'families', or surname groups.

⁵⁹ The problems of family reconstitution are not as great for these surnames as is the case with those which repeat as makers of Castelyn-like wills. This time seven of these nine groups of wills which bear the same surname have been identified as all belonging to the same family, and the remaining two groups of wills are among those above-mentioned repeaters of Castelyn-like wills which have not yet been successfully reconstituted.

⁶⁰ Saints' cults do not appear to have been very popular in Tenterden compared to the new cult of Jesus, at least in terms of testamentary giving. From 1470 to 1534 around 35 per cent of wills contain bequests to confraternities, lights, images, saints' altars, cults and votive masses attached to a saint. Around half of these wills contain bequests to the Jesus mass, and of these, over 80 per cent *only* gave to the cult of Jesus (considering that the Jesus mass only appears in the wills from 1513, this is all the more striking). In terms of popularity, the cult of the Blessed Virgin came next, appearing in around a quarter of these wills, and the cults of St Katherine and St Mildred and gifts to the rood light all trail, at around 10 per cent. Lower down the scale of popularity were a number of other cults such as those of St Stephen and St Erasmus.

⁶¹ Andrew Brown, in his recent work on piety in the diocese of Salisbury, has also drawn attention to the radicalism of the cult of Jesus and, importantly here, to its continuity with later acceptance of reform: *Popular Piety in Late Medieval England*, p. 248.

⁶² Reg. Warham, I, f. 175ᵛ.

⁶³ A glimpse of the family's trade and business activities is provided in the will of Moyse Pellond, dated 1519, in which a substantial amount of clothing and cloth is bequeathed: Cant. Arch. Reg., XIV, f. 47, and by a reference to 'William Pellond, taylor' as a witness in a will of 1501: *ibid.*, IX, f. 70. Information on Pellond landholding in Tenterden has been gleaned from a number of deeds: Maidstone, Kent Archives Office: U55, Knocker Collection, T414; U36, British Record Association Coll., T1454; U442, Gordon Ward Coll., T99; U410, Roberts Mss., T21; BL, Add. Ch. 56982; BL, Add. Mss. 48022, ff. 26ʳ, 27ʳ, 34ʳ.

⁶⁴ The average payment made by the thirty men of the Cinque Ports assessed on goods and chattels in Tenterden hundred on this occasion was 8s: PRO, E179/230, 182.

⁶⁵ This name is entered on the list of freemen beginning in 1529 and probably compiled c. 1558 as part of the Tenterden Custumal, Te/C1, f. 116ʳ. The dating of this entry is reached by comparison with the list of bailiffs, *ibid.*, f. 141ʳ. There is no way of knowing whether this was the same William Pellond who abjured heresies in 1511, or a relative – possibly the William Pellond who died in 1540 and who was the former William's cousin's son: Cant. Arch. Act. Book, VIII, f. 47.

⁶⁶ This would mean that at the youngest, William, was in his thirties at the time of his abjuration.

⁶⁷ Cant. Arch. Reg, III, f. 156.

⁶⁸ *Ibid.*, XI, f. 36.

⁶⁹ *Ibid.*, XIV, f. 47.

⁷⁰ *Ibid.*, XVI, f. 244.

⁷¹ Both Moyse and Richard Pellond left only 12d for their tithes forgotten. Especially given the amount of money bequeathed in Richard's will, this further undermines any notion that in Tenterden these payments offer a reliable index of wealth.

⁷² See, for example, C.L. Burgess, 'By Quick and by Dead', pp. 841–5.

⁷³ D. Plumb, 'The Social and Economic Spread of Rural Lollardy: a Re-Appraisal', *SCH*, 23 (1986), pp. 116 ff.

⁷⁴ See above, p. 200, n. 8.

⁷⁵ Thomson, *LL*, p. 191.

⁷⁶ A. Hope, 'Lollardy: The Stone the Builders Rejected?', in P. Lake and M. Dowling (eds), *Protestantism and the National Church in Sixteenth Century England* (London, 1987), pp. 2–6; Plumb, 'Rural Lollardy'; Brown, *Popular Piety in Late Medieval England*, pp. 217–8. For further comments on the

integration of dissenters into local society, see M. Spufford, 'The importance of religion', in Spufford (ed.), *The World of Rural Dissenters*, pp. 1–23.

⁷⁷ Clark puts the continuity between Lollardy and Lutheranism on the Weald down to the right conditions, namely, good communication through trade with the rest of the country and abroad, and 'the absence of effective ecclesiastical policing', which is to some extent, a combination of Davis's and Everitt's theses. It is then curious that at the same time, Clark refers to 'a strong tradition of multigenerational family loyalty to unorthodoxy' in Kent, which was 'to be one of Lollardy's most valuable legacies to Kentish Protestantism': Clark, *English Provincial Society*, pp. 30–1, 42. The work of the 'Spuffordians' has recently made great headway in demonstrating the descent of dissent within families: see, in particular, Nesta Evans, 'The descent of dissenters in the Chiltern Hundreds', in Spufford (ed.), *The World of Rural Dissenters*, pp. 288–308. However, I have been less concerned here to demonstrate transmission of dissent *per se* within the family, than to identify a semi-separatist 'religious voluntarism' (as Patrick Collinson would call it), which made a certain group of families open to unorthodox ideas: Collinson, 'Critical conclusion', in *ibid.*, p. 396.

⁷⁸ Clark, *English Provincial Society*, p. 31.

⁷⁹ Zell, 'A Wood-Pasture Agrarian Regime', p. 72.

⁸⁰ The wills of Joan, Katherine and Christopher Castelyn all reveal links with the Foules: Cant. Arch. Reg.: VI, f. 96; XI, f. 83; XXI, f. 58. Richard Castelyn witnessed Katherine Foule's will in 1519, and Christopher Castelyn witnessed William Foule's in 1532: *ibid.*, XV, f. 64; XIX, f. 273. There are also instances when Richard and Christopher acted as witnesses or feoffees for other testators in concert with members of the Foule family: Agnes Bocher, 1500, *ibid.*, VII, f. 250; Joan Gerves, widow, 1504, *ibid.*, X, f. 19; Philip Harenden, 1513, *ibid.*, XII, f. 312; George Strekenbold, 1524, *ibid.*, XVI, f. 269.

⁸¹ Thomas Foule witnessed Richard Pellond's will in 1525, and in the same year Bartholomew Pellond acted as witness to George Foule junior's: *ibid.*, XVI, f. 244; XVI, f. 239. In 1495, 'William Pellond senior' is recorded as one of the witnesses to the handing over of a parcel of lands in which, among other persons, William Foughill (or Foule) had been enfeoffed: BL, Add. Ch. 16330. Finally, in 1499, 'William Pellond junior' and George Foughill were feoffees for John at Hell: BL, Add. Mss. 48022, ff. 26ʳ, 27ᵛ.

⁸² KAO, Te/C1, ff. 140ʳ–141ʳ: William Foughill, 1480–81; Bartholomew Foule, 1514–16; George Foule, 1524–5 and 1525–6; John Foule junior, 1535–6, 1539–40 and 1540–1. KAO, U455/T87.

⁸³ Katherine Foule, widow, 1519: Cant. Arch. Reg., XV, f. 64; George Foule junior, 1525: *ibid.*, XVI, f. 239.

⁸⁴ Richard Castelyn was executor with John Hales to John Symme's will of 1498: *ibid.*, VIII, f. 41. In 1500 he was witness with Christopher Hales and George Foughill to Agnes Bocher's: *ibid.*, VII, f. 250. In 1495, John Hales of Tenterden may have been attorney to the family of the late Thomas Elnode, when lands in which William Foughill had been jointly enfeoffed, were passed to Elnode's son – the deed being witnessed by 'William Pellond senior': BL, Add. Ch. 16330. In 1511 John Hales, gent., and Bartholomew Foughill are recorded as two of William Newlond's feoffees in his will: Cant. Arch. Reg., XI, f. 188. They can be seen fulfilling their responsibilities to Newlond in a number of deeds dated up to 1521: KAO, U410, Roberts Mss., T21; U455, Tufton Mss., T88. In 1541 Edward Hales, *generosus*, was involved in land transactions with John Foule, *generosus*: KAO, U455, Tufton Mss., T87.

⁸⁵ Hasted, *The History of Kent*, vii, pp. 200ff., 224.

⁸⁶ KAO, Te/C1, fol. 140ᵛ.

⁸⁷ *DNB*; Hales, Sir James (d. 1554); Clark, *English Provincial Society*, pp. 13, 41, 55.

⁸⁸ *DNB*, Hales, Christopher; Clark, *English Provincial Society*, pp. 37, 40, 54, 57, 62, 63.

⁸⁹ *DNB*, Hales, Sir James; Clark, *English Provincial Society*, pp. 41, 81.

⁹⁰ KAO, Te/C1, f. 141ʳ.

⁹¹ P.W. Fleming, 'Charity, Faith, and the Gentry of Kent 1422–1529', in T. Pollard (ed.), *Property and Politics: Essays in Later Medieval English History* (Gloucester, 1984), p. 36.

[92] In 1524 Christopher Castelyn, George Guildford esquire, and George Foule senior are recorded as three of George Strekenbold's feoffees in his will in which John Hales, 'third baron of the king, esquire', is mentioned: Cant. Arch. Reg., XVI, f. 269. In 1526 George Guildford esquire, John Hales and Christopher Hales were all included in Thomas Wode's will: *ibid.*, XVII, f. 158. Interestingly, in a feoffment of 1475 lands in Tenterden passed from John Guildford, knight, to John Celer of Reading (just outside Tenterden), Katherine Castelyn's father: U55, Knocker Coll., T414. Lastly, Edward Hales, *generosus*, John Foule, *generosus* and George Guildford, *armiger*, appear together in property indentures in 1541: U455, Tufton Mss., T87.

[93] Clark, *English Provincial Society*, pp. 6–7; Hasted, *The History of Kent*, vii, pp. 183ff, 206ff.

[94] Clark, *English Provincial Society*, pp. 14–20, 51–4.

[95] PRO, PCC 29 Dogett, f. 223.

[96] Clark, *English Provincial Society*, pp. 29–30, 42.

11

PENANCES IMPOSED ON KENTISH LOLLARDS BY ARCHBISHOP WARHAM 1511–12

Norman Tanner

Folios 159r–175v of the register of William Warham, archbishop of Canterbury, record his proceedings against suspected Lollards in Kent during the two years 1511 and 1512.[1] They are one of the most informative records of Lollard trials in England on the eve of the Reformation, certainly the best from Kent. I am working on an edition of the proceedings, which I hope will be published in the Kent Records series in a year or so, and the contents will be discussed in the introduction to the edition.[2]

Here, however, I wish to concentrate on just one aspect of the proceedings, namely the penances imposed on those who were found guilty. This sombre subject has been chosen partly because the penances in question were unusually full and detailed, partly because the general topic of penances has been treated relatively little by historians of Lollardy and yet it is important for an understanding of the movement. The sentences were not just following a quantitative tariff, like monetary fines or jail sentences today; they were meant to fit the offences in a more qualitative way. They reveal much about the mentality of the ecclesiastical authorities and something about that of the wider population, insofar as the latter shared the attitudes of the clergy – a factor that is very difficult to gauge but certainly worthy of consideration. They illustrate, too, part of the climate of deterrence and punishment in which Lollards and potential Lollards lived, and which surely affected their behaviour, and probably their beliefs too. John Thomson made a brief and useful survey of the penances imposed throughout the period 1414 to 1520.[3] Now may be the time for a closer look at individual proceedings. What follows, therefore, is intended as a tentative exploration.

Warham's proceedings involved fifty-three suspects. They formed a group with many links among its members, as especially the depositions made by witnesses at the trials make clear. The map on p. 230 shows their geographical distribution. Probably twenty-seven of them, just over half the total, came from Tenterden and the neighbouring villages of Benenden, Rolvenden, Cranbrook, High Halden and Wittersham. Other clusters were eight from Maidstone and adjacent Boxley, Bearsted and East Farleigh; eight from Staplehurst; five from Ashford and

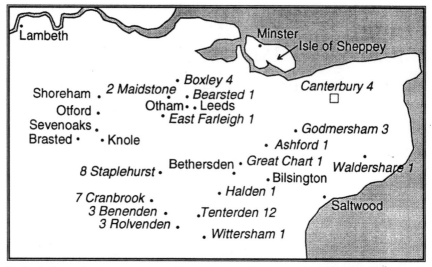

Italics indicate the home town or village of one or more defendants, the numbers indicate how many of them came from the place (in a few cases the figure involves some conjecture).

adjacent Great Chart and Godmersham; four from Canterbury. They were seventeen women and thirty-six men. About half the total belonged to families with two or more suspects, usually husband and wife but sometimes including one or, in the case of the Grebill family, two siblings; and at least some of the families were related to each other.

The ages of fifteen defendants were mentioned, ranging from twenty to seventy-four: five in their twenties, all of whom were sons or daughters of other suspects; a thirty-three year old; one aged forty; seven who were between sixty and sixty-three; one who was seventy-four. Altogether the impression is of a high median age and a well-established Lollard community. There were numerous references in the trials to defendants who had learned their heresies ten, twenty or thirty years earlier, and beyond them to Lollards in the region, no longer living, who had instructed them.

All the defendants were lay men and women. The general impression is of a predominantly artisan group of moderate wealth. None of them appears to have belonged to the gentry class or above. The occupations of ten men were mentioned: three cutlers, probably two weavers, a tailor, a fletcher, a shoemaker, a cordwainer and a glover.[4] The only woman whose occupation was mentioned was described as a servant.[5]

The proceedings were conducted between 28 April 1511 and 28 June 1512, the large majority being concentrated in the five months between 28 April and

23 September 1511. They were held in various places in the diocese of Canterbury, and at Lambeth palace (in the diocese of Winchester): the largest number at the archbishop's residence at Knole near Sevenoaks, a fair number at Lambeth palace, and the remainder variously in Canterbury cathedral, the archbishop's residences in Canterbury, Maidstone and Otford, the collegiate church of All Saints at Maidstone, and the parish church of Saltwood.

Robert Woodward, the commissary general of Archbishop Warham, conducted the proceedings in two cases and Cuthbert Tunstall, the future bishop of Durham and of London, acting as the archbishop's chancellor, in another. In all but these three cases, all of them relatively minor ones, the presiding figure and judge was the archbishop himself. Also attesting to the importance of the trials was the prominent team of clerics assisting him, which frequently included Woodward and Tunstall and John Thornden, the archbishop's suffragan bishop, and on occasions Bishops John Fisher of Rochester and Richard Nykke of Norwich, and the dean of St Paul's cathedral, John Colet.

Of the fifty-three suspects, one was dismissed as not convicted and another was

The great palace of Knole, much of which was built by Archbishop Bourchier in the fifteenth century. Archbishop Warham built the gatehouse, and the largest number of his 1511–12 trials took place here, many in the chapel (lower right corner). (By permission of Kent Messenger Group Newspapers)

The beginning of the record of the trials in Archbishop Warham's register (f. 159r; actual size 17in × 13¼in; parchment). (By permission of the Archbishop of Canterbury and the Trustees of the Lambeth Palace Library) recorded as merely taking an oath to appear before the archbishop when he was summoned, without any indication of the outcome.[6] In one other case the abjuration of the defendant was recorded, but no penance.[7] All the other fifty suspects were found guilty of at least some of the charges brought against them and the penances imposed on them were recorded; though in a few cases it is clear, or seems probable, that the record does not include all the penances imposed.

Five defendants were sentenced to the ultimate penalty of being handed over to the secular arm, in the knowledge that they would be burned to death. Regarding this terrible fate, the present proceedings add nothing new, inasmuch as it was the normal punishment for persistent or relapsed heretics. The four men, Robert Harryson of Canterbury, William Carder of Tenterden, John Browne of Ashford and Edward Walker of Maidstone, and one woman, Agnes Grebill of Tenterden, were confronted with an almost identical set of fourteen charges, which focused on the following topics: the seven sacraments, images of the crucifix and of saints, pilgrimages and relics, prayers to the saints, holy water and blessed bread. All of them initially denied everything in the charges that was incriminating. The depositions against them, however, made clear that all of them had been leading Lollards in the region over a long period of time. One of them, John Browne, admitted a previous conviction for heresy before Cardinal Moreton twelve years previously. When confronted with the depositions and the deponents in person, four of the defendants either rejected outright the allegations made against them or stated that they did not wish to say anything in their defence, and the fifth, William Carder, said he was not aware of any guilt on his part but if there was then he repented of it. None of them, it seems, was willing to make a retraction that was satisfactory to the court. Warham, accordingly, pronounced John Browne a relapsed and incorrigible heretic; the other four he pronounced impenitent and incorrigible heretics and declared that they had incurred major excommunication. All were relinquished to the secular arm. The sentences are formal in their language, yet all of them, apart from the relapsed John Browne's, express forcibly the archbishop's sadness at the outcome: 'with grief and bitterness of heart' he sentenced them after all his efforts to win their repentance had failed.[8]

The relinquishments to the secular arm were recorded also as significations of excommunication addressed by the archbishop to the crown.[9] Watching William Carder being burnt, moreover, was a penance imposed on some other suspects, as will be mentioned shortly. It therefore seems highly likely that the five persons were indeed executed, even though no record of their fate survives.

The other forty-five defendants, all of whom confessed their heresy, at least in some measure and on the basis of charges similar to those brought against the five persons who refused to abjure, received a wide range of penances short of capital punishment. Their penances will be the subject of the remainder of this paper.

First, however, a few words are in order about the context. The archbishop, and English bishops generally, seem to have possessed remarkable freedom regarding the types of penance they imposed on convicted Lollards. As is well known, they could not of themselves order the death penalty; they could only hand over relapsed or obdurate heretics to the secular authority, for the latter to carry out the punishment. Other penalties directly involving the shedding of blood, such as mutilation, were also forbidden to clerics by canon law,[10] though not, it seems, those that involved bloodshed only indirectly, such as flogging, which was imposed at many Lollard trials. Apart from these restrictions the ecclesiastical judges seem to have possessed almost unlimited scope to choose, at least in theory. Earlier trials of Lollards had produced some parameters for penances, but they were flexible ones. There is no evidence to suggest, so far as I am aware, that the English bishops, either collectively or individually, had drawn up official guidelines in the matter. They were not bound, moreover, by the regulations of the Inquisition, since this institution did not function in England. The penances imposed by Archbishop Warham at the present trials, therefore, must be seen as largely the result of the archbishop's own choices. A canon lawyer by training and profession,[11] he appears to have taken much care in working out the penances: indeed they are among the most complex and detailed known of in trials of Lollards.

Of Warham's involvement in other heresy trials, little is known that might provide a background to the present proceedings. John Foxe reported that in 1506, two years after he became archbishop and during a vacancy in the see of London, he received the abjuration of John Brewster of Colchester and sentenced him to wearing a badge representing a faggot on his outer garment for the rest of his life.[12] Between the end of the present proceedings and the archbishop's death in 1532, no further prosecutions of Lollards are known to have taken place in his diocese.[13] The wider context, rather, is provided by the extensive prosecutions of Lollards in other English dioceses in the years 1510 to 1512: those of Bishops Fitzjames of London in 1510–11 and Smith of Lincoln in 1511, for both of which we are largely dependent on Foxe,[14] and that of Bishop Blyth of Coventry and Lichfield in 1511–12, which survives as Lichfield Court Book B/C/13, still unedited and surely now deserving an editor.[15]

To return to the penances of the forty-five defendants, they are listed in the Table of Penances (see opposite), together with the number of defendants upon whom each penance was imposed. The best way in to their examination is through those imposed on a group of ten suspects who appeared before Archbishop Warham on 2 and 5 May 1511: John Grebill senior, who was the husband of

Agnes Grebill mentioned earlier, and their two sons, or 'natural sons' (*filii naturales*) of Agnes as they are described once,[16] John junior and Christopher; Joan Colyn and Robert Hilles from Tenterden; William Riche and Thomas Manning from Benenden; Agnes Ive and Agnes Chetynden from Canterbury; William Olberd senior of Godmersham. Their trials came near the beginning of Warham's proceedings and were the first involving defendants who were not handed over to the secular arm as relapsed or impenitent heretics. The penances formed a basis, probably a model, for most of those that were ordered subsequently.

No depositions against these ten individuals survive: information about the proceedings against them is largely confined to statements that the defendant abjured his or her errors, the abjurations themselves and the penances imposed. Seven of them, however, had appeared as deponents in the trials of the five

Table of Penances

The figures indicate the number of persons upon whom a particular penance was imposed: of the total forty-five persons and, in brackets, of the ten sentenced together on 2 to 5 May 1511 and of the other thirty-five.

33	Carrying a faggot on a public occasion (9* + 24).
31	Confinement to the parish or locality (9 + 22).
25	Informing the archbishop of persons suspected of heresy and of books belonging to them (9 + 16).
17	Wearing a badge with a faggot on it (9 + 8).
13	Surrendering heretical books (9 + 4).
12	Attending divine service in the parish church on Sundays and feast-days (9 + 3).
10	Recitation of the Lord's prayer, Hail Mary and creed (5 + 5).
9	Fasting and/or abstinence in food (2 + 7).
7	Imprisonment (1 + 6).
7	Confession to a priest (7 + 0).
7	Reception of the eucharist (7 + 0).
7	Watching the execution of William Carder (7 + 0).
6	Restrictions in dress (1 + 5)
3	Offering a candle (0 + 3)
1	Treating his wife well (0 + 1).

*   '9' here and below excludes Agnes Chetynden.

persons who were handed over to the secular arm, forming the key witnesses in the first three trials, those of Robert Harryson, William Carder and Agnes Grebill. In the case of Agnes Grebill there was the added poignancy that she was condemned largely on the evidence given against her by her husband and two sons. It seems likely, therefore, that some plea-bargaining went on, although nothing specific was mentioned in this regard.

They made their abjurations at various sessions on 2 and 5 May. The first to abjure, on 2 May, were the three Grebills, William Riche, William Olberd senior, Agnes Ive and Agnes Chetynden. All seven of them were given identical penances to confess to a priest, to receive the eucharist, and to watch William Carder being burned (to death).[17] Confession and reception of the eucharist were presumably linked to the fact that all of them admitted to having previously denied the presence of Christ in the eucharist, and four of them to having denied the value of confession to a priest. Nevertheless the use of the two sacraments as a weapon of penance in this way may seem strange, especially enforced reception of the eucharist. Remedial medicine for the individual and for the wider community are the aspects of penance that are usually emphasised, but the above two penances remind us forcibly of a third aspect, namely that many Christians, perhaps especially the ecclesiastical authorities, believed Christianity to be a system of beliefs that were self-evidently true, so that rejection of any of them implied ignorance or malice. The movement away from Christianity as a mystery to a system of intellectual propositions gathered pace throughout western Christendom from the twelfth century onwards, and is essential to understanding the punishments imposed on religious dissenters in the late Middle Ages, including Lollards. The fourth Lateran council of 1215 had expressed the notion clearly and crudely: 'Heretics . . . have different faces indeed but their tails are tied together inasmuch as they are alike in their pride.'[18] All three aspects were implied in the gruesome penance of having to watch the execution of William Carder – a penalty that appears to be without parallel in other Lollard trials.

Having enjoined these three penances on the seven individuals, the archbishop ordered them to appear before him at eight o'clock in the morning on the following Monday, 5 May, to receive further penances. Meanwhile, at another session on 2 May, Thomas Mannyng and Joan Colyn made their abjurations, and Robert Hilles made his on 5 May. On 5 May, therefore, all ten of them, with the possible exception of Agnes Chetynden,[19] received either their penances in full or a second instalment of them. Appendix 4 (see pp. 247–8) gives the details. There seems to have been no discrimination favouring women, such as occurred at the 1428–31 proceedings in Norwich diocese, for example, where some women were given lighter penances than men for apparently identical offences.[20] Thus Agnes Ive and, if she should be included, Agnes Chetynden, received the same penances as the men concerned. It is not clear why Thomas Mannyng and Joan Colyn received lighter penances, though the probable reason is that they were less involved in Lollardy. This reason, youth, and the pressure he was under may explain why John Grebill junior also received lesser penances. He was only twenty-one years old and, according to his deposition against his mother, Agnes Grebill, he had converted to Lollardy only a year earlier, despite being instructed by his parents in Lollard beliefs since the age of fourteen or fifteen.[21]

The most enduringly public of the penances was the wearing of a badge with a burning faggot on it, clearly visible on the outer garment, for the rest of life unless a dispensation was granted. Also very public was carrying a real faggot, with head, feet and shins bare, on three occasions: in the market-place of Canterbury on the following Saturday, at the front of the procession and during the sermon in Canterbury cathedral on the following Sunday, and at the front of the procession in their parish churches on the Sunday after that. The other penances included confinement to their parish, unless they received the archbishop's permission to travel outside it, surrendering any heretical books they possessed; informing the archbishop of any persons suspected of heresy and of books belonging to such suspects, attending divine service in their parish church on Sundays and feast-days, something that was of course a duty for all Christians. Finally, they were reminded of their obligation to perform all the penances under pain of being treated as relapsed heretics. Joan Colyn alone received the penance of abstinence from meat on each Wednesday of the forthcoming year.

Regarding the other thirty-five defendants (i.e. the forty-five mentioned above, p. 233ff, minus the ten sentenced on 2 and 5 May), most of their penances followed in substance those of the ten individuals just mentioned, but with various additions and details that merit attention. Almost invariably several penances were imposed on a given person. The earliest three penances, however, were abandoned: nobody was ordered to confess to a priest, to receive the eucharist or to watch the punishment of another, capital or otherwise.

Eight of them – two women and six men – were ordered to wear a badge picturing a faggot, clearly visible on their outer garment, for the rest of their lives; though in every case the possibility was mentioned of a dispensation in the future.[22]

Twenty-four of them – seven women and seventeen men – were given the penance of carrying a (real) faggot on some public occasion. All of them were ordered to do this in their parish church on one, two, three or four Sundays and in some cases on various feast-days: Trinity Sunday, Corpus Christi and the Assumption of St Mary. This penance usually began with their being placed in front of the cross-bearer, at the head of the parish procession as it made its way round the outside of the church or through the cemetery, bearing their faggot on their shoulder. Thomas Churche, in a curious alternative arrangement, was 'to sit upon the cross' in the cemetery, bearing his faggot, as the procession went by; the contrasting symbolism of cross and faggot is again apparent.[23] Frequently they were told explicitly to appear with feet and shins bare, and heads uncovered in the case of men, 'in the manner of a penitent'. Once inside the church, they were usually obliged to wait, still bearing their faggot, normally standing but sitting in the case of John Baus and kneeling in the cases of Joan Dodde and Rabage Benet,[24] in some prominent position, often in the middle of the church before the door of the choir, until the end of the mass. Then, according to some instructions, they were to leave the church last, depositing their faggot in the church porch. Joan Dodde had the additional obligation of offering a penny at the high altar during the mass. Two others besides the twenty-four, John Franke and Joan Riche, received similar penances except that they were to carry a candle instead of a faggot, which they were to offer to the priest at the offertory of the mass.[25]

In addition to the penances in parish churches, Joan Olberd and Elizabeth White were assigned similar penances in Canterbury cathedral. They were to walk in front of the procession in the cathedral on Pentecost day, lightly clad as penitents (*'induta sola camisia et uno lintheamine'*; *'induta solomodo camisia et tunica Anglice a kyrtell'*) and carrying a faggot on their shoulders. They were ordered, too, to make a public appearance in Canterbury market on a Saturday, similarly clothed as penitents and carrying a faggot on their shoulders.[26] The choice of Canterbury is not surprising, since Elizabeth White came from that city and Joan Olberd from neighbouring Godmersham. The market-place of Cranbrook was assigned to five others: Thomas and Joan Harwode and their son Philip, who came from neighbouring Rolvenden; Stephen Castelyn and John Boxley, both of whom made their abjurations with the Harwodes, the former coming from neighbouring Tenterden and the latter from more distant Boxley. All of them were ordered to present themselves at the time of the market on a specified Saturday, and once there they were to make three circuits of the market carrying a faggot on their shoulders. Thence they were to proceed to the parish church, where they were to deposit their faggot and to say, on bended knees, the Lord's prayer, the Hail Mary and the creed.[27]

Twenty-two individuals were sentenced to confinement within their locality. Sometimes the restriction followed the formula used on 5 May: they were not to move outside their parish without the permission of the archbishop of the time. More often, though, the formula was somewhat weaker: they were ordered merely to inform the archbishop if they moved. Usually the wording is somewhat imprecise, but it looks as if the prohibition normally concerned only a change of residence, though occasionally even temporary movements seem to have been forbidden.

William Baker, William Olberd junior, Robert Reignold and Thomas Felde, who were sentenced together on 19 May 1511, were ordered to surrender any heretical books that they might possess.[28] They and twelve others were enjoined to inform the archbishop without delay of any persons who were suspected of heresy or who possessed heretical books.

The penance imposed on James Bainham in 1532, of standing before the preacher during the sermon, with a faggot on his shoulder. Bainham relapsed and was burned two months later. (Woodcut in John Foxe, *Acts and Monuments* (1570), vol. 2, p. 1170, by permission of the Bodleian Library, University of Oxford: shelfmark Mason F. 143)

Thomas and Joan Harwode and their son Philip were ordered to attend divine service in their parish church on Sundays and feast-days, 'like good Christians' as they were told.[29]

Regarding abstinence from certain foods, following Joan Colyn mentioned earlier, Margaret Baker was forbidden to eat fish on Fridays for the rest of her life and Joan Bukherst to eat the same on the next five Fridays:[30] measures that would have reduced their diet on that day to a vegetarian one since meat was already forbidden by the general law of the church. All three were women but there does not appear to have been any special significance in this. Rather the penance seems to have been used as a light one, for defendants who were only marginally involved in Lollardy. In the case of Joan Bukherst it was the only penance imposed on her and the reason for it was mentioned, that she had kept her husband's opinions secret. A diet of bread and water featured in the sentences of imprisonment, which will be discussed shortly.

Various other types of penance, which did not feature at the hearings of 2 to 5 May 1511, were imposed. The best way to look at them is through the third instalment of penances given to John Grebill senior, on 3 September of the same year.[31] As mentioned above, John Grebill, the husband of Agnes and the father of Christopher and John junior, was among those sentenced to two separate instalments of penances on 2 and 5 May 1511. On 3 September of that year he appeared before the archbishop to receive a third instalment. No reason was given for these additional penances. Maybe Archbishop Warham regarded him as too dangerous to be left at large, since the earlier depositions showed that his involvement with Lollardy had been long and pronounced, or maybe he relapsed into heresy in some measure during the summer months. The archbishop sentenced him to perpetual imprisonment in the priory of Augustinian canons at Bilsington, Kent. He was forbidden to travel more than a mile outside the priory, under pain of being regarded as a relapsed heretic, and he was given fifteen days to begin his sentence. His diet was to be bread and water, though another part of the sentence suggests the fasting was limited to Fridays: the archbishop moreover, immediately commuted this penance into one of not wearing a linen undergarment (*camisia linea*) on Wednesdays and Fridays. The archbishop also reserved to himself and his successors the right of mitigating or commuting the full sentence in other ways.

Imprisonment was the most severe punishment imposed at the trials, apart from the death penalty. John Grebill and his wife appear to have lived partly in Tenterden, partly in neighbouring Benenden, and of the six other persons who were sentenced to imprisonment, four came from Tenterden; a number that underlines again the centrality of the town in the circle of Lollards. The four from Tenterden were Stephen Castelyn, Robert Franke, William Pelland and Julian Hilles; the other two were Joan Lowes from neighbouring Cranbrook and

Joan Olberd from Godmersham.[32] All of them were sentenced to perpetual imprisonment, though in each case the archbishop explicitly mentioned the possibility of the sentence being relaxed at some time in the future. The places of confinement were religious houses within the diocese except in the case of Joan Olberd, for whom a place was not specified: the priory of Augustinian canons at Leeds for Stephen Castelyn, St Augustine's abbey at Canterbury for Robert Franke, the Cistercian abbey at Boxley for William Pelland, the Benedictine nunnery of St Sepulchre in the suburbs of Canterbury for Julian Hilles, the Augustinian nunnery of St Sexburga at Minster on the isle of Sheppey for Joan Lowes. Their dispersal to different places was presumably intended both to facilitate their return to orthodoxy and to prevent any dangerous concentration of them; though Leeds priory may seem a surprising choice, since the prior regarded his community of canons as rife with heresy, according to a deposition made during a visitation of the priory within a few weeks of Stephen Castelyn being sentenced![33] All the religious houses lay some distance from the prisoner's home town or village.

As was the case with John Grebill, the prisoners were usually given some leeway to move outside the religious house of their confinement, normally a mile but two miles in the case of William Pelland, and a decent interval of time before they had to begin their imprisonment, between fifteen days and a month. Most of them were told explicitly to expect a diet of bread and water, though as with John Grebill the intention may have been to confine the fast to Fridays.

The reasons for this severe punishment of perpetual imprisonment may sometimes be surmised. Robert Franke, Joan Lowes and William Pelland had asked if they might purge themselves of the charges brought against them but had then failed in their purgation, say the records, without giving further details. They were the only defendants known to have attempted purgation, and prison seems to have been, at least in part, the penalty for their failure. The case of Stephen Castelyn paralleled that of John Grebill. He had been sentenced to various penances after his abjuration in May 1511, and then four months later, in September 1511, for reasons that are not explained he was given the further penance of imprisonment. Julian Hilles seems to have been a similar case, though the date of her sentence to prison is uncertain. For Joan Olberd, on the other hand, the order was reversed: she received an initial sentence of imprisonment and various other penances and was told to report three weeks later for a second instalment of penances. The latter, however, are not recorded. All six individuals appear to have been closely involved in Lollardy, like John Grebill, though not more so than some others who received lighter sentences.

John Grebill's third instalment of penances included not wearing a linen undergarment on Wednesdays and Fridays. Five other individuals, all women, were sentenced to similar restrictions of dress. All of them were forbidden to wear a smock on Fridays for the rest of their life, though for some of them exception was made if the Friday coincided with a major feast.[34] There is no apparent reason why these women were singled out for this type of penance.

Recitation of the Lord's prayer, the Hail Mary and the creed in Cranbrook parish church had been imposed on the Harwodes, Stephen Castelyn and John Bampton, as mentioned earlier. Five other individuals, four women and one man, were ordered to say these prayers on various occasions.[35] Margaret Baker appears to have been given a one-off penance of saying the Lord's prayer and the Hail Mary ten times, while the other four were ordered to recite the two prayers five times each and the creed once on every Friday for the rest of their lives. In the cases of Alice Hilles and Agnes Reignold the place was not specified, but for Julian Hilles the recitation was to be made at St Sepulchre's nunnery in the suburbs of Canterbury, which was the religious house in which she was ordered, apparently later, to be imprisoned; and so for William Pelland it was to be made in the place of his imprisonment, before the high altar of the church of Boxley abbey. Again, there is no obvious reason why the recipients were singled out for this penance.

Other penances were assigned to John Dodde. He was ordered to go to his parish church of Staplehurst on the next two Fridays, with head, feet and shins bare, as a penitent, there to offer a candle worth one penny to the image of St Mary. In addition, he was ordered to treat his wife in a kindly and decent manner (*'bene et honeste'*): no hint of a reason is given!

A few observations are in order by way of conclusion. Although the terms 'Lollard' and 'Lollardy' have been used in this paper, they do not appear in Warham's register, nor does the name of John Wycliffe. In the register reference is simply to 'heresy' or 'heretics'. Whether, therefore, the defendants are best described as Lollards, neo-Lollards, Wycliffites or heretics remains a matter of debate, and maybe the archbishop himself was not sure how to categorise them.

Warham described the sentences of imprisonment as 'punishment or penance' (*pena sive penitencia*).[36] They, as well as the other sentences, were both ecclesiastical penances and punishments of a social nature, but the divide between the two may have been hazy. The penalties were meant to speak for themselves, inasmuch as the actions required of the penitents were full of symbolism and, for the most part, very public. 'According to the type of the offence' (*iuxta et secundum criminis qualitatem*) was how the archbishop described the penances he imposed on Joan Olberd.[37] Why, among the variety of penalties imposed, particular ones were chosen for particular individuals may sometimes be surmised but is often not clear, as has been mentioned. Women seem to have been treated in much the same way as men.

Handing over relapsed or obdurate heretics to the secular arm, in the knowledge that they would be executed by burning, was prescribed by the law of the land, principally by the statute *De heretico comburendo* of 1401, and in this sense was outside Warham's control. In other respects the archbishop eschewed physical violence, noticeably avoiding the punishment of flogging. Touches of mercy are to be seen within the sentences of imprisonment – the permitted mile or two outside the place of confinement and the interval of time before the sentence had to be begun – and especially in the possibility, often mentioned explicitly, of a penance being dispensed from, mitigated or commuted at some time in the future. In general, at least the intention seems to have been corrective and preventive rather than of great severity.

How the penances were carried out, or indeed whether most of them were ever performed at all fully, as well as the attitudes to them of the convicted persons and other interested parties, are issues that remain mysterious. Though it is worth noting that in the case of John Brewster of Colchester, whom Archbishop Warham had sentenced earlier to wear a badge with a faggot on it, as mentioned above, John Foxe tells us that he wore the badge for two years until the comptroller of the earl of Oxford, under whom he was working, plucked it away![38]

Penitential discipline is a significant though neglected aspect of the study of Lollardy. It contributes to an understanding of how the ecclesiastical authorities thought the movement ought to be treated and, what is of equal importance, of the environment in which Lollards, their sympathisers and other people lived. Warham's proceedings may prove to be the fullest and most sophisticated collection of penances enacted, so they are a reasonable place to begin. Other trials and relevant material need to be examined in order to fill out the picture. This brief paper, therefore, ends, hopefully and penitentially, with a plea for further study.

Notes

[1] The register is kept in Lambeth Palace Library, London. The relevant folios run 159r–167v, 167*r–v, 168r–175v. Hereafter references to the register are given by folio numbers only. For recent discussions of the proceedings, see Thomson, *LL*, pp. 183–90 and Hudson, *PR*, pp. 134–6, 143, 150–1 and 156. For John Foxe's treatment, see Foxe *A&M*, iv, pp. 181–2 and 722–3, and v, pp. 647–54.

[2] Subsequently published as *Kent Heresy Proceedings 1511–12*, ed. N. Tanner, Kent Records, 26 (Kent Archaeological Society, Maidstone, 1997).

[3] Thomson, *LL*, pp. 231–6.

[4] Respectively: John Browne, Stephen Castelyn and Edward Walker; John Grebill senior and William Carder; Christopher Grebill; John Dodde; William Bukhurst; Robert Bright; William Riche.

[5] Agnes Reignold or Raynold.

[6] James Bukherst, f. 167*r, and William Bukherst, f. 167*r–v.

[7] Simon Piers, f. 175r–v.

[8] Ff. 171v–175r for the proceedings against the five persons. See Appendix 1 for the sentence of Robert Harryson, which was the first of the five sentences and was followed closely, regarding its form, in the other four. See Appendix 2 (p. 246) for the relinquishing of Robert Harryson, William Carder and Agnes Grebill to the secular arm.

[9] PRO, C/85/24, nos. 20–22 and 24–25.

[10] The fourth Lateran council of 1215, canon 18 (*Decrees of the Ecumenical Councils*, ed. N.P. Tanner (London, 1990), i, p. 244); *Decretales Gregorii Papae IX*, 3.50.9 (*Corpus Iuris Canonici*, ed. E. Friedberg (Leipzig, 1879, reprinted Graz, 1955), ii, pp. 659–60).

[11] Emden, *BRUO*, iii, pp. 1988–9 (William Warham); *DNB*, 59, pp. 378–9 (William Warham).

[12] Foxe, *A&M*, iv, pp. 215–16. See Hope, below, p. 262.

[13] Thomson, *LL*, p. 190.

[14] *Ibid.*, pp. 87–8, 162 and 238; Foxe, *A&M*, iv, pp. 123–6, 173–82, 208 and 214–15.

[15] J. Fines, 'Heresy Trials in the Diocese of Coventry and Lichfield, 1511–12', *JEH*, 14 (1963), pp. 160–74; I. Luxton, 'The Lichfield Court Book: a Postscript', *BIHR*, 44 (1971), pp. 120–5.

[16] F. 170^v.

[17] See Appendix 3 (pp. 246–7).

[18] Canon 3 (*Decrees of the Ecumenical Councils*, ed. Tanner, i, p. 233).

[19] Her name is omitted, though the omission may be a scribal error.

[20] Tanner, *HT*, p. 24.

[21] F. 174^r.

[22] Ff. 162^r (Stephen Castelyn), 162^v (William Baker and Robert Reignold), 163^v (Elizabeth White), 164^r (Thomas Churche and Joan Olberd), 165^v (John Lynche and Thomas Browne).

[23] F. 164^r.

[24] Ff. 167^r and 167*^{r}.

[25] Ff. 165^r and 166^r.

[26] F. 163^{r-v}

[27] F. 162^r.

[28] F. 162^v.

[29] F. 162^r.

[30] Ff. 164^v and 167*^{r}.

[31] See Appendix 5 (pp. 248–9).

[32] Ff. 163^r (Joan Olberd), 167*^{v} (Joan Lowes), 168^r (Stephen Castelyn), 168^v–169^r (Robert Franke), 175^v (William Pelland), 175^v (Julian Hilles).

[33] *Kentish Visitations of Archbishop William Warham and his Deputies, 1511–12*, ed. K.L. Wood-Legh, Kent Records, 24 (Kent Archaeological Society, Maidstone, 1984), pp. xv and 40.

[34] Ff. 163^v (Agnes Reignold), 164^v (Alice Hilles), 165^r (Joan Riche), 167*^{v}–168^r (Joan Lowes), 168^v (Julian Hilles). In four cases the word 'smock' was used, in one case *camisia*.

[35] Ff. 163^v (Agnes Reignold), 164^v (Alice Hills and Margaret Baker), 168^v (Julian Hilles), 175^v (William Pelland).

[36] Ff. 167*^{v}, 168^v, 175^v.

[37] F. 163^r.

[38] Foxe, *A&M*, iv, pp. 215–16. See Hope, below, p. 264.

Appendices
For the original texts, from which the translations below have been made, see *Kent Heresy Proceedings*, pp. 6–7 (Appendix 1), p. 25 (Appendix 2), p. 36 (Appendix 3), pp. 39–40 (Appendix 4), and pp. 98–9 (Appendix 5).

1 Sentence of Robert Harryson, 2 May 1511 (f. 172ᵛ)

In the name of God, Amen. We, William by divine permission archbishop of Canterbury, primate of all England and legate of the apostolic see, are sitting in judgement, having invoked the name of Christ and having before our eyes God alone, duly and canonically proceeding in virtue of our office – after the merits of the case have been heard and understood, seen, investigated and scrutinised, and with fitting deliberation discussed and pondered, preserving in and throughout everything in the said business whatever the law requires to be observed or is called for in any way – in a matter of heresy against you, Robert Haryson: layman of our city of Canterbury, known to be placed under and subject to our jurisdiction, who are appearing in person before us in court, having been disclosed and reported to us regarding the said heresy, and after good and responsible people have proclaimed your ill repute in the said matter extensively and publicly all over our diocese of Canterbury.

On account of what has been done, deduced, proved and shown before us in this matter, we have found, by legitimate proofs cited in judicial manner in our presence, that you have held, believed, affirmed, preached and taught various errors, heresies and condemned opinions that are opposed, contrary and repugnant to divine and ecclesiastical law, against the orthodox faith as defined and observed by the universal, catholic and apostolic church, especially against the sacraments [*sic*, in the plural] of the altar or the eucharist and other sacraments and teachings of holy mother church. Following the example of Christ, who desires not the death of a sinner but rather that he be converted and live, we have tried repeatedly to correct you and to lead you back, by lawful and canonical means, in so far as we have been able and known how, to the orthodox faith as defined and observed by the universal, catholic and apostolic church and to the unity of the same holy mother church. We have found you, however, so stiff-necked that you are unwilling either to confess your errors and heresies of your own accord and immediately, or to return to the said catholic faith and unity of holy mother church. Rather, like a son of iniquity and darkness, you have hardened your heart to such an extent that you are not willing to listen to the voice of your pastor, who with paternal affection offers you peace. Nor will you be influenced by affectionate and paternal warnings or brought back by wholesome persuasions.

We are unwilling that you, wicked as you are, should become worse and in future infect the Lord's flock with the disease of your heresy, something that we fear greatly. Acting on the advice of experts who have assisted us in this matter and with whom we have communicated, we pronounce and declare by way of sentence and definitively in this ordinance, with grief and sadness of heart, that you, the aforesaid Robert – whose faults and sins have been aggravated by your damnable obstinacy, who have been convicted of the detestable crime of heresy and refuse to return as a penitent to the unity of the church – that you have been and are, in virtue of the above things, a heretic and one who believes in, supports and gives refuge to heretics. We relinquish you henceforth to the judgement and court of the secular arm. We also pronounce, decree and declare by this ordinance that you Robert, heretic as mentioned above, have also fallen into and incurred the sentence of major excommunication by reason of the above and that you have been and are excommunicated.

Present are the reverend father lord John, bishop of Cyrene, and the venerable masters Cuthbert Tunstall, doctor of both laws, Thomas Welles, Gabriel Silvester and Clement Browne, professors of sacred theology, together with the aforesaid notaries and many others.

2 Relinquishing of William Carder, Agnes Grebill and Robert Harryson to the secular arm, 2 May 1511 (ff. 172ᵛ–173ʳ)

To the most excellent prince and lord, lord Henry by the grace of God most illustrious king of England and France and lord of Ireland, William, by divine permission archbishop of Canterbury, primate of all England and legate of the apostolic see, sends greetings in him by whom kings reign and princes have dominion.

We signify to your royal highness, by this present decree, that certain sons and daughters of iniquity, William Carder, Agnes Grebill and Robert Haryson, on account of their various condemned and manifest errors and heresies and damnable opinions against the catholic faith and holy mother church, which they and each one of them taught and preached by various ways and means, have been legitimately and canonically convicted and judged to be heretics by us, and each one of them has been thus convicted and judged. Since, therefore, holy mother church may not do what ought to be done further in this matter, we relinquish the said heretics, and each one of them, to your royal highness and your secular arm.

Given in our manor of Knoll on 2 May in the year of the Lord 1511 and in the eighth year of our translation.

3 Penances imposed on 2 May 1511 (f. 160ᵛ)

Thereupon the same most reverend father absolved them from the sentence of excommunication that they had incurred by reason of the aforesaid things and restored them to the sacraments of the church and communion with the faithful. Then he enjoined upon them and each one of them, as part of their penance, that first they confess to a priest and receive the eucharist; and that they go to watch William Carder being burnt on account of his incorrigibility. And then the same reverend father fixed for them the following Monday, at eight o'clock in the morning, to receive the remainder of their penance.

4 Penances imposed on 5 May 1511 (f. 161ʳ)

On the said following Monday, namely on the second day of the aforesaid month of May, in the same place as above, in the presence of the above-named witnesses, the same most reverend father, sitting judicially in court, enjoined the following penance upon Christopher Grebill, Robert Hilles, William Riche, William Olberd senior, Agnes Ive and John Grebill senior, namely:

First, each of them will wear a representation of a burning faggot – that is, men on the upper arm, on the left sleeve of their outer garment, women on the left sleeve of their outer garment – publicly and without any concealment for their rest of their life, unless the same most reverend father or his successors dispense otherwise with them in the matter.

Next, each of them will carry a faggot of wood on their shoulder in the market-place of the city of Canterbury next Saturday, and at the front of the procession on next and the following Sunday in the cathedral church of Christ at Canterbury. They shall remain there during the sermon, with the faggot on their shoulder, until the sermon is finished. On the following Sunday each of those who have abjured in this way will carry the same bundle of wood in a similar manner at the front of the procession in their parish church. During the above, their head, feet and legs shall be bare.

Next, henceforth none of them shall dwell outside the parish in which they now live, unless they obtain explicit permission beforehand from the said most reverend father or his successors.

Next, if they have any heretical books, they will bring them to the said most reverend father without delay.

Next, if they know of now, or shall in the future, persons who are suspected of heresy or possess heretical books, they shall inform without delay the said most reverend father of their names.

Next, on Sundays and feast-days each of them shall frequent their parish church and attend divine worship, like a good Christian.

Furthermore, he warned them to perform their penance and each part of it under pain of becoming a relapsed heretic.

Then the same most reverend father enjoined upon Thomas Mannyng and John Grebill junior that on the following Sunday each of them should go before the procession in their parish church carrying a faggot of wood, and leave it there after the procession.

Then the same most reverend father enjoined upon Joan Colyn that henceforth she must not conceal anybody whom she knows to be suspected of heresy or teaching or holding heresy; that she must not move to other places, in order to remain in them, unless she first informs the same most reverend father or his successors as to where she will stay; and that she should not eat meat on Wednesdays throughout the next year.

5 Penances of John Grebill senior, 3 September 1511 (f. 168ᵛ)

In the name of God, Amen. We, William by divine permission archbishop of Canterbury, primate of all England and legate of the apostolic see, are sitting in judgement, having before our eyes God alone, duly and canonically proceeding in virtue of our office – after the merits of the case have been heard and understood, seen, investigated and scrutinised, and with fitting deliberation discussed and pondered, preserving in and throughout everything in the said business whatever the law requires to be observed or is called for in any way – in a matter of heresy against you, John Grebill of Benenden of our diocese of Canterbury, who are known to be placed under and subject to our jurisdiction.

On account of what has been done, deduced and proven before us in the aforesaid matter, confessed by you, recognised and shown before us too, we have found, by your confession and other legitimate proofs cited in judicial manner, that you have held, believed, asserted, affirmed and taught various errors, heresies and condemned opinions that are opposed, contrary and repugnant to divine and ecclesiastical law, against the orthodox faith as defined and observed by the universal, catholic and apostolic church, that you have infected many others of Christ's faithful with the disease of heresy, by your perverse and insane teaching, that you have taught them continuously and diligently the said errors, heresies and condemned opinions against the orthodox faith and determination of the holy Roman and universal church, thereby turning them away and separating them from the unity of the catholic faith and of holy mother church, and that you have turned them away and separated them in so far as you have been able to. Now, however, relying on better advice, you wish to return to the unity of the church, as you affirm, with a pure and good heart and unfeigned faith.

Acting on the advice of experts with whom we have communicated in this matter – after you abjured all heresy according to the customary form of the church, and pledged yourself to obey the law and to abide by the church's commandments and the injunctions that we had imposed on you, or would do so, on account of the above things, and to perform faithfully the penance that we had assigned to you, or would do so, in this affair – we absolve you from the sentence of excommunication that you incurred thereby and we restore you to the church's sacraments and communion with the faithful. In the name of the Father, the Son and the holy Spirit.

In the above ways you have rashly departed from almighty God and the holy catholic church and have infected with the disease of heresy, by your perverse and insane teaching, many innocent people and other Christians. Lest you infect the Lord's flock in the future with the contagious disease of heresy, something that we fear greatly, we pronounce and decree that, after you have first carried out the other injunctions and penances that we have already assigned judicially to you or are about to do so, you shall be confined to the priory of canons at Bilsington in our diocese of Canterbury, there to do perpetual penance. We wish, decree and order by this our definitive sentence, which we promulgate and publish in this ordinance, that your confinement shall be such that you do not move beyond one mile outside the said priory at Bilsington, and there you are to be sustained for the rest of your life on bread that mortifies and water that punishes. To us and our successors as archbishops of Canterbury is reserved the power of mitigating or otherwise commuting the above punishment or penance, if it seems right to us or our successors to do so.

Then the same most reverend father commuted the penance of the said John Grebill regarding fasting on bread and water, into not wearing a linen under-garment on Wednesdays and Fridays during his life, so that as long as the said John was alive he should not wear a linen under-garment on any Wednesday or

12

THE LADY AND THE BAILIFF: LOLLARDY AMONG THE GENTRY IN YORKIST AND EARLY TUDOR ENGLAND

Andrew Hope

R eports of martyrdoms in early sixteenth-century England take many forms. Here are two from 1511. The first report is by Andrea Ammonio, newly appointed Latin secretary of Henry VIII and an Italian humanist from Lucca.[1] Erasmus was also in England at this time, and he and Ammonio established a correspondence oiled by mutual complaints about their host society. On 8 November 1511 Ammonio wrote:

> I am not surprised that the price of firewood has gone up: every day there are a great number of heretics to make bonfires for us, and still their number continues to grow. Why even my servant Thomas's own brother, who is more like a lump of wood[2] than a human being, has instituted a sect of his own, if you please, and has followers too.[3]

Carriers – for this was one of Thomas's functions – were stock objects of abuse in Erasmus's circle.[4] Nothing more is known of Thomas or his brother's activities in this respect, nor can their identities be traced. There can, however, be little doubt about the heretics to whose burning Ammonio referred.[5] They were William Sweeting,[6] a sometime bailiff and holy water clerk, and James Brewster, a carpenter, and they had been burned together at Smithfield on 18 October 1511.[7]

The second report is by Joan Baker, wife of the London upholsterer Gervase Baker.[8] In her abjuration for heresy, probably in May of 1511, she recalled a conversation with John Cawood, the parish priest of St Margaret's Bridge Street, about 'the brennyng of the Lady Yong for suche opinions as she toke. The said

*I wish to thank Margaret Aston and Colin Richmond and all members of the conference for their encouragement and helpful discussion of this paper. I wish to thank similarly members of the John Foxe Colloquium in Cambridge (5 July 1995) and the Medieval Church History Group in Oxford (19 October 1995) where parts of this paper were also presented.

Johan saide that she dyed a martir be fore god and she besought god that she myght dy no wors then she did . . .'[9]

The first of these encapsulates many of the features of one traditional picture of English Lollardy: low social status and intellectual vacuity – and even the patronising tone which Lollards often elicit. The second introduces something altogether different. Lady Jane Young was the widow of a lord mayor of London.

A number of recent accounts have pointed to the existence of Lollardy in more elevated social settings than the proverbial humble craftsmen.[10] Is this, however, merely to introduce one more dimension of incoherence and to provide yet more evidence of Lollardy's supposed fragmentation?[11]

The two reports are not, of course, chosen at random. Their histories are intertwined, and suggest both the persistence of Lollardy among the gentry, and something of the ways in which Lollards of different social backgrounds related to each other.

Despite her high social status, Lady Jane Young was, and to some extent remains, a shadowy figure. Moreover there is doubt, as we shall see, that she was indeed a martyr. What is not in doubt is that her mother was a martyr. Joan Boughton, aged over eighty, was burnt at Smithfield on 28 April 1494, an event recorded by a number of chroniclers.[12] Apart from the chronicle evidence that her mother's name was Boughton, Jane Young's origins are unknown. It would be reasonable to speculate that Jane's marriage to Sir John Young indicates a background of some status. The Youngs were a wealthy Bristol family, closely associated with that of the legendary Cannings. John followed his half-brother and fellow grocer Thomas Canning first to London, and then in the office of lord mayor, to which Young was elected in October 1466.[13] Gregory's *Chronicle* recorded that 'menne callyd hym the good mayre',[14] and Fabyan described Young's humiliation of an alderman who refused either to remove or to pay for the removal of a dead dog from his own doorway.[15] He later went to unusual lengths to prevent a fraud being practised on an apprentice, who does, however, seem to have been some kind of relative.[16]

Politically the Youngs were closely identified with the Yorkist cause. John's eldest brother Thomas was a lawyer and an MP, and was an intimate adviser of Richard duke of York. His proposal in the Commons in 1451 that York should be declared heir presumptive to the throne resulted in his imprisonment in the Tower.[17] John was among those London aldermen knighted by Edward IV in 1471 as reward for their loyalty to him in his campaign to recover the throne in that year.[18]

There were Boughton families of status in Warwickshire and Kent, but Jane cannot be shown to have come from either.[19] A Thomas Boughton of Hungerford was prosecuted for Lollard heresies in 1499, but he was a shoemaker and a marriage alliance of his family with the Youngs may be thought unlikely.[20] Perhaps, however, their marriage *was* unlikely. They were married one May between 1467 and 1470, but it was probably a clandestine marriage. The question of whether Sir John was or was not married was oddly made a condition for the repayment of an obligation. An aldermanic court decided he was married at the date of the obligation, despite one party producing a priest who claimed to have performed the marriage two months after the date of the obligation.[21] At the time Sir John was probably living in the parish of St Botolph's, Billingsgate.[22] He died early in 1482, leaving an impeccably orthodox will,[23] and was buried in the church of St Michael Paternoster.[24]

Some time in the next two or three years Lady Jane remarried. She became the second wife of Sir Thomas Lewkenor, a member of a prolific and powerful Sussex family.[25] By his first marriage Thomas Lewkenor had a son Roger, born about 1468, and a daughter Katherine.[26] He was probably already a widower when, in 1478, his father Sir Roger, and then the following year his stepmother Katherine, died.[27] He had thus just inherited his father's estate and had it freed from the encumbrance of a dowager at the time of his remarriage.

For her part Lady Jane Young brought to the marriage (or so she was later to claim) £2000 in goods and credit. In return she received from Sir Thomas a jointure of manors and lands to the value of 100 marks, and he entered into an obligation of 1,000 marks with his uncle Thomas Lewkenor of Goring, Sir Thomas Bourchier, and Sir Thomas and Humphrey Tyrell, to the use of his wife.[28] It seemed on all sides a prosperous match.

William Sweeting's origins are almost equally obscure. Nothing is known of his parentage, but he received an education which provided him with the considerable literacy and numeracy necessary conscientiously to perform the duties of bailiff on important estates over a period of several decades. He is first known in the service of Lady Elizabeth Lucy at Dallington near Northampton. Elizabeth was a Percy and it may be that the Sweetings were Percy retainers, since Sweeting referred to her by her maiden name. She first married Thomas Burgh, by whom she had a son in about 1431.[29] She then married Sir William Lucy of Dallington.[30] Lady Elizabeth died in 1455,[31] but it would seem likely from the chronology of his life which he was to give at his trial that Sweeting continued in the service of Sir William after her death.[32]

Sir William Lucy's second wife was Margaret John alias Margaret FitzLewis. It was a marriage by which Sir William became the Uriah the Hittite of the Wars of the Roses. According to Gregory's *Chronicle*, he arrived late at the Battle of Northampton and 'the fylde was done or that he come; an one of the Staffordys was ware of hys comynge, and lovyd that knyght ys wiffe and hatyd hym, and anon causyd his dethe'.[33] The spoils did not go to the victor, however, for when Margaret remarried it was to Thomas (or John) Wake. She died in 1466.[34]

The Lucys were no strangers to heresy. Their roots were in Herefordshire and the central Welsh marches, where their neighbours included Sir John Oldcastle, Sir John Clanvow and the Talbots, to the last of whom at least the Lucys were related.[35] Northamptonshire too was the county of the Lollard knights Sir John Trussell and Sir Thomas Latimer.[36] Sir William's father, Walter Lucy, was a leading counsellor of Edmund Mortimer earl of March, the strength of whose

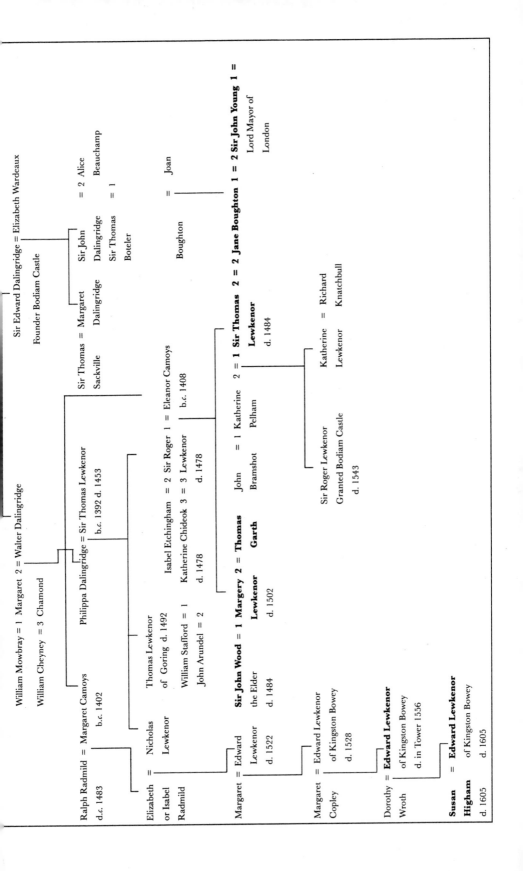

Sir Edward Dalingridge = Elizabeth Wardeaux

Founder Bodiam Castle

William Mowbray = 1 Margaret 2 = Walter Dalingridge

William Cheyney = 3 Chamond

Sir Thomas = Margaret
Sackville   Dalingridge

Margaret   Sir John
Dalingridge   Dalingridge   = 2 Alice
                  Sir Thomas   Beauchamp
                  Boteler   = 1

Boughton   = Joan

Philippa Dalingridge = Sir Thomas Lewkenor
                       b.c. 1392 d. 1453

Ralph Radmild = Margaret Camoys
d.c. 1483   b.c. 1402

Thomas Lewkenor
of Goring d. 1492

Nicholas
Lewkenor

Isabel Etchingham = 2 Sir Roger 1 = Eleanor Camoys
Katherine Chideok 3 = 3 Lewkenor   b.c. 1408
d. 1478   d. 1478

William Stafford = 1
John Arundel = 2

John   = 1 Katherine   2 = 1 Sir Thomas   2 = 2 Jane Boughton 1 = 2 Sir John Young 1 =
Bramshot   Pelham   Lewkenor   Lord Mayor of
                                d. 1484   London

Elizabeth =
or Isabel
Radmild

Margaret = Edward 1 Margery 2 = Thomas
           Lewkenor Lewkenor   Garth
           d. 1522   d. 1502

Sir John Wood = 1 Margery 2 = Thomas
the Elder   Lewkenor   Garth
d. 1484   d. 1502

Sir Roger Lewkenor
Granted Bodiam Castle
d. 1543

Katherine = Richard
Lewkenor   Knatchbull

Margaret = Edward Lewkenor
           of Kingston Bowey
           d. 1528

Dorothy = Edward Lewkenor
Wroth   of Kingston Bowey
          d. in Tower 1556

Susan   = Edward Lewkenor
Higham   of Kingston Bowey
d. 1605   d. 1605

FITZLEWIS, LUCY, PERCY AND DE VERE FAMILIES

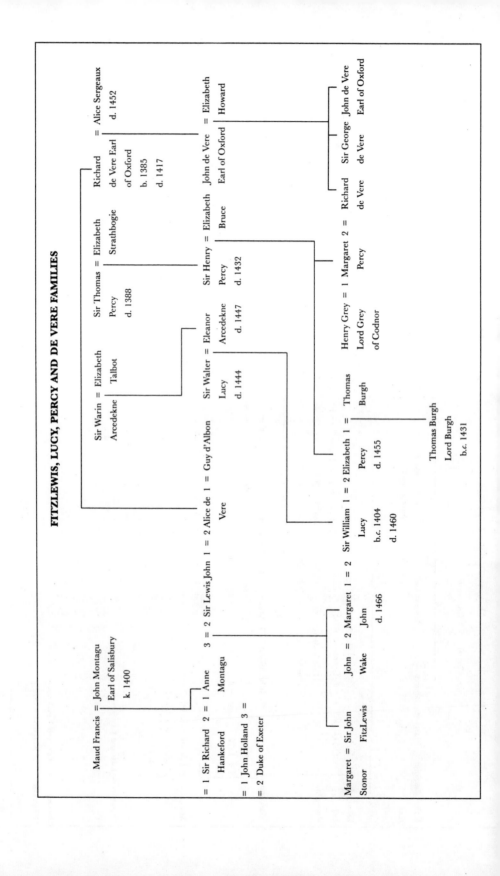

claim to the throne was more than matched by his incapacity for resolute political action.[37] In the fragmentary depositions which survive from Cambridge's 1415 plot against Henry V, it seems that while Lucy may have steered March away from any involvement, it was necessary for the devout Henry Lord Scrope to warn Lucy unequivocally against alliance with the fugitive Oldcastle and the remnants of the Lollard rising of the previous year.[38]

Lady Elizabeth Lucy seems to have had no exceptional Lollardy connections, though in a much intermarried aristocracy it is always possible to find connections of some kind. Such connections are much more evident with Sir William's second wife Margaret John alias FitzLewis. She was the granddaughter of the Lollard knight John Montagu, third earl of Salisbury, who was lynched at Cirencester in 1400.[39] His daughter Anne Montagu married Sir Lewis John alias John FitzLewis.[40] Sir Lewis left a will in which he spoke of his 'wretched body' in the manner characteristic of the Lollard knights.[41]

About the year that Margaret died, Sweeting moved on to Boxted in Essex. He became holy water clerk at the parish church. He held the post for seven years, probably between about 1467 and 1474. It was long enough for 'Clerk' to become an alias.[42] By the fifteenth century the duties of holy water clerk had broadened to those of parish clerk in general.[43] Sweeting would have been responsible for much of the day-to-day administration of the parish.[44] His duties included the preparation of the church for services, especially cleaning the choir (the Faversham clerk in 1506 was reminded to 'brusshe away the cobwebbis'[45]), laying out the books and vestments, and dressing the altar. He was to see the font was cleaned and prepared for baptisms. When required he was to ring the church bells and take holy water around to parishioners' houses. His liturgical duties (again as they were set out for the parish clerk of Faversham in 1506) required that he 'intende upon the Vicar or his depute in mynystracion of the Sacraments and Sacramentallis at all tymes, both be daie and nyghte as oft as nede shall requyre'.[46] On these occasions he was liturgically attired in a rochet, a surplice-like garment, and required to lead in singing the responses.

The post might seem inappropriate for someone of a Lollard disposition. Sweeting had, at least later in life, as we shall see, a particular aversion to images, and his duties probably included a requirement to 'swepe all the ymagys and glass wyndowys of the chirch ij tymes of the ȝere'.[47] There were compensations though. He had a highly active role in parish affairs; he kept track of christenings, weddings and burials;[48] he could, if effective, carve out for himself some kind of pastoral niche. His pivotal position in the parish is brought out by the requirements at the church of St Stephen, Coleman Street, in London. There, the clerk was to be an 'exemplar of devocion'. Moreover, they (the parish had two clerks):

shal make no contencon nor baat nor hevenesse betwene the curate and the parisschoners nor of no other preste. And if thei here any confeterice or imagynacon or sklawndyr of malice agaynce the curatte or any other preste that longs to the said chirch in all haste thei shal in confession tell hit to the curate and the namys of the personys that so ymagyn.[49]

The post also brought educational duties: the requirement 'to teche childern to rede and synge in the quyer' could offer many opportunities to nudge a new generation in an heretical direction.[50] He may well have had responsibility for reading the liturgical epistle during the mass[51] which raises the possibility that Sweeting read epistles in church in Latin and in people's houses in English – Lollardy indeed as the English heresy. Such Latin–vernacular, public–private, ecclesiastical–domestic discontinuities were portentous.[52]

In about 1475 Sweeting moved on to become bailiff to Margery Wood at the local manor of Rivers Hall in Boxted. He was there for thirteen years, probably until about 1488. Margery was the second wife of the Yorkist exchequer official John Wood the elder.[53] His tenure of Rivers Hall had come to him in right of his first wife, Elizabeth Michell. The Wood family's ancestral lands were in west Sussex.[54] It is possible there was some history of friction with their Lancastrian neighbours, the Lewkenors. Both had claims to Bodiam Castle in the east of the county. In the 1470s, however, such rivalries were subsiding. A marriage alliance was concluded: Margery Wood was the sister of Sir Thomas Lewkenor.[55] The dispute over Bodiam was resolved: it went to the Lewkenors.[56]

While William Sweeting was bailiff at Rivers Hall, Sir John Wood was establishing a successful career as a Yorkist administrator and parliamentarian. He became speaker of the House of Commons in Edward IV's last parliament and was Richard III's first treasurer.[57] In consequence he was perhaps not often at his Essex seat, which may give added point to the remark in Foxe's account that Sweeting was not just bailiff of the estate, but farmer as well. Under these circumstances it was not at all unusual for close relations to develop between the woman who had charge of the estate and her leading official. There were advantages on both sides: he was an essential ally in her dealings with other men whilst not threatening her position; she could add to his standing and prestige. Although in this instance probably both parties were married, marriage was an occasional outcome.[58] Another might be that kind of relationship of trust in which discussion of potentially dangerous religious topics became possible.[59]

The duties of bailiff could vary from manor to manor, and the court rolls of Rivers Hall seem not to have survived. However, as bailiff Sweeting would have been in charge of much of the day-to-day outdoor running of the manor. He would have been responsible for managing the workforce, for deciding upon and allotting tasks, and for making all the necessary decisions about sowing and harvesting and stock rearing. He had in addition to defend the lord's interests in the manorial court and to render accounts at the end of the year.[60] As the monks of Canterbury described it, their bailiff was: 'to cause the land to be ploughed, sown, reaped, manured and cultivated, and all the wagons and ploughs and cattle together with the sheep, lambs, hogs, and all other head of stock there to be managed and tended as shall seem best for our profit, rendering thereof such an account as it behoves bailiffs to render . . .'[61] The post might in fact be seen as the secular manorial counterpart to that of holy water clerk in a parish.

It is during the twenty-year period at Boxted that the first clear evidence of Sweeting's Lollardy emerges. He was reading the Gospel of Matthew with William Man, and learnt from Man that the sacrament of the altar was not the very body of Christ, but was bread in substance and received in memorial of Christ.[62] Although he attributes his eucharistic heresies to Man, given the background of his time in the Lucy household it is probable that it was no religious innocent who read Matthew's Gospel with William Man and discussed the sacrament of the altar. It may be that at his trial the court came to the same conclusion. It is difficult to see why otherwise such biographical details were investigated and recorded.

Many sections of the political nation were less ready than Sir John Wood to acquiesce in Richard III's assumption of the crown. Sir Thomas Lewkenor was among the disaffected, despite being made a Knight of the Bath at Richard's coronation.[63] When armed rebellion broke out in the Weald of Kent in the second week of October 1483, Sir Thomas, holding Bodiam Castle near the Kent–Sussex border, was quickly drawn in.[64] The rebellion, however, faltered. In the west Buckingham was thwarted by the weather and the sullen refusal of his own tenantry to turn out. Henry Tudor, having sailed from Brittany, declined to land. The Kent–Surrey–Sussex rebels, after three weeks or so, were forced back to Bodiam.[65] On 8 November Richard in Exeter issued a summons to a list of southern gentry – including Richard Lewkenor of Brambletye who was probably a first cousin of Sir Thomas – to besiege Bodiam.[66] On the same day the king ordered Sir Thomas's Middlesex lands at South Mimms and elsewhere to be placed in the custody of Sir John Elrington of Hoxton.[67] Bodiam, according to some recent estimates, was not as well designed to withstand siege action as it looked, and it probably did not hold out for long.[68]

Sir Thomas Lewkenor was still at large in the second week of December when Richard III issued a lengthy proclamation to the people of Kent in which he listed the rebels and offered rewards for their capture. Three hundred marks or £10 of land was offered for Sir Thomas.[69]

The date of Sir Thomas's submission is unknown. He was attainted by act of parliament in January 1484.[70] Richard, however, had been precipitate in granting away the rebels' lands and offices.[71] As has been seen, forfeitures began even while the rebellion was in progress. At some subsequent date Lewkenor's London possessions in Christopher Alley were entrusted to Richard Gough.[72] His manor of Stoke Doyle in Northamptonshire was granted to William Sapcottes, and the constableship of Bodiam Castle granted to Nicholas Rigby.[73] The act of attainder went some way to protecting the inheritances of the wives of those attainted, but perhaps already the revenues of the lands of Lady Jane Young which she enjoyed as a gift of Sir John Young, had been placed in the hands of Sir Christopher Ward.[74]

With few exceptions, however, the rebels were to suffer in their estates and their purses rather than in their bodies. In May 1484 Sir Thomas submitted to a bond of 1,000 marks and was placed under house arrest in the custody of his sister Margery and brother-in-law Sir John Wood.[75] In the summer of 1484 therefore, Sir Thomas Lewkenor and, we may assume, his wife the former Lady Jane Young, were resident at Rivers Hall where Sweeting was the bailiff. A pardon was issued to Sir Thomas some time during the summer, which restored his legal status, but probably did not rescind the requirement for him to remain with the Woods.[76] In the autumn, however, both Sir Thomas Lewkenor and his host Sir John Wood died, which perhaps suggests an epidemic disease.[77]

Lady Jane Young and William Sweeting therefore both spent the summer of 1484 at Rivers Hall. Was Lady Jane Young thus one of William Sweeting's converts, either that summer or through some other contact between the Lewkenors and the Woods? It would seem most likely that she was, although it is just possible to argue the alternative hypothesis, that Lady Jane converted Sweeting, since it is uncertain when either of them first became Lollards.

Bristol, the home of the Youngs, was the one place in England, if anywhere, where Lollardy was endemic. There is, however, no evidence that the Youngs were anything other than orthodox.[78] In contrast to Bristol, West Sussex, the home of the Lewkenors, was comparatively stony ground for Lollards. However, in 1470 there was an isolated case of heresy at Rogate, where the Lewkenors held a manor, a mere two miles or so from their principal seat at Trotton.[79] John Hodd, the vicar of Rogate, was summoned to answer for his 'lollardries and heresies' and faced with outlawry if he did not appear.[80]

Against this can be set some positive indication of the Lewkenors' orthodoxy. Most interesting is Lambeth Library MS 545, a book of hours which belonged to Sir Thomas's father and which descended through his brother Roger's family. They heavily personalised it with entries of family births and deaths, and with a souvenir of pilgrimage to Bromholm.[81] The will of Lady Joan Lewkenor points in a similar direction. A widow for nearly a quarter of a century after her husband Sir John, an uncle of Sir Thomas Lewkenor and Margery Wood, fell at the battle of Tewkesbury, her will of 1494 is suffused with a quiet Catholic piety and almost exclusively taken up with other-worldly matters.[82]

If it is unlikely that either of her two husbands' families were channels of Lollard influence, the probable sources of her Lollardy are reduced to two. Given her mother's heresy, it is possible that Lady Jane was a Lollard throughout her life. If this was so, it was a life of remarkable dissembling. On balance, however, it may seem more likely that when she and Sweeting met it was Sweeting who was the Lollard, and that it was Sweeting who was then responsible, directly or indirectly, for her mother's conversion as well.

Her husband's death left Lady Jane's affairs in considerable confusion. In December 1484 by a grant from Richard III she retrieved possession of her first husband's lands in London and Hertfordshire, perhaps those whose revenues had previously been assigned to Sir Christopher Ward.[83] The Tudor victory at Bosworth the following summer brought in its train a reversal of her second husband's attainder, but she may not have benefited greatly by it.

The considerable wealth which both parties brought to the Lewkenor–Young match seems to have been dissipated in the rebellion or lost in confiscation.[84] Lady Jane claimed that at his death Sir Thomas left neither goods of his own, nor those which were hers by right of her first husband, Sir John Young.[85] She may have been exaggerating, but marriage to Sir Thomas had probably cost her dear. Lady Jane was also finding it difficult to defend herself amid a throng of predatory male Lewkenors. Her stepson Sir Roger was occupying some of her jointure and, along with her brother-in-law Richard Lewkenor, had appropriated some of the bills of monies still owing to Sir John Young, including a long-outstanding £300 from the draper Richard Langton.[86] She seems to have needed money more than land at this time, for in August 1486 she alienated most of her lands in South Mimms and Cheshunt to another draper, Sir William Capell, for £300.[87] Nothing is known of her affairs thereafter until her mother's martyrdom in 1494. It is described in gloating detail by the author of *The Great Chronicle*.[88] Another chronicler, Robert Fabyan – who, as one of the two sheriffs of that year, would have been one of those officiating at the execution – is less informative.[89]

Joan Boughton was tried on 27 April and considerable attempts were made to return her to orthodoxy. She believed Wycliffe to have been a saint and held resolutely to eight of the twelve articles of heresy put to her.[90] What these were the chronicler says he will 'pass over for the hearing of them is neither pleasant nor fruitful'. On being told that if she persisted in her obstinacy she would be burned, she retorted that 'she was so beloved with God and his holy angels that all the fire in London should not hurt her'. She was burned the next day, the chronicler taking some pleasure that, far from 'all the fire in London', all that was needed was a 'quateron of faggot and a few reeds'. Others reacted differently, and in the night ashes from the fire were removed and kept in an earthenware pot as a precious relic.[91]

According to *The Great Chronicle* Lady Jane was 'soon reported [to have] a great smell of an heretic after the mother'.[92] Two years or so after her mother's martyrdom, that is, probably in late 1496 or early 1497, she entered a bill of complaint in chancery in an attempt to recover goods and lands still, she maintained, wrongfully detained by her stepson and brother-in-law, including the £300 Langton debt.[93] If heresy accusations or charges were brought against her, the responsibility might well lie with the Lewkenors who had reason to do this as a counter to her chancery suit. She was, however, still alive in June 1501 when she alienated further lands in Cheshunt to Hugh Clopton, his wife, and others.[94]

There is then no information about Lady Jane Young until Joan Baker's recorded conversations of 1511. Joan's remark that Lady Jane Young 'dyed a martir' has already been quoted. When Joan hoped that 'she myght dy no wors then she [Lady Young] did', it is her priest's reply, that then Joan Baker 'shulde be brent as she [Lady Young] was, and as many as takyth hur opinions',[95] which adds the detail that she was burned. Under interrogation for her views, Joan Baker also recollected another conversation. Although she could remember the words, she was unable to recall who the conversation had been with, a fine piece of selective amnesia. She had said to this person that all honour and worship which is given to images should be given to God; he or she had replied that for such sayings Lady Young had been burnt. Joan then said that if she died for that saying then she died well.[96] There are thus two different conversations about the burning of Lady Young. However, the lack of corroborative evidence does make its historicity questionable.[97] Since it is not known where she was living at this time, it is possible her burning may have taken place outside London, which could explain the silence of London chroniclers.[98] On the other hand Joan Baker's words could be the result of a scribal error similar to the one which produced the note to page 7, line 15, on page 710 of volume 4 of Townsend's edition of Foxe, in which Fabyan is quoted as saying the martyr 'was called mother Yongue', when in fact he wrote 'moder to the lady Yonge'.[99] Alternatively, it is conceivable that by some process of generational osmosis Joan Boughton became popularly known as 'Lady Young'. There are reasons therefore to justify speculation that Joan Baker's words were really a reference to Joan Boughton and not to her daughter, especially with their implied admiration for a spirit of defiance. The author of *The Great Chronicle*, however, was evidently fascinated by the case and was well informed, and there seem to be no grounds for doubting his remark that the orthodoxy of Lady Jane Young was suspect, just as her mother's had been.

Any formal links between William Sweeting and Lady Jane Young were probably ended about 1489. In that year Margery Wood married Sir Thomas Garth, a member of Parliament and an accomplished soldier.[100] At about the same time Sweeting moved on to become servant of the prior of St Osyth's, a house of Augustinian Canons near Colchester. The steward of the abbey, to whom Sweeting may have owed his appointment, was Sir George de Vere, brother of the earl of Oxford.[101] It may be that here we have a glimpse of the web of patronage within which William Sweeting moved. Sir George was related both to the Lucys and to the FitzLewises, and the FitzLewises were also an important client family of the de Vere earls of Oxford.[102]

Sweeting was a servant of the abbey for more than sixteen years, from about 1489 until his arrest early in 1506. It was here that he achieved his most famous coup. He converted the prior, George Laund, to his Lollard views. St Osyth's close social and economic ties with Colchester[103] may have meant that Colchester Lollards had contacts with the house. The accounts of the house for 1511–12, for example, mention John Pygas as purchasing sea coal. He may be, or have been related to, the Colchester Lollard John Pykas, who was a baker, and therefore had need of fuel. The house collected rents from members of the Page and Bocher families, both of which were implicated in Colchester Lollardy.

It was probably during this time that Sweeting began his association with James Brewster the carpenter, with whom he was to be martyred. Brewster had probably been taught both carpentry and Lollardy by Henry Hart in Westminster, before arriving in Colchester in about 1501.[104] At their trial in 1511 Brewster was slightly freer with his evidence than Sweeting. The fourth accusation he faced was that:

> he, hearing upon a time one Master Bardfield of Colchester thus say: 'He that will not worship Maozim in heart and thought shall die in sight', he asked afterwards of William Man, what that word Maozim should mean? who told him, that it signified as much as the masing God, to wit, the sacrament of the altar.

This passage goes some way to exposing the intellectual and social texture of Colchester Lollardy in the years prior to the reformation. It is clear that we are not here dealing with a few unthought-out elemental prejudices against popular religious practices, but with a theology with its own technical vocabulary and an organised (if perhaps limited) structure of ideas.

Maozim occurs once in the whole bible, in the eleventh chapter of Daniel, and refers to a strange God which is worshipped by a blasphemous ruler: 'Forsoþe he shal worshipe god of Maosym in his place, & he shal honor god whom his faders knewen not, in gold & silver & precious stoon, & preciouse þingis'.[105] Those who abet the ruler in his apostasy are rewarded with honour and authority.[106] Those who remain faithful to the true God are destroyed by violence.[107] But the result is a purged and purified remnant 'maad whijt til to a tyme determyned, for ʒit another tyme schal be'.[108] Here was a template which Lollards could use to order and understand their own experiences. And the false god ('whom his faders knewen not') was the mass.[109]

When these ideas were being expounded by Master Bardfield there was a distance of some kind between him and Brewster, such that Brewster had afterwards to ask Man what Bardfield had meant. The distance may have been formal, that is, Bardfield was giving an address which Brewster felt unable to interrupt; or it may have been social, that Brewster felt easier asking Man. In either case we are a long way from alehouse ribaldry.

There can be little doubt about the family of 'Master Bardfield'. The title 'master' may indicate either academic attainment or social status. There are no records of any Bardfields at Cambridge or Oxford in this period. However, there are two Essex families to whose senior male members 'master' might have been applied. The Bardfields of Margaretting were of considerable wealth and standing, but it is not possible to trace any Lollard connections for them.[110] The other Bardfield family, however, came from Colchester as Brewster specified, and they take us to the heart of a Lollard group entrenched high in Colchester society.[111] At the beginning of the century the head of the family was John Bardfield, who was to be elected one of the bailiffs of Colchester in 1505. By his first wife he had had a daughter Marion and by his second a son, John, and another daughter, Maud. His son John married as his second wife Katherine Cowbridge, daughter of another bailiff of Colchester, Robert Cowbridge.[112] According to Foxe, the Cowbridges had been Lollards since Wycliffe's day. Robert Cowbridge died in 1510 but his widow Margaret was forced to abjure in 1528 and their unstable son William was burned by Longland in 1536.[113] Marion married Thomas Matthew, the Lollard Colchester town councillor, and they hosted one of the most significant of Colchester conventicles. Bardfield's other daughter, Maud, predeceased him, but had married Henry Barker. Bardfield's wife Margery remarried Thomas Reveley. Corpus Christi College, Oxford possesses a Wycliffite Bible inscribed in an early sixteenth-century hand 'Thomas Reveley'.[114] Margery named Thomas Bowgas as one of her executors.[115] Thomas Bowgas abjured a series of Lollard heresies in London on 4 May 1528, and did penance in his parish church of St Leonard's, Colchester, on 10 May 1528.[116] His wife was obliged to find six compurgators to clear herself of similar accusations in July.[117] She was the daughter of Alice Gardner.[118] Alice was the godmother of John Tyball who was the inspiration behind the Steeple Bumpstead Lollards, and she taught Lollard heresy to both Tyball and John Pykas. Pykas, as we saw, may have had dealings with St Osyth's. He taught heresy in the presence of, among others, Thomas and Margaret Bowgas, and was another of those attending Thomas Matthew's conventicle.[119]

In the autumn of 1505 Bardfield was elected one of the two bailiffs of Colchester, the highest municipal office. Probably early the next year Sweeting's Lollard group was uncovered by the authorities. Sweeting, Brewster, their joint mentor William Man, Sabine Man (who was most likely the wife or a relative of William Man), Henry Cole, and George Laund the prior of St Osyth's were all arrested.[120] They were sent to London where they abjured and did penance at Paul's Cross on 15 March,[121] before returning for another penitential ceremony in Colchester. Sweeting and Brewster were condemned to wear a faggot badge on their left arm or shoulder for life.

Bardfield's participation had either gone undetected, or he had been able to use his wealth or political power to extricate himself. The church authorities may have colluded: it was no doubt bad enough indicting the prior of St Osyth's

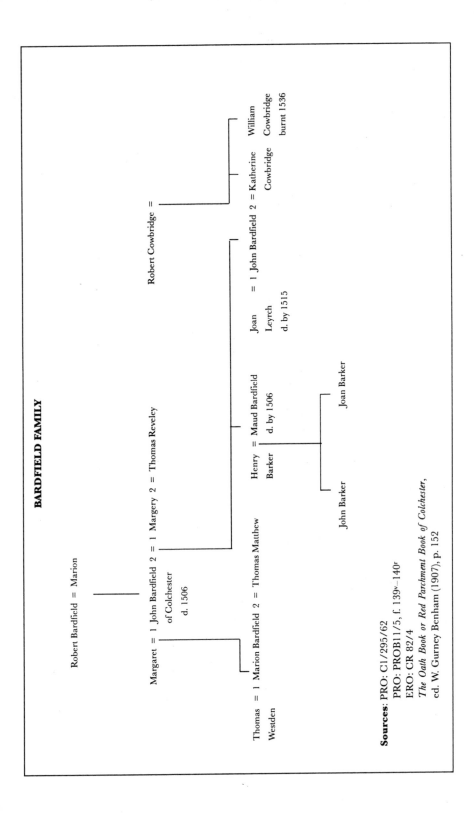

BARDFIELD FAMILY

Robert Bardfield = Marion

Robert Cowbridge =

Margaret = 1 John Bardfield 2 = 1 Margery 2 = Thomas Reveley
of Colchester
d. 1506

Joan = 1 John Bardfield 2 = Katherine
Leyrch   Cowbridge
d. by 1515

William
Cowbridge
burnt 1536

Thomas = 1 Marion Bardfield 2 = Thomas Matthew
Westden

Henry = Maud Bardfield
Barker   d. by 1506

John Barker   Joan Barker

Sources: PRO: C1/295/62
PRO: PROB11/5, f. 139ᵛ–140ʳ
ERO: CR 82/4
The Oath Book or Red Parchment Book of Colchester,
ed. W. Gurney Benham (1907), p. 152

without adding a serving bailiff of Colchester. He may anyway have already been a sick man. He made his will in June and died before he could serve out the full municipal year. He left his field by Parsonage Lane in Colchester to his parish church of St Leonard, the proceeds of which were to pay for obits for him, his parents' and his wives' souls for a hundred years, after which the money was to go to chantry priests who were to continue the office in perpetuity. It may have been a price exacted from Bardfield for being left unmolested. He was to finance *Maozim* for ever.[122] Before two years were up, however, both Sweeting and Brewster had had the badges they were commanded to wear removed by their employers.

Sweeting again found work as a holy water clerk, this time at St Mary Magdalen, Colchester. St Mary Magdalen was a small and barely viable parish outside the walls, on the road which led to Bardfield's parish of St Leonard's at the Hythe. In Morant's time it had fewer than sixty houses. It was a dependency of St John's Abbey.[123] The parson evidently found Sweeting's faggot badge an embarrassment rather than an impediment, and removed it. After two years Sweeting left to become holy water clerk for a year at Rotherhithe.

Brewster meanwhile had been employed as a carpenter in the household of John de Vere, earl of Oxford and elder brother of Sir George, the steward of St Osyth's. The comptroller of the earl's household, who had probably once been and perhaps was still Philip FitzLewis of the same FitzLewis-alias-John family, removed Brewster's badge.[124]

Sweeting then moved on to Chelsea to become a neatherd. The episodes in which Sweeting is seen relating to the more conventional Lollard conventicle date from this period, although this may be simply a feature of the record rather than any new practice. He was especially close to Roger Hellier of Stratford Langthorn, and in about 1508 or 1509 he was meeting him in his house along with Thomas Goodred, and discussing the Gospels, especially the eleventh chapter of Matthew.[125] It is a chapter which might have been written for Lollards to chew over. It contains the proofs of Jesus's ministry as adduced by John the Baptist's followers, which include, in the Wycliffite translation, that 'pore men ben taken to prechynge of the gospel'.[126] It includes too Jesus's condemnation of his generation as 'like to children sittynge in Chepynge, that crien to her peeris and seien, we han sungen to ʒou & ʒe han not dauncid'.[127] (They could picture it: Cheap was where John Barrett, a goldsmith and one of the leading London Lollards, lived.) It would be worse on the day of judgement for cities which had been shown the way and rejected it than for Tyre and Sidon. Jesus thanked God for having 'hidde these thingis fro wise men & prudent: & hast schewid hem to litil children'.[128]

Sweeting and Brewster met again when Brewster travelled up from Colchester to attend conventicles which Sweeting held in the fields outside Chelsea. Sweeting read 'many good things out of a certain book' to Brewster and

Goodred, who were both carpenters, a netmaker named John Woodruff, who like Brewster was a protégé of Henry Hart, Woodruff's wife, and Sweeting's brother-in-law. These readings seem to have had some liturgical structure, for Foxe preserves what may be a rare Lollard antiphon:

> James Brewster should thus say:
> 'Now the son of the living God help us';
> unto whom William Sweeting again should answer:
> 'Now Almighty God so do'.[129]

Sweeting therefore was still giving the responses, just as he had in Boxted church forty years before, even though he was literate and Brewster was not.

In the late spring of 1511 both Sweeting and Brewster were probably engaged in instructing the Forge family in their beliefs. John Forge was a London wiredrawer with two sons, John, who was fifteen, and Thomas, who may have been older. Once, when he and Thomas were alone together, Sweeting related in great detail an account of the conversion of St Paul. Brewster, accompanied by Thomas Goodred, told John Forge senior of Moses and the brazen calf, the Salutation of the Virgin Mary, and the story of Tobias and his son. Whether intended or not, John junior listened.[130]

On 25 July 1511 the church authorities questioned John Forge the son about what he had seen and heard. He described James Brewster telling his father the stories of Moses, the Virgin, and Tobias. Thomas Forge was then also questioned and he described his conversations with Sweeting.[131] Brewster was arrested the same day, which happened to be St James's Day. Sweeting was arrested the following morning, St Anne's Day, as he went out to attend to his animals in Chelsea. His room was searched for books. Sweeting and Brewster were imprisoned in the Lollards' Tower at St Paul's, where their gaoler was Charles Joseph, the summoner who was to achieve infamy three years later as the chief suspect in the Hunne case. In the weeks which followed a series of their associates were arrested and examined: Thomas Ansty on 29 July, Richard Woolman and John Calverton on 7 August, Thomas Walker alias Thomas Talbot on 8 August, and his wife the next day, Thomas Goodred on 11 and 12 August, Elizabeth Bate and Thomas Ansty's wife Joan also on 12 August. William Sweeting and James Brewster were examined on 13 August. Sweeting's close associates Roger Hellier and Robert Bennet were examined on 20 August, William Mason on 2 September, and Elizabeth Matthew on 8 September.[132]

Sweeting and Brewster were far more at risk than the others since they had previously abjured the errors which they were now charged with teaching. They both submitted themselves to the church again, a failure of nerve which was held to be greatly to their discredit by Victorian historians.[133] The two were burned together in a single fire in Smithfield on 18 October 1511.[134]

William Sweeting was a man of considerable ability. His long periods of employment, for example with Margery Wood or at St Osyth's, are evidence of his capacity successfully to carry out demanding jobs. He seems too to have sought out the same kinds of work, requiring administration, direction and responsibility, whether it was as a holy water clerk or a bailiff. His final post as neatherd may reflect nothing more than his increasing age. It was fifty-five years since the death of Elizabeth Lucy, his first employer. There seems also to be a pattern about his employers: they are always women or celibate men. His employment and his employers may give some clues as to his own conception of the kind of role to which he aspired. In the religious sphere the question which then presents itself is whether the attempted and ultimately successful conversion of Prior George Laund was repeated in the case of others he came across. That Lady Jane Young was probably resident for a period at Rivers Hall does seem to make Sweeting's conversion of her, and perhaps her mother, very likely. So it is additionally suggestive that the court should have enquired into his service with Elizabeth Lucy and Margery Wood. Such biographical investigations in heresy cases usually have some point to them. Both the women were dead by then so that no good could come of publishing any religious lapses they might have had, but investigation might reveal something of Sweeting's activities. That the workplace was the setting for most of Sweeting's recorded heretical activity is given added significance by what is known of his wife. She was notably unimpressed by his religious teachings. She revered images and set up candles before them. She enjoyed her pilgrimages too, and in Sweeting's recorded belief that she should 'keep at home and . . . attend her business' we may have an authentic fragment of their domestic exchanges.[135]

Some care should be exercised over words like 'conversion', which carry with them notions of polar opposites. Joan Boughton was undoubtedly a Lollard: she believed Wycliffe was a saint. William Sweeting, however, would not have lasted long as a holy water clerk expounding such ideas. It would surely be right to view his approach to that office as more subtle. He could encourage some forms of devotion and discourage others, he could promote some practices and discourage others. He could give this or that reading or festival a doctrinal slant. In short, he could influence. At his death Sir George de Vere, who may have been responsible for Sweeting's appointment to St Osyth's and whose brother's comptroller removed Brewster's faggot badge, left a will which, though orthodox, stipulated that prayers at his funeral should be said in English.[136] The de Veres also owned a Wycliffite bible, although it is not known when they acquired it.[137]

As suggested earlier, Lollardy is not unknown in gentry circles at this time. The case of Alice Wilmot-Cottesmore-Doyly, who married her way through three Oxfordshire gentry families, offers a number of parallels. Her family, Eden alias Clydesdale, presents similar problems of identification to that of the Boughtons. She greatly revered the religious teaching of John Hacker, socially her inferior although not her employee.[138] The Durdants, a gentry family at Iver, seem to have had a wide reputation among Lollards to judge by the gathering which assembled to celebrate a Durdant wedding.[139] Of equivalent status in towns there were, as we have seen, the Bardfield, Cowbridge and Matthew families in Colchester. In Coventry Richard Cook, twice mayor and member of Parliament for the city, a member of the Pysford family, and others were associated with the town's Lollards.[140] In London Joan Baker defended Lady Young, and Richard Hunne defended Joan Baker. The goldsmith John Barrett taught his apprentices Lollardy and they found their way to Amersham, where the leading families of Saunders and Bartlett were, or became, Lollards.[141] The examples can be multiplied.

A central question, however, is where this Lollardy among the élite has come from. Is it percolating up from some artisan stratum, or is there a direct descent from the gentry Lollardy of the late fourteenth and early fifteenth centuries?

The career of William Sweeting would give some weight to the former suggestion. Not only does he seem to be influencing his social superiors, but if Joan Boughton really was his convert, it would eliminate one of the few possible examples of continuity from the first half of the century. However, there is here a real danger of generalising from a single and possibly exceptional example. We simply do not know from where the Durdants or the Saunders or the Clydesdales or the Barretts or any of the others derived their heresy. There is, moreover, some evidence of a social gulf between the Lollards Sweeting was mixing with in London in the last years of his life and the probably relatively small circle of well-off London Lollards. Alice Ray, grand-daughter of the Lollard Thomas Walker alias Thomas Talbot, was proud of her son's apprenticeship with one member of this Lollard élite, Richard Wright. 'He is a prevy man', Alice said of Wright, 'and grett with my master Barret and his wife', but added that 'he will deele with no poer folkes'. It may be that Alice was exaggerating Wright's exclusivity since it reflected well on her and her son. Nevertheless both Wright and Barret seem to have been cautious in their practice of Lollardy. They had much to lose. They were probably not found at meetings in fields.[142]

The same problems of generalisation attend the question of gender. That on this reconstruction of Sweeting's activities women seem largely to be recipients rather than providers or initiators should not be taken as typical, if only because there is strong contrary evidence from the Chilterns and Essex.[143]

Finally, it is appropriate to look forward to the reformation. What was the legacy of Sweeting's long and audacious Lollard career? In some ways it might seem surprisingly thin. The gentry families among whom he spread his beliefs seem to have taken no obvious lead in furthering the same ideas when orthodoxy began to come apart in the decades after his death. He might have been gratified to know the extent to which Edward Lewkenor – a great-grandson of Sir Thomas's cousin Edward – was instrumental at the end of the century in promoting puritan ideals not only in Sussex, but also at Denham, a parish whose tithes Sweeting probably once collected, since they were impropriated to St Osyth's Abbey.[144] The link is not as remote as it might appear. Edward's father, also named Edward Lewkenor, had been a ward of, and married the daughter of, Robert Wroth (c. 1489–1535), who had been Lady Jane's neighbour in Enfield.[145] This Edward Lewkenor conspired against Mary I and was imprisoned in the Tower. He died there of natural causes in 1556, refusing the sacrament on his death bed.[146]

Nothing more is known of George Laund, the prior of St Osyth's. It is possible that William Barlow, through whose hands the Anglican church was to claim apostolic descent, was a canon of St Osyth's at the time but, as with all things in the early career of Bishop Barlow, equally possible that he was not.[147]

Sweeting's time in Boxted probably bore fruit in the Lollard community which seems to have flourished there into the reformation. In the early 1520s that most stalwart of Lollard families, Richard and Alice Collins of Ginge in western Berkshire, presumably along with their learned daughter Joan and certainly with their substantial collection of Lollard books, arrived in Boxted. They were fugitives from Longland and Audley's episcopal justice in the dioceses of Lincoln and Salisbury, across whose borders they had operated and where they were no longer safe. Settled in Boxted, they called themselves Johnson instead of Collins and proceeded to rebuild in the Boxted area that reputation for Lollard learning which they had previously enjoyed around Burford.[148] A decade later they were caught again, this time by Stokesley, but it was a different world now. Whereas in the early 1520s they had fled across the country and changed their name, in the early 1530s they secured their release and wrote a letter of complaint to Thomas Cromwell.[149]

It was a different world in other ways too. John Mell was a Boxted Lollard who was probably a tenant of Rivers Hall. When he was arrested in the early 1530s he possessed not only the Lollard *ABC* but also printed books from Antwerp: Tyndale's *English New Testament* and George Joye's *English Psalter*.[150]

Sweeting was to have his literary memorial in Foxe's *Acts and Monuments*, but he may also have left another faint trace in Erasmus. This paper began with Ammonio's joke about heretics sending up the price of firewood. Erasmus replied three days later. He had no wish openly to contradict his fellow humanist, but equally he had no wish to endorse religious persecution. His solution was to play along with Ammonio's conceit. Erasmus discussed the bellicose Julius II, upon whose sanity he cast some doubt, and went on: 'I have less sympathy with those heretics you mention if only because they have chosen the moment when winter is upon us to send up the price of fuel'.[151]

Years later, in his 1529 colloquy 'Charon', Erasmus described this new world of a Christendom racked by war, religious conflict and persecution, and fantasised again about a shortage of wood. Charon, who ferries the souls of the newly dead across the Styx, sets out to build new boats to accommodate all the extra traffic expected from wars in Christendom and from what will happen 'if these controversies, that are now managed by the tongue and the pen, come to be decided by arms', but finds all the woods in the Elysian fields have been used for the burning of heretics. This time Erasmus left his reader in no doubt that responsibility for the depletion lay with the persecutors and not with the persecuted.[152]

Notes

[1] Thomas B. Deutscher, 'Andrea Ammonio', in Peter G. Bietenholz (ed.), *Contemporaries of Erasmus: A Biographical Register of the Renaissance and Reformation*, vol. 1 (Toronto, 1985), pp. 48–50; Desiderius Erasmus, *Letters*, vol. 2, in *Collected Works of Erasmus* (Toronto, 1975–), introduction to letter 218, p. 156.

[2] It is not clear whether the implication that Thomas's brother is therefore combustible is conscious or unconscious. The Latin words used are *lignum* (firewood) and *stipes* (wood, log). Terence uses the latter similarly as a term of abuse. *Opus Epistolarum Des. Erasmi Roterdami*, ed. P.S. Allen, I, (Oxford, 1906), p. 481.

[3] Erasmus, *Letters*, vol. 2, p. 189 (letter 239; Ammonio to Erasmus, London, 8 November 1511). Little weight can be placed on the evidence of letter 239 for London Lollardy. Ammonio was a florid writer who would not allow precision to obscure effect.

[4] See for example *Letters*, vol. 2, p. 256 (letter 276; Erasmus to [William] G[onnell?] and H[umphrey Walkden?], Cambridge, October 1513). A couple of years later, however, Erasmus had a good word for Thomas 'who is such a sensible and wide awake servant that he looks after your interests better than you do'. See *Letters*, vol. 2, letter 283, p. 269; Erasmus to Ammonio, Cambridge, 2 December [1513]; and for the incident which provoked it, *ibid.*, letter 282, p. 265; Erasmus to Ammonio, Cambridge, 28 November [1513], ll. 18–19).

[5] There was, however, one intervening letter from Ammonio (*Letters*, vol. 2, pp. 179–182, letter 236; Ammonio to Erasmus, London, 27 October) which did not mention the burnings.

[6] The account presented here of William Sweeting is an expansion, with additional material, of pp. 6–8 of Andrew Hope 'Lollardy: the stone the builders rejected?', in P. Lake and M. Dowling (eds), *Protestantism and The National Church in the Sixteenth Century* (London, 1987). The original narratives of his life are in Foxe, *A&M*, IV, pp. 180–1, 214–15. A narrative of Brewster follows on pp. 215–16. These references will not be systematically footnoted hereafter.

[7] F.D. Logan, *Excommunication and the Secular Arm in Medieval England: A study in legal procedure from the thirteenth to the sixteenth century* (Toronto, 1968), p. 192.

[8] On Gervase Baker see PRO, C1/473/29 (Baker v. Mayor and Sheriffs of London), a dispute about a partially repaid debt.

[9] E. Jeffries Davis, 'The Authorities for the Case of Richard Hunne (1514–15)', *EHR*, 30 (1915), p. 486. Foxe's summary is in *Actes and Monuments* (1563), p. 373. His later truncated version is the basis of the Victorian Townsend and Pratt texts, IV, p. 175, the fuller version appearing in the Addenda, p. 773. See also III, pp. 704n, 706, and IV, pp. 7, 710. There is some additional material among Archbishop Ussher's transcripts, TCD, MS 775, ff. 122v–124v. I am most grateful to Susan Brigden for providing me with copies of relevant Ussher entries. These will not be systematically footnoted hereafter.

[10] See, for example, Imogen Luxton, 'The Lichfield Court Book: a Postscript', *BIHR*, 44 (1971), pp. 120–5; Andrew Hope, 'Lollardy: the stone the builders rejected?', pp. 2–10; and Derek Plumb, 'The Social and Economic Spread of Rural Lollardy: A Reappraisal', *SCH*, 23 (1986), pp. 111–29. Margaret Spufford (ed.), *The World of Rural Dissenters, 1520–1725* (Cambridge, 1995) appeared after

the conference.

[11] On fragmentation see Jeremy Catto, 'Religious Change under Henry V', in G.L. Harriss (ed.), *Henry V: The Practice of Kingship* (Oxford, 1985), pp. 114–15, and *idem*, 'Wyclif and the Lollards: Dissidents in An Age of Faith?', *History Today*, 37, no. 11 (1987), p. 52; and Greg Walker, 'Heretical Sects in Pre-Reformation England', *History Today*, 43, no. 5 (1993), pp. 42–8. For the contrary view see Hudson, *PR*, and Richard G. Davies, 'Lollardy and Locality', *TRHS*, 6th series, 1 (1991), pp. 191–212.

[12] *The Great Chronicle of London*, eds A.H. Thomas and I.D. Thornley (London, 1938), pp. 252–3; Robert Fabyan, *The New Chronicles of England and France*, ed. Henry Ellis (London, 1811), p. 685; and *Chronicles of London*, ed. Charles Lethbridge Kingsford (Oxford, 1905), p. 200.

[13] Thomas Canning was elected mayor in 1456. *Calendar of Letter-Books preserved among the Archives of the Corporation of the City of London at the Guildhall: Letter-Book K. Temp. Henry VI*, ed. R.R. Sharpe (London, 1911), p. 381, and *Letter-Book L. Temp. Edward IV–Henry VII* (London, 1912), p. 68; Sylvia L. Thrupp, *The Merchant Class of Medieval London (1300–1500)* (Ann Arbor, 1948), pp. 328, 376–7; E.M. Carus-Wilson, *Medieval Merchant Venturers* (London, 1967), pp. 80–81 (curiously omitting John as one of his mother's distinguished children).

[14] William Gregory, *Chronicle of London*, in *Historical Collections of a Citizen of London*, ed. James Gairdner (Camden Society, 1876), p. 233.

[15] Fabyan, *New Chronicles*, p. 656.

[16] *CCR, 1476–85*, p. 126; PRO, C1/64/568; E.W. Ives, *The Common Lawyers of Pre-Reformation England; Thomas Kebell: A Case Study* (Cambridge, 1983), p. 318.

[17] P.A. Johnson, *Duke Richard of York 1411–1460* (Oxford, 1988), pp. 73, 98–100, 241.

[18] J. Warkworth, *A Chronicle of the First Thirteen Years of the Reign of King Edward the Fourth* (Camden Society, 1839), p. 21; Charles Ross, *Edward IV* (London, 1974), pp. 165–75. There are accounts of the Cannings and of John and Thomas Young in Josiah C. Wedgwood, *History of Parliament: Biographies of the Members of the Commons House 1439–1509* (London, 1936), pp. 151, 980–2; and of Thomas Young in E.W. Ives, *The Common Lawyers; Thomas Kebell*, p. 480. See also John MacLean, 'Notes on the family of Yonge or Young, of Bristol, and on the Red Lodge', *Transactions of the Bristol and Gloucestershire Archaeological Society*, 15 (1890–1), part 2, pp. 228–30, 244. In addition see (published since the conference) Pamela Nightingale, *A Medieval Mercantile Community: The Grocers' Company and the Politics and Trade of London, 1000–1485* (New Haven, CT, 1995), pp. 414, 434, 443, n. 3, 451–2, 475, 491–4, 496–7, 502, 504–5, 507–11, 513 and n. 2, 514–15, 529–30, 534, 536, 541, 543, 552.

[19] There is something to be said for each. The Warwickshire family produced two MPs which would have brought them into contact with the Youngs (Wedgwood, *History of Parliament: Biographies*, pp. 94–5). The Kent family contracted a marriage alliance with the Lewkenors (*The Visitations of Kent*, ed. W. Bruce Bannerman, part 1 (Harleian Society, 74, 1923), p. 2), as Jane Young was to do.

[20] On Boughton see Hudson, *PR*, pp. 149, 166, 275, 470.

[21] PRO, C1/46/212 (Osbern v. the Mayor and Aldermen of London). John Osbern based an appeal to chancery on the unreasonableness of the court's dismissal of the priest's evidence. The other party comprised a gentleman, Ambrose Grysaker, and a mercer, John Lambard the younger. The 'May' given here is based on the priest's evidence. Grysaker and Lambard argued that Young was married by March. Lambard may have fancied he had inside information since he was probably the younger brother, or possibly son, of the John Lambard, mercer, who was an alderman from 1460 to 1470 (Thrupp, *Merchant Class*, p. 352). He was thus an uncle (or brother) of Elizabeth 'Jane' Shore, the mistress of Edward IV. Nicholas Barker, 'Jane Shore: part 1. The Real Jane Shore', *Etoniana*, no. 125 (4 June 1972), pp. 385–6, 389–90; W.E. Hampton, *Memorials of the Wars of the Roses: A Biographical Guide* (Upminster: Richard III Society, 1979), pp. 85–6. The wide range of years possible on the basis of the address to the chancellor is narrowed since the case is datable to after Young became an alderman and before he was knighted.

[22] PRO, C1/31/501 (Young v. Walwyn) shows he was living there in September 1465.

[23] *The Great Chronicle*, p. 440; PRO, C1/32/327 (Langton v. Mayor and Aldermen of London)

shows he was alive in January 1482; Thomson, *LL*, pp. 156–7.

24 John Stow, *A Survey of London*, ed. Charles Lethbridge Kingsford (Oxford, 1908), i, p. 243. Buried in the same church were his daughter Agnes, whom Stow records as the wife successively of Robert Sherington, Robert Mulleneux, and William Cheyney. Her mother was Sir John's first wife. Also buried in the church was Sir William Oldhall, a close associate of Richard duke of York and of Thomas Young.

25 See William Durrant Cooper, 'Pedigree of the Lewkenor Family', *Sussex Archaeological Collections*, 3 (1850), pp. 89–102.

26 *Ibid.*, pp. 96–7; *Calendar of Inquisitions Post Mortem Henry VII*, vol. 2, no. 629; Frank Ward, 'The divorce of Sir William Barentine', *Sussex Archaeological Collections*, 68 (1927), pp. 179–81 (which suggests Roger was born a year or two earlier). Katherine married the Kentish gentleman Richard Knatchbull of Mersham. See also the pedigree at the back of Sir Hughe Knatchbull-Hugessen, *Kentish Family* (London, 1960).

27 His father died before Michaelmas 1478. Detailed arrangements for Katherine's widowhood were then made in January 1479 by an indenture between Katherine and her stepson. They were confirmed by Thomas in chancery the following month, but Katherine was dead by May. See PRO, C54/330, m. 7d, calendared in *CCR, 1476–85*, no. 474, pp. 134–6. (The calendar entry is in error in making Thomas the son of Sir Roger and Katherine. The roll makes clear he was the son and heir of Sir Roger only.) See also *CFR, 1471–85*, nos. 511, 512 (p. 173), 539 (p. 183), 565 (p. 197).

28 PRO, C1/211/65 (Lewkenore v. Leukenore and Leukenore). The lands and manors are not named in the chancery bill. On Humphrey Tyrell see W.E. Hampton, *Memorials of the Wars of the Roses: A Biographical Register* (Upminster, Richard III Society, 1979), p. 55 (no. 72).

29 GEC, vol. 2, p. 422.

30 For a brief account of Dallington manor in this period see Philip J. Randell, *Old Dallington* (Dallington, 1955), 2nd edn, pp. 8–9.

31 The date of her death precludes her from being the Elizabeth Lucy who was the mistress of Edward IV. See *The Lisle Letters*, ed. Muriel St Clair Byrne (Chicago, 1981), 1, pp. 14, 142–4, 393.

32 Sweeting accounts for thirty-six years of his life before 1506, the date of his first trial. Allowing for a certain rounding down in months to produce complete years and for some intervals during the three changes of employment, a starting date of 1466 is both possible and produces a chronology which fits well with other datable events.

33 Gregory, *Chronicle of London*, p. 207.

34 GEC, vol. 8, pp. 261–2; W.E. Hampton, 'Roger Wake of Blisworth', *The Ricardian*, 4, no. 52 (March 1976), p. 10.

35 Elizabeth Talbot, the daughter of John Talbot of Richards Castle, Herefordshire, was Sir William Lucy's maternal grandmother. A connection of this family with the Sir Thomas Talbot who participated in Oldcastle's rebellion is implied by K.B. McFarlane, *JW*, p. 153, and is asserted by Hugh Talbot, *The English Achilles: An account of the Life and Campaigns of John Talbot, 1st Earl of Shrewsbury (1383–1453)* (London, 1981), pp. 36, 42. John Talbot, William Lucy's cousin and the future earl of Shrewsbury, was imprisoned in the Tower at the time of Oldcastle's rebellion, and Hugh Talbot (pp. 42–3) accepts this as evidence of complicity. John Talbot's subsequent commission to try Lollards in Shropshire (p. 42) is not in this context unusual, and would bear comparison with Nicholas Hereford (McFarlane, *JW*, p. 114), or John de Stourton, later Lord Stourton (GEC, vol. 12, part 1, pp. 301–2), who was the son of William Stourton, one of McFarlane's possible Lollard knights (*LK*, p. 215). Either their loyalty was being tested, or use being made of inside information, or both.

36 McFarlane, *LK*, pp. 152–60, 166–7.

37 T.B. Pugh, *Henry V and the Southampton Plot of 1415* (Gloucester, 1988), pp. 81, 82, 114–15 and *passim*.

38 *Ibid.*, pp. 115, 126, 168–9.

39 On Montagu's career see McFarlane, *LK*, pp. 167–8, 175, 177–81, 208.

40 On Sir Lewis John's career see H.L. Elliot, 'FitzLewis of West Horndon and the Brasses at

Ingrave', *Transactions of the Essex Archaeological Society*, n.s. 6 (1898), pp. 28–59. In 1442 he was serving in Normandy with John Talbot, the future Earl of Shrewsbury (PRO, C47/2/49/42). Cf. n. 35.

[41] PRO, PROB 11, 14 Rous; McFarlane, *LK*, pp. 207–20.

[42] Foxe, *A&M*, IV, p. 214.

[43] J.S. Craig, 'Co-operation and initiatives: Elizabethan churchwardens and the parish accounts of Mildenhall', *Social History*, 18, no. 2 (October 1993), p. 357, notes the need for more study of the office of parish clerk.

[44] There are useful summaries of duties in E.L. Cutts, *Dictionary of the Church of England* (London, n.d.), pp. 444–6 (*s.v.* Parish Clerk) and Joyce Youings, *Sixteenth Century England* (Harmondsworth, 1984), p. 39. See also Peter Heath, *The English Parish Clergy on the Eve of the Reformation* (London, 1969), pp. 19–20, 84–5.

[45] F.F. Giraud, 'On the Parish Clerks and Sexton of Faversham A.D. 1506–1593', *Archaeologia Cantiana*, 20 (1893), pp. 204–6.

[46] *Ibid.* Note the similar provisions at the church of St Stephen Coleman Street: the clerk was 'to be at noo tyme owt of the way, but one to be alwayes ready to mynester Sacramentes and Sacramentalls what soo ever shall nede to wayet upon the Curat and give hym warnyng'; Edwin Freshfield, 'Some Remarks upon the Book of Records and History of the Parish of St Stephen, Coleman Street, in the City of London', *Archaeologia*, 50 (1887), p. 51.

[47] *Ibid.*, p. 51.

[48] *Ibid.*

[49] *Ibid.*, p. 52.

[50] Giraud, 'On the Parish Clerks of Faversham', pp. 204–6.

[51] Cuthbert Atchley, *The Parish Clerk, and his Right to Read the Liturgical Epistle* (Alcuin Club Tracts, 4, 1903, new edn, 1924).

[52] Anne Hudson, 'Lollardy: the English Heresy', *SCH*, 18 (1982), pp. 261–83, reprinted in Hudson, *LB*, pp. 141–63; Colin Richmond, 'Religion and the fifteenth century English gentleman', in Barrie Dobson (ed.), *The Church, Politics, and Patronage in the Fifteenth Century* (Gloucester, 1984), pp. 193–208.

[53] On Sir John Wood see J.S. Roskell, 'Sir John Wood of Molesey, Speaker in the Parliament of 1483', *Surrey Archaeological Collections*, 56 (1959), pp. 15–28, reprinted in J.S. Roskell (ed.), *Parliament and Politics in Late Medieval England* (London, 1981–3), III, pp. 383–96; F. Leslie Wood, 'Sir John Wood, Treasurer', *Notes and Queries*, 12th ser., 8 (1921), pp. 206–7, 253, with further notes by John B. Wainewright and by James Seton Anderson, in 11 (1922), p. 460. John Wood the younger was his younger brother.

[54] Roskell, 'Sir John Wood of Molesey', pp. 383–5.

[55] *Ibid.*, p. 384; F. Leslie Wood, 'Sir John Wood, Treasurer,' p. 207.

[56] On the Lewkenor–Wood Bodiam dispute see PRO, C1/41/35–8. Mark Anthony, *Lower Bodiam and its Lords* (London, 1871), pp. 9–13, makes significant corrections to the Dalingridge genealogy given by Cooper, 'Pedigree of the Lewkenor Family' (see above, n. 25).

[57] See Roskell, 'Sir John Wood of Molesey', pp. 383–96.

[58] Rowena E. Archer, '"How ladies . . . who live on their manors ought to manage their households and estates": Woman as Landholders and Administrators in the Later Middle Ages', in P.J.P. Goldberg (ed.), *Woman is a Worthy Wight: Women in English Society c. 1200–1500* (Stroud, 1992), pp. 149–51, 170.

[59] See Hope, 'Lollardy: the stone the builders rejected?', p. 10; Hudson, *PR*, pp. 131, 134–7; and Davies, 'Lollardy and Locality', pp. 195–8.

[60] T.F.T. Plucknett, *The Medieval Bailiff* (London, 1954), pp. 2–13; H.S. Bennett, *Life on the English Manor* (Cambridge, 1937), pp. 162–6; Dorothea Oschinsky, *Walter of Henley and other Treatises on Estate Management and Accounting* (Oxford, 1971), pp. 268–75 (demanding duties as set out by the anonymous *Seneschaucy*), 290–3, 317, 395.

[61] Quoted in Bennett, *Life on the English Manor*, p. 163.

62 Foxe, *A&M*, IV, p. 214; TCD, MS.775, f. 123ᵛ.

63 Samuel Bentley (ed.), *Excerpta Historica, or, Illustrations of English History* (London, 1831), p. 384, printing BL, Harl. MS 2115, f. 152; Charles Ross, *Richard III* (London, 1981), p. 112. Conway identifies the knighthood as given to Thomas's namesake and uncle, but this seems to be an error (Agnes Conway, 'The Maidstone Sector of Buckingham's Rebellion', *Archaeologia Cantiana*, 37 (1925), pp. 103–20).

64 On Sir Thomas Lewkenor's participation in the rebellion and possible family beliefs about the fate of Edward V, see Philip Morgan, 'The Death of Edward V and the Rebellion of 1483', *Historical Research*, 68 (1995), pp. 229–32. I am most grateful to Dr Morgan for sending me an advance copy of his article.

65 *CPR, 1476–85*, p. 370; Rosemary Horrox, *Richard III: A study of service* (Cambridge, 1989), p. 158; Conway, 'The Maidstone Sector', pp. 103–20.

66 *CPR, 1476–85*, p. 370; William Page *et al.*, 'The Hundred of Staple: Bodiam', in *VCH Sussex*, 9, p. 263. Conway suggests Richard Lewkenor was Sir Thomas's uncle.

67 *British Library Harleian Manuscript 433*, ed. Rosemary Horrox and P.W. Hammond, 4 vols (Gloucester, 1979–83); vol. 2, p. 33. On Elrington see Horrox, *Richard III*, pp. 180, 240, citing PRO, PROB 11/7, f. 59ʳ⁻ᵛ. On the Lewkenors at South Mimms where they had held land since the thirteenth century see F. Brittain *et al.*, *The Story of Potters Bar and South Mimms* (Potters Bar, 1966), pp. 35–7, 39, 54–8.

68 Nigel Saul, 'Bodiam Castle', *History Today*, 45, no. 1 (1995), pp. 16–21.

69 *BL Harl. MS 433*, vol. 2, pp. 48–9; also printed in James Gairdner, *History of the Life and Reign of Richard the Third* (Cambridge, 1898), pp. 342–4 (Appendix, note v.), and in P.W. Hammond and Anne F. Sutton, *Richard III: The road to Bosworth Field* (London, 1985), pp. 148–50. I am most grateful to Rosemary Horrox for dating this proclamation. It has usually been assigned to January 1484 on the basis that it was issued at Richard's 'commyng now into this his said countie [of] Kent', and Richard's next known visit to Kent was in January 1484 (Gairdner, *History of Richard the Third*, p. 147; Conway, 'The Maidstone Sector', p. 105; Rhoda Edwards, *The Itinerary of King Richard III 1483–1485* (London, 1983), pp. 12–13). A further complication is Paul Murray Kendall's suggestion in *Richard the Third* (London, 1955), p. 275, that Richard visited Kent on his way back to London from the West Country after the collapse of the rebellion. However, he seems to have been misled by a calendaring error in 'The Records of the City of Canterbury' by J. Brigstocke Sheppard, *Ninth Report of the Royal Commission on Historical Manuscripts* (1883), p. 177, where Lord Cobham and his party apparently ride to meet the king in Sandwich, but in fact rode (perhaps taking ship at Sandwich) to meet the king before his entry into London. Dr Horrox writes: 'There's no doubt that [the proclamation] was issued in the second week of December – although it's undated this bit of Harley 433 is chronological, give or take a day or two either way. It looks as if Richard was planning to go into Kent himself before Christmas and didn't. The reference to his "now coming" is only in the context of subjects approaching him for redress, none of the rest is contingent upon his presence. Its issue is, I'm sure, primarily linked with the activity of the royal commissioners in Kent, and they are certainly active at this point – they crop up in all the extant borough records. So the information it gives about which rebels were still at large does reflect early December rather than January.' (Personal communication.)

70 *Rot. Parl.*, VI, pp. 244–9; *CFR, 1471–85*, no. 891 (pp. 313–14).

71 Horrox, *Richard III*, pp. 186–8.

72 *BL Harl. MS 433*, vol. 2, pp. 33, 108–9. On Elrington and Gough see Horrox, *Richard III*, pp. 180, 239, 240.

73 *BL Harl. MS 433*, vol. 1, pp. 101, 200; *CPR, 1476–85*, p. 535.

74 *BL Harl. MS 433*, vol. 2, p. 108; Horrox, *Richard III*, p. 195. Lady Jane's lands are not unfortunately further specified.

75 *CCR, 1475–85*, no. 1242 (p. 365); Horrox, *Richard III*, pp. 173, 274; Ross, *Richard III*, pp. 180–1. It was suggested by Kendall, *Richard the Third* (pp. 149 and 184), that Wood was a close

friend of the king's, although on what grounds is uncertain (cf. Ross, *Richard III*, p. 76).

[76] *BL Harl. MS 433*, vol. 1, p. 191. On pardons see Horrox, *Richard III*, pp. 273–4.

[77] Sir Thomas Lewkenor who rebelled in 1483 cannot therefore be the member of Lady Margaret Beaufort's household of that name in 1494, as suggested in Michael K. Jones and Malcolm G. Underwood, *The King's Mother: Lady Margaret Beaufort, Countess of Richmond and Derby* (Cambridge, 1992), p. 277. Conflicting dates are given for the death of Sir John Wood. According to his widow's inquisition post mortem (*Calendar of Inquisitions Post Mortem Henry VII*, vol. 2, no. 629) he died on 20 August 1484, but according to documents in the Garth–Ernley dispute in *The Notebook of Sir John Port*, ed. J.H. Baker (Selden Society, 102, 1986), p. 98, he died either on 23 (text) or 25 (footnote) October 1484.

[78] Although a Bristol priest named John Young was in trouble for Lollard heresy in mid-century; see *The Register of Thomas Bekynton Bishop of Bath and Wells 1443–1465*, eds H.C. Maxwell-Lyte and M.C.B. Dawes (Somerset Record Society, 49–50 1934), I, no. 458, pp. 120–7. See also Hudson, *PR*, pp. 133, 144.

[79] The advowson of the church was, however, held by the abbey of Durford at this time. See Olive M. Moger, 'The Hundred of Dumpford: Rogate' and 'The Hundred of Dumpford: Trotton', in *VCH Sussex*, 4, pp. 24, 27, 35.

[80] *Year Books of Edward IV: 10 Edward IV and 49 Henry VI, A.D. 1470*, ed. N. Neilson (Selden Society, 1931), p. xxvii.

[81] Montagu Rhodes James and Claude Jenkins, *A Descriptive Catalogue of the Manuscripts in the Library of Lambeth Palace*, part 5, no. 545, pp. 746–50; Richmond, 'Religion and the Fifteenth Century English Gentleman', p. 202.

[82] PRO, PROB 11/23 Voxe. Joan was the daughter of Richard Halsham and granddaughter of the poet John Halsham. She is easily confused with Lady Jane Lewkenor, as in the index to *BL Harl. MS 433*.

[83] *BL Harl. MS 433*, vol. 2, p. 181. Again, the lands are not specified.

[84] Land recovered after a reversal of attainder might not of course be of the same value as it was when it was lost, especially if it was possible for the new tenants to anticipate that their tenure might be short.

[85] PRO, C1/211/65 (Lewkenore v. Leukenore and Leukenore).

[86] PRO, C1/211/65 (Lewkenore v. Leukenore and Leukenore). For Langton's debts see C1/32/327 (Langton v. Mayor and Aldermen of London), which can be dated to 1482. In December 1481 Young, through an intermediary, offered to sell Langton 95 butts of malmsey for £475, £100 to be paid on 1 March 1482 followed by two instalments of £187 10s 0d at the two following Christmases (assuming the £177 10s 0d stated to be due at Christmas 1483 to be a scribal error). A dispute then arose about Langton's sureties. Young died soon after the deal was concluded, which perhaps gave Langton the opportunity to stall on repayment. If the £300 which was still outstanding 15 years later was not part of this sum, then Langton was already in debt to Young, and the sum had been owing for even longer.

[87] *CCR, Henry VII*, vol. 1, no. 128, p. 35. Capell had dealings with Margery Wood's second husband, Sir Thomas Garth (PRO, SP46/123, f. 43. Accounts of William Capell.)

[88] *Great Chronicle of London*, pp. 252–3.

[89] Fabyan, *New Chronicles of England and France*, p. 685.

[90] Or nine, according to BL, MS Vitellius A.16, in *Chronicles of London*, ed. Kingsford, p. 200.

[91] *Great Chronicle of London*, pp. 252–3. The *Great Chronicle* seems to be the basis ('my author') of Foxe's account in *A&M*, IV, p. 7. Foxe placed her in his Church Calendar to be commemorated on 14 February, for which he became embroiled in a controversy with Nicholas Harpesfield (I, 'Kalender'; A & M, III, pp. 704–9)

[92] *Great Chronicle of London*, p. 252.

[93] PRO, C1/211/65 (Lewkenor v. Leukenore and Leukenore). The bill states that Sir Thomas 'died 12 years and more past'. Lady Jane's stepson Sir Roger Lewkenor's estate was valued at 500

marks per annum in the mid-1530s when he was about seventy and his potential heirs intriguing for the inheritance. See Frank Ward, 'The divorce of Sir William Barentine', *Sussex Archaeological Collections*, 68 (1927), pp. 179–81.

[94] *CCR, Henry VII*, vol. 2, no. 134, p. 46.

[95] E. Jeffries Davis, 'The Authorities for the Case of Richard Hunne (1514–15)', *EHR*, 30 (1915), p. 486.

[96] TCD, MS.775, f. 122ᵛ.

[97] As noted by Susan Brigden, *London and the Reformation* (Oxford, 1989), p. 97.

[98] Since she was alive in 1501, she cannot, for example, have been Fabyan's 'old heretic brent in Smithfield' in July 1500 (*The New Chronicles of England and France*, p. 687).

[99] Foxe, *A&M*, IV, p. 710; Fabyan, *The New Chronicles of England and France*, p. 685.

[100] On Thomas Garth's adventurous career see Agnes Conway, *Henry VII's Relations with Scotland and Ireland 1485–1498* (Cambridge, 1932), pp. 49–61, 85, 87–90, 112–14, 130, 173, 189, 219. Margery Wood died in 1502 (*Cal. Inq. P. M. Hen. VII*, vol. 2, p. 629; F. Leslie Wood, 'Sir John Wood, Treasurer', [above, n. 53]) not 1526, as in Philip Morant, *The History and Antiquities of the County of Essex* (London, 1768), p. 241 (probably mistaking 18 Henry VII for 18 Henry VIII), followed by Roskell, 'Sir John Wood of Molesey', p. 396. After her death Rivers Hall became the subject of a protracted and complex dispute between Thomas Garth and John Ernley. See *Calendar of Letter-Books . . . London: Letter-Book L*, p. 280; *Notebook of Sir John Port*, ed. Baker, pp. 96–9. Cf. Essex Record Office, D/Dfa F12. Garth died in June 1505 (PRO, C1/373/52, Wylkynson v. Lancaster).

[101] R.C. Fowler, 'A Balance Sheet at St Osyth Abbey', *Transactions of the Essex Archaeological Society*, n.s. 19 (1927), pp. 190–1.

[102] I am grateful to Rowena Archer for advice on the de Vere genealogy. Philip FitzLewis drew up some of the extant de Vere accounts for 1490–1; Melvin J. Tucker, 'Household Accounts 1490–1491 of John de Vere, earl of Oxford', *EHR*, 75 (1960), p. 472. He was also a feoffee of Sir Thomas Lewkenor's father Sir Roger; PRO, C54/330, m. 7d.

[103] See, for example, PRO, C1/545/1.

[104] Foxe, *A&M*, IV, pp. 215–16. Brewster lived in Colchester for ten years before his arrest in 1511. It is reasonable to assume his period of residence at Westminster was prior to his coming to Colchester.

[105] Daniell 11:38, in Corpus College Oxford, MS 4.

[106] Daniell 11:39. And land according to modern translations, but not in the Wycliffite. None of the Wycliffite versions manages a very clear narrative in this part of Daniel.

[107] Daniell 11:33.

[108] Forshall & Madden, *HB*, III, p. 659 (Daniell 11:35).

[109] Although this was not the reading of the long scholarly gloss on this passage printed in Forshall & Madden, *HB*, III, pp. 659–62, where (p. 659) 'Maosym is interpretid strong hold, ether help', as it still is. The gloss identifies the evil ruler as Antichrist.

[110] Their last adult male, John Bardfield, died in 1497 after a successful career as a Duchy of Lancaster official. See Horrox, *Richard III*, p. 126. His heirs were his nephews John and Thomas Bardfield, neither of whom lived to be 22. (PRO, PROB 11/6/52–53; C1/334/43 Lyttefote v. Suthwell).

[111] The two families are easily confused since they tended to use the same Christian names. They are not known to have been related.

[112] His first wife had been Joan Leyrch, who was dead by 1515. See PRO, C1/295/62.

[113] Foxe, *A&M*, V, pp. 251–3; Andrew Hope, 'Lollardy: the stone the builders rejected?', pp. 5–6.

[114] Corpus Christi College, Oxford, MS4; Forshall & Madden, *HB*, I, Preface, no. 94, p. li.

[115] PRO, C1/577/2 (Sawier *et al.*, v. Boggas and Brice). For all their apparent unity the family was split by John Bardfield's will and fought the issue out in chancery. See also *Feet of Fines for Essex*, IV, 1423–1547, eds P. Reaney and M. Fitch (Essex Archaeological Society, Colchester, 1964), p. 186, no. 17.

[116] John Strype, *Ecclesiastical Memorials relating chiefly to Religion, and the Reformation of it, and the Emergencies of the Church of England, under King Henry VIII, King Edward VI and Queen Mary I* (Oxford, 1822), vol. 1, part 1, no. 18, pp. 56–8.

[117] *Letters and Papers, Foreign and Domestic, of the Reign of Henry VIII*, eds J.S. Brewer *et al.* (London, 1862–1932), IV, no. 4545.

[118] Essex Record Office, D/A CR 4/70–71 (Will of Alice Garner).

[119] *Letters and Papers*, IV, no. 4029; Hope, 'Lollardy: the stone the builders rejected?', p. 11. Walker, 'Heretical Sects in Pre-Reformation England', denies the existence of a self-conscious heretical group in Essex in the 1520s, but on a cursory and insufficient examination of the evidence.

[120] Their identities can be deduced from the long list given by Foxe, *A&M*, IV, pp. 206–7, of those who abjured in the diocese of London early in the sixteenth century. At one point the list reads 'William Gosse, George Laund prior of St Osyth, Henry Coll, William Manne, William Sweeting, Jacob Brewster, Sabine Mann'. Foxe indicates elsewhere (*A&M*, IV, p. 180) that Brewster abjured at the same time as Sweeting, and Manne is presumably Sweeting's old associate from Boxted, William Man. If this list is in order the fifth of the six abjurers in 1506 was Henry Coll (or Henry Cole). The choice of the final name would appear to be between the first or the last name. Sabine Manne is probably to be preferred as she may have been the wife or a relative of William, and was arrested with him, and this would also have the merit of leaving the list headed by its most prominent member, George Laund. See also Fabyan, *New Chronicles of England and France*, p. 689. On the Man family see Margaret Aston, 'Iconoclasm at Rickmansworth, 1522: Troubles of Churchwardens', *JEH*, 40 (1989), reprinted in *FF*, pp. 251–2. There do seem, however, to be rather too many Mans around in south-east England in this period to be very confident about locating the family of the highly peripatetic Lollard evangelist Thomas Man.

[121] *Great Chronicle of London*, p. 331.

[122] PRO, PROB 11/15 Adeane (139ᵛ); *The Oath Book or Red Parchment Book of Colchester*, ed. W. Gurney Benham (Colchester, 1907), p. 144. An alternative to the above would be if 'Master Bardfield' were to be John the younger. The 'master' appellation would seem slightly more appropriate to the father than the son, as would the evident function of Lollard teacher. If John Bardfield the elder was not a Lollard it also becomes necessary to explain the total absorption of the rest of his family in Lollardy.

[123] Morant, *History . . . of Essex 1768*, I, pp. 125–6; 'Religious Houses: The Hospital of St Mary Magdalen', in *VCH Essex*, 2, pp. 184–5.

[124] Tucker, 'Household Accounts of John de Vere', p. 472.

[125] TCD, MS 775, f. 123. The other chapter recorded as being especially studied was John 24, which is an error of some kind since this book has only seventeen chapters. Sweeting probably knew the area around Stratford Langthorn well since St Osyth's owned properties in Stratford-at-Bow and Whitechapel, which were useful stopping-off points for men and animals on the way to London. See Kevin McDonnell, *Medieval London Suburbs* (Chichester, 1978), pp. 23, 160.

[126] Matthew 11:5 (Forshall & Madden, *HB*).

[127] Matthew 11:16–17 (Forshall & Madden, *HB*).

[128] Matthew 11:25 (Forshall & Madden, *HB*).

[129] Foxe, *A&M*, IV, p. 216.

[130] TCD, MS 775, f. 123; Brigden, *London and the Reformation*, p. 88. To Ussher's summary may be added the additional information from Foxe that Alice Forge was part of this group. However, since Foxe erroneously gives the family as 'Thomas Forge, Alice Forge his wife, and John Forge their son', it is not possible to be sure whose wife Alice was.

[131] TCD, MS 775, f. 123. There is uncertainty about the date of Thomas Forge's examination.

[132] TCD, MS 775, ff. 122ᵛ–124ᵛ.

[133] For example, James Gairdner, *The English Church in the Sixteenth Century from the Accession of Henry VIII to the Death of Mary* (London, 1902), pp. 51, 53–4.

[134] Foxe, *A&M*, IV, pp. 180, 214–16. Contrary to the comment on this case in Thomson, *LL*, p. 137, that 'the details of Foxe's account may . . . be regarded with some degree of caution', it is the

details which prove reliable and open the story up to further historical investigation.

135 Foxe, *A&M*, IV, p. 215.

136 S.A.A. Majendie, *Some Account of the Family of De Vere* (Castle Hedingham, [1904?]), p. 34.

137 *Standard*, 30 December 1868, notes its sale to the British Museum.

138 Hope, 'Lollardy: the stone the builders rejected?', pp. 8–10.

139 Foxe, *A&M*, IV, p. 228; Plumb, 'Social and Economic Spread of Rural Lollardy', pp. 123–6.

140 Luxton, 'The Lichfield Court Book', pp. 120–5. The reference to 'magister Pisford' is a neat parallel to that of 'master Bardfield' (p. 122).

141 Hope, 'Lollardy: the stone the builders rejected?', pp. 2–5; Plumb, 'Social and Economic Spread of Rural Lollardy', pp. 121–3, 126–8.

142 TCD MS 775, f. 124; Foxe, *A&M*, IV, p. 224; Brigden, *London and the Reformation*, pp. 96–8.

143 Notwithstanding Shannon McSheffrey 'Women and Lollardy: A Reassessment', *Canadian Journal of History*, 26 (1991), pp. 199–223. Her *Gender and Heresy: Women and Men in Lollard Communities, 1420–1530* (Philadelphia, 1995) appeared after the conference.

144 Patrick Collinson, 'Magistracy and Ministry: A Suffolk Miniature', in R.B. Knox (ed.), *Reformation, Conformity and Dissent: Essays in Honour of Geoffrey Nuttall* (London, 1977), pp. 77–91, reprinted in P. Collinson, *Godly People: Essays on English Protestantism and Puritanism* (London, 1983), pp. 445–66, describes the activities of Sir Edward Lewkenor and his family and associates.

145 There had been a previous marriage alliance between the Wroths and the Lewkenors. D.O. Pam, *Protestant Gentlemen: The Wroths of Durants Arbour, Enfield, and Loughton, Essex* (Edmonton Hundred Historical Society, 1973), pp. 3–4 (which, however, confuses this Edward with his son). In 1572 the Wroths leased from the crown Lady Jane's old manor of Honeylands and Pentriches which the Capels had bought, and subsequently bought it in 1600 (G.C. Tyack, 'Enfield', *VCH Middlesex*, 5, p. 228).

146 *Historical Manuscripts Commission*, vol. 3, p. 239. Other branches of the Sussex Lewkenors were Catholic. See Roger B. Manning, *Religion and Society in Elizabethan Sussex: A study of the enforcement of the religious settlement 1558–1603* (Leicester, 1969).

147 John Bale, *Scriptorium Illustrium Maioris Brytanniae Catalogus*, I, p. 715. Still the best guide is E.G. Rupp, *Studies in the Making of the English Protestant Tradition* (Cambridge, 1949), where it is suggested (p. 68, n. 1) that Bale had no evidence for his assertion.

148 On the Collins family see Margaret Aston, 'Lollardy and Literacy', *History*, 49 (1964), reprinted in *idem, LR*, p. 201 and n. 37; Hudson, *PR*, pp. 463–4. Their cover was blown by John Pykas in 1528 (though the authorities appear not to have spotted it) when he referred under examination to 'Richard Collins alias Jonson, wever de Boxtede' (Strype, *Ecclesiastical Memorials*, vol. 1, part 1, p. 122; Foxe, *A&M*, IV, pp. 234–9, V, p. 41). On their reputation compare the estimates of Robert Pope (Foxe, IV, p. 234) and John Tyball (Strype, *Ecclesiastical Memorials*, vol. 1, part 2, no. 17, p. 54).

149 Foxe, *A&M*, V, p. 41; *Letters and Papers . . . Henry VIII*, IX, no. 1115. The letter is undated. It has been calendared under 1535, but it could be earlier.

150 Foxe, *A&M*, V, p. 38. The Mells were tenants of Rivers Hall later in the century; see Francis W. Steer, 'A manorial dispute in the 16th century', *The East Anglian Magazine*, 8, no. 3 (November 1948), pp. 156–9.

151 Erasmus, *Letters*, vol. 2, p. 192 (letter 240; Erasmus to Ammonio, Cambridge, 11 November [1511]).

152 W.T.H. Jackson (ed.), *Essential Works of Erasmus* (New York, 1965), pp. 35–40, esp. p. 39; Christopher Robinson, *Lucian and his Influence in Europe* (London, 1979), p. 176; Roland H. Bainton, *Erasmus of Christendom* (London, 1969), p. 260; Geraldine Thompson, *Under Pretext of Praise: Satiric Mode in Erasmus' Fiction* (Toronto, 1973), pp. 116–19.

INDEX